DATA STRUCTURES AND ALGORITHMS

AUTHOR

Dr. Ranbir Singh Sanasam

Professor,

Department of Computer Science and Engineering,

IIT Guwahati, Assam

REVIEWER

Dr. Kuldeep Kumar

Assistant Professor,

Department of Computer Engineering,

NIT, Kurukshetra

KHANNA BOOK PUBLISHING CO. (P) Ltd.

4C/4344, Ansari Road, Darya Ganj, New Delhi, India

All India Council for Technical Education

Nelson Mandela Marg, Vasant Kunj, New Delhi, India

Dear Readers,

To prevent the piracy, this book is secured with HIGH SECURITY HOLOGRAM on the front title cover. In case you don't find the hologram on the front cover title, please write us to at contact@khannabooks.com or whatsapp us at +91-99109 09320 and avail special gift voucher for yourself.

Specimen of Hologram on front Cover title:

Moreover, there is a SPECIAL DISCOUNT COUPON for you with EVERY HOLOGRAM.

How to avail this SPECIAL DISCOUNT:

Step 1: Scratch the hologram

Step 2: Under the scratch area, your "coupon code" is available

Step 3: Logon to www.khannabooks.com

Step 4: Use your "coupon code" in the shopping cart and get your copy at a special discount

Step 5: Enjoy your reading!

ISBN: 978-93-5538-542-0

Book Code: UG413EN

Data Structures and Algorithms

by Dr. Ranbir Singh Sanasam

First Edition: 2026

Originally Published by:

All India Council for Technical Education, Ministry of Education, GOI

Exclusively Published & Distributed by:

Khanna Book Publishing Co. (P) Ltd.
4C/4344, Ansari Road, Daryaganj,
New Delhi (INDIA)

Visit us at: **www.khannabooks.com**
Write us at: **contact@khannabooks.com**

To view complete list of books, Please scan the QR Code:

KPH

Printed in Bharat.

प्रो. टी. जी. सीताराम
अध्यक्ष
Prof. T. G. Sitharam
Chairman

सत्यमेव जयते

आज़ादी का अमृत महोत्सव

अखिल भारतीय तकनीकी शिक्षा परिषद्
(भारत सरकार का एक सांविधिक निकाय)
(शिक्षा मंत्रालय, भारत सरकार)
नेल्सन मंडेला मार्ग, वसंत कुंज, नई दिल्ली–110070
दूरभाष : 011–26131498
ई–मेल : chairman@aicte-india.org

ALL INDIA COUNCIL FOR TECHNICAL EDUCATION
(A STATUTORY BODY OF THE GOVT. OF INDIA)
(Ministry of Education, Govt. of India)
Nelson Mandela Marg, Vasant Kunj, New Delhi-110070
Phone : 011-26131498
E-mail : chairman@aicte-india.org

FOREWORD

Engineers are the backbone of any modern society. They are the ones responsible for the marvels as well as the improved quality of life across the world. Engineers have driven humanity towards greater heights in a more evolved and unprecedented manner.

The All India Council for Technical Education (AICTE), have spared no efforts towards the strengthening of the technical education in the country. AICTE is always committed towards promoting quality Technical Education to make India a modern developed nation emphasizing on the overall welfare of mankind.

An array of initiatives has been taken by AICTE in last decade which have been accelerated now by the National Education Policy (NEP) 2020. The implementation of NEP under the visionary leadership of Hon'ble Prime Minister of India envisages the provision for education in regional languages to all, thereby ensuring that every graduate becomes competent enough and is in a position to contribute towards the national growth and development through innovation & entrepreneurship.

One of the spheres where AICTE had been relentlessly working since past couple of years is providing high quality original technical contents at Under Graduate & Diploma level prepared and translated by eminent educators in various Indian languages to its aspirants. For students pursuing 2nd year of their Engineering education, AICTE has identified 87 books, which shall be translated into 12 Indian languages - Hindi, Tamil, Gujarati, Odia, Bengali, Kannada, Urdu, Punjabi, Telugu, Marathi, Assamese & Malayalam. In addition to the English medium, books in different Indian Languages are going to support the students to understand the concepts in their respective mother tongue.

On behalf of AICTE, I express sincere gratitude to all distinguished authors, reviewers and translators from the renowned institutions of high repute for their admirable contribution in a record span of time.

AICTE is confident that these outcomes based original contents shall help aspirants to master the subject with comprehension and greater ease.

T. G. Sitharam

(Prof. T. G. Sitharam)

ACKNOWLEDGEMENT

The authors are grateful to the authorities of AICTE, particularly Prof. T. G. Sitharam, Chairman; Dr. Abhay Jere, Vice-Chairman; Prof. Rajive Kumar, Member-Secretary; Dr. Ramesh Unnikrishnan, Advisor-II and Dr. Sunil Luthra, Director, Training and Learning Bureau, for their planning to publish the books on Data Structures and Algorithms. We sincerely acknowledge the valuable contributions of the reviewer of the book Dr. Kuldeep Kumar, Assistant Professor, Department of Computer Engineering, National Institute of Technology Kurukshetra for valuable suggestions and thorough checking of the contents.

This book is an outcome of various suggestions of AICTE members, experts and authors who shared their opinions and thought to further develop the engineering education in our country. Acknowledgements are due to the contributors and different workers in this field whose published books, review articles, papers, photographs, footnotes, references and other valuable information enriched us at the time of writing the book.

Dr. Sanasam Ranbir Singh

PREFACE

The book titled "Data Structures and Algorithms" has been written considering the specific topics recommended by AICTE, in a very systematic and orderly manner. Efforts have been made to explain the fundamental concepts of the subject in the simplest possible way. Various standard text books and reference books have been considered while preparing the contents in different sections and subsections. The book covers all the topics specified in the AICTE syllabus. Each topic has been illustrated with appropriate pictorial examples, algorithms, and program segments. All the illustrative worked out programs (source codes) are written in C programming language. Though the book has been written targeting students with diverse academic backgrounds in general with or without programming knowledge, a reader with C programming knowledge may have added advantage in regards to the example source codes. Apart from the illustrative examples, the book also provides numerous solved problems in every unit for proper understanding of the related topics.

The book has been divided into four units as specified in the AICTE syllabus. The Unit 1 provides basic introduction to data structures and algorithms, and different approaches of estimating time complexity and space complexity of a given problem solution, with various worked out examples. The Unit 2 defines three data structures namely array, stack and queue, and their operations. The Unit 3 presents linked list, tree, binary tree, and various special types of binary trees. The Unit 4 explains different sorting algorithms, hashing and a brief introduction to graph. As recommended in the AICTE syllabus, the book covers only a limited topics on graph – only the terminologies, representation and traversal.

Every unit is enriched with numerous MCQ, short, long practice problems for the readers to check their understanding of the topics in respective units. At the end of every unit, a QR code linking to an external web page has been provided. Readers are encouraged to visit the external linked for additional reading materials, exercise and worked out solutions. The external web page will be updated time to time with additional resources. As the books has been focused on mostly understanding the basics, concepts and fundaments, the additional materials on the external web link will be beneficial for further exploration on the topics and challenges.

As the book has been prepared considering the precised topics recommended by AICTE, we sincerely hope that the book will provide a one-stop point for understanding the concepts and fundamentals of data structures and algorithms, and help to explore the relevant advanced topics. I would be thankful to all beneficial comments and suggestions which will contribute to the improvement of the future editions of the book. The QR Code below provide the web link for additional reading materials, and other resources of the book.

Dr. Sanasam Ranbir Singh

OUTCOME BASED EDUCATION

For the implementation of an outcome based education the first requirement is to develop an outcome based curriculum and incorporate an outcome based assessment in the education system. By going through outcome based assessments evaluators will be able to evaluate whether the students have achieved the outlined standard, specific and measurable outcomes. With the proper incorporation of outcome based education there will be a definite commitment to achieve a minimum standard for all learners without giving up at any level. At the end of the programme running with the aid of outcome based education, a student will be able to arrive at the following outcomes:

PO1. **Engineering knowledge**: Apply the knowledge of mathematics, science, engineering fundamentals, and an engineering specialization to the solution of complex engineering problems.

PO2. **Problem analysis**: Identify, formulate, review research literature, and analyze complex engineering problems reaching substantiated conclusions using first principles of mathematics, natural sciences, and engineering sciences.

PO3. **Design / development of solutions**: Design solutions for complex engineering problems and design system components or processes that meet the specified needs with appropriate consideration for the public health and safety, and the cultural, societal, and environmental considerations.

PO4. **Conduct investigations of complex problems**: Use research-based knowledge and research methods including design of experiments, analysis and interpretation of data, and synthesis of the information to provide valid conclusions.

PO5. **Modern tool usage**: Create, select, and apply appropriate techniques, resources, and modern engineering and IT tools including prediction and modeling to complex engineering activities with an understanding of the limitations.

PO6. The engineer and society: Apply reasoning informed by the contextual knowledge to assess societal, health, safety, legal and cultural issues and the consequent responsibilities relevant to the professional engineering practice.

PO7. Environment and sustainability: Understand the impact of the professional engineering solutions in societal and environmental contexts, and demonstrate the knowledge of, and need for sustainable development.

PO8. Ethics: Apply ethical principles and commit to professional ethics and responsibilities and norms of the engineering practice.

PO9. Individual and team work: Function effectively as an individual, and as a member or leader in diverse teams, and in multidisciplinary settings.

PO10. Communication: Communicate effectively on complex engineering activities with the engineering community and with society at large, such as, being able to comprehend and write effective reports and design documentation, make effective presentations, and give and receive clear instructions.

PO11. Project management and finance: Demonstrate knowledge and understanding of the engineering and management principles and apply these to one's own work, as a member and leader in a team, to manage projects and in multidisciplinary environments.

PO12. Life-long learning: Recognize the need for, and have the preparation and ability to engage in independent and life-long learning in the broadest context of technological change.

COURSE OUTCOMES

After completion of the course the students will be able to:

CO-1: For a given algorithm student will able to analyze the algorithms to determine the time andcomputation complexity and justify the correctness.

CO-2: For a given Search problem (Linear Search and Binary Search) student will able to implement it.

CO-3: For a given problem of Stacks, Queues and linked list student will able to implement it and analyze the same to determine the time and computation complexity.

CO-4: Student will able to write an algorithm Selection Sort, Bubble Sort, Insertion Sort, Quick Sort, Merge Sort, Heap Sort and compare their performance in term of Space and Time complexity

CO-5: Student will able to implement Graph search and traversal algorithms and determine thetime and computation complexity.

Course Outcomes	Expected Mapping with Programme Outcomes *(1- Weak Correlation; 2- Medium correlation; 3- Strong Correlation)*											
	PO-1	PO-2	PO-3	PO-4	PO-5	PO-6	PO-7	PO-8	PO-9	PO-10	PO-11	PO-12
CO-1	3	2	2	2	1	-	-	-	-	-	-	-
CO-2	3	1	2	1	-	-	-	-	-	-	-	-
CO-3	3	3	2	1	-	-	-	-	-	-	-	-
CO-4	3	3	3	2	1	-	-	-	-	-	-	-
CO-5	3	3	2	1	1	-	-	-	-	-	-	-
CO-6	3	3	3	2	1	-	-	-	-	-	-	-

GUIDELINES FOR TEACHERS

To implement Outcome Based Education (OBE) knowledge level and skill set of the students should be enhanced. Teachers should take a major responsibility for the proper implementation of OBE. Some of the responsibilities (not limited to) for the teachers in OBE system may be as follows:

- Within reasonable constraint, they should manoeuvre time to the best advantage of all students.
- They should assess the students only upon certain defined criterion without considering any other potential ineligibility to discriminate them.
- They should try to grow the learning abilities of the students to a certain level before they leave the institute.
- They should try to ensure that all the students are equipped with the quality knowledge as well as competence after they finish their education.
- They should always encourage the students to develop their ultimate performance capabilities.
- They should facilitate and encourage group work and team work to consolidate newer approach.
- They should follow Blooms taxonomy in every part of the assessment.

Bloom's Taxonomy

Level	Teacher should Check	Student should be able to	Possible Mode of Assessment
Create	Students ability to create	Design or Create	Mini project
Evaluate	Students ability to justify	Argue or Defend	Assignment
Analyse	Students ability to distinguish	Differentiate or Distinguish	Project/Lab Methodology
Apply	Students ability to use information	Operate or Demonstrate	Technical Presentation/ Demonstration
Understand	Students ability to explain the ideas	Explain or Classify	Presentation/Seminar
Remember	Students ability to recall (or remember)	Define or Recall	Quiz

GUIDELINES FOR STUDENTS

Students should take equal responsibility for implementing the OBE. Some of the responsibilities (not limited to) for the students in OBE system are as follows:

- Students should be well aware of each UO before the start of a unit in each and every course.
- Students should be well aware of each CO before the start of the course.
- Students should be well aware of each PO before the start of the programme.
- Students should think critically and reasonably with proper reflection and action.
- Learning of the students should be connected and integrated with practical and real life consequences.
- Students should be well aware of their competency at every level of OBE.

LIST OF FIGURES

Unit 1 Introduction

Unit 2 Array, Stack and Queue

Unit 4 Sorting, Hash and Graph

CONTENTS

Unit 2: Array, Stack, and Queue

Unit 3: Linked List and Trees

Unit 4: Sorting, Hash and Graph

1 Introduction

UNIT SPECIFICS

In this unit, we introduce the concept of data structure and algorithm, and their importance in solving a problem through computer programming. Broadly, the following aspects of data structures and algorithms are discussed in this unit:

- *Concept of data structure and its constituents;*
- *Operations on data structures;*
- *Types of data structures;*
- *Concept of algorithm and its properties;*
- *Evaluation of an algorithm through asymptotic notations;*
- *Time and space complexity;*
- *Estimating best case, worst case, and average case complexities of an algorithm;*

The topics and discussions are organised in a conceptual flow to understand the relationship between data structure and algorithm while solving a computer problem. The topics are explained with relevant examples for easy understanding and generating curiosity. Concepts are also illustrated pictorially using appropriate examples. After reading this unit, one should able to relate the importance of selecting appropriate data structure, and appropriate algorithm for efficiently solving a problem through computer programming.

Besides giving a large number of multiple-choice questions, short and long answer type questions, a number of numerical problems are also provided at the end of the unit. The list of references and suggested readings will allow the readers to further explore the topics deeper. To help the readers to implement the examples reported in this unit, additional reading materials, exercises and QR code have been provided at the end of the unit. The QR code can be scanned and navigated to an external web page, where additional the materials are uploaded.

The Know More section, provided after the related practical problems, has also been provided to understand addition background and related topics for the reader to explore further.

RATIONALE

Data structures and algorithms are fundamental concepts that need to be understood for solving problems through computer programming. While data structures deal with different methods of storing data into memory and ways of accessing the stored data in the memory, algorithms deal with the process of solving a problem which uses a specific data structure for storing the data required by the problem. Complexity of an algorithm may depend on the underlying data structure used, and depending on the data structure used, the way of solving a problem may also be different. Therefore, this introductory unit explains the need of studying different data structures which will provide a broader view of the available choices in regards to data storage for solving a target problem efficiently.

The process/approach of solving a problem defines an algorithm. While there exist several possible approaches for solving a target problem, which one among the possible approaches is the most efficient one? This introductory unit not only explains properties of an algorithms, but also discuss different metrices of measuring its efficiency. Understanding of the topics presented in this unit is necessary to conceptually link different data structures reported in other units, and understand the estimates related to different operations associated with each of the data structure. In other words, this introductory unit is the fundamental unit for understanding subsequent units in this book.

PRE-REQUISITES

Programming: C programming language (Many of the examples are given in C like statements)

Computer System: Main Memory

UNIT OUTCOMES

The list of outcomes of this unit is as follows:

U1-O1: Understand the concept of data structure

U1-O2: Understand different classes of data structures

U1-O3: Understand the concept of algorithm and its relation with data structure

U1-O4: Learn different evaluation metrics of an algorithms

U1-O5: Learn the way of estimating the efficiency of an arbitrary algorithm

Unit-1 Outcomes	EXPECTED MAPPING WITH COURSE OUTCOMES (1- Weak Correlation; 2- Medium correlation; 3- Strong Correlation)					
	CO-1	CO-2	CO-3	CO-4	CO-5	CO-6
U1-O1	2	3	1	1	1	-
U1-O2	2	3	1	1	1	-
U1-O3	3	3	1	1	1	-
U1-O4	3	3	2	1	1	-
U1-O5	3	3	2	1	1	-

1.1 INTRODUCTION

Assume that you are asked to write a computer program to calculate the *factorial* of a positive integer number n. The factorial of the number n can be defined as $n! = n \times (n-1) \times (n-2) \times \ldots \times 3 \times 2 \times 1$. For writing this program, as the required input data is just a single value, a variable which can hold a positive integer is sufficient (say, *int n;* in C programming language) to store the input n. On the other hand, if you are asked to write a program to search an element (say 5) in a given set of n integer numbers (say, $\{6, 3, 7, 2, 1, 8, \ldots, 10\}$, then the program need to store all the elements of the set and the element to be searched (that means, memory to store $n+1$ numbers). Now, several questions related to data have arisen. *How should the numbers be stored in the memory? Are the numbers organized in an ordered or unordered list? If the numbers are stored in a particular way in memory, how should the elements be accessed?* and so on. These questions, in regard to the second problem, are important because based on the way the input data elements are stored and arranged in the memory, the corresponding program needs to be designed. Whereas, such questions may not be relevant for the first problem, as it has only one input value. Therefore, the concern of data structure generally arises when the underlying problem deals with a collection of data elements. To understand the above two scenarios, example 1.1 and example 1.2 show C programs for estimating the factorial of an integer number and searching of an element in a collection of elements.

Example 1.1: Write a C program to find the factorial of an integer number. Assume the number is 6.

Algorithm: $n! = n \times (n-1) \times (n-2) \times \ldots \times 3 \times 2 \times 1$.

```
#include <stdio.h>
main(){
        int n = 6, fac = 1;
        while (n >= 1) {
                fac = fac * n;
                n = n-1;
        }
        printf("The factorial is %d", fac);
}
```

Output:

```
The factorial is 720
```

In the above example, the program needs a variable n to hold the single-valued input data element 6, and a temporary variable *fac* to hold intermediate estimates. As there are only two independent single valued data elements, the question of structural representation and logical relationships between data elements of a collection do not arise.

Further, the program in example 1.2 takes a multi-valued data, and a single-valued data to be searched as inputs, and search the occurrence of the single-valued data in the multi-valued data.

Example 1.2: Write a C program to search for a value in a given collection.

Algorithm: Check every element in the collection and compare it with the searched value.

```
#include <stdio.h>
main(){
        int find = 10, collection[]={3, 10, 4, 6, 7}, i;

        /* check every element in the collection and check the occurrence of 10. */
        for(i=0; i<5; i++) {
            if(collection[i] == find)
                break;
        }
        if(i<5)
            printf("Found");
        else printf("Not found");
}
```

Output:

```
Found
```

In this example, the program takes two types of inputs – a collection of integers and an integer to be searched. For storing the integer value to be searched, we can simply define an integer variable (*find* in this example). However, for storing the collection of integers, we need a data structure (this example uses *array* data structure and defines an instance `collection[]`. Arrays are defined in section 1.3.1 of this unit).

The above two examples describe two scenarios – one which does not require a data structure to store the input data (use *primitive data type* instead of data structure), and another which needs a data structure to store the input data.

A program may often deal with two types of data – *explicit data given to the program as input* and *intermediate data generated by the program during its execution for solving the problem.* In example 1.1, the value n is the explicit input data, whereas the value fac is the intermediate data generated by the program during its execution to assist in estimating factorial n. Both the types of data can be single-valued data or multi-valued data. A program should be concerned of the data structure/primitive data type to be used to store both the types of data. Therefore, the nature of such data will affect the storage requirement of a program. Example 1.3 illustrates another program that takes single-value data, but generate a set of values, which needs a data structure to store intermediate values.

Example 1.3: Write a C program to print binary representation of an integer number n. Assume $n = 10$.

Algorithm: Assign the number to quotient. Divide the quotient by 2, and collect the corresponding quotient and remainder. Repeat the first operation until the quotient becomes 1. Print the collected remainders in the reverse order of their collections.

```
#include <stdio.h>
main(){
    int n = 10, q, i=0;
    int bits[10];

    q = n;                      /* Assign the number to quotient */
    while (q!=0) {
        bits[i++] = q%2;        /* remainders are collected in an array; */
        q = q/2;                /* q denotes quotient */
    }
    printf("The binary representation of %d is ", n);
    while(i>0)
        printf("%d", bits[--i]);
}
```

Output:

```
The binary representation of 10 is 1010
```

The above example program explains two aspects of handling data – *single-valued input data* and *multi-valued intermediate data*.

(i) *Explicit input data:* The number, that we want to convert to binary, is just one integer number. Hence, an integer variable is sufficient to store the number. Similarly for the temporary single-valued data q and i.

(ii) *Intermediate multi-valued data generated by the program:* The remainders need to be collected, stored, and retrieved in a specific order, because the remainders should be printed in the reverse order of the collections. **An array data structure** is needed to store and arrange the remainder. Before formally defining **Array** data structure, it has been used. An array is a linear data structure which stores values in consecutive memory locations.

Though the amount of storage for the input data is constant, the storage size for the intermediate data depends on the number of remainder bits generated while running the program. The number of remainder bits depends on the input data. If n is the input value, then the number of bits is $\lceil \log_2 n \rceil$.

From the above examples, it is noticed that the data which a program will require, may be provided as inputs to the program or generated intermediately by the program during its execution. A program needs to allocate memory for storing such data (both the input or intermediate), and devise mechanisms for accessing the stored data. While the underlying data consists of more than one data element, the organization of the data elements in the memory should also be taken care of by the program so that the data elements can be accessed or modified or inserted.

What is data? Data is often defined as raw facts which does not carry any specific information. For example, a collection of values $\{5, 4, 6, 5.1, 4.6, 4, 6, ...\}$. Let us say, the above values are the heights of a population in a given town. Until the context is associated with them i.e., *height of the population in a town*, these values have no specific meaning. The collection is termed as *data* and the data with the context is termed as *information*.

The definition of data has been evolved over time with the growing applications of computer programming in diverse fields. Accordingly, different answers to the question "*what is data*" have also been evolved. Data can come in various forms, such as numbers, texts, symbols, figures, images, bytes, bits, etc., depending on the source of the raw facts. Without worrying much about the form of data, the study of data structure generalizes the concept of data as a collection of facts which may be in one of the above-mentioned forms, and focuses on the way of storing, organizing, processing, and retrieving the collection. In this book, we will refer to data, if not explicitly mentioned, as a generalized collection of facts without considering their contexts.

What is data structure? Data structure defines a *structural representation of logical relationships between the data elements of a data*. It not only defines storage for the data elements constituting a data in memory, but also the logical relationship between them, and also the methods for inserting, deleting, updating and accessing the data elements. The `collection[]` in example 1.2 or `bits[]` in example 1.3 are instances of a data structure name *array* (defined in Section 1.3.1).

Data structures are the building blocks of any program or software. Given a problem, two different aspects are evolved from the above examples. One is *the data on which the problem will be applied*, and another is *the approach of solving the problem*. The first aspect is referred to as *data structure*, and the second aspect is referred to as *algorithm*. *Algorithms + Data Structures = Programs,* as suitably captured in a popular book by Niklaus Wirth, expresses that *algorithms* and *data structures* are inherently related. The choice of an algorithm to solve a problem should depend on the underlying data structure used for storing and organizing the data required by the problem. Suppose, if you are asked to sort a given set of numbers which is stored using a *particular data structure*, then among many possible sorting algorithms, you should choose the one that is suitable for the given data structure. Likewise, if you are given an algorithm to sort a collection of numbers, among many possible data structures which can be used to store the data, you should choose the one that is suitable for the given algorithm. Therefore, data structures and algorithms go hand-in-hand. This book presents different types of data structures, the algorithms to manipulate the data structures, the methods of estimating and representing the efficiency of algorithms, and applications of different data structures.

1.2 BASIC TERMINOLOGIES

As discussed in Section 1.1, data structures are defined considering two aspects – (i) *storage structure for storing the data elements in computer memory*, and (ii) *operations for processing, deleting, manipulating, and retrieving the data elements from the data structure*. Every data structure should have the associated *storage structure* and *set of operations*. For a given data structure, further, the amount of storage required for storing the associated data in memory (*space complexity*) and the amount of time each associated operation will take to perform a unit operation (*time complexity*) should also be studied.

1.2.1 Data, Data Elements, Data type

Data structure is defined by its data and the set of operations which can be performed on the data. It should hold the following conceptual properties.

Data: Collection of raw facts, which could be collection of *homogeneous elements* or *heterogeneous elements*. Few examples are – a collection of integer numbers, a collection of characters, or a collection of student records where each record consists of name, roll number, address, etc.

Data element: It is a logical unit constituting a data. It can be formed by a single-valued element or a multiple valued element. For a data representing a collection of integer numbers, each data element is a single-valued integer, whereas for the data representing student records, a record consisting of name, roll number, and address may define a data element. In some books, data elements and *data items* are used interchangeably.

Data type: It specifies the type of value or values of data elements constituting a data. For example, integer, character, float, boolean, user-defined data type (using `struct` in C programming language), etc.

Name: An instance of a data structure should be assigned a name.

For example, when an instance of *array* (defined in Section 1.3.1) data structure is defined as $int\ A[10]$; in C programming language. Then, A denotes the name of the instance, int defines the data type that each data element should hold, the number 10 defines the number of data elements that A can hold.

1.2.2 Storage Structures

From the application programming aspects, programmers need to understand two types of computer memory – *primary memory* (also referred to as main memory or RAM) and *secondary memory* (usually the hard disk). The programs (the source codes, object codes, executable codes, etc.) are stored in secondary storage, and the process states of a program in execution (the required instructions and data) are stored in main memory. When we refer to memory in this book while discussing data structures, it means computer's main memory if not explicitly specified. As the required data of an instruction need to be in main memory at the time of execution of the instruction, data structures are assumed to be defined in main memory, if not explicitly defined.

Main memory of a computer can be abstracted as a long strip of linearly arranged memory cells. Each cell can store information defined by a certain number of bits (usually 1 byte) and each has a unique address ranging from 0 to $n - 1$, where n is the number of memory cells. For a given data structure, the required amount of memory cells is allotted in main memory either at **contiguous** or **non-contiguous** memory locations, depending on the type of data structure. Example 1.4 shows an illustrative example of memory allocation of integer variables in main memory.

Further, the amount of memory required for storing data of a data structure also depends on the associated **data type** of its data elements. For a data structure defining a collection of character, 1 byte of memory will be needed for storing each of the data element. Whereas for a data structure defining a collection of integer numbers, two bytes of memory (assuming short integer) will be needed for storing each of the data element. In example 1.2, the collection variable needs 10 bytes of memory.

Example 1.4: Abstracted view of Main Memory in a computer and allocation of memory for single-valued data. Integer data type is assumed to take 2 bytes of memory.

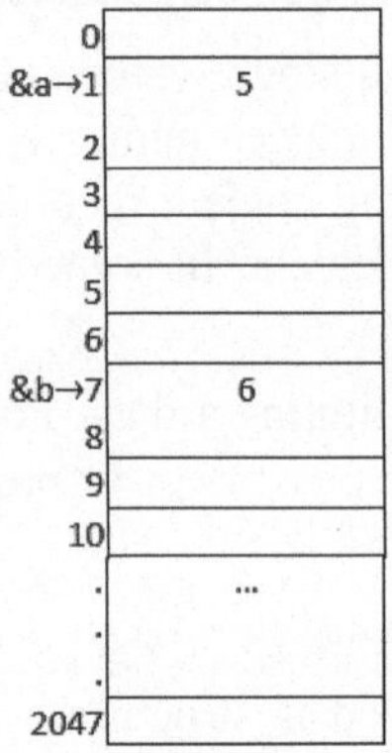

Memory

```
#include<stdio.h>
main(){
    int a=5, b=6;

    printf("Sum of %d and %d is %d", a, b, a+b);
}
```

The above figure shows a conceptual main memory of 2k bytes that has 2048 number of memory locations and each location has 8 bits (1 byte). The program on the right side needs two single-valued data (variables *a* and *b*), and each of them is allotted two bytes (assuming that an integer data type needs two bytes of memory). A block of two bytes required for a variable is allotted at contiguous locations, but the blocks of memory for different variables may be allotted **at arbitrary locations** in memory. Byte locations 1 and 2 are allotted to variable *a* (1 being the address of the variable), and byte locations 7 and 8 are allotted to variable *b* (7 being the address of the variable). The address of the variable is defined by the cell address of the first byte of the reserved block.

Different data types require different amount of memory to store an instance of the data type. Further, different programming languages may define the memory requirement of different data types differently. A typical C programming language memory requirement for different data types is listed below.

Data type	char	int	float	bool	double	long int	short int	long double
Memory	1 byte	4 bytes	4 bytes	1 byte	8 bytes	4 bytes	2 bytes	16 bytes

Contiguous Memory Allocation

Storage structure with contiguous memory locations means that the data elements of the data structure will be stored at contiguous memory locations in memory. Let us consider a data structure which holds n number of character type data elements, and each memory location holds one byte. If the first element of the data is allotted at i^{th} location in memory, then the second element will be allotted at $(i+1)^{th}$ location, the third element at $(i+2)^{th}$ and so on, and the last element at $(i+n-1)^{th}$ location. A contiguous block of n locations (i.e., contiguous n bytes of memory for this example) is allotted to the data structure. Similarly, if the data structure holds n number of integer type data elements, a contiguous block of $2n$ locations (assuming that each integer will need two bytes) is allotted to the data structure. Two illustrative examples are shown in Example 1.5.

Example 1.5: Illustration of contiguous memory allocation of two typical data structures in memory.

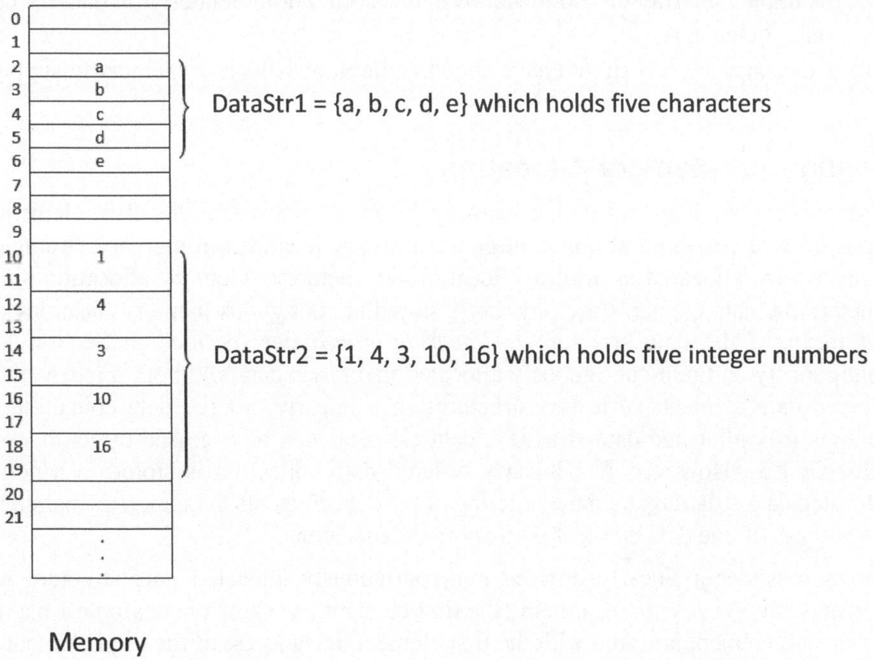

Contiguous storage structures have the following advantages over non-contiguous storage structures.

(i) The data elements are generally ordered linearly, i.e., first, second, third, fourth, and so on.

(ii) If the address of the first data element is known, the address of any data element can be directly derived by its index without scanning the other data elements. If the address of the first element is pt, then the address of the kth data element is $pt + (k-1)b$, where b is the byte size of the data type of the data element. A memory allocation with such accessing method is known as **random access memory**.

(iii) No additional memory is needed, other than the memory required for storing the data elements.

While contiguous storage is easier and efficient in terms of data access and memory consumption, it may also have the following limitations.

(i) Once the contiguous memory is allocated, it cannot be changed. As a result, the number of data elements in a data structure is limited to its allocated size of the memory. It cannot be changed in run time.

(ii) If sufficient contiguous space for storing the data elements is not available, it may result in operating system defragmentation and additional system I/O operations. However, programmers do not need to worry about it, as it will be handled by the operating system.

(iii) The programmer may have reserved a large block of memory, but actually used only a small portion of the reserved memory, resulting in underutilization of the allotted storage. For example, an array of 100 locations is reserved, but the underlying data of the program has only 5 elements.

(iv) Computer's RAM should have enough contiguous block of memory to support the storage.

Non-contiguous Memory Allocation

Storage structure with non-contiguous memory location means that the data elements of the data structure will be stored at non-contiguous arbitrary locations in memory. Storages for the data elements are allocated at arbitrary locations in memory. Memory allocation simply indicates whether the data elements are *physically* stored at contiguous memory locations or not. It does not mean, if the data structure is *linear* or *non-linear* (defined in Section 1.3). Both the contiguously and non-contiguously allocated memories can hold both *linearly* and *non-linearly* ordered data elements of a data structures. If a linearly ordered data collection is stored in a contiguously allocated data structure, data elements can be accessed by its index (as shown in example 1.5). However, if a linearly ordered data collection is stored in a non-contiguously allocated data structure, then the ordering of the data elements in memory is maintained by storing the address of one data element with another data element.

Let us consider a linearly ordered non-contiguously allocated data structure with five data elements, say *{a, b, c, d, e}*, *a* being the first element. As shown in example 1.6.a, the address of the second element is stored with the first element, the address of the third element is stored with the second element, and so on.

Further, if we consider another non-linearly ordered non-contiguously allocated data structure with five data elements as shown in example 1.6.b. The address of the elements *b* and *c* are stored with the element *a*, the address of *d* with *c,* and the address of *e* with *d*.

Example 1.6: Illustration of Non-Contiguous Storage Structure for linearly and non-linearly ordered data

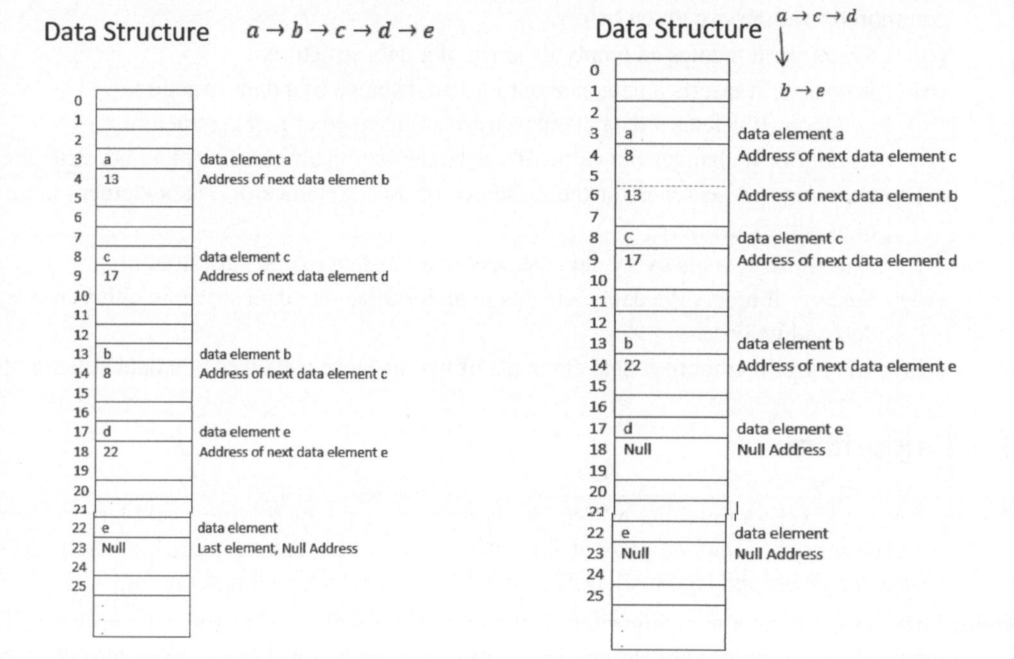

(a) Linear (b) Non-Linear

A Non-Contiguous storage structure has the following advantages.

(i) Data can grow in run time. Any number of data elements can be added to the existing structure in run time, as long as RAM supports it.

(ii) Availability of large contiguous block of memory for storing the data elements is not required.

While non-contiguous storage has more flexibilities in terms of memory allocation and number of data elements, it has the following disadvantages.

(i) Additional memory is needed to store the addresses of other data elements. It has higher storage requirement as compared to its contiguous counterpart. In the example 1.6.b, the address of elements b and c are allocated with the storage of data element a.

(ii) For accessing an element, one may need to traverse through the other data elements to get the address of the target element. For example, for accessing the element e, one needs to access the data elements a and b to get the address of the element e in example 1.6.a.

A constituent unit of a data structure with non-contiguous memory allocation is generally defined by a tuple consisting of the associated data element and the addresses of other data elements linked with it.

1.2.3 Operations on Data Structures

Several operations can be performed over the data stored in an instance of a data structure. Some of the common operations are given below.

(i) *Creation:* It creates an empty instance of a data structure.

(ii) *Insertion:* It inserts a data element into an instance of a data structure.

(iii) *Deletion:* It deletes a data element from an instance of a data structure.

(iv) *Updation:* It changes the value of a data element in an instance of a data structure.

(v) *Searching:* It searches for the existence or non-existence of a data element in an instance of a data structure.

(vi) *Traversal:* It visits every data element in an instance of a data structure.

(vii) *Sorting:* It orders the data elements in an instance of a data structure either in ascending or descending order.

(viii) *Merging:* It combines data elements of two or more instances of a data structure to one.

1.2.4 Algorithm

An algorithm is a well-defined list of *finite unambiguous* steps for solving a problem. As provided in the classic book, *Fundamentals of Algorithms*, by Donald Knuth in his book series, *The Art of Computer Programming*, an algorithm should satisfy the following properties.

Input Specified: An input to an algorithm is the data that will be used to solve the problem. The set of inputs to the algorithm should be clearly specified. An algorithm can have zero or more inputs. These are the data that are given initially before the algorithm begins, or dynamically as the algorithm runs.

Output Specified: An output of an algorithm is a data that will be returned by the algorithm after solving the problem. The output should be clearly specified. An algorithm has one or more outputs. These are the quantities that have a specified relationship with the inputs.

Definiteness: Every step of an algorithm should be unambiguous. A step in an algorithm generally represents a logical unit of computation, which may involve one or more numbers of low-level computations. For instance, in example 1.7, the statement *fact=fact*n* in Step 3 involves one multiplication operation and one assignment operation.

Finiteness: Every algorithm should terminate after a finite number of steps.

Effectiveness: The steps of an algorithm should be sufficiently basic and doable by a person in a finite time with pencil and paper.

In the book, *Formal Languages and their Relation to Automata*, by Hopcroft and Ullman, an algorithm is also defined as a *procedure* that halts. A procedure is a finite sequence of instructions that *may or may not terminate*. For example, Operating System, an operating system in execution does not terminate by its own.

Algorithms are generally written using *pseudocodes,* where the steps are written in informal natural language that are easily understandable to humans and can be easily converted to computer programs. An algorithm can also be pictorially represented using a *flowchart.* A flowchart shows the sequence of steps of execution pictorially. An example algorithm, program, and flowchart for calculating the factorial of an integer number are given in Example 1.7.

Example 1.7: Estimate the factorial of an integer number.

Computation: $n! = n \times (n-1) \times (n-2) \times \ldots \times 3 \times 2 \times 1.$

Name: Factorial

Input: Integer number n

Output: Factorial of n

BEGIN

1. *Initialize fact = 1*
2. *Repeat till n >= 1*
3. *fact = fact * n*
4. *n = n - 1*
5. *End Repeat*
6. *Print fact*

END

(a) Algorithm

```
#include <stdio.h>
main() {
    int n = 10, fac = 1;
    while (n >= 1) {
        fac = fac * n;
        n = n-1;
    }
    printf("The factorial is %d", fac);
}
```

(c) Program in C

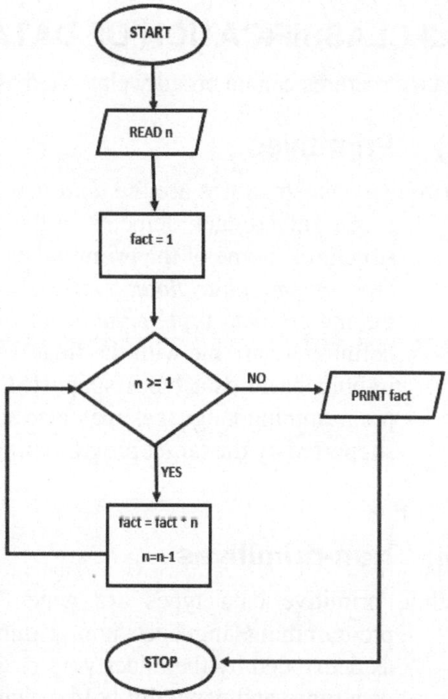

(b) Flowchart

1.2.5 Complexity of an Algorithm

The efficiency of an algorithm is measured generally in terms of *time complexity* (or *time efficiency)* and *space complexity* (or *space efficiency)*. Time complexity is the amount of time the algorithm takes to complete its execution. It is defined as the rate of growth of running time with respect to the size of the input. The interpretation of the size of the input depends on the nature of the underlying problem. The size of the input may be the value of the input (e.g., factorial of n) or the number of data elements (e.g., searching for an element in a collection of elements). Similarly, space complexity is the amount of memory consumed by the algorithm, and defined as the rate of growth of memory consumption with respect to the input size. The memory consumption includes the storage requirement for storing both the explicit and intermediate data. The time complexity and space complexity are represented using *Asymptotic Notations* $(\theta, O, o, \Omega, \omega)$. Readers can refer to *Concrete Mathematics: A Foundation for Computer Science*, by Ronald Graham, Donald Knuth, and Oren Patashnik, about the meaning of Asymptotic in complexity.

1.3 CLASSIFICATION OF DATA STRUCTURES

Data structures can be broadly classified as *primitives* and *non-primitives*.

(i) Primitives

Primitive data structures are the *data types* generally provided by programming languages for storing single-valued data elements in the memory. They are the fundamental building block of data structures. Some of the primitive data structures which are provided by programming languages are – *integer, char, float, bool*. For example, in C programming, *int* is for defining a variable with the integer data type, *char* is for defining a variable with the character data type, *float* is for defining a variable with the float data type, and so on. Though integer, char, float, and bool are in-built basic data types supported with a general purposed programming language, different programming languages may also support other data types. One needs to refer to the data types supported by the target programming language.

(ii) Non-primitives

While primitive data types are generally the default data types supported by the underlying programming languages, non-primitive data types refer to the data types created by programmers as demanded by the underlying programs. Primitive data structures generally refer to primitive data types and generally hold a single-valued data element. Whereas, a non-primitive data type may hold single data or multiple data members/attributes. Data members of a non-primitive data type may be defined with primitive data types or using non-primitive data types.

The following example defines a non-primitive data type named `Record` using `struct` with the data members `int age`, `char name`, `char rollNo`. The size of the `Record` data type is defined by the size of its constituent data members.

```
struct Record{
        char name[50];
        char rollNo[10];
        int age;
};
```

Likewise, a single member non-primitive datatype can also be defined in C programming language as follows.

```
typedef int Integer;
```

While data type defines the type of a data element in a data structure, the data structures (which can hold single value or composite values) which are not defined by default with the underlying programming languages are non-primitive. In general, the standard data types such as int, char, float, bool are primitive data structures and others are non-primitives. All the data structures which will be discussed in this book for storing and organizing data with multiple data elements are generally referred to as non-primitives.

(iii) Linear Vs Non-linear

Depending on the way its data elements are arranged, a data structure can be of *linear* or *non-linear* types. In a linear data structure, its data elements are ordered sequentially. The elements may be ordered as first, second, third, fourth, and so on, or top to bottom, or head to tail. Whereas, in a non-linear data structure, its data elements are not ordered sequentially. The data elements may be ordered, but not sequentially. The **arrays, queues, stacks, linked lists** are common linear data structures, and **trees, graphs** are common non-linear data structures.

Note that linear or non-linear structure defines how the underlying data elements are logically arranged, not the memory allocations as contiguous or non-contiguous. A linear data structure can be implemented with contiguous as well as non-contiguous memory allocation. Like-wise, a non-linear data structure can also be implemented with contiguous as well as non-contiguous memory allocation.

(iv) Random Access Vs Sequential

In random access, the data elements can be directly accessed/visited with any condition on other data elements in equal time. In sequential, an element can be accessed/visited after visiting the elements which appear before the target elements. Array is a random access data structure, where as linked list, stack, queue are sequential data structure.

(v) Homogeneous Vs Heterogeneous

Depending on the nature of the data type associated with the data elements of a data structure, it can be either a *homogeneous* or *heterogeneous* data structure. A homogeneous data structure holds date elements of same data type, whereas data elements of a heterogeneous data structure are generally compound elements which can hold more than one element of same or different data types. An array of integers is of homogeneous type, whereas an array of student records with attributes such as name, roll no, age is heterogeneous type. Each record can hold elements of different data types, making a record heterogeneous. An array of heterogeneous elements is also heterogeneous.

(vi) Static Vs Dynamics

Depending on whether the number of data elements of a data structure can be changed in run time or not, a data structure can be of *static* or *dynamic* type. In static data structure, the storage for its *probable* data elements is defined prior and it cannot be changed in run time. Whereas, in dynamic data structure, the storage of its data element can be allotted or removed in run time depending on their existence.

1.3.1 Different Non-Primitives Data Structures

Though different types of data structures will be discussed in details in the respective units, conceptually different types of data structures are briefly defined below.

(i) Arrays

An array is the simplest type of data structure whose elements are ordered linearly and stored at consecutive memory locations. It is a homogeneous data structure which means that the data elements of an array are of same data type. An array can be of one dimensional or multi-dimensional. In C programming language, a one-dimensional array a of size n with *integer* data type can be defined as $int\ a[n]$; A two-dimensional array of size $n \times m$ can be defined as $int\ a[n][m]$;. Similarly, it can be defined for different data types such as char, float, etc. Array data structures are generally static in nature. Though memory allocation of an array is generally done in compile time (above examples), it can also be done dynamically in run time (using *malloc* or *calloc* functions in C programming). However, once the memory is allocated, it cannot be changed. Therefore, array is inherently a static data structure. The data elements of an array can be accessed using its positional *index*. In C programming, index starts from 0, and first logical element has index 0, second has 1 and so on. A data element at any arbitrary location can be accessed using its index, without visiting other elements in the data structure (also referred to as *random access*).

Though array is access efficient, it may not be memory efficient. Once a block of memory is reserved for the array to store the element, the following scenarios may happen.

- The actual number of data elements in the array is smaller than what it can accommodate, resulting in underutilization of the memory space. The unused memory cannot be claimed during the life-time of the variable by other variables, resulting in a wastage of memory space.
- If the number of data elements is larger than the number supported by the allocated memory, array overflow happens. As additional space cannot be allocated in run time, the array cannot hold data elements beyond the number supported by the allocated space.

The examples 1.8 and 1.9 shows examples of compile time and run time memory allocation.

Example 1.8: Array – compile time memory allocation

```
#include <stdio.h>
main(){
        int a[10];
        a[0] = 3;
        a[1] = 1;
        a[2] = 7;
        printf("The first element is %d\n",a[0]);
        printf("The second element is %d\n",a[1]);
        printf("The third element is %d",a[2]);
}
```

Output:

```
The first element is 3
The second element is 1
The third element is 7
```

A homogeneous one-dimensional array which can hold upto 10 integer values can be defined as $int\ a[10]$;. This declaration cannot hold more than 10 elements. The statement $a[0] = 3$; stores integer 3 at index 0, $a[1] = 1$; stores integer 1 at index 1, $a[2] = 7$; stores integer 7 at index 2. Though memory for 10 elements is reserved at compile time, it uses on the first three locations. Once the values are assigned, the values are retrieved using the index, i.e., $a[0]$ in the statement `printf("The first element is %d\n",a[0]);`.

Example 1.9: Array – run time memory allocation

```
#include <stdio.h>
main(){ int n=3;
        int *a = (int *)malloc(sizeof(int)*n);
        a[0] = 3;
        a[1] = 1;
        a[2] = 7;
        printf("The first element is %d\n",a[0]);
        printf("The second element is %d\n",a[1]);
        printf("The third element is %d",a[2]);
}
```

Output:

```
The first element is 3
The second element is 1
The third element is 7
```

The above program defines an array of size 3 with run time memory allocation using *malloc*. Once the memory is allotted, it cannot be changed. Though memory allocation is dynamically done in run time by the value of *n*, as it cannot be changed once allocated, array is naturally a static data structure.

While an array is of homogeneous data structure in nature, we often see arrays of heterogeneous data elements, where data elements consist of multiple values (*compound type*). Such a data element is often referred to as a *record*. The array of records is often referred to as a *file*. An example of record and file is illustrated in example 1.10, where each record consists of three elements - name, roll and age of char and int data types, and a file of two records. Mathematically, a record (compound type) is called *cartesian product* of its constituent element types. If A and B are two constituent types, then the cartesian product of A and B is defined as $\{(a,b)|a\epsilon A, b\epsilon B\}$. If there are three constituent types A, B, C, the cartesian product is $\{(a,b,c)|a\epsilon A, b\epsilon B, c\epsilon C\}$. So, a file is a subset of the cartesian product.

Example 1.10: Heterogeneous one-dimensional array (a file of records) – static allocation

```
#include <stdio.h>
#include <string.h>
struct element{
        char name[50];
        char roll[10];
        int age;
};

main(){
        struct element a[10];
        strcpy(a[0].name,"Ram");
        strcpy(a[0].roll,"CSE01");
        a[0].age  =17;

        strcpy(a[1].name,"John");
        strcpy(a[2].roll,"CSE02");
        a[3].age  =17;

        printf("The first element is %s\n",a[0].name);
        printf("The second element is %s\n",a[0].roll);
        printf("The third element is %d",a[0].age);
}
```

Output:

```
The first element is Ram
The second element is CSE01
The third element is 17
```

Above program defines an array of `struct element` which can hold upto 10 data elements (10 records). Each data element (`record`) holds three different values – name, roll and age. Let us say, the `element` has only `name` and `roll` of same data type `char`, it will still be treated as heterogenous.

(ii) Linked Lists

Linked list is a *linear* data structure where its data elements are arranged sequentially. The first element is generally referred to as *head*, and the last element is generally referred to as *tail*. Each data element of a linked list is generally called *node*. A node consists of two fields; *information* field which holds the values of the corresponding data element, and *address* field which holds the address of another node. The *head* stores the address of the first element. The address field of the first node holds the address of the second node. Similarly, the address field of the second node holds the address of the third node, and so on. The address field of the last node holds *null.* As each data element maintains the data and the address of the next data element, it is inherently a *heterogeneous* data structure. Figure 1.1 illustrates pictorial representation of a linked list. The linear arrangement of data elements is maintained in a linked list by the address of the next node stored in each node. If one wants to access the second element, as the address of this node is stored only with the first node, the first node needs to be visited to obtained the address of the second node. Similarly, to access the third node, one needs to visit the first and second nodes to get the address of the third node. As the address of a data element is not directly available, for accessing an arbitrary data element, all the previous data elements need to be visited starting from the head node. Therefore, the access mechanism is sequential, not random access.

For many of the real-world applications, the number of data elements that will be stored in a data structure is not known prior. It may grow or shrink during program execution. In an array, the maximum number of possible data element is assumed and allocate the required memory prior to the application. Once memory is allocated, it cannot be changed. Unlike array, the idea in linked list data structure is to accommodate as many numbers of data elements as required by the program and allocate memory only for the data elements held by the data structure. A node in a linked list can be created, inserted, deleted in run time, and any number of nodes can be inserted as long as it is supported by main memory. Unlike array, in linked list, the space allocated to a node can be released once it is deleted. While linked list is flexible in terms of memory storage and number of data elements it can hold, processing of the data elements is expensive as compared to array.

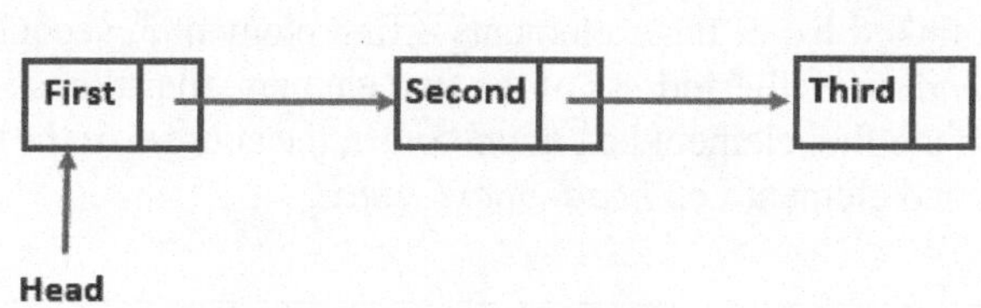

Figure 2.1: An example linked list

Though a linked list can be implemented using both the static memory allocation in contiguous memory locations (i.e., array) and the dynamic memory allocation in non-contiguous memory locations, it is generally implemented (or convenient to implement) using dynamic memory allocation at non-contiguous memory location. Example 1.11 shows an implementation of a linked list using dynamic memory allocation, which can store a set of integer numbers. The program creates three nodes, each holding an integer value, and displays the elements in the order of the node sequence. Further, in example 1.12, the same is implemented using array. Details of linked list are discussed in Unit - 3.

Example 1.11: Linked list – dynamic memory allocation

```
#include <stdio.h>
struct node{
      int info;
      struct node *next;
};

main(){
      struct node *head;
      head = (struct node *)malloc(sizeof(struct node));
      head->info = 3;
      head->next= (struct node *)malloc(sizeof(struct node));
      head->next->info = 1;
      head->next->next    =    (struct    node    *)malloc(sizeof(struct
    node));
      head->next->next->info= 7;

      printf("First element: %d\n",head->info);
      printf("Second element: %d\n",head->next->info);
      printf("Third element: %d\n",head->next->next->info);
}
```

Output:

```
First element: 3
Second element: 1
Third element: 7
```

Above program defines a linked list of three elements – first element 3, second element 1, and third element 7. The variable *head* stores the address of the first element, the address of the second element is stored in the *next* field of the first element i.e., *head->next*, the address of the third element is stored in the *next* field of the second element i.e., *head->next->next.*

In Example 1.12, the linked list is created in a two dimensional array `int a[10][2];`. Each row of the array defines each possible node in the list. The information part of the node is stored in the first column, and the address (index in the array) of the next node is stored in the second column, as illustrated in the figure in Example 1.12. Unlike dynamic allocation, the number of nodes that can be accommodated in the list is defined by the space allocated in the array.

Example 1.12: Link list – static memory allocation

```
#include <stdio.h>

main(){
   int a[10][2], head=5;

   /* first node */
   a[head][0] = 3; // data
   a[head][1] = 2; // address of next node

   /* second node */
   a[2][0] = 1; // data
   a[2][1] = 8; // address of next node

   /* third node */
   a[8][0] = 7;   // data
   a[8][1] = -1; // last node

   printf("First element: %d\n",a[head][0]);
   printf("Second element: %d\n", a[a[head][1]][0]);
   printf("Third element: %d\n", a[a[a[head][1]][1]][0]);
}
```

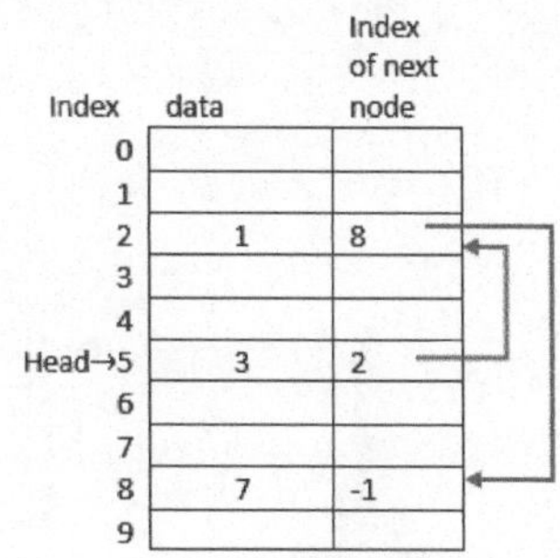

Output:

```
First element: 3
Second element: 1
Third element: 7
```

Above program implements a linked list with three elements using a two-dimensional array of size 10 × 2 – first element 3, second element 1, and third element 7.

(iii) Stacks

Stack, also known as *Last-in First-out (LIFO)*, is a linear data structure in which insertions and deletions of data elements are done only at one end, known as *top*. Operation of this structure is similar to a stack of rings placed as shown in Figure 1.2.a. The rings can be inserted or removed only from the top. The operation of inserting a data element into a stack is called *push*, and the operation of removing a data element from a stack is called *pop*. A stack data structure can be implemented using either an array or a linked list, as illustrated in Figures 1.2.b and 1.2.c, respectively. Given the state of a stack with few already stored elements, the figure shows the status of the stack after a push operation or a pop operation. Depending on the nature of data elements that a stack can hold, a stack can be either homogeneous or heterogeneous.

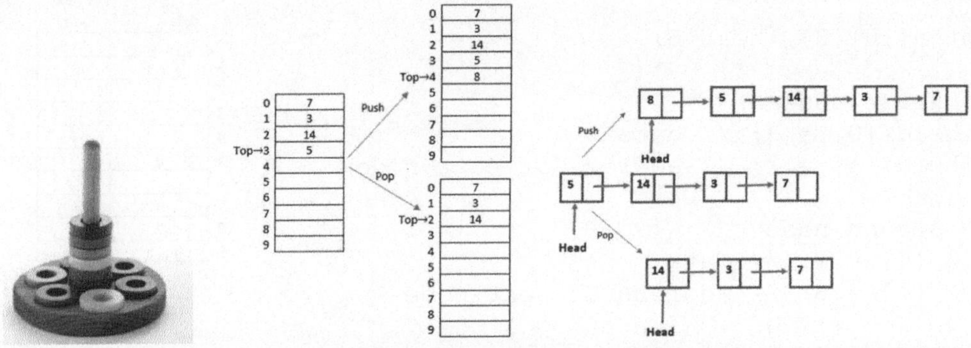

(a) Stack of Rings (b) Array implementation of stack (c) Linked list implementation of stack

Figure 2.2: Description of Stack

(iv) Queues

Queue, also known as *First-in First-out (FIFO)*, is a linear data structure in which insertions of data elements are done from one end, called *head*, and deletions of data elements are done from another end, called *tail*. Operation of this structure is similar to queue in a bank counter where people enter into the queue from the back and exit from the front. A queue data structure can be implemented using either an array or a linked list, as illustrated in Figures 1.3.a and 1.3.b, respectively. The operation of inserting a data element in a queue is called *enqueue*, and the operation of removing a data element from queue is called *dequeue*. Given the state of a queue with few already stored elements, the figure shows the status of the queue after an enqueue operation or a dequeue operation. Depending on the nature of data elements that a queue can hold, a queue can be either homogeneous or heterogeneous.

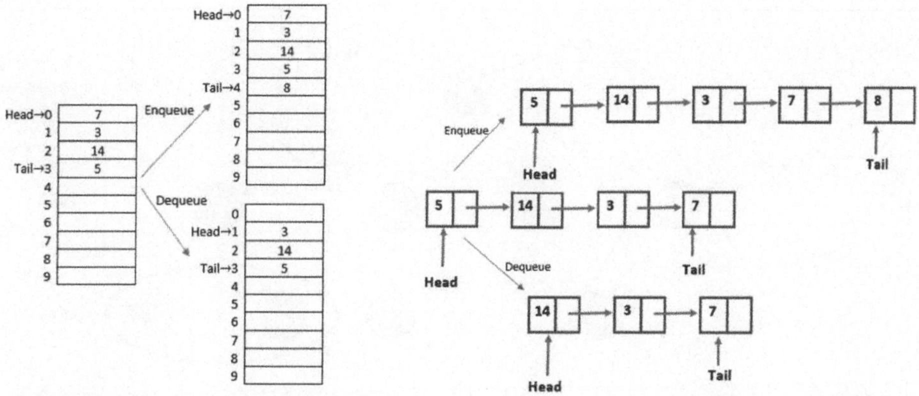

(a) Array implementation of queue **(b) Linked list implementation of queue**

Figure 2.3: Illustration of queue implementation using array and linked list implementation

(iv) Trees

A tree is a *non-linear* data structure in which the data elements are arranged in a *parent* and *children* hierarchical relationship. The data elements in a tree are called *nodes,* and the connections between the nodes as *edges*. A tree has a special node called *root* which acts like the head of the data structure. The node which are connected to root node are called *children* of the root node. Further, these children nodes may also have their own children, and recursively these nodes may have their own children, and so on. Therefore, every node in a tree other than the root represents a sub-trees with their own zero or more children. All the children of a node are called *siblings*. The node with no child is called *leaf* node. Figure 1.4 illustrates visualization of a tree. Depending on the nature of a tree, it might be implemented using an array data structure or linked data structure.

Binary tree is a special type of tree, where nodes of the tree will have at the most two children, and children are ordered as *left child* or *right child*. Discussion on tree in this book mostly focuses on binary tree. Various types of binary tree will be discussed in Unit - 3.

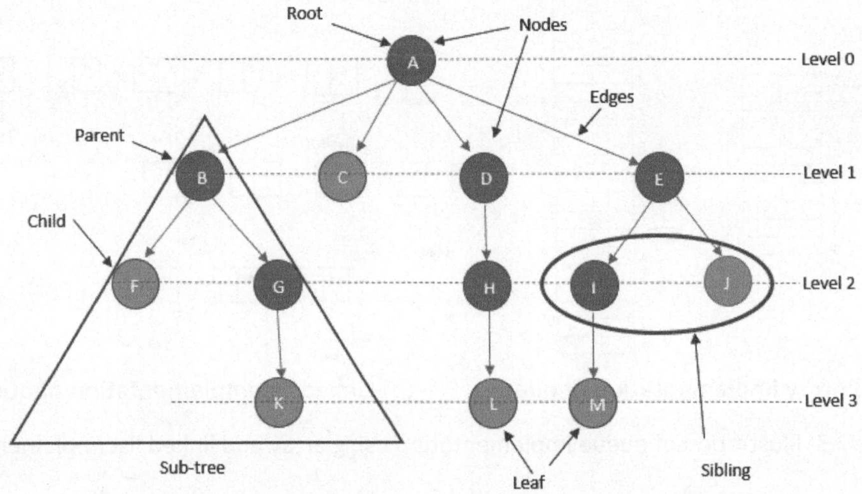

Figure 2.4: A brief description of a tree data structure

(v) Graphs

A graph is a *non-linear* data structure which is defined by a set of nodes and set of edges, without any specific ordering. A node represents a data element, and an edge represents a connection between two nodes. Friendship network in Facebook where nodes are the users and edges are the friendship relation between users is an example of a graph. Depending on whether the edges have directions or not, a graph can be a *directed* or *undirected* graph. Further, depending on whether the edges have strength of the connection (close friends or casual friends) or not, a graph can also be a *weighted* graph or *unweighted* graph. An example graph is shown in Figure 1.5.

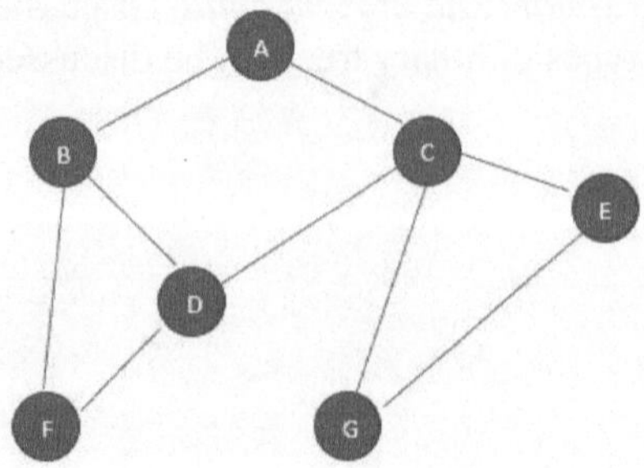

Figure 2.5: An example of a graph

1.4 ANALYSIS OF ALGORITHMS

Let us consider the algorithm of estimating factorial given in example 1.7 to start a discussion on *how to analyse an algorithm*. The algorithm of estimating factorial is shown below.

Name: Factorial
Input: Integer number n
Output: Factorial of n
Description: $n! = n \times (n-1) \times (n-2) \times \ldots \times 3 \times 2 \times 1.$

```
BEGIN
1.  Initialize fact = 1          Executed 1 time
2.  Repeat till n >= 1           Executed n+1 times
3.          fact = fact * n      Executed n times
4.          n = n - 1            Executed n times
5.  End Repeat
6.  Print fact                   Executed 1 time
END
```

To simplify the analysis, let us assume that each of the basic computation in the algorithm takes constant amount of time, *say c*. Now, let us ask a basic question on *how many times, the basic operations will be computed?* Without difficulty, it can be seen that the initialization statement *fact = 1* in Step-1 will be executed only one time. The comparison statement $n >= 1$ in Step-2 will be executed $n + 1$ times. The statement $fact = fact * n$ in Step-3 will be executed n times. The statement $n = n - 1$ in Step-4 will be executed n times. Step-6 will be executed only one time. The total time for execution is $T(n) = 1c + (n+1)c + nc + nc + 1c = 3nc + 3c$. If c is considered to be unit time, it can be further simplified as $T(n) = 3n + 3$, which is a polynomial of degree one. It basically means, the running time of the algorithm linearly increases with the increase in the value of the input. Further, if the expression $T(n) = 3n + 3$ is looked at deeper, the second term 3 also means that there are three statements which are independent of the input value, and the coefficient 3 of independent variable n also means that there are three statements which will be repeated n times. Depending on the value of n, the running time will also be different, i.e., linearly increases with the increase in *n*.

What about the space consumption? Space complexity of an algorithm will be defined not only by the storage requirement of the data that the algorithm needs during its computation, but also by the process of the program of the algorithm during its execution. To understand memory consumption of a program, let us briefly review memory allocation of a process during its execution. When a process is created by the operating system, a chunk of memory is allocated to the process. This chunk is broadly divided into four sections as shown in Figure 1.6 – *text/code, data, heap,* and *stack*. The text/code section stores the executable code of the program that the process will run. The data section stores the global variables defined in the program. The heap will store all the dynamically allocated memory during the execution of the program. The stack section stores the local variables of all the active functional calls. While the code and data sections are static, the stack and heap may grow. When the process performs any dynamic memory allocation (for example, using *malloc* or *calloc* in C programming), it will be added to heap. When a function is called by a process, a record (known as *activation record*) containing all the local variables (including function parameters) defined within the scope of the function, return address to the caller function will be pushed in the stack. The top of the stack will have the information about the currently active function. When the process completes execution of a function, the corresponding records will be popped from the stack. For example, when a C program starts executing its *main()* function, its activation record containing information about its local variables, return address etc. will be pushed into the stack. Likewise, when main function or any function calls another function, the activation record of the newly called function will be pushed into the stack. When process exits the function, its record will be popped from the stack. Thus, the stack at a particular instance will have the records of all the functions whose executions are yet to be completed. The stack and heap will grow in the opposite direction as shown in Figure 1.6. When they touch, either a stack overflow or memory allocation error will occur. Space complexity defines the rate of growth of the memory consumed by the process in execution (in the data section, heap section and stack section) with respect to the input *n*.

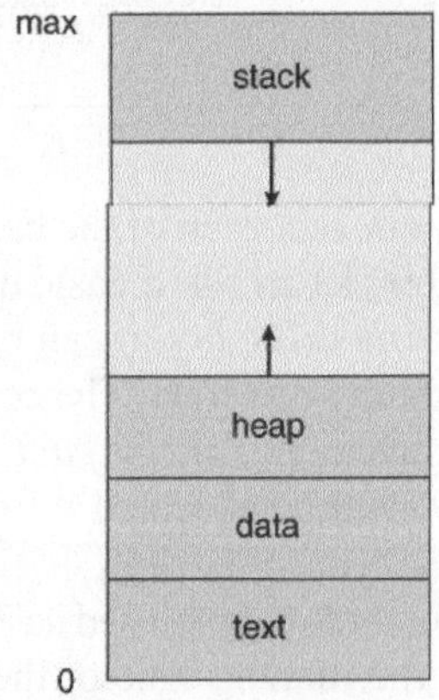

Figure 2.6: A process in memory

Let us estimate space complexity of the above factorial algorithm/program. As described above, the text section will consume a fixed amount of memory, *say c*. As there is no global variables or dynamic memory allocations, the data and heap section consume zero memory. Only one record, *say r*, for *main()* function will be pushed into stack. Therefore, the algorithm/program will consume a constant size space of $S(n) = c + r$, which does not grow with *n*.

Now, let us change the above algorithm for calculating the factorial of n from iterative $n! = n \times (n-1) \times (n-2) \times \ldots \times 3 \times 2 \times 1$ to a recursive form as

$$fact(n) = \begin{cases} n \times fact(n-1), & if\ n > 1 \\ 1, & if\ n = 1 \end{cases}$$

The recursive algorithm and its respective recursive program in C is given below.

```
//ALGORITHM
Name: Factorial (n)
Input: Integer number n
Output: Factorial of n
Description: fact(n) = n × fact(n − 1)
BEGIN
1. IF n == 1 THEN
2.     RETURN 1
3. RETURN n * Factorial(n-1)
END
```

```
//PROGRAM
#include <stdio.h>
int fact(int);
main(){
   int n = 10;
   printf("The factorial is %d", fact(n));
}
int fact(int n){
     if(n == 1)
      return 1;
     return n*fact(n-1);
}
```

For the above recursive algorithm, its running time can be defined using the recursive expression $T(n) = T(n-1) + c$ and $T(1) = c$, where c is the time for executing one operation. If $n = 1$, it just returns 1. i.e., it involves one comparison operation i.e., $T(1) = c$. If $n > 1$, then time for one comparison operation (i.e., c) plus time for one multiplication operation (i.e., c) plus time for Factorial(n-1) (i.e., $T(n-1)$). Therefore, $T(n) = T(n-1) + c + c$. Let us now, simplify the recursive expression and see what we get.

$$T(n) = T(n-1) + c + c = T(n-2) + 2c + 2c = T(n-3) + 3c + 3c = \ldots$$
$$= T(1) + (n-1)c + (n-1)c = c + (n-1)c + (n-1)c = 2nc - c$$

Since c is constant, execution time $T(n) = 2n - 1$ is a polynomial of degree one. It means that the execution time grows linearly with n, which is similar to the above iterative algorithm.

Now, let us estimate its space consumption. Like in iterative algorithm, except for the stack section, the code, data and heap sections of the process will consume fixed memory, i.e., c + 0 + 0, c for code, zeros for heap and data. However, unlike its iterative algorithm, the stack will grow as the process executes the recursive function. As the process starts execution, one record for main function will be pushed into the stack. When main function calls the recursive function for the first time, i.e., *fact(n)*, a record for the fact function will be pushed into the stack. When the fact function calls itself for *fact(n-1)*, another record of fact function will be pushed into the stack. Likewise, one record each will be pushed for every recursive call into the stack, and the stack grows till *fact(1)* is called. At the time the process executes *fact(1)*, the stack has $n + 1$ records.

As the recursive function terminates in the reverse order, corresponding records will also be popped from the stack in reverse order. So, the space consumption will be $S(n) = (n+1)r + c$, where r is the fixed memory for each record. For simplicity, if we assume all the constant parameters as 1, then $S(n) = n + 2$, a polynomial of degree one. Unlike, the iterative algorithm, the space consumption of the recursive algorithm grows linearly with input *n*.

1.4.1 Running Time and Space consumption of the Example 1.3 Program

The example program 1.3 convert an integer number to its binary equivalent. The corresponding algorithm is also given below. The variable *q* is initialized to *n*, and in every iteration, the value of q is reduced by half i.e., $,\frac{n}{2^1},\frac{n}{2^2},\frac{n}{3},\ldots,\frac{n}{2^k}$. The subsequent values of q are divided by 2 for k times and k is equal to $\lceil \log_2 n \rceil$. The running time of this algorithm is equivalent to $T(n) = 5\lceil \log_2 n \rceil + 2$. Therefore, running time grows logarithmically with n. In this program, the size (number of elements) of the local variable *bits* depends on input *n*. The array needs at least $\lceil \log_2 n \rceil$ number of elements. Therefore, the size of the record for storing the local variables of the *main()* function of the program will depend on the value of *n*. Except for the Stack section of the process, all other sections are independent of *n*. Therefore, space consumption may be defined as $S(n) = \log_2 n + c = O(\log_2 n)$, which grows logarithmically with *n*.

Algorithm: Decimal-to-Binary
Input: integer n
Output: binary of n

BEGIN	
Initialize q = n	1 time
Initialize i = 0	1 time
WHILE q != 0	$\lceil \log_2 n \rceil$ times
bits[i] = q%2	$\lceil \log_2 n \rceil$ times
q = q/2	$\lceil \log_2 n \rceil$ times
i = i + 1	$\lceil \log_2 n \rceil$ times
END WHILE	
PRINT bits	$\lceil \log_2 n \rceil$ times – read all the elements in *bits* array
END	**Total:** $5\lceil \log_2 n \rceil + 2$

1.4.2 Running time with loop and nested loops

From the above examples, it can be seen that the rate of growth of running time of an algorithm depends on the number of iterations in the loops present in the algorithm. Some more cases of loops are discussed in this section. These examples show segments containing the loops (C codes for convenience).

In the example below, let us say, there are few constant time statements before, within and after the *for loop*, and they take constant time *c*. As the loop iterate for n times, its running time can be defined as $T(n) = cn + 2c$, which is a polynomial of degree one. As the value of i in the *for loop* is incremented by one, the statements inside the for loop will be iterated for n times. The iteration can also be mathematically defined as $\sum_{i=1}^{n} c = cn$. Thus, $T(n) = \sum_{i=1}^{n} c + 2c = cn + 2c$.

```
....
for(i=0; i<n; i++){
        [few constant time statements]
}
......
```

In the above estimate, we have not explicitly considered the three statements - $i = 0;$, $i < n;$, and $i++;$ associated with the *for loop* statement. As these statements also contribute to the constant factors, it has been generalized by the constant time factor c. Let us consider these statements and also see the estimate. In the for loop, the initialization part $i = 0$ will be executed for 1 time, the comparison part $i < n$ will be executed for $n + 1$ times, and the increment part $i++$ will be executed for n times i.e., a total of $2n + 2$. It means, on an average, two additional statements on top of the statements with the loop in each iteration. As it is yet another constant factor, it does not affect in the asymptotic growth of the algorithm. Therefore, for simplicity, we consider only the number of iterations, if not explicitly specified in the subsequent discussion.

```
....
for(i=1; i<=n; i=i*2){
        [few constant time statements]
}
......
```

In the above example, the value of i is incremented by its double (i.e., $i = i * 2$). Therefore, the *for loop* will iterate for $\log_2 n$ times. The iteration can be mathematically defined as $\sum_{i=1}^{\log_2 n} c = c \log_2 n$. Thus, its running time can be defined as $T(n) = c \log_2 n + 2c$, which is logarithmic.

```
....
for(i=0; i<n; i++){
      for(j=0; j<n; j++)
            [few constant time statements]
}
......
```

In the above example, there is a nested for loop, each loop iterating for n times. The iteration in the nested loop can be defined mathematically as $\sum_{i=1}^{n}\sum_{j=1}^{n} c = cn^2$. Therefore, its running time can be defined as $T(n) = cn^2 + 2c$, which is a polynomial of degree 2. The n^2 in the expression means that statements in the inner for loop will be iterated for n^2 times.

```
....
for(i=0; i<n; i++){
      [few constant time statements]
}
......
for(j=0; j<n; j++){
      [few constant time statements]
}
......
```

In the above example, though there are two for loops, as they are not nested, the effect of the loops will be additive, i.e., $T(n) = cn + cn + 3c = 2cn + 3c$, still a polynomial of degree 1.

Generalization: From the above examples, it can be seen that each loop in an algorithm/program defines another function of n, and the following cases can be realized.

1. If there is one loop defined by $f(n)$, then running time can be defined as $T(n) = f(n) + b$, where b is the constant parameter defined by the statements before and after the loop.
2. If there are a number of unnested loops defined by $f(n)$, then running time can be defined as $T(n) = af(n) + b$.
3. If there are a_1 number of loops defined by $f_1(n)$ and a_2 number of loops defined by $f_2(n)$, then running time can be defined as $T(n) = a_1f_1(n) + a_2f_2(n) + b$.
4. A nested loop of $f(n)$ within another loop $g(n)$ can be defined as $T(n) = g(f(n)) + b$.
5. Similarly, k number of deep nested loops can be defined as $T(n) = f_1\left(f_2\left(f_3(\dots f_k(n))\right)\right) + b$.

1.4.3 Best, Average and Worst Cases

For the examples such as factorial or integer to binary conversion, there is only one input scenario i.e., the given value n. However, for some classes of problem, there could be multiple input scenarios, and the running time of the algorithm will be different for different input scenarios. An example of such problems is linear search. *Given an array of elements, the task is to check the occurrence of an element.* For searching an element in the given array, the elements in the array need to be checked linearly one-by-one until the target element is found or all the elements are checked. One such algorithm is given below.

```
Algorithm: LinearSearch
Input: integer e, integer array A
Output: Print the index of the element if FOUND
Assumption: A has n elements
BEGIN
    Initialize i = 0, loc = -1          1 time for two statements
    WHILE i < n                         upto n+1 times
        IF A[i] == e THEN               upto n times
            i = i + 1                   1 time
            Break
        END IF
    END WHILE
    IF i != -1 THEN                               1 time
        PRINT FOUND at i-1                1 time
    ELSE
        Print NOT FOUND                 1 time
    END IF
END                                     Total: T(n) ≤ 2n + 5
```

For this problem, we have the following three cases.

Best Case: The element to be searched is the first element of the array. In this case, the WHILE loop iterates only one time, and $T(n) = \sum_{i=1}^{1} c + d = c + d$, where c is the constant number of steps within the loop, and d is the constant number of steps before and after the loop. Best case takes constant running time.

Worse Case: The worst case occurs when the element is not found (or the element is the last element of the array). If the element is not found, the running time is $T(n) = \sum_{i=1}^{n} c + d$, which is a polynomial of degree 1. That means, running time linearly increases with the size of the array.

Average Case: In average case analysis, it is assumed that the element to be searched may occur at any position in array with equal probability. If the element is present at the i^{th}position, the number of iterations of the while loop is i, i.e., $\sum_{j=1}^{i} c$. If $Pr(i)$ is the probability of occurring the searched element at the position i, then its running time can be defined as $\Pr(i)\sum_{j=1}^{i} c = \frac{1}{n}\sum_{j=1}^{i} c$, where $Pr(i) = \frac{1}{n}$. So, the expected average case running time can be defined as follow.

$$T(n) = \frac{1}{n}\sum_{j=1}^{1} c + \frac{1}{n}\sum_{j=1}^{2} c + \frac{1}{n}\sum_{j=1}^{3} c + \cdots . + \frac{1}{n}\sum_{j=1}^{n} c + d$$

$$T(n) = c\frac{1}{n} + 2c\frac{1}{n} + 3c\frac{1}{n} + \cdots . + nc\frac{1}{n} + d = \frac{n(n+1)c}{2n} + d = \frac{(n+1)c}{2} + d$$

The "+ d" in the above expression is for the constant steps executed before and after the while loop. The above average running time is also a polynomial of degree one.

Let us take another example of sorting elements in an array to understand another scenario of best, average and worst cases. The given algorithm is known as *bubble sort*, which is discussed in detailed in unit 4 of this book. Given an array, the algorithm will sort the elements in the array in ascending order.

```
Algorithm: bubbleSort
Input: Array a
Output: Sorted array A
BEGIN
  FOR (i = 0; i < n - 1; i++)
    FOR (j = 0; j < n - i - 1; j++)
      IF (a[j] > a[j + 1])
        swap(a[j], a[j + 1])  //a function to exchange the values at a[j] and a[j+1]
      END IF
    END FOR
  END FOR
END
```

In the above algorithm, the outer loop iterates for $n - 1$ times and the inner loop iterates for $n - i$ times. If the time for the constant steps inside the inner loop is c, then running time of the nested loop can be defined as $T(n) = \sum_{i=1}^{n-1}\sum_{j=i}^{n-i} c + d = c\sum_{i=1}^{n-1}(n-i) + d = c((n-1) + (n-2) + (n-3) + .. + 3 + 2 + 1) + d = c\frac{n(n-1)}{2} + d$, where d is for any other constant steps if any. It is a polynomial of degree two.

In the above algorithm, for the cases where $(a[j] > a[j+1])$ is false, the swap operation is ignored. If the given array is already in sorted order, the condition $(a[j] > a[j+1])$ will always be false, and no swap operation will be performed. However, in the given algorithm above, as we do not check for the case of already sorted input array, irrespective of the ordering of the elements in the input array, both the outer and inner loop will iterate for their complete cycles and perform $(a[j] > a[j+1])$ comparison for $\frac{n(n-1)}{2}$ times. As the number of comparison operations dominates swap operations, we consider comparison operation as the basic operation inside the loop.

Can we do better? In the algorithm given above, let us assume that for a given i in the outer loop, the condition $(a[j] > a[j+1])$ inside the inner loop always false, i.e., no swap operation happens for a given i in the outer loop. It indicates that all the elements in the array are already in order at the time of processing of the inner loop for the given i. At this point, if we terminate the algorithm, we can avoid un-necessary iteration for the remaining i. The following algorithm modifies the above algorithm to check, if the elements in the array are already in sorted order, before completing the outer loop. A flag `swapped` is set to 0 before the inner loop. If any consecutive pair of elements are not in ordered, the inner loop will set the flag `swapped` to 1. After completing the inner loop for a given i, if the value of `swapped` is 0, it means that the array is already in sorted order. If the part of the array to be processed by the inner loop is in already sorted order, the algorithm terminates. With this modification, we have the following three cases.

Algorithm: bubbleSortModified
Input: Array a
Output: Sorted array A

```
BEGIN
FOR (i = 0; i < n-1; i++)
    swapped = 0;
    FOR (j = 0; j < n-i-1; j++)
        IF (a[j] > a[j+1])
            swap(a[j], a[j+1]);
            swapped = 1;
        END IF
    END FOR
    IF (swapped == 0)
        break;
    END IF
END FOR
END
```

Best Case: The elements in the given array are already in ascending order. In this scenario, the outer loop will iterate only one time, and inner loop will iterate for n-1 times without performing any swap operation. So, running time of this algorithm can be expressed as $T(n) = (n-1)c + d$, which is a polynomial of degree one. It means, the algorithm performs n-1 number of comparison operations.

Worst Case: The elements in the given array are in reverse order i.e., descending order. In this scenario, the outer loop will iterate for $n-1$ times, and for each value of i in outer loop, the inner loop iterates for $n-i$ times. For every inner loop iteration, $n-i$ number of swap operations are performed. So, the running time of the algorithm for this case can be expressed as $T(n) = \sum_{i=1}^{n-1}\sum_{j=i}^{n-i} c + d = c\frac{n(n-1)}{2} + d$, which is a polynomial of degree two. It means, the algorithm performs $\frac{n(n-1)}{2}$ number of comparison operations (also swap operations).

Average Case: The elements in the given array are in any random order. Without proving mathematically, we can roughly say, in average case, there are about half the number of swap operation as that of the worst case, that is, $\frac{n(n-1)}{4}$ number of swap operations on average. In other words, in worst case, we have seen that $n-1$ number of swap operations are performed for the last index in the sorted array, $n-2$ number of swap operations for the last but one index, and so on. So, on an average, from the first index till the last applicable index, there are $\frac{1}{2} + \frac{2}{2} + \frac{3}{2} + \cdots + \frac{n-3}{2} + \frac{n-2}{2} + \frac{n-1}{2} = \frac{n(n-1)}{4}$ number of swap operations. Therefore, average case running time for bubble sort algorithm is also a polynomial of degree two.

1.5 ASYMPTOTIC NOTATIONS

In the above discussion, the running time and space consumption have been defined as a function of n i.e., $T(n)$ for running time and $S(n)$ for space consumption. As mentioned in section 1.2.5, the time complexity and space complexity are represented using *Asymptotic Notations* $(\theta, O, o, \Omega, \omega)$. As we are interested in the rate of growth, the idea of using asymptotic notations is to represent complexity in terms of a prior known class of rate of growth such as $\log_2 n, n, n\log_2 n, n^2, n^3, 2^n$ etc. Readers may refer *Introduction to Algorithms, by Thomas Cormen, Charles Leiserson, Rolard Rivest, and Clifford Stein* for extended study on the analysis of algorithms.

1.5.1 Big Oh Notation (O)

Definition: Let $f(n)$ be the function defining efficiency of an algorithm, say $T(n)$ or $S(n)$ above. Now, $f(n)$ can be written as $O(g(n))$ i.e., $f(n) = O(g(n))$ if and only if there exist two positive constants C and n_0 such that $0 \le f(n) \le Cg(n), \forall n \ge n_0$.

Let us illustrate the above definition with the following example. Let $f(n) = 2n + 4$ and $g(n) = n$. To prove $f(n) = O(g(n))$, we just need to find the existence of any C and n_0 satisfying the condition $f(n) \le Cg(n), \forall n \ge n_0$. Let us assume $C = 3$, and estimate $f(n)$ and $Cg(n)$ for different values of n, as shown in the following table.

Different values of *n*	$f(n) = 2n + 4$	$Cg(n) = 3n$	$f(n) \le Cg(n)$
1	6	3	No
2	8	6	No
3	10	9	No
4	12	12	

Different values of n	$f(n) = 2n + 4$	$Cg(n) = 3n$	$f(n) \leq Cg(n)$
5	14	15	For all values of $n \geq 4$, the condition $f(n) \leq Cg(n)$ holds. So, n_0 is 4.
6	16	18	

For $C = 3$ and $n_0 = 4$, as the condition $f(n) \leq Cn$ holds, $f(n)$ can be written as $O(n)$ i.e., $f(n) = O(n)$. *What about* $g(n) = n^2$? For the same value of C, we can estimate the following.

Different values of n	$f(n) = 2n + 4$	$Cg(n) = 3n^2$	$f(n) \leq Cg(n)$
1	6	3	No
2	8	12	For all values of $n \geq 2$, the condition $f(n) \leq Cg(n)$ holds. So, n_0 is 2.
3	10	27	
4	12	48	
5	14	75	
6	16	108	

For $C = 3$ and $n_0 = 2$, as the condition $f(n) \leq Cn^2$ holds, $f(n)$ can also be written as $O(n^2)$ i.e., $f(n) = O(n^2)$. Without loss of generality, we can see that $f(n)$ holds for all higher degrees of n, such as $O(n \log n), O(n^2), O(n^2 \log n), O(n^3)$ etc. Among these possible $g(n)$, the $O(n)$ is the tight most one. Therefore, we generally say $f(n) = 2n + 4 = O(n)$. *What about* $g(n) = \log n$? Without difficulty, it can be seen that for any value of C, the condition $f(n) \leq Cg(n)$ may not hold for large value of n. Therefore, $f(n) \neq O(\log n)$. Similarly, $f(n) \neq O(1)$. The $O(1)$ means *asymptotic constant*. For example, $T(n) = 3 = O(1)$.

In the approach of finding asymptotic complexity of an algorithm defined by a function of n, we first *guess a bound and then prove that the guess is correct.* This way of finding the boundary function is known as the *substitution method.*

Remarks: As the definition indicates, Big Oh says that the growth of $f(n)$ is always smaller or equal to that of $g(n)$. Thus, $g(n)$ defines an *upper bound* of $f(n)$. Therefore, Big Oh may or may not represent an asymptotically tight upper bound. For example, the bound $2n + 3 = O(n)$ is tight, but $2n + 3 = O(n^2)$ is not tight.

1.5.2 Big Omega Notation (Ω)

Definition: Let $f(n)$ be the function defining efficiency of an algorithm. Then, $f(n)$ can be written as $\Omega(g(n))$ i.e., $f(n) = \Omega(g(n))$ if and only if there exist two positive constants C and n_0 such that $0 \leq f(n) \geq Cg(n), \forall n \geq n_0$.

Let $f(n) = 2n + 4$ and $g(n) = n$. To prove $f(n) = \Omega(g(n))$, we just need to find existence of any C and n_0 satisfying the condition $f(n) \geq Cg(n), \forall n \geq n_0$. Let us assume $C = 2$, and estimate $f(n)$ and $Cg(n)$ for different values of n as shown in the following table.

Different values of n	$f(n) = 2n + 4$	$Cg(n) = 2n$	$f(n) \leq Cg(n)$
0	4	0	No
1	6	2	For all values of $n \geq 1$, the condition $f(n) \geq Cg(n)$ holds. So, n_0 is 1.
2	8	4	
3	10	6	
4	12	8	
5	14	10	
6	16	12	

For all values of $C = 2$ and $n_0 = 1$, as the condition $f(n) \geq Cn$ holds, $f(n) = \Omega(n)$. Similarly, $f(n)$ will hold for lower degrees $\Omega(1)$ and $\Omega(\log n)$, but **will not hold for higher degrees** such as $\Omega(n \log n), \Omega(n^2), \Omega(n^2 \log n), \Omega(n^3)$ etc.

Remarks: As the definition indicates, Big Omega says that the growth of $f(n)$ is always greater or equal to that of $g(n)$. Thus, $g(n)$ defines a *lower bound* of $f(n)$. Therefore, Big Oh may or may not represent an asymptotically tight upper bound. For example, the bound $2n + 3 = \Omega(n)$ is tight, but $2n + 3 = O(\log n)$ is not tight.

1.5.3 Theta Notation (θ)

Definition: Let $f(n)$ be the function defining efficiency of an algorithm. Then, $f(n)$ can be written as $\boldsymbol{\theta}(g(n))$ i.e., $f(n) = \boldsymbol{\theta}(g(n))$ if and only if there exist three positive constants C_1, C_2 and n_0 such that $0 \leq C_1 g(n) \leq f(n) \leq C_2 g(n), \forall n \geq n_0$.

From the above examples, it can be seen that $f(n) = 2n + 4$ can be written as $\theta(n)$. Let $C_1 = 2$ and $C_2 = 3$, and estimate as follows

Values of n	$f(n) = 2n + 4$	$C_1 g(n) = 2n$	$C_2 g(n) = 3n$	$C_1 g(n) \leq f(n) \leq C_2 g(n)$
0	4	0	0	No
1	6	2	3	No
2	8	4	6	No
3	10	6	9	No
4	12	8	12	

Values of n	$f(n) = 2n + 4$	$C_1g(n) = 2n$	$C_2g(n) = 3n$	$C_1g(n) \leq f(n) \leq C_2g(n)$
5	14	10	15	For all values of $n \geq 4$, the condition holds. So, $f(n) = \theta(n)$.
6	16	12	18	

Therefore, $f(n) = 2n + 4 = \theta(n)$. From the above examples, it can be seen that $f(n) = \theta(g(n))$ if and only if $f(n) = O(g(n))$ and $f(n) = \Omega(g(n))$.

Remarks: As the definition indicates, Theta says that the growth of $f(n)$ should not be smaller or greater than that of $g(n)$. Thus, $g(n)$ defines a *tight bound* of $f(n)$. Figure 1.7 presents an example illustrating relationship between $f(n)$ and $g(n)$ for different asymptotic notations.

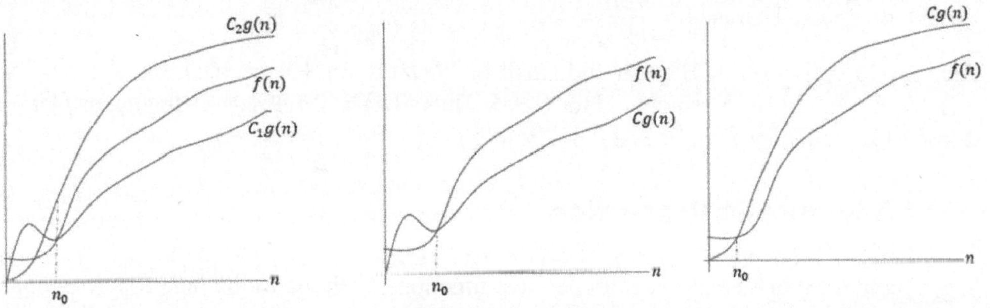

(a) $f(n) = \theta(g(n))$ (b) $f(n) = \Omega(g(n))$ (c) $f(n) = O(g(n))$

Figure 2.7: An illustration of the relationship between f(n) and g(n) for different asymptotic notations.

Further, the following table shows the rate of growth for some of the common functions with approximate values. It clearly shows that the growth rates of these functions hold the following relationships.

$$1 < \log n < n < n \log n < n^2 < n^3 < 2^n < n!$$

input	1	$\log_2 n$	n	$n\log_2 n$	n^2	n^3	2^n	$n!$
10	1	3.3	10	3.3×10	10^2	10^3	10^3	3.6×10^6
10^2	1	6.6	10^2	6.6×10^2	10^4	10^6	1.3×10^{30}	3.6×10^{157}
10^3	1	10	10^3	10^4	10^6	10^9		
10^4	1	13	10^4	13×10^4	10^8	10^{12}		
10^5	1	17	10^5	17×10^5	10^{10}	10^{15}		
10^6	1	20	10^6	20×10^6	10^{12}	10^{18}		

Table 1.1: Approximate values of some of the functions for different values of n

1.5.4 Small Oh and Small Omega Notations (o, ω)

Definition Small Oh (o): A $f(n)$ can be written as $o(g(n))$ i.e., $f(n) = o(g(n))$ if and only if for any positive constants C, there exists a positive constant n_0 such that $0 \leq f(n) < Cg(n), \forall n \geq n_0$. That is, $\lim_{n\to\infty} \frac{f(n)}{g(n)} = 0$.

In the case of Big Oh, the condition $f(n) < Cg(n)$ should hold for a particular C, whereas the condition should hold for all C in the case of small oh. Therefore, $f(n) = 2n + 4 = O(n)$, but $f(n) = 2n + 4 \neq o(n)$ as the condition does not hold for C<=2. Thus, $f(n) = 2n + 4 = o(n \log n)$ or $f(n) = 2n + 4 = o(n^2)$. In this, $g(n)$ defines a loose bound $f(n)$.

Definition Small Omega (ω): A $f(n)$ can be written as $\omega(g(n))$ i.e., $f(n) = \omega(g(n))$ if and only if for any positive constants C, there exists a positive constant n_0 such that $0 \leq f(n) > Cg(n), \forall n \geq n_0$. That is, $\lim_{n\to\infty} \frac{f(n)}{g(n)} = \infty$.

Analogy to definition of Big Oh and small oh, $f(n) = 2n + 4 = \Omega(n)$, but $f(n) = 2n + 4 \neq \omega(n)$ as the condition does not hold for C>=5. Thus $f(n) = 2n + 4 = \omega(\log n)$, or $f(n) = 2n + 4 = \omega(1)$. In this, $g(n)$ defines a loose bound $f(n)$.

1.5.5 Few Asymptotic Properties

If $f(n)$, g(n) and $h(n)$ are asymptotically positive functions, then the following properties hold.

Reflexive:

- $f(n) = O(f(n))$
- $f(n) = \theta(f(n))$
- $f(n) = \Omega(f(n))$

Symmetric:

- $f(n) = \theta(g(n))$ if and only if $g(n) = \theta(f(n))$

Transitive:

- If $f(n) = \theta(g(n))$ and $g(n) = \theta(h(n))$, then $f(n) = \theta(h(n))$
- If $f(n) = O(g(n))$ and $g(n) = O(h(n))$, then $f(n) = O(h(n))$
- If $f(n) = \Omega(g(n))$ and $g(n) = \Omega(h(n))$, then $f(n) = \Omega(h(n))$
- If $f(n) = o(g(n))$ and $g(n) = o(h(n))$, then $f(n) = o(h(n))$
- If $f(n) = \omega(g(n))$ and $g(n) = \omega(h(n))$, then $f(n) = \omega(h(n))$

Transpose Symmetric:

- $f(n) = O(g(n))$ if and only if $g(n) = \Omega(f(n))$
- $f(n) = o(g(n))$ if and only if $g(n) = \omega(f(n))$

1.5.6 Solving Recurrence Equation

Running time of a recursive algorithm can be represented by a *recurrence expression*. In section 1.4, we have taken an example of estimating the factorial of n using a recursive algorithm, whose running time can be represented using a recurrence expression $T(n) = T(n-1) + c, T(1) = 1$. We have expanded the expression to obtain the expression $T(n) = cn$. Then, by substitution, we can prove that $T(n) = \theta(n)$. Some more examples of recurrence expression and their solutions using substitution methods are discussed.

Example 1.13: $T(n) = \begin{cases} 2T(n-1) + 1, & if\ n > 1 \\ 1 & , if\ n = 1 \end{cases}$

Description: The algorithm has two recursive calls with n-1 data size

$$T(n) = 2T(n-1) + 1 = 2[2T(n-2) + 1] + 1 = 2^2T(n-2) + 2^1 + 2^0$$

$$= 2^2[2T(n-3) + 1] + 2^1 + 2^0 = 2^3T(n-3) + 2^2 + 2^1 + 2^0$$

$$= 2^3[2T(n-4) + 1] + 2^2 + 2^1 + 2^0 = 2^4T(n-3) + 2^3 + 2^2 + 2^1 + 2^0$$

....

....

$$= 2^{n-1}T(1) + 2^{n-2} + \cdots + 2^3 + 2^2 + 2^1 + 2^0$$

$$= 2^{n-1} + 2^{n-2} + \cdots + 2^3 + 2^2 + 2^1 + 2^0$$

$$= 2^n - 1 = O(2^n)$$

Execution of above recurrence expression can also be visualized in the form of a binary tree (a node in the tree can have at most two children). $T(n) = 2T(n-1) + 1$ means, the task of solving the problem is divided into two sub-tasks with size reduced by one, and the cost of dividing the task and other constant computations is 1. Running time can also be estimated from the figure as well as given below.

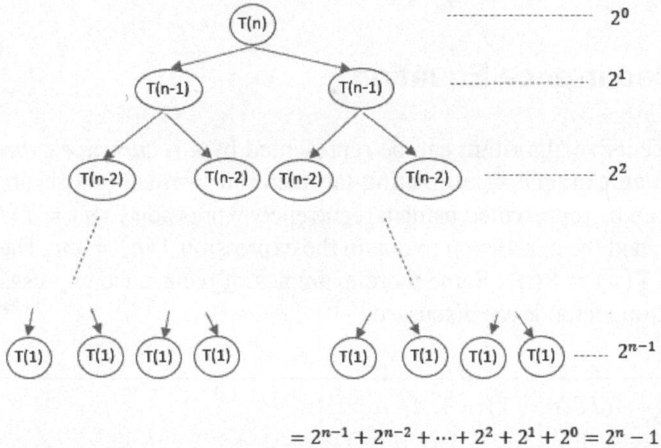

Each node in the above tree represents a function call, and two children represent two instances of recursive calls from each function. At level $i \geq 0$ of the tree, there are 2^i number of nodes, and each node consumes a constant computation cost of 1. Therefore, level i of the tree consumes a computation cost of 2^i. There are n number of levels. Therefore, the total cost is $2^{n-1} + 2^{n-2} + \cdots + 2^2 + 2^1 + 2^0 = O(2^n)$. The estimation using the above tree approach is known as *Recursion Tree Method.*

Example 1.14: $T(n) = \begin{cases} 2T(n-1) + 3, & if\ n > 1 \\ 1 & , if\ n = 1 \end{cases}$

Description: The algorithm has two recursive calls with n-1 data size

$$T(n) = 2T(n-1) + 3 = 2[2T(n-2) + 3] + 3 = 2^2T(n-2) + 3.2^1 + 3.2^0$$

$$= 2^2[2T(n-3) + 3] + 3.2^1 + 3.2^0 = 2^3T(n-3) + 3.2^2 + 3.2^1 + 3.2^0$$

$$= 2^3[2T(n-4) + 3] + 3.2^2 + 3.2^1 + 3.2^0 = 2^4T(n-3) + 3.2^3 + 3.2^2 + 3.2^1 + 3.2^0$$

......

....

$$= 2^{n-1}T(1) + 3.2^{n-2} + \cdots + 3.2^2 + 3.2^2 + 3.2^1 + 3.2^0$$

$$\approx 3.2^{n-1} + 3.2^{n-2} + \cdots + 3.2^2 + 3.2^2 + 3.2^1 + 3.2^0$$

$$\approx 3(2^n - 1) = O(2^n)$$

Using recursion tree method, the running time of $T(n) = 2T(n-1) + 3$ can be estimated as follows. The computation cost at i^{th}level is 3×2^i, and there are n number of levels.

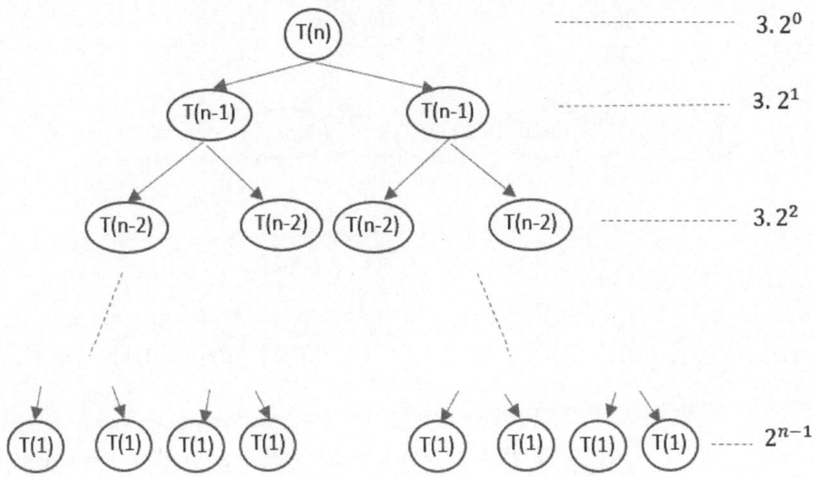

$$= 2^{n-1} + 3.2^{n-2} + \cdots + 3.2^2 + 3.2^1 + 3.2^0 \approx 3.2^n - 1$$

Example 1.15: $T(n) = \begin{cases} 2T(n/2) + 1, & if\ n > 1 \\ 1 & , if\ n = 1 \end{cases}$

Description: The algorithm has two recursive calls with n/2 data size

$$T(n) = 2T(n/2) + 1 = 2[2T(n/2^2) + 1] + 1 = 2^2T(n/2^2) + 2^1 + 2^0$$

$$= 2^2[2T(n/2^3) + 1] + 2^1 + 2^0 = 2^3T(n/2^2) + 2^2 + 2^1 + 2^0$$

$$= 2^3[2T(n/2^4) + 1] + 2^2 + 2^1 + 2^0 = 2^4T(n/2^4) + 2^3 + 2^2 + 2^1 + 2^0$$

....

....

$$= 2^kT(n/2^k) + 2^{k-1} + \cdots + 2^2 + 2^2 + 2^1 + 2^0$$

$$= 2^kT(1) + 2^{k-1} + \cdots + 2^2 + 2^2 + 2^1 + 2^0, Assume\ that n = 2^k$$

$$= 2^kT(1) + 2^{k-1} + \cdots + 2^2 + 2^2 + 2^1 + 2^0 = 2^{k+1} - 1 = 2^k + 1 = n + 1 = O(n)$$

Using recursion tree method, the running time of can be estimated as follows. The computation cost at i^{th}level is 2^i, and there are $\log_2 n$ number of levels.

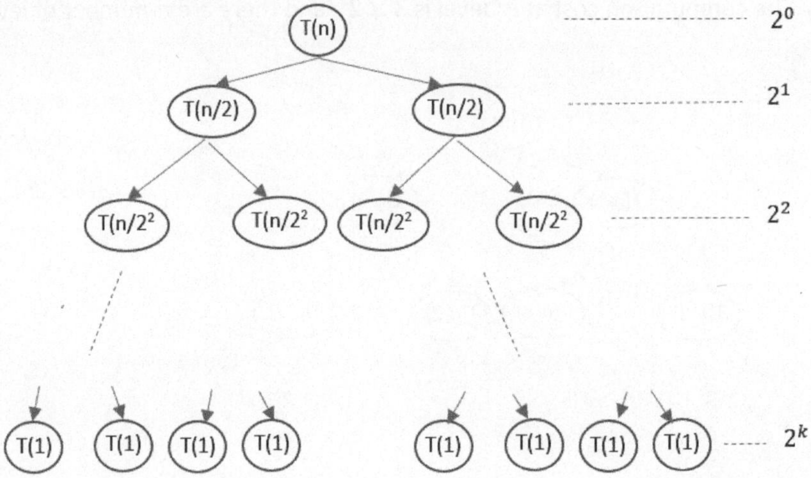

$$= 2^k + 2^{n-1} + \cdots + 2^2 + 2^1 + 2^0 = 2^k + 1 = n + 1$$

Example 1.16: $T(n) = \begin{cases} 2T(n-1) + n, & if\ n > 1 \\ 1 & , if\ n = 1 \end{cases}$

Description: The algorithm has two recursive calls with n-1 data size

$$T(n) = 2T(n-1) + n = 2[2T(n-2) + (n-1)] + n = 2^2T(n-2) + (n-1)2^1 + n2^0$$

$$= 2^2[2T(n-3) + (n-2)] + (n-1)2^1 + n.2^0$$
$$= 2^3T(n-3) + (n-2)2^2 + (n-1)2^1 + n2^0$$

$$= 2^4T(n-4) + (n-3)2^3 + (n-2)2^2 + (n-1)2^1 + n2^0$$

....

....

$$= 2^{n-1}T(1) + (n-n-2)2^{n-2} + \cdots + (n-3)2^3 + (n-2)2^2 + (n-1)2^1 + n2^0$$

$$\approx (n-(n-1))2^{n-1} + (n-(n-2))2^{n-2} + \cdots + (n-3)2^3 + (n-2)2^2 + (n-1)2^1 + (n-0)2^0$$

$$= n(2^{n-1} + 2^{n-2} + \cdots + 2^3 + 2^2 + 2^1 + 2^0) - [(n-1)2^{n-1} + (n-2)2^{n-2} + \cdots + 3.2^3 + 2.2^2 + 1.2^1]$$

$= n(2^n - 2) - 2(1 - n2^n + (n-1)2^n)$ as $\sum_{k=1}^{n} kz^k = z\frac{1-(n+1)z^n+nz^{n+1}}{(1-z)^2}$

$= O(n2^n)$

Using recursion tree method, the running time of $T(n) = 2T(n-1) + n$ can be estimated as follows. The computation cost at i^{th} level is $n2^{i-1} - (i-1).2^{i-1}, i \geq 1$, and there are n number of levels.

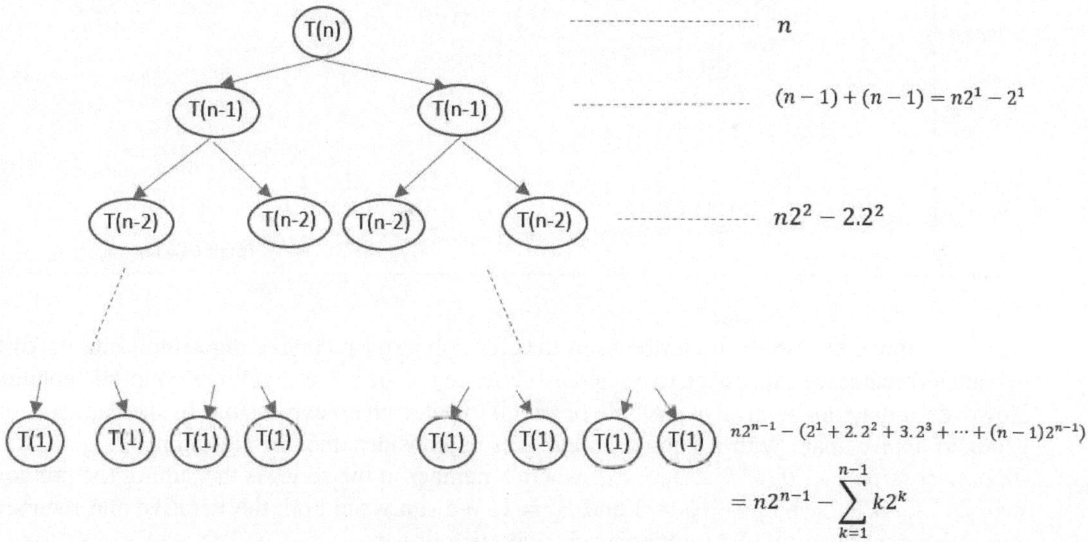

Example 1.17: $T(n) = \begin{cases} 2T(n/2) + n, & if\ n > 1 \\ 1 & , if\ n = 1 \end{cases}$

Description: The algorithm has two recursive calls with n-1 data size

$T(n) = 2T(n/2) + n = 2[2T(n/2^2) + n/2] + n = 2^2T(n/2^2) + n + n$

$= 2^2[2T(n/2^3) + n/4] + n + n = 2^3T(n/2^2) + n + n + n$

$= 2^3[2T(n/2^4) + n/8] + n + n + n = 2^4T(n/2^4) + n + n + n + n$

....

....

$= 2^kT(n/2^k) + n + \cdots + n + n + n + n$

$= 2^kT(1) + n + \cdots + n + n + n + n, Assume\ that n = 2^k$

$$= n\log_2 n + n = O(n\log_2 n)$$

Using recursion tree method, the running time of $T(n) = 2T(n/2) + n$ can be estimated as follows. The computation cost at every level is n, and there are $\log_2 n$ number of levels.

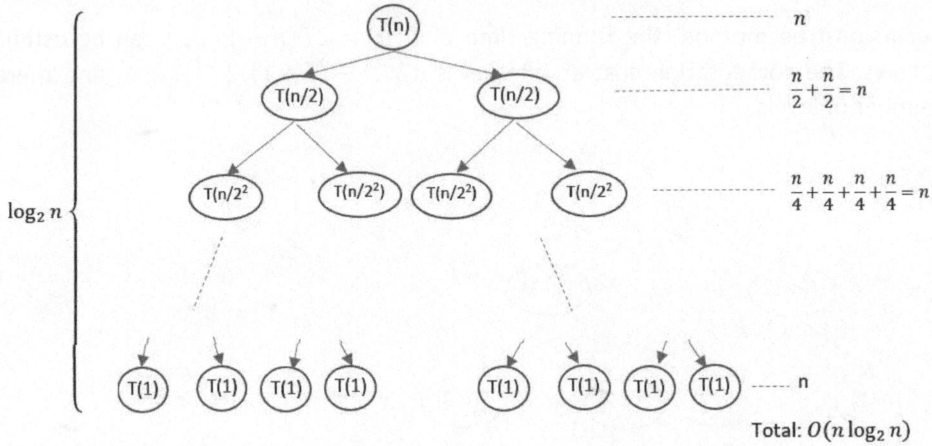

From the above examples, it can be seen that for solving a recursive algorithm, one needs to expand its recurrence expression to a standard series to get the corresponding asymptotic notation. However, it may not be always possible or trivial to get such an expression. In such as case, one needs to approximate with a known bound. Let us consider another algorithm for generating *Fibonacci series i.e., 0, 1, 1, 2, 3, 5, ...,* where a number in the series is the sum of the previous two, i.e., $F_n = F_{n-1} + F_{n-2}$, $F_0 = 0$ and $F_1 = 1$. We can write both the iterative and recursive algorithms for generation first *n* Fibonacci series as follows.

Name: FibonacciSeries
Input: Integer number n
Output: First n Fibonacci series
Description: $F_n = F_{n-1} + F_{n-2}, F_0 = 0, F_1 = 1$

```
BEGIN
Initialize F1 = 0, F2=1 and i=2
PRINT F1, F2
WHILE (i < n)
        F3 = F1 + F2
        PRINT F3
        F1=F2
        F2=F3
        i = i+1
END WHILE
END
```

Name: Fib (n)
Input: Integer number n
Output: First n Fibonacci series
Description: F(n)=F(n-1)+F(n-2)

```
BEGIN
IF n==1 OR n==0 THEN
        PRINT n
        RETURN n
ELSE
        PRINT Fib(n-1)+ Fib (n-2)
END IF
END
```

Without difficulty, it can be seen that the iterative algorithm has a linear bound i.e., O(n), as the while loop iterates for n times and there are constant running time steps within the while loop. However, the recursive algorithm has a recursive expression of the form $T(n) = T(n-1) + T(n-2) + c$. Because, it has two recursive calls of the size n-1 and n-2, and a constant computation time for splitting the task and other constant steps. If we expand the recurrence expression, we may not be able to get a standard series easily. For simplicity, let us assume $c = 1$.

$$T(n) = T(n-1) + T(n-2) + 1$$
$$= T(n-2) + T(n-3) + 1 + T(n-3) + T(n-4) + 1 + 1$$
$$= T(n-2) + 2T(n-3) + T(n-4) + 3$$
$$= T(n-3) + T(n-4) + 1 + 2T(n-4) + 2T(n-5) + 2 + T(n-5) + T(n-6) + 1 + 3$$
$$= T(n-3) + 3T(n-4) + 3T(n-5) + T(n-6) + 1 + 2 + 1 + 3$$

....

.....

The above expression needs to be expanded till every recursive call reduces to T(1). It is not easy to converse to a standard expression/series. In such a scenario, one can approximate with a known upper bound to get its asymptotic notation. It may be easier to use a pictorial tree-based expansion to approximate its asymptotic relation.

From the Figure 1.8, which computes fib(7), it can be seen that the nodes in a level is complete only upto 4^{th}level. That means, given *n*, only upto $\lceil n/2 \rceil$ levels will be complete, the rest of the levels will be incomplete. However, as it is a binary tree, we know that the number of nodes cannot be more than 2^i. So, we can assume the bound as 2^i, and approximate the series as $T(n) < 2^{n-2} + 2^{n-1} + \cdots + 2^2 + 2^1 + 2^0 \approx 2^{n-1} - 1$, and obtain the asymptotic complexity as $O(2^n)$. The assuming 2^n bound above may be a loose bound, as we know that the last levels will have nodes lesser that 2^n. The reader may attempt to get a better bound.

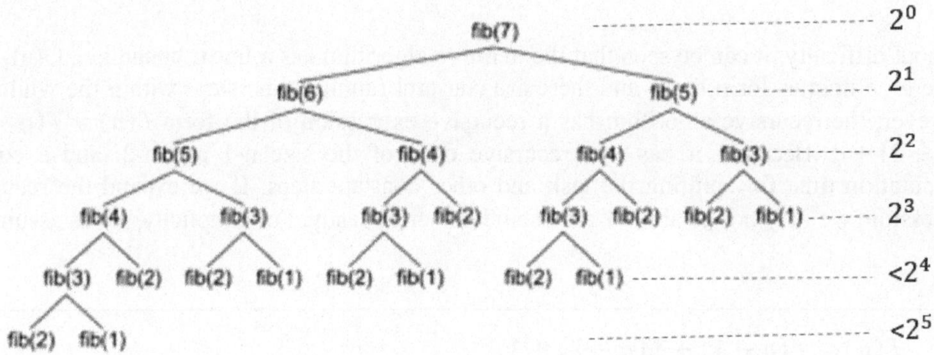

$$T(n) < 2^{n-2} + 2^{n-1} + \cdots + 2^2 + 2^1 + 2^0 \approx 2^{n-1} - 1$$

Figure 2.8: Tree representation of time complexity computation for fib(7)

What about the space complexity? As seen in Figure 1.7, the height of the tree is at the most $n - 1$. It means that the stack sector of the process running this algorithm will grow at the most by $n - 1$ records. At any instance in time, the stack will hold at the most $n - 1$ number of records of the recursive function. Therefore, space complexity is $O(n)$.

Similarly, let us take another example $T(n) = T\left(\frac{n}{3}\right) + T\left(\frac{2n}{3}\right) + n$. It divides the task into two, but with unequal sizes. Figure 1.8 illustrates the recursive expansion.

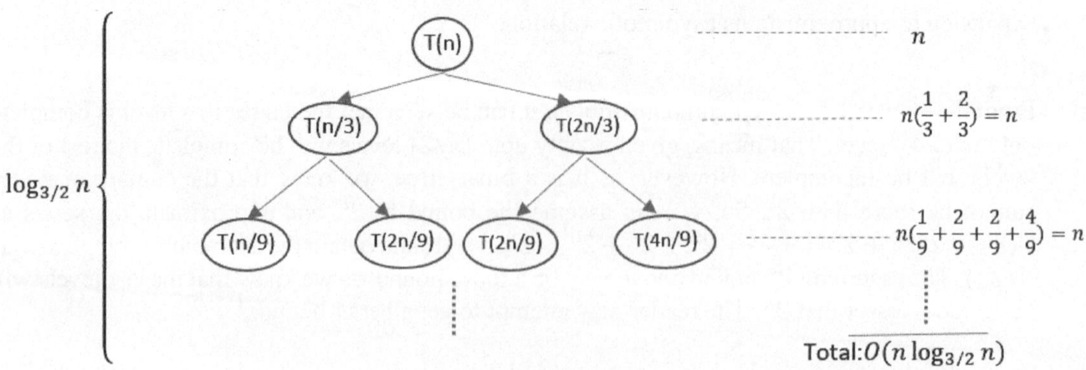

Figure 2.9: Recussive expansion for T(n)=T(n/3)+T(2n/3)+n

Every level has n computational cost and there are $\log_{3/2} n$ levels. Therefore, asymptotic complexity is $O(n \log_{3/2} n)$. It will have the space complexity of $O(\log_{3/2} n)$, i.e., the height of the tree.

1.5.7 Master Theorem

As discussed in the classic book, *Introduction to Algorithms, by Thomas Cormen, Charles Leiserson, Rolard Rivest, and Clifford Stein, the* asymptotic complexity of some of the standard recurrence expressions can be directly obtained using Master Theorem, which is briefly defined below.

Let $T(n)$ be a recurrence expression of the form $T(n) = aT\left(\frac{n}{b}\right) + f(n)$ defined over a non-negartive integer n, where $a \geq 1$ and $b > 1$ are constent, and $f(n)$ is a function of n. The $\frac{n}{b}$ in the recurrence expression represents either $\left\lfloor\frac{n}{b}\right\rfloor$ or $\left\lceil\frac{n}{b}\right\rceil$. Then, the $T(n)$ has the following asymptotic complexity bounds.

1. If $f(n) = O(n^{\log_b a-\varepsilon})$ for some constant $\varepsilon > 0$, then $T(n) = \theta(n^{\log_b a})$.
2. If $f(n) = \theta(n^{\log_b a})$ for some constant $\varepsilon > 0$, then $T(n) = \theta(n^{\log_b a} \lg n)$.
3. If $f(n) = \Omega(n^{\log_b a+\varepsilon})$ for some constant $\varepsilon > 0$, and if $af\left(\frac{n}{b}\right) \leq cf(n)$ for all sufficiently large n and some constant $c < 1$, then $T(n) = \theta(f(n))$.

In all the above three cases, the function $f(n)$ is compared with the function $n^{\log_b a}$. If one if asymptotically larger than the another, the asymptotic complexity of $T(n)$ is defined as θ of the larger function. If they are same, then multiply $T(n)$ by $\lg n$. In case 1, $n^{\log_b a}$ is asymptotically larger than $f(n)$, so, $T(n) = \theta(n^{\log_b a})$. In case 3, $f(n)$ is asymptotically larger than $n^{\log_b a}$, so $T(n) = \theta\big(f(n)\big)$. In case 2, they are asymptotically same, so $T(n) = \theta(\lg n\, f(n))$.

Let us take the following examples to understand the above conditions.

1. For $T(n) = T\left(\frac{n}{2}\right) + 1$, $a = 1, b = 2$ and $f(n) = 1$. Now, $f(n) = n^{\log_b a} = n^{\log_2 1} = 1$. Therefore, $T(n) = \theta\big(\lg n\, n^{\log_2 1}\big) = \theta(\lg n)$. If you recursively expand the expression $T(n) = T\left(\frac{n}{2}\right) + 1$ with $T(1) = 1$, you will also see that $T(n) = \log_2 n + 1 = \theta(\log_2 n)$.
2. For $T(n) = 2T\left(\frac{n}{2}\right) + 1$, $a = 2, b = 2$ and $f(n) \leq n^{\log_b a-\varepsilon} = n^{\log_2 2} = n$ for $\varepsilon = 0$. Therefore $T(n) = \theta\big(n^{\log_2 2}\big) = \theta(n)$. You have also seen in Example 1.15 that $T(n) = 2T\left(\frac{n}{2}\right) + 1 = \theta(n)$.
3. For $T(n) = 2T\left(\frac{n}{2}\right) + n$, $a = 2, b = 2$ and $f(n) = n^{\log_b a} = n^{\log_2 2} = n$. Therefore $T(n) = \theta\big(\lg n\, n^{\log_2 2}\big) = \theta(n \lg n)$. You have also seen in Example 1.17 that $T(n) = 2T\left(\frac{n}{2}\right) + n = \theta(n \log_2 n)$.
4. For $T(n) = 2T\left(\frac{n}{2}\right) + n^2$, $a = 2, b = 2$ and $f(n) \geq n^{\log_b a+\varepsilon} = n^{\log_2 2} = n$ for $\varepsilon = 0$. Therefore, $f(n) = \Omega\big(n^{\log_2 2}\big) = \Omega(n)$, and $T(n) = \theta(f(n)) = \theta(n^2)$.
5. For $T(n) = 5T\left(\frac{n}{2}\right) + n$, $a = 5, b = 2$ and $f(n) \leq n^{\log_b a-\varepsilon} = n^{\log_2 5-0.322} = n^2$ for $\varepsilon = 0.322$. Therefore $T(n) = \theta\big(n^{\log_2 5}\big)$.

1.6 LINEAR AND BINARY SEARCH

Given an array of elements, a linear search algorithm will scan all the elements in the array one-by-one from the first element till the last element and check if the element to be searched is present or not. A sample linear search program which scans the entire array is discussed in example 1.2. As this program scans all the elements in the array, its running time can be defined as $T(n) = an + b$ where a and b are positive constant, and its asymptotic complexity can be defined as $T(n) = \theta(n)$.

Further in Section 4.3, a variant of the linear search algorithm is discussed with its best case, worst case and average case scenarios. In the best case, the loop iterates only one time and hence $T(n)$ is some constant and its asymptotic complexity is $T(n) = \theta(1)$. In the worst case, the loop iterates for n times with running cost $T(n) = an + b$, and its asymptotic complexity is $T(n) = \theta(n)$. In the average case, it has $T(n) = an + b$ running time (see Section 4.3 for a detailed estimate), and has $T(n) = \theta(n)$ asymptotic complexity.

In the above case of linear search, the elements in the array are allowed to be in any arbitrary order. Now, let us assume that the elements are in **ascending order** (it can also be in descending order). Under this assumption, the scanning of the element can be restricted till we find an element in the array which is equal to or greater than the element to be searched and modify the algorithm as follows.

Algorithm: LinearSearch

Input: An element *e*, a sorted array A

Output: Print the index of the element if FOUND

Assumption: A has *n* elements

```
BEGIN
Initialize i = 0
WHILE i < n
    IF A[i] == e THEN
        Break
    END IF
    i = i+1
END WHILE
IF i < n THEN
    PRINT FOUND at i
ELSE
    Print NOT FOUNT
END IF
END
```

Similar to the earlier version of linear search given in Section 4.3, the above algorithm also will its best case if the element is found at the first location, average case if the element is found at the arbitrary location, and worst case if the element is not found or found at the last location of the array. Accordingly, its best case, worst case, and average case time complexity are $\theta(1), \theta(n)$ and $\theta(n)$ respectively.

If we mandatorily assume that the elements are in sorted order, can we do better? Unlike linear search, instead of scanning the array from first to last, we can check the middle element directly. If the element to be searched is found in the middle, we stop searching. If the element to be searched is smaller than the middle element, then the element could be in the first half of the array. In such a case, we search only the elements in the first half and elements in the second half are ignored. If the element to be searched is larger than the middle element, then the element could be in the second half of the array. In such a case, we search only the elements in the second half and the elements in the second half are ignored. In this manner, the above search conditions are successively applied over the selected half of the intermediate array till the size of the array is 1 or element is found. This approach is called *binary search*. It is binary because larger array is divided into two smaller halves and search the element. Such an approach of dividing a bigger problem size into a smaller problem size(s) and solve the target problem is known as *divide and conquer*. Using divide and conquer, a complex problem may be able to solve more easily and efficiently and effectively. Recursive algorithms are generally *divide and conquer*. The above binary search approach is illustrated with the example below.

Input Array: A ={3, 5, 6, 10, 13, 17, 19, 20}, index start from 0

Element to be search: 4

Number of elements: n=8

Step 1: As array size is not 1, perform the following operations.

(i) Check the middle i.e., $A\left[\left\lceil\frac{8}{2}\right\rceil - 1\right] = A[3]$ and compare with searched element i.e., 4

(ii) The middle element i.e., 10 is not the searched element. Divide the array into two halves {3, 5, 6} 10 {13, 17, 19, 20}

(iii) As middle element 10 larger than the searched element 4, select the first half i.e., {3, 5, 6}

Step 2: As array size is not 1, perform the following operations.

(i) Check the middle i.e., $A\left[\left\lceil\frac{3}{2}\right\rceil - 1\right] = A[1]$ and compare with searched element i.e., 4

(ii) The middle element i.e., 5 is not the searched element. Divide the array into two halves {3} 5 {6}

(iii) As middle element 5 smaller than searched element 4, select the first half i.e., {3}, 5, 6}

Step 3: As the array size is 1, the element is not the search element, **Print NOT FOUND** and terminate.

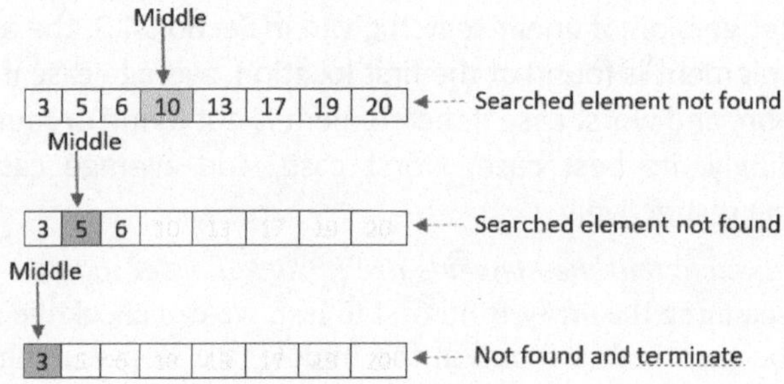

In the above scenario, comparisons with only three number of elements (out of 8 elements in the array) are performed. This three is nothing but $\lceil \log_2 8 \rceil = 3$. Instead of 4, if we search 10, we can find in the first step itself, i.e., one comparison. Likewise, if we search 5, it needs two comparisons. For search element 3, it needs three comparisons.

If we search for 6, we get the element in three steps as shown in the following figure.

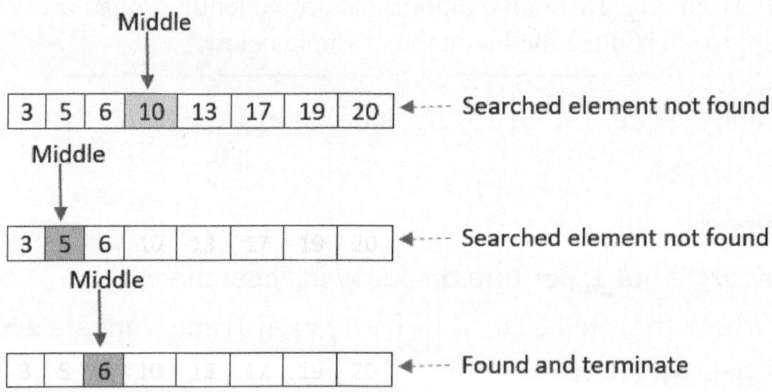

For 13, we get in three steps, For 17, we get in two steps as shown in the following figure.

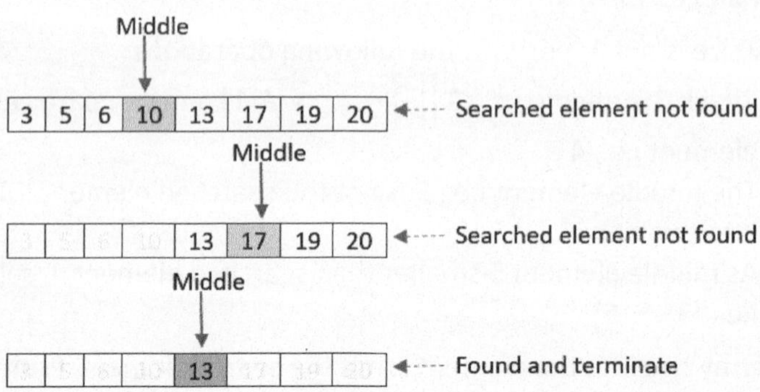

For 19, we get in three steps.

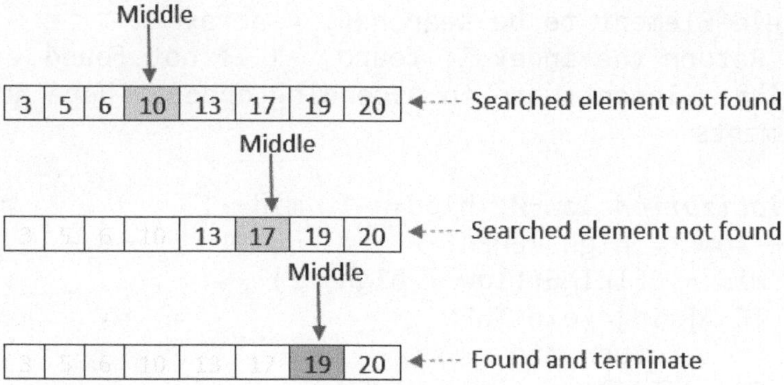

For 20, we get in four steps as shown below. Likewise, if we search any element larger than 20, it will take four steps.

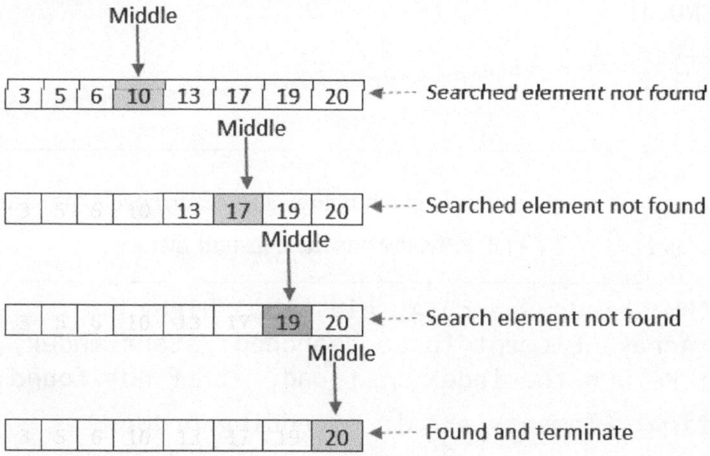

An iterative binary search algorithm is given below. In every iteration of the while loop, the size of the array is reduced by half by updating the low or high variable by mid+1 or mid-1. Therefore, the while loop will iterate at the most upto $\log_2 n$.

```
Algorithm: binarySearch
Input: ele-Element to be searched, A-array
Output: Return the index if found, -1 if not found
Assumption: Elements are in ascending order. There are n number of
   elements
BEGIN
Initialization low=0, high=n-1, mid=-1
WHILE low <= high REPEAT
      mid = CEILING((low + high)/2)
      IF A[mid]==ele THEN
           return mid
      ELSE IF ele > A[mid] THEN
           low = mid + 1
      ELSE THEN
           high = mid - 1
     END IF
     mid = -1
END WHILE
END
```

A recursive binary search algorithm is given below. The recurrence expression of the algorithm can be defined as $T(n) = T\left(\frac{n}{2}\right) + c$, where c is the constant factors.

```
Algorithm: binarySearch(A, ele, low, high)
Input: Array, Element to be searched, start index, end index
Output: Return the index if found, -1 if not found
Assumption: Elements are in ascending order.
BEGIN
IF low > high THEN
    return -1
ELSE
    mid = (low + high) / 2
    IF A[mid] == ele THEN
           return mid
    ELSE IF A[mid] < ele THEN
          return binarySearch(A, ele, mid + 1, high)
    ELSE THEN
          return binarySearch(A, ele, low, mid - 1)
      END IF
      END IF
END
```

Best case: the element is found in the middle. It will take asymptotic constant time i.e., $T(n) = \theta(1)$.

Worst Case: The element is not found or found in the last step. It will take asymptotic $\log_2 n$ i.e., $T(n) = \theta(\log_2 n)$.

Average case: Given an array with n elements, we observe the following generalizations from the above examples.

- There is 2^0 index in the array that needs one comparison.
- There are 2^1 indexes in the array that need two comparisons.
- There are 2^2 indexes in the array that need three comparisons.
- There are 2^{i-1} indexes in the array that need i comparisons.
- There are $2^{\log_2 n-1}$ indexes in the array that need $\log_2 n$ comparisons.

Given n indexes, probability of an index with i number of comparisons is $\frac{2^{i-1}}{n}$. Therefore, average number of comparisons is $T(n) = 1\frac{2^0}{n} + 2\frac{2^1}{n} + 3\frac{2^2}{n} + \cdots + k\frac{2^{k-1}}{n}$, where $n = 2^k$ i.e, $k = \log_2 n$.

Therefore, $T(n) = \frac{1}{n}\sum_{i=1}^{k} i2^{i-1} = \frac{1}{2n}\sum_{i=1}^{k} i2^{i} = \frac{1}{2n}\left[2\frac{1-(k+1)n+2kn}{(1-2)^2}\right] = \frac{1}{n} - k - 1 + 2k$

$$= k - 1 + \frac{1}{n} \approx \log_2 n - 1 = O(\log_2 n)$$

So, the average case time complexity is $O(\log_2 n)$.

UNIT SUMMARY

In this unit, the concept of data structure and algorithm, their relationship from the aspect of solving a problem through a computer program have been discussed in detail with appropriate examples. The contents of the unit have been logically organised for understanding the following thematic concepts:

- What is a data structure, and what are the terminologies related to data structure?
- Categorization of data structures based on the
  - Structural relationship between the data elements (linear or non-linear).
  - Memory allocations (static or dynamic, and contiguous or non-contiguous).
  - Different types of data structures (array, linked list, stack, queue, tree, graph)
- What is an algorithm and what are the properties of algorithm?
- Approaches of evaluating an algorithm?
  - Asymptotic notations
  - Time complexity and space complexity
  - Best case, worst case, and average case
- Estimating complexity of a given algorithm
  - Iterative and recursive
  - Recurrence expression, recursive tree and Master's theorem
- Searching – linear search and binary search

EXERCISES

Many of these questions have been compiled from various sources including past GATE examinations.

Multiple Choice Questions

Q1. Consider the following C program segment:

```
int i=1, n;
while (i <=n)
      i = i*2;
```

The number of comparisons made in the execution of the loop for any $n > 0$ is:

(A) $\lceil \log_2 n \rceil + 1$ (B) n (C) $\lceil \log_2 n \rceil$ (D) $\lfloor \log_2 n \rfloor + 1$

Q2. Consider the following C program segment:

```
int i=1, n;
while (i <=n)
      i = i*2;
```

For any $n > 0$, the time complexity of the above program segment is:

(A) $\theta(\log_2 n)$ (B) $\theta(n)$ (C) $\theta(1)$ (D) $\theta(n^2)$

Q3. Consider the following C program segment:

```
int i=1, n;
while (i <=n)
        i = i*2;
```

For any $n > 0$, the space complexity of the above program segment is:

(A) $\theta(\log_2 n)$ (B) $\theta(n)$ (C) $\theta(1)$ (D) $\theta(n^2)$

Q4. The following C function determines GCD of two positive integer numbers n and m. Let $n \geq m$.

```
int gcd(n,m) {
        if (n % m ==0) return m;
        return gcd(m, n%m);
}
```

How many recursive calls are made by this function?

(A) $\theta(\log_2 n)$ (B) $\Omega(n)$ (C) $\theta(\log_2 \log_2 n)$ (D) $\theta(\sqrt{n})$

Q5. What is the time complexity of the following recursive function:

```
int do (int n) {
  if (n <= 2) return 1;
  else return (do(floor(sqrt(n))) + n);
}
```

(A) $\theta(\log_2 n)$ (B) $\theta(n \log_2 n)$ (C) $\theta(\log_2 \log_2 n)$ (D) $\theta(n^2)$

Q6. Consider the following code segment:

```
int isPrime(n) {
        int i,n;
        for(i=2;i<=sqrt(n);i++)
                if(n%i == 0) {
                        printf("Not Prime\n");
                        return 0;
                }
    return 1;
}
```

Let $T(n)$ denote the number of times the for loop is executed by the program on input n. Which of the following is TRUE?

(A)	$T(n) = O(\sqrt{n})$ and $T(n) = \Omega(\sqrt{n})$	(B)	$T(n) = O(\sqrt{n})$ and $T(n) = \Omega(1)$
(C)	$T(n) = O(n)$ and $T(n) = \Omega(\sqrt{n})$	(D)	None of above

Q7. Consider the recurrence equation $T(n) = 2T(\sqrt{n}) + 1, T(1) = 1$. Which one of the following is true?

(A) $T(n) = \theta(\log \log n)$ (B) $T(n) = \theta(\log n)$ (C) $T(n) = \theta(\sqrt{n})$ (D) $\theta(n)$

Q8. Consider the functions. $f(n) = 2^n$, $g(n) = n^n$, and $h(n) = n^{\log n}$. Which one of the following statements about the asymptotic behavior of the functions $f(n)$, $g(n)$ and $h(n)$ is true?

(A)	$f(n) = O(g(n))$ and $g(n) = O(h(n))$	(B)	$f(n) = \Omega(g(n))$ and $g(n) = O(h(n))$
(C)	$g(n) = O(f(n))$ and $h(n) = O(f(n))$	(D)	$h(n) = O(f(n))$ and $g(n) = \Omega(f(n))$

Q9. The minimum number of comparisons required to determine if an integer appears more than n/2 times in a sorted array of n integers is

(A) $\theta(n)$ (B) $\theta(\log n)$ (C) $\theta\left(\frac{n}{2}\right)$ (D) $\theta(1)$

Q10. Let W(n) and A(n) denote respectively, the worst case and average case running time of an algorithm executed on an input of size n. Which of the following is ALWAYS TRUE?

(A) $A(n) = \Omega(W(n))$ (B) $A(n) = \theta(W(n))$ (C) $A(n) = O(W(n))$ (D) $A(n) = o(W(n))$

Q11. The recurrence relation capturing the optimal execution time of the Towers of Hanoi problem with *n* discs is

(A)	$T(n) = 2T(n-2) + 2$	(B)	$T(n) = 2T(n-1) + n$
(C)	$T(n) = 2T\left(\frac{n}{2}\right) + 1$	(D)	$T(n) = 2T(n-1) + 1$

Q12. Find the returned value of the following function.

```
int unknown(int n) {
    int i, j, k = 0;
    for (i  = n/2; i <= n; i++)
        for (j = 2; j <= n; j = j * 2)
            k = k + n/2;
    return k;
}
```

(A) $\theta(n^2)$ (B) $\theta(n^2 \log n)$ (C) $\theta(n^3)$ (D) $\theta(n^3 \log n)$

Q13. Find the returned value of the following function.

```
int unknown(int n) {
    int i, j, k = 0;
    for (i  = 1; i <= n; i++)
        for (j = 1; j <= n; j++)
            k = k + 1;
    return k;
}
```

(A) $\theta(n^2)$ (B) $\theta(n^2 \log n)$ (C) $\theta(n^3)$ (D) $\theta(n^3 \log n)$

Q14. Find the returned value of the following function.

```
int unknown(int n) {
    int i, j, k = 0;
    for (i  = n/2; i <= n; i++)
        for (j = 2; j <= n; j = j * 2)
            k = k + 1;
    return k;
}
```

(A) $\theta(n^2)$ (B) $\theta(n^2 \log n)$ (C) $\theta(n \log n)$ (D) $\theta(n)$

Q15. Which one of the following correctly determines the solution of the following recurrence relation?

$$T(n) = \begin{cases} 2T\left(\frac{n}{2}\right) + \log n, & n > 1 \\ 1, & n = 1 \end{cases}$$

(A) $\theta(n)$ (B) $\theta(n^2)$ (C) $\theta(n \log n)$ (D) $\theta(\log n)$

16. Which of the following statements best describes the relationship between algorithms and data structures?

A) Algorithms are used to define the structure of data in a program.

B) Data structures are used to define the approach of using the data to solve a problem.

C) Algorithms and data structures are inherently related and go hand in hand.

D) Data structures are more important than algorithms in developing efficient programs.

17. Which of the following is not true about contiguous memory allocation-based data structure?
    (A) The non-linear data structures can be implemented.
    (B) Contiguous memory allocation does suffer from internal fragmentation.
    (C) The size of the storage structure can be changed during runtime.
    (D) If the address of the first data element is known, the address of any data element can be directly derived by its index without scanning the other data elements

18. Which of the following is NOT a common operation that can be performed over the data of a data structure?
    (A) Addition
    (B) Deletion
    (C) Updation
    (D) Creation

19. Which one of the following is NOT true regarding Linear and Non-Linear Data Structures?
    (A) A linear Data structure stores its data sequentially.
    (B) A non-linear data structure orders its data elements non-sequentially.
    (C) Arrays, queues, and stacks are common examples of linear data structures.
    (D) Non-linear data structures cannot be implemented using contiguous memory allocation.

20. What is the output of the following code?

```
main(){
    int a[10];
    a[0] = 3;
    a[1] = 1;
    a[2] = 7;
    printf("%d",a[10]);
}
```

    (A) Segmentation fault
    (B) 7
    (C) 9999999
    (D) 0

21. Analyse the time and space complexity of the following program.

```
int fact(int n){
    if(n == 1)
    return 1;
    return n*fact(n-1);
}
```

    (A) $T(n) = \theta(n)$ and $S(n) = \theta(1)$
    (B) $T(n) = \theta(n)$ and $S(n) = \theta(n)$
    (C) $T(n) = \theta(1)$ and $S(n) = \theta(n)$
    (D) $T(n) = \theta(1)$ and $S(n) = \theta(1)$

22. The Best case, Worst case and Average case of a Binary search algorithm given in respective order is given by
    (A) $\theta(n), \theta(\log n), \theta(n)$
    (B) $\theta(n), \theta(n^2), \theta(\log n)$
    (C) $\theta(1), \theta(\log n), \theta(\log n)$
    (D) $\theta(\log n), \theta(\log n), \theta(\log n)$

Short and Long Answer Type Questions

Q1. Consider the following function and determine the functionality of foo. Estimate time complexity and space complexity of the function.

```
int foo(int a, int b){
        if(a == b)
                return a;
        if (a > b)
                foo(a - b, b);
        else
                foo(a, b - a);
}
```

Q2. Consider the following function and determine the functionality of foo. Estimate time complexity and space complexity of the function.

```
int foo(int a, int b, int res){
      if(a == b) return res*a;
      else if((a%2 == 0) && (b%2 == 0))
        return foo(a//2, b//2, 2*res);
      else if (a % 2 == 0)
        return foo(a // 2, b, res);
      else if (b % 2 == 0)
      return foo(a, b // 2, res);
      else if (a > b)
        return foo(a - b, b, res);
      else return foo(a, b - a, res);
}
```

Q3. Prove or disprove

1. If $f(n) = O(n^{\log_2 c})$ for some constant positive c, then $T(n) = \theta(n^{\log_2 c})$.
2. If $f(n) = \theta(n^{\log_2 c})$ for some constant $c > 0$, then $T(n) = \theta(n^{\log_2 c} \lg n)$.
3. $f(n) = O(g(n))$ if and only if $g(n) = \Omega(f(n))$.
4. $f(n) = o(g(n))$ if and only if $g(n) = \omega(f(n))$.
5. $\log_8 n = \frac{1}{2} \log n$

Q4. If the time complexity of an algorithm is defined by $T(n) = 1 \times 2 + 2 \times 2^2 + 2 \times 2^3 \ldots + 2 \times 2^n$. What is the asymptotic time complexity of $T(n)$ in term of big-O?

Q5. If the time complexity of an algorithm is defined by $T(n) = \sum_{i=1}^{n} \lfloor \log_2 i \rfloor$. What is the asymptotic time complexity of $T(n)$ in term of big-O?

Q6. If the time complexity of an algorithm is defined by $(n) = 1 + \left(1 - \frac{1}{1!}\right)n + \left(1 - \frac{1}{1!} + \frac{1}{2!}\right)n(n - 1) + \left(1 - \frac{1}{1!} + \frac{1}{2!} - \frac{1}{3!}\right)n(n-1)(n-2) + \cdots$. What is the asymptotic time complexity of $T(n)$ in term of big-O?

Q7. If the time complexity of an algorithm is defined by $T(n) = 1^2 + 2^2 + 3^2 + \cdots + n^2$. What is the asymptotic time complexity of $T(n)$ in term of big-O?

Q8. Prove or disprove

1. $cO(f(n)) = O(f(n))$ for some constant positive c.
2. $O(f(n)) + O(f(n)) = O(f(n))$
3. $O\left(O(f(n))\right) = O(f(n))$
4. $O(f(n)g(n)) = O(f(n)g(n))$
5. $O\big(f(n)g(n)\big) = f(n)O(g(n))$

Q9. Prove or disprove: $O\big(f(n) + g(n)\big) = f(n) + O(g(n))$, if $f(n)$ and $g(n)$ are positive for all n.

Q10. Prove or disprove: $\theta(e^n) \leq \theta(n^m)$ for an arbitrary m.

Numerical Problems

Q1. Find the asymptotic time complexity in terms of $O, \theta, \Omega, o, \omega$, wherever feasible, of the following expression.

1. $T(n) = 2T\left(\frac{n}{2}\right) + 3T\left(\frac{n}{3}\right) + 1, T(1) = 1$
2. $T(n) = T\left(\frac{n}{3}\right) + T\left(\frac{2n}{3}\right) + 1, T(1) = 1$
3. $T(n) = T\left(\frac{n}{2}\right) + T\left(\frac{n}{3}\right) + \theta(n), T(1) = 1$
4. $T(n) = T\left(\frac{n}{3}\right) + 3T\left(\frac{2n}{3}\right) + \theta(n), T(1) = 1$
5. $T(n) = T(n-1) + 2T(n-2) + 1, T(0) = 0, T(2) = 1$

Q2. Consider the following recurrence equation and estimate its asymptotic complexity in terms of O.

$$T(n) = 3T\left(\frac{n}{4}\right) + n, T(1) = 2$$

Q3. Consider the following recurrence equation and estimate its asymptotic complexity in terms of O.

$$T(n) = 2T\left(\left\lfloor\frac{n}{2}\right\rfloor\right) + \sqrt{n}, \quad T(1) = 2$$

Q4. How many substrings of different non-zero length (but less than or equal to n) can be formed from a string of length n?

Q5. Given an array with n number of integer numbers. What is the minimum number of exchanges required in worst case, if we want to arrange the numbers in the array such that all negative numbers occur before all positive numbers.

PRACTICAL

Q1. Consider two matrices of orders $n \times k$ and $k \times m$. Write a program to multiply the two matrices and estimate the time complexity of the algorithm.

Q2. Consider two matrices of orders $n \times m$. Write a program to add the two matrices and estimate the time complexity of the algorithm.

Q3. Write a program to find second smallest element in an array of n elements, and estimate its time complexity.

Q4. Write a program to solve Tower of Hanoi problem, and estimate its time complexity.

Q5. Write a program to find LCM of two positive integer numbers, and estimate its time complexity.

Q6. Write a program to find prime factors of a positive integer number and estimate its time complexity.

Q7. Write a program to convert a number with radix a to its equivalent number with radix b and estimate its time complexity.

Q8. Consider a set with n integer numbers. Write a program to generate all permutations of size $k \leq n$, and estimate its time complexity.

Q9. Write a program to find square root of a given positive integer number, and estimate its time complexity.

Q10. Write a program to find $log\ a$ given positive integer number based b, and estimate its time complexity.

KNOW MORE

Loop Invariant: Given a program, the problem of guaranteeing the correctness of the program is one of the core challenges in software development. Researchers and practitioners use a variety of techniques to validate correctness of the program. For an iterative problem, *loop invariant* is one of the approaches which can be used to help understanding correctness of an algorithm/program. *The loop invariant of a given loop is a Boolean condition which is true – (i) before the loop starts, (ii) during the execution of the loop, and (iii) after the loop.*

A loop can be realized as the following template.

```
while E {
      S
}
```

where E is the loop condition also known as *loop guard*, and S is the loop body. The loop invariant should be true – (i) before the execution of the `while` loop, (ii) before the execution of S and after the execution of S during each iteration of the loop, and (iii) after exiting the loop. Let us illustrate the above conditions with the following algorithm which estimates the sum of the elements in an array.

```
Algorithm: SUM
Input: A - an array of integers
Output: sum - sum of the elements in A
Begin:
i = 0
sum = 0
while (i < len(A))
      sum = sum + A[i]
      i = i + 1
return sum
END
```

For a given problem, identifying an appropriate loop invariant condition is the most crucial task. One needs to identify the condition which will hold for before, within and after the loop justifying the correctness of the program. For the above example, we define the loop invariant as follows.

$\boldsymbol{Invariant(i, sum)}$: $0 \leq i \leq len(A)\ AND\ sum = \sum_{j=0}^{i-1} A[j]$

The above invariant condition ensures that at a particular instance of loop iteration, the *sum* will hold the sum of all the effected elements in the array. The above loop invariant holds true during the following stages.

1. Before the start of the loop, the value of i is 0 and sum is also 0. The invariant is true.
2. For an arbitrary value of i while iterating the loop i.e., $0 \leq i < len(A)$, the sum is equal to $\sum_{j=0}^{i-1} A[j]$ before the start of S and after executing S. Thus, the invariant is true.
3. After the exiting the loop, $i = len(A)$ and $sum = A[0] + A[1] + \cdots + A[len(A) - 1]$. Thus, the invariant is true.

The above algorithm can be annotated as follows.

```
Algorithm: SUM
Input: A - an array of integers
Output: sum - sum of the elements in A
Begin:
i = 0
sum = 0
// loop invariant holds here
while (i < len(A))
      // loop invariant holds here
      sum = sum + A[i]
      i = i + 1
      // loop invariant holds here
```

```
return sum
    // loop invariant holds here
END
```

Prove of Correctness of a Program: Prove of correctness of a program can be performed using *induction on the invariant*. The following three steps are generally performed.

1. *Base Step:* The loop invariant is true just before entering the loop.
2. *Induction Step:* Assume that the loop invariant and loop guard are true at an arbitrary iteration in the loop. Then, prove that they are also true in the next iteration.
3. *Postcondition Step:* The loop invariant and negation of the loop guard are true after exiting the loop. Satisfying negation of loop guard is important to ensure successfully exiting the loop.

Let us illustrate the above steps with the example program above.

1. *Base Step:* Just before entering the loop, $i = 0$ and $sum = 0$. Now let us check the invariant

   $$\boldsymbol{Invariant(0,0)}: 0 \leq 0 \leq len(A)\ AND\ 0 = \sum_{j=0}^{-1} A[j]$$

   Both the conditions are true.
2. *Induction Step:* Let us assume that the invariant is true at the time of entering an arbitrary iteration k, that is $\boldsymbol{Invariant(0,k)}: 0 \leq k \leq len(A) AND\ sum_k = \sum_{j=0}^{k-1} A[j]$ is true.
   Now, we need to prove for $\boldsymbol{Invariant(0,k+1)}: 0 \leq k+1 \leq len(A) AND\ sum_{k+1} = sum_k + A[k]$.

   Given that loop guard holds during the iteration. The next iteration of k is $k+1$.
   At the kth iteration, sum_k is equal to the sum of the first k elements in the array. Now, $sum_{k+1} = sum_k + A[k]$ i.e., $\sum_{j=0}^{k} A[j]$. Therefore, sum_{k+1} is the sum of the first $k+1$ elements in the array. Hence, the induction is proved.
3. *Postcondition Step:* When $i = len(A)$, the loop guard fails i.e., negation of loop guard is true. At this instance, $sum = \sum_{j=0}^{len(A)-1} A[j]$. That is, the sum of all the elements in the array. Then, the loop invariant and negation of the loop guard are true.

Additional Examples on Loop Invariant:

Example 1:

```
Algorithm: Balance decrement and increment of two variables
 i = n
j = 0
while(i > 0){
     i = i-1
     j = j+1
}
```

```
Print the values of i and j
```

$$\boldsymbol{Invariant(i,j,n)}: 0 \le i \le n \; AND \; 0 \le j \le n \; AND \; i + j = n$$

Example 2:

```
Algorithm: Find maximum value in an array A
Assumption: few positive values(at least one) are present
            in A
max = 0;
for (int i = 0; i < len(A); i++) {
    if (A[i] > max) {
        max = A[i];
    }
}
Print max
```

$$\boldsymbol{Invariant(i, max)}: 0 \le i \le len(A) \; AND \; max = \max(A[0 \ldots (len(A) - 1)])$$

Further Reading

Readers are encouraged to explore the following E-Books/E-Resources for additional examples, and discussions on related topics.

1. Complexity of Algorithms. Chapter 1, Electronic Lecture Notes - DATA STRUCTURES AND ALGORITHMS, by Y. Narahari (https://gtl.csa.iisc.ac.in/hari/wp-content/uploads/2021/10/dsa.pdf)
2. Arrays, Iteration, Invariants. Chapter 2, Lecture Notes for Data Structures and Algorithms, John Bullinaria, School of Computer Science, University of Birmingham, UK (https://www.cs.bham.ac.uk/~jxb/DSA/dsa.pdf)
3. Algorithm Analysis, Chapter 2, Data Structures and Algorithm Analysis in C++, Weiss, Mark Allen, 4th Ed. (https://www.uoitc.edu.iq/images/documents/informatics-institute/Competitive_exam/DataStructures.pdf).

REFERENCES AND SUGGESTED READINGS

- [Adamson, 1996] I. T. Adamson. (1996), Data structures and Algorithms: A first Course, Springer.
- [Aho, 1983] A. V. Aho, J. E. Hopcroft, and J D. Ullman. (1983), Data Structures and Algorithms, Addison-Wesley.
- [Cormen, 2001] Cormen, T. H.; Leiserson, C. E.; Rivest, R. L. & Stein, C. (2001), *Introduction to Algorithms* , The MIT Press .
- [Donald, 2009] Donald E. Knuth. (2009), The Art of Computer Programming: Fundamental Algorithms, Vol. 1, 3rd Edition, Pearson.

- [Graham, 1994] R. L. Graham, D. E. Knuth and O. Patashnik. (1994) Concrete Mathematics: A Foundation for Computer Science, 2nd Edition. Addison -Wesley.
- [Greene, 1988] D. H. Greene and D. E Knuth. (1988) Mathematics for the analysis of Algorithms, Birkhauser.
- [Hopcroft, 1969] J. E. Hopcroft and J. D. Ullman. (1969) Formal language and their relation to automata. Addison-Wesley.
- [Horowitz, 1983] E. Horowitz and S Sahni. (1983) Fundamentals of data Structure, Computer Science Press
- [Horowitz, 1993] E. Horowitz, S Sahni and A. Freed. (1993) Fundamentals of data Structure in C, Computer Science Press.
- [James, 2009] James A. Storer. (2009), An Introduction to Data Structures and Algorithms, 1st Edition, Birkhauser Springer.
- [Kingston, 1990] J. H. Kingston. (1990), Algorithms and data structures, Addison-Wesley.
- [Kozon, 1992] D. C. Kozen. (1992), The design and Analysis of Algorithms, Springer.
- [Lewis, 1991] H. R. Lewis and L. Denenberg. (1991) Data Structures and Their Algorithms, Harper Collins.
- [Wirth, 1976] Wirth, N. (1976), *Algorithms + Data Structures = Programs* , Prentice-Hall.

Dynamic QR Code for Further Reading

Scan the following QR Code to navigate to an external page to explore additional materials, and listen to lecture of prominent scientists.

2 Array, Stack and Queue

UNIT SPECIFICS

This unit discusses the following linear data structures:

- *Array;*
- *Stack;*
- *Queue;*

Each data structure is first conceptually introduced and then followed by storage structure, applicable operations with appropriate examples and diagrams. The algorithm for each of the operations is also discussed. The complexity of each algorithm is also discussed. Initially, array data structure and its properties are discussed in details. Storage structures of different types of arrays – multidimensional arrays, sparse arrays are presented with appropriate visualization. After that, implementations of Stack and Queue data structure using array are given in details along with their algorithms and sample programs. Few applications of Stack data structure are also discussed. Implementation of circular queue using array is also presented. The conceptual understanding of Abstract Data Type (ADT) is briefly introduced, and generalized definitions of Stack and Queue ADTs are provided.

A large number of exercise questions of different types - multiple choice, short and long answer typed questions, practice questions are also given. For additional questions and reading materials, a QR code has been provided which is linked to a web page, for further reading and exercises.

RATIONALE

This unit discusses three of the most fundamental data structures. Among the data structures (discussed in this unit and later units), array is the most fundamental data structure, which may be used further implementing other data structures. For instance, the other two data structures – Stack and Queue discussed in this unit are implemented using array (they can also be implemented using another data structure called linked list discussed in Unit-III). Therefore, array data structure, its types, operations on array, etc. are first introduced. It is followed by the conceptual definitions of stack and queue, their implementations using array.

PRE-REQUISITES

Programming: C programming language (Many of the examples are given in C like statements)
Computer System: Main Memory

UNIT OUTCOMES

List of outcomes of this unit is as follows:

U2-O1: Understanding Array data structure, different types of arrays
U2-O2: Algorithms of different types of operations on array, and estimating their complexities
U2-O3: Understand stack data structure
U2-O4: Algorithms of different types of operations on stack, and estimating their complexities
U2-O5: Understand stack data structure
U2-O6: Algorithms of different types of operations on queue, and estimating their complexities

Unit-2 Outcomes	EXPECTED MAPPING WITH COURSE OUTCOMES (1- Weak Correlation; 2- Medium Correlation; 3- Strong Correlation)					
	CO-1	CO-2	CO-3	CO-4	CO-5	CO-6
U2-O1	1	-	3	-	-	-
U2-O2	1	-	3	-	-	-
U2-O3	1	-	3	-	-	-
U2-O4	1	-	3	-	-	-
U2-O5	1	-	3	-	-	-
U2-O6	1	-	3	-	-	-

2.1 ARRAYS

An array is a collection of finite number of *homogeneous* data elements stored at *contiguous* memory locations. Homogeneous means, the data elements are of the *same type*. It is a *linear* data structure, because its data elements are ordered as first, second, third, and so on. The data elements of an array are stored at contiguous memory locations linearly.

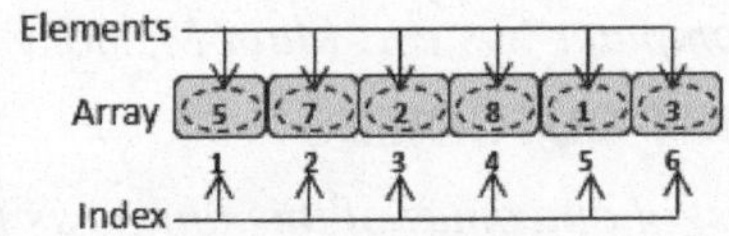

Figure 2.1: Array

Index defines the location and ordering of the data elements. If the index of the first element is 1, the index of the second element is 2, the index of the third element is 3 and so on. The indexes of the first and last elements of an array are often referred to as *lower bound (LB)* and *upper bound (UB)* respectively. Figure 2.1 illustrates an example of an array with $\{5, 7, 2, 8, 1, 3\}$ data elements, and its *LB* and *UB* as 1 and 6, respectively. The first element 5 is stored at index $LB = 1$. The second element 7 is stored at the index *LB+1*, the third element 2 at the index *LB+2* and so on. The last element 3 is stored at the index *UB*. The number of data elements in an array is defined by $(UB - LB + 1) = (6 - 1 + 1) = 6$.

The data element at any arbitrary location can be accessed using its index, without visiting other elements in the array. Therefore, the method of accessing data elements of an array is also referred to as *random access method.* If the name of an array is *A*, the first element of *A* can be accessed as $A[LB]$, second element as $A[LB + 1]$ and so on. The number of the elements in the array is limited by the amount of memory allotted for the array in the memory.

2.1.1 Types of Arrays

An array can be defined as an *one-dimensional (1D)* array or a multi-dimensional array (more than one dimension). Figure 2.1 defines an example of a 1D array. A two-dimensional (2D) array is defined as an *array of 1D arrays*. Likewise, a three-dimensional array is defined as an *array of 2D arrays*, and so on. Figure 2.2 illustrates 1D, 2D and 3D types of arrays pictorially.

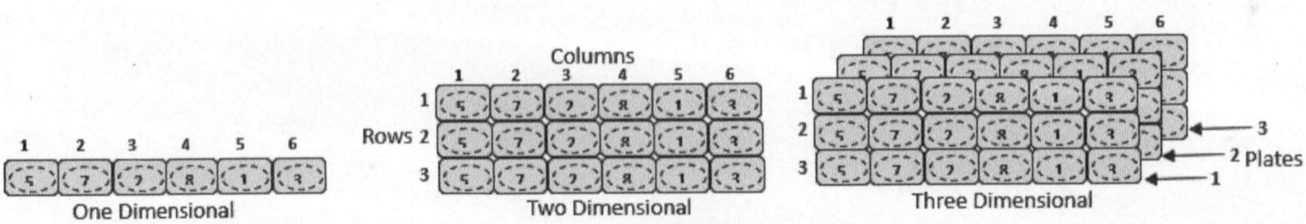

Figure 2.2: Types of Arrays

While 1D array is defined as $A[Columns]$ where *Columns* represent the number of data elements, a 2D array is defined as $A[Rows][Columns]$, where *Rows* represents the number of 1D arrays. The sizes of constituent 1D arrays are same. Likewise, 3D array is defined as $A[Plates][Rows][Columns]$, where *Plates* represents the number of 2D arrays of same sizes. In the similar way, higher order array can be defined. In C/C++ programming language, 1D, 2D, and 3D arrays of integer types can be defined like *int A[10]*, *int A[5][10]*, and *int A[3][5][10]* respectively. The number of data elements that can be accommodated in each dimension is also referred to as the order of the constituent array. In the above example, the order of the 1D array is 10, 2D array is 5×10 and 3D array is $3 \times 5 \times 10$. In general, the order of an array of *k*-dimensional array is $n_k \times n_{k-1} \times n_{k-2} \times ... n_2 \times n_1$ where n_i represents the size of the ith dimension.

2.1.2 Representation of Arrays in Memory

One-dimensional Array: Let *A* be an array of size *n*. Let the datatype of its data elements be *Type*, which needs *k* number of bytes. While defining the array *A*, a memory of size $n \times k$ will be allocated in a contiguous memory location in the computer's memory (i.e., main memory). Figure 2.3 illustrates allocation of an integer array of 5 elements. It is assumed that an integer datatype needs 2 bytes of memory. In this example, the *base address*, the starting memory address of the array is 1000. Each memory location has one byte of storage. Therefore, the bytes at the location 1000 and 1001 together store the first element of the array i.e., *A[0], assuming LB=0.* Similarly, successive two bytes of storage store the successive elements.

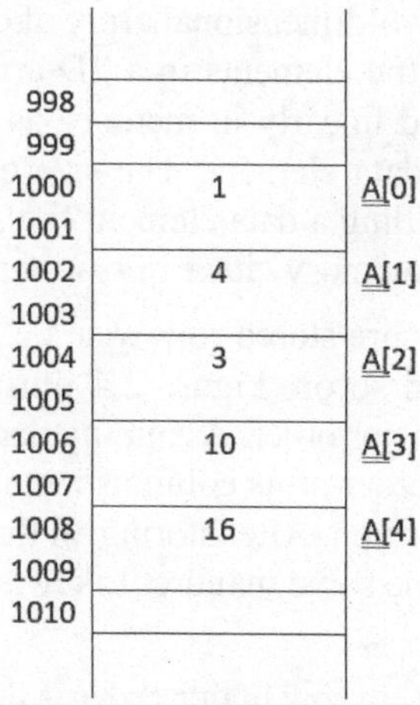

Figure 2.3: Allocation of an integer array of 5 elements in memory. The lower bound is assumed to start from 0, and {1, 4, 3, 10, 16} are the elements in the array. Each element consumes two bytes of memory.

Since the elements are stored at consecutive memory locations, the memory address of the ith element of the array can be estimated as below.

$$Address\ of\ A[i] = base\ address + (i - LB) \times k$$

where k is the byte required for the underlying datatype. In the above example, *base address* is 1000, $k = 2$ and $LB = 0$. The address of A[3] is $1000 + (3 - 0) \times 2 = 1006$. If the LB is 1, the address of A[3] will be $1000 + (3 - 1) \times 2 = 1004$. In general, the name of the array represents the address of the first element.

Example 2.1: Understanding memory allocation of a 1D array.

Let us consider the following array declaration in C/C++ programming language to define the example shown in figure 2.3. The index starts from 0, i.e., $LB = 0$.

```
int A[5];
```

The array variable name A represents the address of the first element in the array. Therefore, the following two *printf* statements will print the same data element 1.

```
printf("%d", A[0]);
printf("%d",*A);
```

Similarly, $A[1]$ and $*(A + 1)$ will point to the second data element 4. Therefore, $A[i]$ and $*(A + i)$ point to the same i^{th} data element.

Two-dimensional Array: Let A be a two-dimensional array of order $n \times m$, i.e., n number of rows and m number of columns. Though the elements in a 2D array is pictorially arranged as rows and columns, they are actually stored linearly in memory as a sequence of $n \times m$ memory blocks. Each memory block holds one data element. The size of the memory block is defined by the number of bytes required for holding a data element (i.e., size of the datatype of the array). The 2D elements can be arranged in memory either in *row major order* or *column major order*.

In row major order, the elements are stored row-wise i.e., the elements in the first row, then the elements in the second row, and so on. Figure 2.4 illustrates storage of a 3×6 integer array sequentially in memory in row major order. Assuming that the base address is 1000, the elements in the first row are stored in the order of its columns i.e., first element at 1000, second element at 1002, third element at 1004, and so on. After storing all the elements in the first row, the elements in the second row are stored in the same manure. Likewise, elements in the subsequent rows are stored.

The address of an element $A[i][j]$ in row major order is defined as below.

$$Address\ of\ A[i][j] = Base\ address + ((i - LB_R) \times Col + (j - LB_C))k$$

where k is the number of bytes required for a memory block, Col is the number of columns in the array, LB_R is the lower bound of the row index, and LB_C is the lower bound of the column index. The $(i - LB_R) \times Col$ in the above expression defines the number of affecting elements till the $(i-1)^{th}$ row, and $(j - LB_C)$ defines the number of affecting elements in the ith row. Figure 2.4

assumes 2 bytes of memory for an integer datatype. Therefore, the address of $A[1][3]$ in Figure 2.4 is $1000 + ((1 - 0) \times 6 + (3 - 0)) \times 2 = 1018$, where $LB_R = 0$ and $LB_C = 0$.

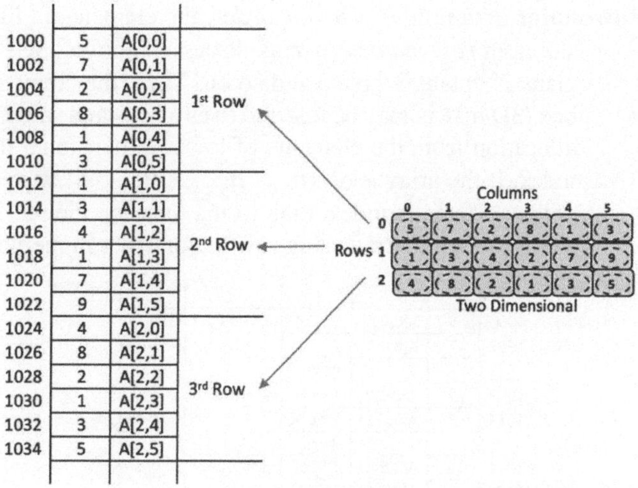

Figure 2.4: Storing elements in two-dimensional array in memory using row major order.

In column major order, the elements are stored column-wise i.e., the elements in the first column, then the elements in the second column, and so on. Figure 2.5 illustrates the storage of a 3×6 integer array sequentially in memory column major order. The address of an element $A[i][j]$ in column major is defined as below.

$$Address\ of\ A[i][j] = Base\ address + ((j - LB_C) \times Row + (i - LB_R))k$$

where k is the number of bytes required for a memory block and Row is the number of rows in the array. The $(j - LB_C) \times Row$ in the above expression defines the number of affecting elements till the $(j-1)^{th}$ columns, and $(i - LB_R)$ defines the number of affecting elements in the jth column. The address of $A[1][3]$ in Figure 2.5 is $1000 + ((3 - 0) \times 3 + (1 - 0)) \times 2 = 1020$, where $LB_R = 0$ and $LB_C = 0$.

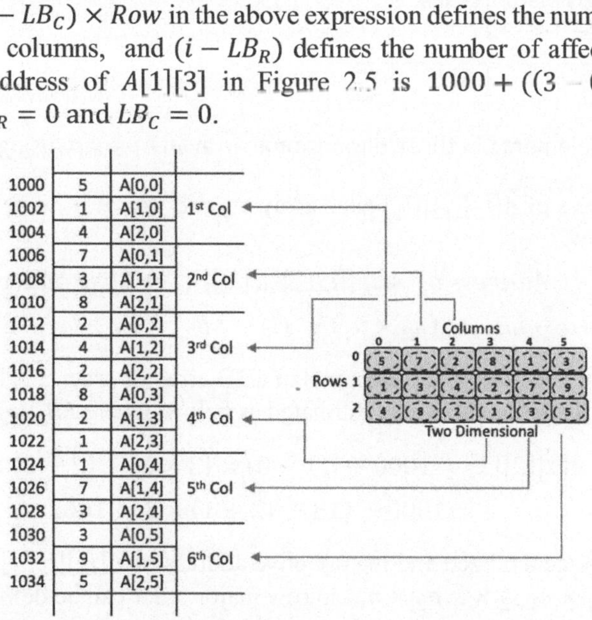

Figure 2.5: Storing elements in two-dimensional array in memory using column major order.

Multidimensional Array: As mentioned above, an array could be conceptually of any order, $n_k \times n_{k-1} \times n_{k-2} \times \ldots n_2 \times n_1$. Like in 2D array, the elements in high dimensional array can be stored in memory either in *row major order* or *column major order*.

Row-major order: In *row major order,* the elements in the first two dimensions i.e., $n_2 \times n_1$ will be stored in *row major order* as discussed above, then store the elements in n_3 in the order of 1st plate, 2nd plate, 3rd plate and so on. Then, the elements in n_4 in the order of 1st box, 2nd box, 3rd box (3D matrix may be referred to as a box) and so on. The idea is to maintain contiguous memory allocation from the elements of lower dimensional index to the elements in higher dimensional index. If the array is of $(n_k \times n_{k-1} \times n_{k-2} \times \ldots n_2 \times n_1)$ orders, contiguous memory allocation will start from $n_1$index, then to n_2, then n_3, then n_4, and so on till n_k. Figure 2.6 illustrates the storage of a 3D array using row major order in memory.

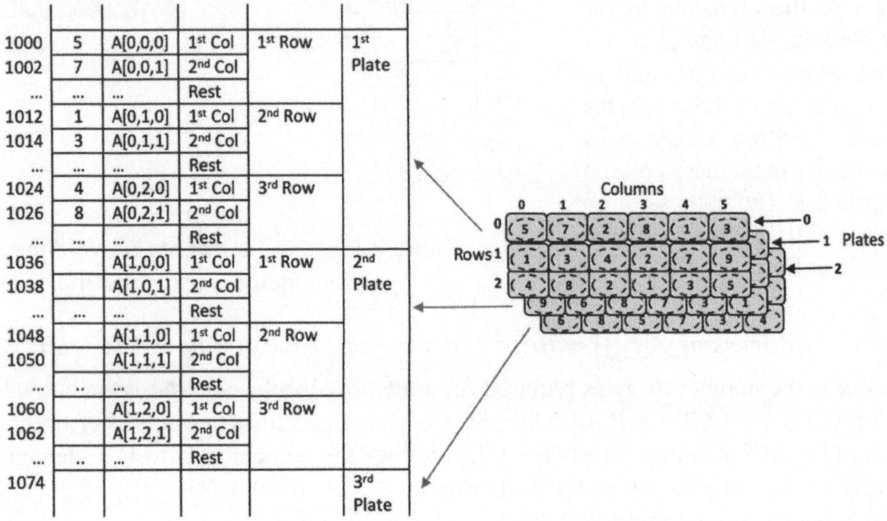

Figure 2.6: Storing elements in three-dimensional array in memory using row major order.

The effective address of $A[i_3][i_2][i_1]$ in an array of order $(n_3 \times n_2 \times n_1)$ in row major order can be defined as below.

$$Address\ of\ A[i_k][i_{k-1}] \ldots [i_2][i_1] = Base\ address$$
$$+ (i_3 - LB_3) \times (n_2 \times n_1) + (i_2 - LB_2) \times n_1 + (i_1 - LB_1)] \times k$$

Figure 2.6 illustrates storage of the elements in a 3D array of order $3 \times 3 \times 6$ in memory. The address of $A[1][2][1]$ element can be estimated as below, where $LB_3 = 0$, $LB_3 = 0$ and $LB_3 = 0$.

$$Address\ of\ A[1][2][1] = 1000 + [(1-0) \times (3 \times 6) + (2-0) \times 6 + (1-0)] \times 2$$
$$= 1000 + (18 + 12 + 1) \times 2 = 1062$$

Similarly, it can be generalized and the effective address of $A[i_k][i_{k-1}] \ldots [i_2][i_1]$ in an array of orders $(n_k \times n_{k-1} \times n_{k-2} \times \ldots n_2 \times n_1)$ in row major order can be defined as below.

$$Address\ of\ A[i_k][i_{k-1}] \ldots [i_2][i_1] = Base\ address$$
$$+ [(i_k - LB_k) \times (n_{k-1} \times n_{k-2} \times \ldots n_2 \times n_1)$$
$$+ (i_{k-1} - LB_{k-1}) \times (n_{k-2} \times n_{k-3} \times \ldots n_2 \times n_1)$$

$$+ (i_{k-2} - LB_{k-2}) \times (n_{k-3} \times n_{k-4} \times \ldots n_2 \times n_1)$$

$$\ldots \ldots \ldots$$

$$+ (i_3 - LB_3) \times (n_2 \times n_1) + (i_2 - LB_2) \times n_1 + (i_1 - LB_1)] \times k$$

If we closely look at the above allocation pattern, we observe that the idea is to keep the elements in the lower dimension in contiguous location before the higher dimension, it keeps n_1 before n_2, keeps $n_2 \times n_1$ before n_3, keeps $n_3 \times n_2 \times n_1$ before n_4, and so on. That means, contiguous memory allocation in row major order is maintained from lower order index to higher order index.

Column-major order: Before we discuss *how are the elements in multidimensional array are stored in memory using column major order*, let us first look a typical way of storing the elements in a 3D array in memory to justify storage pattern of column major order in memory. In this example, we store the array in the way we visualise a 3D matrix as array of 2D arrays i.e., store 2D in column major order, and store them in the sequence of plates. That is, the elements in the first two dimensions i.e., $n_2 \times n_1$ are stored in *column major order* as discussed above. The elements in n_3 are stored in the order of 1st plate, 2nd plate, 3rd plate and so on, following column major order in 2D. The following figure illustrates such a storing pattern.

1000	5	A[0,0,0]	1st Raw	1st Col	1st Plate
1002	1	A[0,1,0]	2nd Raw		
1004	4	A[0,2,0]	3rd Raw		
1006	7	A[0,0,0]	1st Raw	2nd Col	
1014	3	A[0,1,1]	2nd Raw		
1016	8	A[0,2,1]	3rd Raw		
1018	2	A[0,0,2]	1st Raw	3rd Col	
1020	4	A[0,1,2]	2nd Raw		
...	...	...	Rest		
1036		A[1,0,0]	1st Raw	1st Col	2nd Plate
1038		A[1,1,0]	2nd Raw		
...	...	A[1,2,0]	3rd Raw		
1048		A[1,0,1]	1st Raw	2nd Col	
1050		A[1,1,1]	2nd Raw		
...	..	A[1,2,1]	3rd Raw		
1060		A[1,0,2]	1st Raw	3rd Col	
1062		A[1,1,2]	2nd Raw		
...	..	...	Rest		
1074					3rd Plate

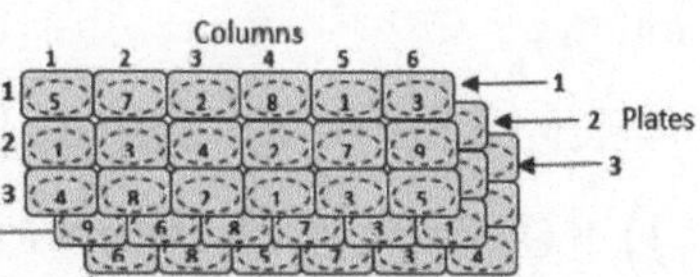

Three Dimensional Array

The above storage pattern is easy to visualize and understand, but it lacks generalization. That means, the elements in n_2 index are stored in contiguous locations based on the index values, do not follow continuity for n_1 and n_3, whereas in the row major order the continuity is maintained from n_1 till n_k. As a result, an application on such storage pattern needs to take special attention to take care of the irregular continuity pattern.

To take care of the above issue, in *column-major order,* contiguous memory allocation is maintained from higher order index to the lower order index. This concept is first illustrated using the following diagram, where contiguous memory allocation is maintained from the plate index.

First element in first plate, first row and first column is stored, then the element in second plate, first row and first column is stored, and so on. In this case, generalization on contiguous memory allocation from higher dimensional index to lower dimensional index is maintained.

Address	Value	Element	Plate	Row	Column
1000	5	A[0,0,0]	1st Plate	1st Raw	1st Col
1002	4	A[1,0,0]	2nd Plate		
1004	3	A[2,0,0]	3rd Plate		
1006	1	A[0,1,0]	1st Plate	2nd Raw	
1008		A[1,1,0]	2nd Plate		
1010		A[2,1,0]	3rd Plate		
1012	4	A[0,2,0]	1st Plate	3rd Raw	
1014		A[1,2,0]	2nd Plate		
1016		A[2,2,0]	3rd Plate		
1018	7	A[0,0,1]	1st Plate	1st Raw	2nd Col
1020	7	A[1,0,1]	2nd Plate		
1022	7	A[2,0,1]	3rd Plate		
1024		A[0,1,1]	1st Plate	2nd Raw	
1026		A[1,1,1]	2nd Plate		
1028	..	A[2,1,1]	3rd Plate		
1030		A[0,2,1]	1st Plate	3rd Raw	
1032		A[1,2,1]	2nd Plate		
1034	..	A[2,2,1]	3rd Plate		
1036					3rd Col

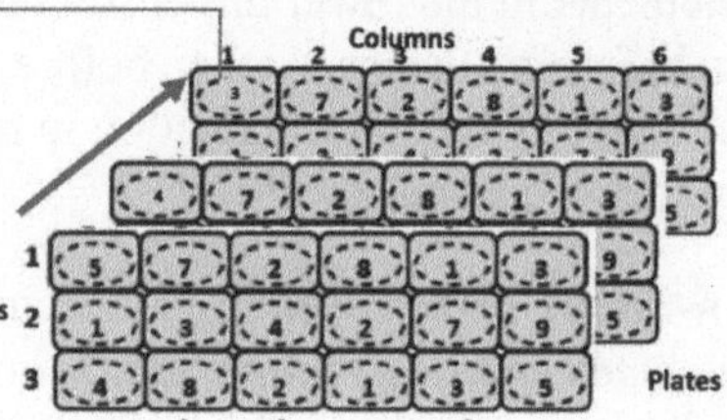

Considering the above memory allocation approach, effective address of an element $A[k][j][i]$ in a 3D array of order $n_3 \times n_2 \times n_1$, where n_3 is the number of plates, n_2 is the number of rows in each plate, and n_1 is the number of columns in each row, in column major order can be defined as follows.

$Effective\ address\ of\ A[k][j][i] = Base\ address + \left[\left(n_3 \times n_2 \times (i - LB_i)\right) + \left(n_3 \times (j - LB_j)\right) + (k - LB_k)\right] \times k$, where k is the bytes required for each element in array.

Considering the above estimate, the effective address of A[0][1][1] in column major order is $1000 + [3 \times 3 \times 1 + 3 \times 1 + 0] \times 2 = 1024$.

In the similar manner, contiguous memory allocation for higher dimensional matrix of order $n_k \times n_{k-1} \times n_{k-2} \times \ldots n_2 \times n_1$ in column major order is also maintained. The effective address of $A[i_k][i_{k-1}] \ldots [i_2][i_1]$ in an array of order $(n_k \times n_{k-1} \times n_{k-2} \times \ldots n_2 \times n_1)$ can be defined as follows.

$$\begin{aligned} Effective\ address\ of\ A[i_k][i_{k-1}] \ldots [i_2][i_1] &= Base\ Address \\ +\big[\left(n_k \times n_{k-1} \times \ldots \times n_2 \times (i_1 - LB_1)\right) &+ \left(n_k \times n_{k-1} \times \ldots \times n_3 \times (i_2 - LB_2)\right) \\ &+ \left(n_k \times n_{k-1} \times \ldots \times n_4 \times (i_3 - LB_3)\right) + \cdots \ldots \ldots + n_k \times (i_{k-1} - LB_{k-1}) \\ &+ (i_k - LB_k)\big] \times k \end{aligned}$$

Considering the above estimate, the effective address of A[0][0][2][0] in an array of order $3 \times 3 \times 3 \times 6$ in column major order is $1000 + [3 \times 3 \times 3 \times 0 + 3 \times 3 \times 2 + 3 \times 0 + 0] \times 2 = 1036$.

2.1.3 A Special Case of 2D Array: Sparse Matrix

Sparse matrix is a special type of matrix with a relatively high proportion of zero elements. Different sources define sparse matrix differently. Some of the definitions are – *more number of zero entries than non-zero entries*; *matrix with more than two third zeroes entries*, etc. In this book, if a matrix has high proportion of zero entries (say, close to half), it is referred to as a sparse matrix. For a sparse matrix with a large number of zero entries, *is it necessary to store the zero entries in memory, as it is known to have zero values*? This section briefly discusses ways of representing sparse matrices by ignoring the majority or all of the zero elements of the array from storing into memory, and reducing storage requirements. Some of the standard sparse matrices such as *triangular matrix*, *diagonal matrix*, *tri-diagonal matrix*, etc. have known index positions with zero values. For such matrices, we can predetermine the position of zero values and directly ignore them from storing into the memory. Some of these standard sparse matrices are discussed below.

Left lower triangular matrix: Figure 2.7 illustrates an example representing a *left lower triangular matrix* in memory. As shown in the figure, a left lower triangular matrix A has zero entries for all the indices where row index is smaller than the column index i.e., $A[i][j] = 0$ if $i < j$. That means, non-zero elements reside only at the index where $i \geq j$. As we know that entries at $A[i][j]$, $i < j$ *are zeros, we store only the elements at* $i \geq j$ *in the memory. Assuming that the elements* are stored in *row major order*, the effective address of $A[i][j]$ in the memory can be defined as follows.

$$A[i][j] = base\ address + \left(\frac{(i - LB_R)(i - LB_R + 1)}{2} + (j - LB_C)\right) \times k$$

where base address (BA) is the address of the $A[LB_R][LB_C]$.

In the example shown in Figure 2.7(a), the lower bounds LB_R and LB_c are set to 0, and the base address is 1000. With these values, we can estimate the effective address of a random element $A[i][j]$ in the array using the above expression, if $j \leq i$. Some estimates are given below.

The address of $A[3][2] = 1000 + \left(\frac{(3-0)(3-0+1)}{2} + (2-0)\right) \times 2 = 1000 + 16 = 1016.$

The address of $A[4][3] = 1000 + \left(\frac{(4-0)(4-0+1)}{2} + (3-0)\right) \times 2 = 1026$

The address of $A[2][2] = 1000 + \left(\frac{(2-0)(2-0+1)}{2} + (2-0)\right) \times 2 = 1010$

For the elements $A[i][j]$ with $j > i$, by the definition of a left lower triangular matrix, $A[i][j]$ has zero value, and such element is not stored in the memory. For example, the elements $A[3][4], A[2][4], A[0][3]$ etc. are not stored in memory, as they have zeros.

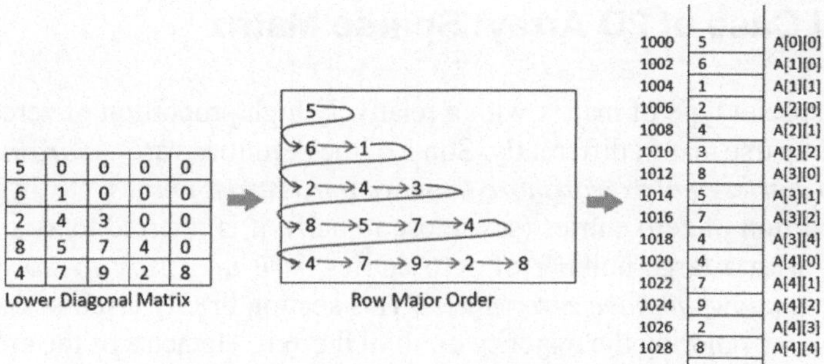

Figure 2.7: Left Lower Triangular Matrix

Right lower triangular matrix (Figure 2.8): Assuming that the elements are stored in row major order, the address of $A[i][j]$ in the memory is

$$A[i][j] = base\ address + \left(\frac{(i - LB_R)(i - LB_R + 1)}{2} + ((j - LB_C) - (UB_R - i))\right) \times k$$

For instance, the address of $A[2][3] = 1000 + \left(\frac{(2-0)(2-0+1)}{2} + ((3-0) - (4-2))\right) \times 2 = 1000 + (3+1) \times 2 = 1008$.

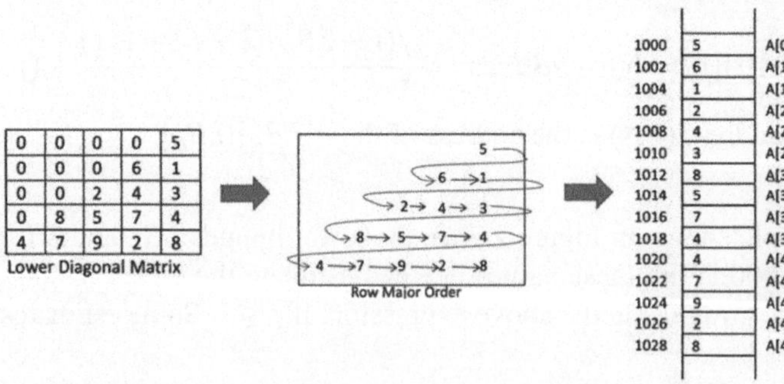

Figure 2.8: Right Lower Triangular Matrix

Diagonal matrix (Figure 2.9): The address of $A[i][i]$ in the memory is

$$A[i][i] = base\ address + (i - LB_R) \times k$$

For instance, the address of $A[3][3] = 1000 + (3 - 0) \times 2 = 1000 + 6 = 1006$

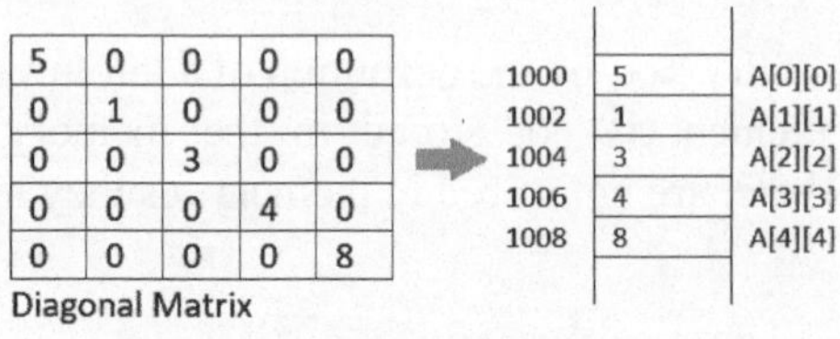

Figure 2.9: Diagonal Matrix.

Tri-diagonal matrix (Figure 2.10): Assuming that the elements are stored in row major order, the address of $A[i][j]$ in the memory is

$$A[i][j] = base\ address + \big((i - LB_R - 1) \times 3 + 2 + (j - i + 1)\big) \times k$$

For instance, the address of $A[0][0] = 1000 + ((0 - 0 - 1) \times 3 + 2 + (0 - 0 + 1)) \times 2 = 1000.$

For instance, the address of $A[0][1] = 1000 + ((0 - 0 - 1) \times 3 + 2 + (1 - 0 + 1)) \times 2 = 1002.$

For instance, the address of $A[2][2] = 1000 + ((2 - 0 - 1) \times 3 + 2 + (2 - 2 + 1)) \times 2 = 1012.$

For instance, the address of $A[3][2] = 1000 + ((3 - 0 - 1) \times 3 + 2 + (2 - 3 + 1)) \times 2 = 1016.$

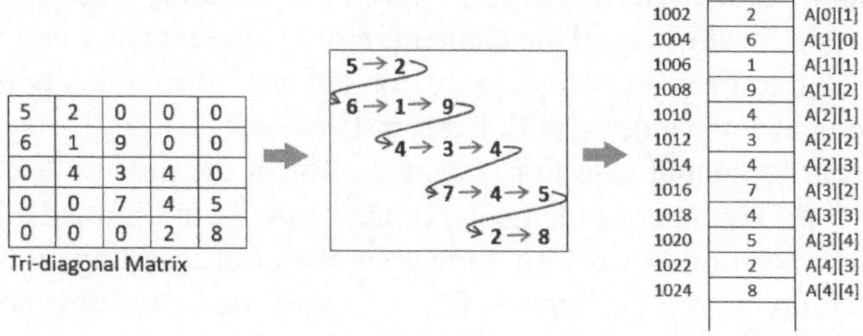

Figure 2.10: Tri-diagonal Matrix in Row Major Order.

In the similar manner, addresses of the elements stored using column major order may be estimated. Further, effective addresses of other types of triangular matrices (left upper, right upper) can also be defined, but left as exercises to the readers. Searching of an element in the above standard sparse matrixes should be done by following the corresponding effective address estimates described above. Further, given an effective address in memory of a standard sparse matrix, the corresponding row and column indexes of the array can also be estimated, but left as exercises to the readers.

Representation of Sparse matrices: For the above sparse matrices with regular patterns, the effective address of an element in memory may be estimated by following the storage sequence. However, for a random sparse matrix without any pattern, such estimate may not be feasible. In such a scenario, the non-zero elements may be stored in an array or linked list along with their corresponding row and column information as shown in Figure 2.11.

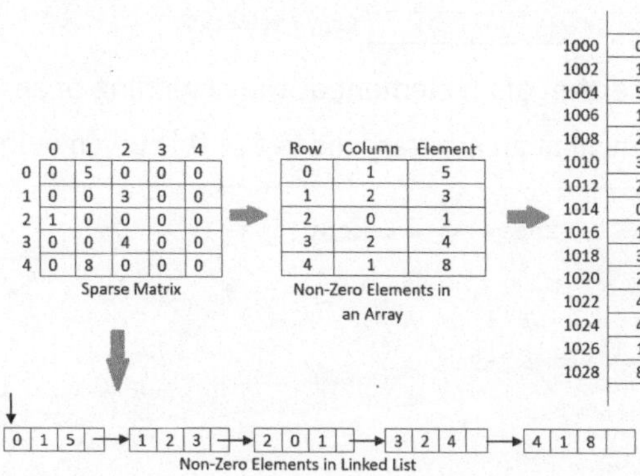

Figure 2.11: Representation of sparse matrix using an array or linked list in row major order.

Searching Operation: Since only the non-zero elements in the sparse matrix may be present at arbitrary locations, the effective address of a non-zero element (in its respective representation – array or linked list) cannot be estimated following the approaches discussed above. Linear search, as applicable on array or linked list, needs to be applied.

2.1.4 Operations on a Linear Array (1D Array)

Insertion: An insertion operation on an array is referred to as adding an element at a particular index position in the array. Insertion can be made at the first position, intermediate position or after the last element. The number of elements that can be accommodated in an array is defined by the contiguous memory storage that has been reserved for the array. Insertion of an element at the index $i \geq 0$ will result in shifting all the elements stored at the index i and higher by one position towards the tail of the array to create space for the new element. Figure 2.12 illustrates the insertion of an element at the index $i = 0$. Let $n = UB - LB + 1 = 7 - 0 + 1 = 8$ be the number of elements in the array before insertion, then insertion at the index $i \geq 0$ will result in shifting $n - i$ (i.e., $UB - i + 1$) number of elements. In the example in Figure 2.12, eight elements need to be shifted by one position. Therefore, time complexity of inserting an element at an arbitrary index $i \geq 0$ in an array with n elements is $O(n)$. It holds best case time complexity (insertion at the end i.e., no shifting, but only storing the element) of $O(1)$, and average (half of the elements are moved) and worst case (all the elements are moved) time complexity of $O(n)$.

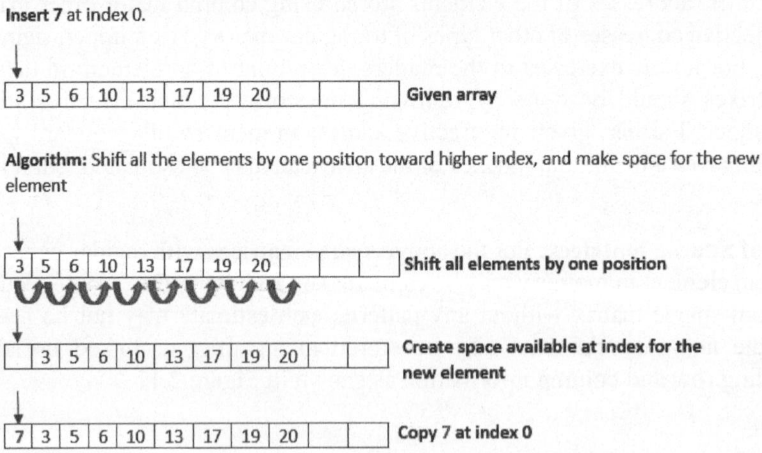

Figure 2.12: Insertion of an element at the beginning of an array.

An algorithm for inserting an element at an arbitrary index $i \geq 0$ is given below.

```
Input: Array A, index i, element ele
BEGIN
    Repeat for k=UB-1 to i
            A[k+1]=A[k]
    End Repeat
    A[i] = ele
    UB=UB+1
END
```

Deletion: A deletion operation on an array will remove an element from the array at a particular index i. Deleting an element at the end will not disturb the other elements, except that UB will be reduced by 1. Whereas, deleting an element at an arbitrary index i will result in shifting all the elements from $i + 1$ to UB by one position towards the beginning. Figure 2.13 illustrates deleting an element at an arbitrary index i. If there are n number of elements in an array, the time complexity for deleting an element at an arbitrary index $i \geq 0$ is $O(n)$. It holds best case time complexity (deleting at the end i.e., no shifting, but UB update) of $O(1)$, and average (half of the elements are moved) and worst case (all the elements are moved) time complexity of $O(n)$.

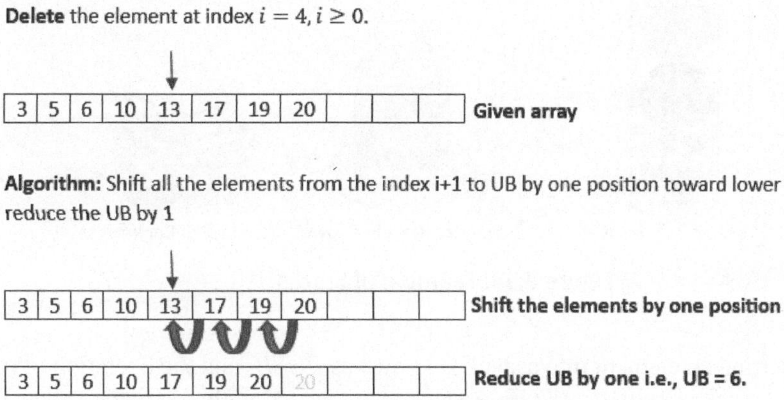

Figure 2.13: Deleting an element at an arbitrary index.

An algorithm for deleting an element at an arbitrary index $i \geq 0$ is given below.

```
Input: Array A, index i
BEGIN
1. Repeat for k=i to UB-1
2.          A[k]=A[k+1]
3. End Repeat
4. UB=UB-1
END
```

Searching of an element in an array (search operation) is discussed in Section 1.4.3.

Update operation of an element at index i simply changes the value at i with a new value. It does not affect the elements at the other indices. For example, $A[i] = new\ value$. As it needs only one assignment, it holds a time complexity of $O(1)$ irrespective of the index position.

2.2 STACKS

Stack is a linear data structure in which data elements can be inserted and removed only from one end. It follows *Last-in First-out (LIFO)* or *First-in Last-out (FILO)* operations. LIFO implies that the element which is inserted at last can only be removed first before removing others. Similarly, LIFO implies that the element which was inserted at first can only be removed at last. LIFO or FILO means that elements can only be removed from a stack in the reverse order of their insertion. A few examples of stack are shown in Figure 2.14.

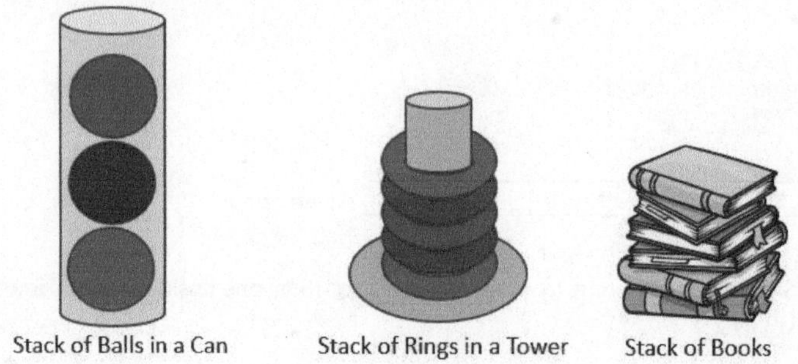

Figure 2.14: Example of Stacks

The operation of inserting an element into a stack is known as *PUSH*, and the operation of removing an element from a stack is known as *POP*. A stack is associated with a variable called TOP (top of the stack), which points to the last inserted element in the stack. After a PUSH operation, the TOP will point to the new element which is just inserted into the stack. Similarly, after a POP operation, the TOP will point to the element which was inserted just before the removed element. Pictorially, PUSH and POP operations are illustrated in Figure 2.15.

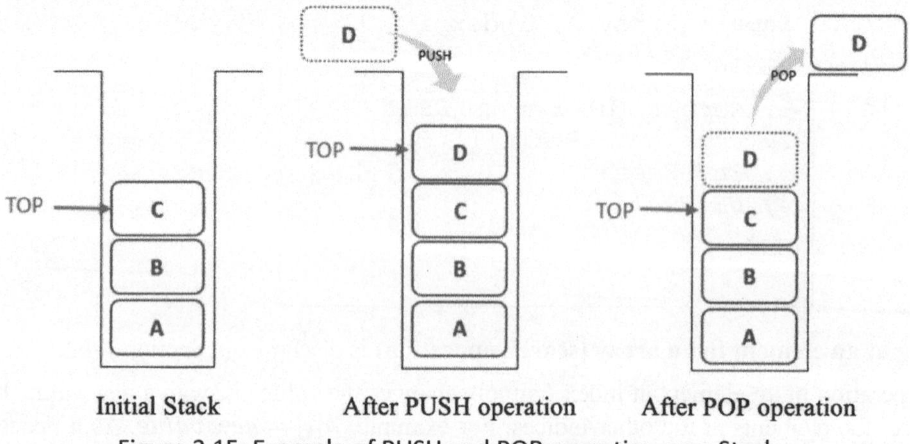

Figure 2.15: Example of PUSH and POP operation on a Stack

2.2.1 Implementation of Stack

A stack can be implemented using either an Array or a Linked List data structure. In this unit, implementation of a stack using one-dimensional array is discussed. Let an array of size MAX (`int storage[MAX];` in C programming language) be defined to hold the elements in the stack. That means, the stack can hold upto MAX number of elements. Initially, the stack is empty and the TOP is initialized to -1 i.e., TOP = -1. Now, the PUSH operation can be defined as follows.

```
Algorithm: PUSH
Assumption: The storage array and TOP are global variables
Input: element
BEGIN
1. IF (TOP < MAX-1) THEN
2.       TOP = TOP + 1
3.       storage[TOP] = element
4. ELSE
5.       PRINT "STACK FULL"
END
```

Similarly, POP operation can be defined as follows.

```
Algorithm: POP
Assumption: The storage array and TOP are global variables
Output: the popped element
BEGIN
1. IF (TOP > -1) THEN
2.       out = storage[TOP]
3.       TOP = TOP - 1
4.       RETURN out
5. ELSE
6.       PRINT "STACK EMPTY"
END
```

The top of the stack can also be read using `storage[TOP]` directly. Since the elements can be inserted or removed directly by using the index TOP, the time complexity for both the PUSH and POP operations is $O(1)$. In some applications, the need of scanning the elements in the stack may arise. In such a case, the following function can also be defined to display all the elements in the stack. The time complexity of the DISPLAY function is $O(MAX)$.

```
Algorithm: DISPLAY
Assumption: The storage array and TOP are global variables
BEGIN
1. i=0
2. REPEAT(i<= TOP) THEN
3.        PRINT storage[i]
4.        i = i + 1
5. END REPEAT
END
```

Putting everything together, the following stack implementation can be realised in C programming language.

```c
#include <stdio.h>
#define MAX 10
// Global variables
int storage[MAX];
TOP = -1;

void PUSH(int ele){   // insert an element
    if(TOP < MAX-1){
        TOP = TOP + 1;
        storage[TOP] = ele;
    } else{
        printf("Stack FULL");
    }
}

int POP(){       // Remove an element
    int out;
    if(TOP > -1){
        out = storage[TOP];
        TOP = TOP - 1;
    } else{
```

```
                printf("Stack EMPTY");
                out = -1;   // Assuming that -1 is not a
                            // valid element.
            }
            return out;
        }

        int topOfStack(void){   // Get top of the stack
            return storage[TOP];
        }

        void DISPLAY(void){   // Display all the elements
            int i=0;
            while(i<=TOP){
                printf("%d ", storage[i]);
                i++;
            }
        }

        main(){
            PUSH(5);
            PUSH(7);
            printf("%d ",POP());
            printf("%d ",POP());
        }
```

The above program will display "7 5 ".

2.2.2 Applications of Stack

Stack data structure is used in various computer applications - recursive function, context switching in operating system, memory management, etc. One of the popular applications of stack is conversion of *infix* expression to *postfix* expression, and evaluation of postfix expressions. Few of these examples are discussed in this section.

Infix to Postfix Conversion: Let E be an arithmetic expression in *infix* form which involves operands and operators. Some examples of infix expressions are given below.

$a + b,\ a - b, a * b, a/b, (a - b) * (c + d), a/(c * a) + c * b, a - b + c$

The operators may have different *precedence* and *associativity*. The table below summarises the precedence and associativity of a few of the commonly used operators. In this example, lower the value, higher is the precedence. The precedence of some operators like exponent and unary may be interpreted differently in different programming languages and tools. In this discussion, the following precedence and associativity are used. Whenever there is an ambiguity in representing the expression, it is always good to use parenthesis.

Precedence	**Operators**	**Associativity**	**Example**
1	( )	Left-to-Right	$(a + b) + (c + d)$; $(a + b)$ will be estimated before $(c + d)$
	[ ]	Left-to-Right	$[a + b] + [c + d]$; $[a + b]$ will be estimated before $[c + d]$
2	↑(Exponent operator)	Right-to-Left	$a \uparrow b \uparrow c = a \uparrow (b \uparrow c)$
	+/- (Unary plus or minus)	Right-to-Left	$-a + -b = -a + (-b)$
3	*, /, % (Multiplication, division, Modulo)	Left-to-Right	$a * b\ /c\%d = (((a * b)/c)\%\ d)$
4	+/- (binary Addition, Subtraction operators)	Left-to-Right	$a + b - c = ((a + b) - c)$

For converting an infix expression to a postfix expression, the infix expression is scanned from left to right, and the following steps are followed. Initially, we consider to have an empty stack and an empty postfix expression.

Step 1: If the current token is operand, append it to the postfix expression.

Step 2: If the current token is operator, and stack is empty, PUSH the operator

Step 3: If the current token is "(", PUSH it into the stack.

Step 4: If the current token is ")", POP tokens from the stack till "("and append them to the postfix expression, other than '(".

Step 5.1: POP tokens from the stack as long as the popped token is an operator with higher or equal precedence than the current token. If popped token is '(', PUSH '('. Else Append the popped tokens to the postfix. PUSH the current token.

Step 5.2: Else PUSH current token into Stack

Step 6: If scanning of the infix expression is complete, POP all the tokens from the stack and append them to the postfix.

The above infix to postfix conversion procedure is illustrated below considering an infix expression $a + b - (c + d) * e/f$.

Token	Stack	Step	Postfix
a		1	a
+	+	2	a
b	+	1	ab
-	-	5.1	ab+
(	-(	3	ab+
c	-(	1	ab+c
+	-(+	5.2	ab+c
d	-(+	1	ab+cd
)	-	4	ab+cd+
*	-*	5.2	ab+cd+-
e	-*	1	ab+cd+-e
/	-/	5.1	ab+cd+e*
f	-/	1	ab+cd+e*f
		7	ab+cd+c*f/-

The following program shows the above procedure in C programming language.

```
int precedence(char c){
        if(c=='('||c==')'||c=='['||c==']')return 1;
        /* p and m denote unary plus and unary minus */
        else if(c=='^'||c=='p'||c=='m')return 2;
        else if(c=='*'||c=='/')return 3;
        else if(c=='+'||c=='-')return 4;
        else return 5;
}

int isOperator(char){
        if  (c=='^'  ||  c=='p'||  c=='m'||  c=='*'||  c=='/'||
c=='+'|| c=='-'|| c=='('|| c==')'|| c=='['|| c==']') return 1;
        else return 0;
}
```

```
void infixToPostfix(char infix[], int n){
        /* Assume that a global stack is implemented like the
one shown in section 2.2.1. PUSH(), POP(), isEmpty(), topOfStack()
are implemented.
            The parameter infix is the infix expression and n is
the number of characters in infix expression. */
        char postfix[n];
        int j=0;

        for(i=0; i<n;i++){
            if(isOperator(infix[i])==0){
                postfix[j++]= infix[i];
            }
            else{
                if(infix[i]=='('||infix[i]=='[')
                    PUSH(infix[i]);
                else if(infix[i]==')'||infix[i]==']'){
                    while(topOfStack()!='(' ||
                        topOfStack()!='['){
                        postfix[j++]=POP();
                    }
                    POP();
                }
                else{
                    while(!isEmpty() &&
                    precedence(infix[i])>= topOfStack()){
                        postfix[j++]=POP();
                    }
                    PUSH(infix[i]);
                }


            }
        }
        while(!isEmpty()){
            postfix[j++]=POP();
        }
        postfix[j]='\n';
        printf("PostFix Expression is %s", postfix);
}
```

Postfix Evaluation: Evaluation of a postfix expression can also be done using stack. Let $2 + 5 - (3 + 6) * 2/3$ be an infix expression. The postfix of the expression is $2\,5 + 3\,6 + 2 * 3\,/-$. The following steps can be followed to evaluate the postfix expression.

Step 1: Scan the postfix expression.

Step 2: if the token is an operand, PUSH the token into the stack

Step 3: If the token is a binary operator, POP two tokens from the stack. Apply the operator on the popped tokens (in the sequence <2nd popped token><operator><1st popped token>), and PUSH the result into the stack.

Step 4: if the token is an unary operator, POP a token from the stack. Apply the operator on the popped token, and PUSH the result into the stack.

Step 5: Continue till the last operator in the postfix.

The above procedure is illustrated below.

Token	Stack	Step	Remaining token in postfix
2	2	2	$5 + 3\,6 + 2 * 3\,/-$
5	2 5	2	$+3\,6 + 2 * 3\,/-$
+	7	3	$3\,6 + 2 * 3\,/-$
3	7 3	2	$6 + 2 * 3\,/-$
6	7 3 6	2	$+2 * 3\,/-$
+	7 9	3	$2 * 3\,/-$
2	7 9 2	2	$* 3\,/-$
*	7 18	3	$3\,/-$
3	7 18 3	2	$/-$
/	7 6	3	$-$
–	1	3	

The following function shows implementation of postfix evaluation in C programming language.

```
void evaluatePostfix(char postfix[], int n){
        /* Assume that a global stack is implemented like one
shown in section 2.2.1. PUSH(), POP(), isEmpty(), topOfStack()
are implemented.
            The parameter postfix is the postfix expression and
n is the number of characters in postfix expression.
```

```
        We assume to have functions is isBinary() and
evaluate() to check the operator is binary or unary operator, and
evaluate */

        int i;
        float a, b;
        for(i=0; i<n; i++){
            if(isOperator(postfix[i])==0) PUSH(postfix[i])
            else{
                if(isBinary(postfix[i])){
                    a=POP();
                    b=POP();
                    PUSH(evaluate(a, b, postfix[i])
                }
                else{
                    a=POP();
                    PUSH(evaluate(a, postfix[i]);
                }
            }
        }
        printf("The value is %f", POP());
}
```

2.2.3 Abstract Data Type (ADT)

While primitive data types or the traditional data structures define data from the perspective of storage and organization, abstract data type (ADT in short) defines data from the point of view of the users of the data – *possible values, possible operations, and behaviour of the operations*. While using primitive data types or the traditional data structures, the application programmer needs to take care of everything – from the storage to organization to accessing. Whereas, while using ADT, the application programmer only needs to know possible values, possible operations, and behaviour of the operations. Usage of ADT is conceptually separated from the implementation of the ADT. In ADT, the underlying data storage, and the necessary functions for operating the data are encapsulated under one data type, which is conceptually illustrated below by defining an stack ADT.

Let us assume that the keyword `<ADT>` is used to define an abstract data type, and STACK is the name of the data type. An ADT will often conceptually have two members – data storage, and the methods/functions to operate on the data type.

```
<ADT> STACK{
        DATA:
            int storage[MAX]; // MAX is a global variable
                              //assume that stack stores
                              // integer values
            int TOP=-1;
        METHODS:
            void PUSH( int ele);
            int POP(void);
            int topOfStack(void);
            bool isEmpty(void);
            bool isFull(void);
};
```

Once the above ADT is declared, the definitions of the associated member functions can be conceptually illustrated as follows. The syntax of the defining the ADT will be different for different programming languages.

```
void STACK::PUSH(int ele){
        if(TOP < MAX-1){
            TOP = TOP + 1;
            storage[TOP] = ele;
        } else{
            printf("Stack FULL");
        }
}
int STACK::POP(void){
        int out;
        if(TOP > -1){
            out = storage[TOP];
            TOP = TOP - 1;
        } else{
            printf("Stack EMPTY");
            out = -1;   // Assuming that -1 is not a
                        // valid element.
        }
        return out;
}
int STACK::topOfStack (){
        if(TOP == -1){
            printf("Stack Empty")
```

```
                return -1; // Assuming that -1 is not a
                               // valid element.
            } else{
                return storage[TOP];
            }
}
bool STACK::isEmpty (){
            if(TOP == -1){
                return true;
            } else{
                return false;
            }
}


bool STACK::isFull (){
            if(TOP == MAX-1){
                return true;
            } else{
                return false;
            }
}
```

Once the definition of the ADT is developed, an application programmer can directly use the ADT by declaring instances of the ADT in the application program as follows.

```
<ADT> STACK st;
st.PUSH(10) // for inserting 10 into the stack
st.POP() // for removing an element from the stack
```

By separating the definition and usage of the ADT, application programmers conceptually do not worry about the storage, and implementation of the accessing methods. They only need to understand the type of data that can be stored, and the syntax of using the access methods.

Though in several occasions, while defining a customed ADT, the programmer needs to implement the costumed ADT of his/her own, imagine a case where some developers have implemented the STACK ADT and distributed for use by application programmers. In such a scenario, application programmers just need to know the way of using the ADT. They do not have to worry about whether the storage has been defined using array or linked list, how the methods have been implemented.

In the above example, the members of the ADT are not protected. Application programmers can access all the members of the ADT. There will be cases where some of the members should be protected from application programmers. In the above definition, the `storage` variable is accessible to application programmers, and the element of the `storage` can be directly manipulated. `For example, st.storage[2]=5;`. The philosophy behind an ADT is also to protect accessing of the data directly from the programmers, and access only through few permissible access methods. To support this, an ADT is generally defined along with the access control such as PRIVATE and PUBLIC as illustrated below.

```
<ADT> STACK{
        PRIVATE:
            int MAX;
            int storage[MAX];
            int TOP;
            void init(int max){
                  MAX = max;
                  TOP=-1;
            }
        PUBLIC:
            void initiate(int n){
                  init(n);
            }
            void PUSH( int);
            int POP(void);
            int topOfStack(void);
            int isEmpty(void);
            int isFull(void);
};
```

The PRIVATE members are not allowed to access from the application program. They can be only accessed by the member functions of the ADT. Only the members listed under PUBLIC can be accessed from the application program. Conceptually, both the storage and accessing methods can be placed under both the PRIVATE and PUBLIC category. But, in practice data storages are often protected from the public access. In the above example, a private method `init()` is defined to initialize the private variables of the ADT. The `init()` function is in turn called from the `initiate()` public member. Object-oriented programming languages generally support a function called *constructor* for such purpose. Likewise, *destructor* can also be defined to clear data stored in private variables.

```
<ADT> STACK st;
st.initiate(100);  //define stack size to 100 and initiate other
                   //ADT private variables
st.PUSH(10) // for inserting 10 into the stack
st.POP() // for removing an element from the stack
```

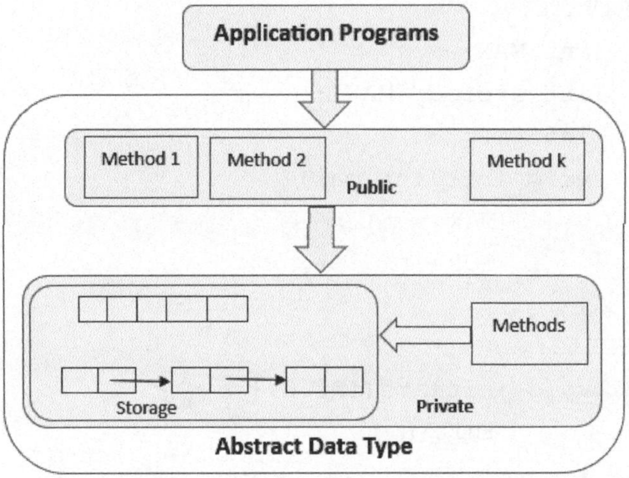

Figure 2.16: Conceptual Visualization of ADT

Figure 2.16 summarises the concept of Abstract Data Type. ADT provides a way of defining a data type which encapsulates the associated data elements and necessary access methods together. *Encapsulation* and *information hiding* are the principal components of an ADT. Encapsulation defines data elements, storage and access methods together under one unit. Information hiding defines data access controls by separating the members of the ADT into public and private. Different programming languages may support additional access control policies. Implementation of an ADT is defined as a *class* in programming languages like C++, Java, Python etc. As discussed above, conceptually, *Stack* can also be defined as an ADT with public access methods such as push(), pop(), isEmpy(), isFull(), topOfStack(). The data storage information of the data elements can be hidden from the application programs, and implemented using different mechanisms such as array, linked list, pointer, etc.

2.3 QUEUES

Queue is a linear data structure in which data elements can be inserted from one end and removed from another end. It follows *First-in First-out (FIFO)* or *Last-in Last-out (LILO)* operations. FIFO implies that the element which is inserted at first can only be removed first before removing others. Similarly, LILO implies that the elements which was inserted at last can only be removed at last. Few examples of queues are shown in Figure 2.17.

Figure 2.17: Examples of Queues

The process of inserting an element into a queue is called *enqueue* and the process of removing an element from the queue is called *dequeue*. Figure 2.18 pictorially illustrates enqueue and dequeue operations. A queue maintains two pointers named *Head* (also referred to as *Front*) and *Tail* (also referred to as *Rear*). The Head pointer points to the element which was first inserted among the elements in the queue. The Tail pointer points to the element which was last inserted among the elements in the queue. Upon a dequeue operation, the Head pointer will be updated to point to the second element (the element which was inserted next to the dequeued element). Similarly, upon an enqueue operation, the Tail pointer will be updated to point to the just inserted element. A queue may be implemented using an array, or a linked list or a tree. In this unit, the implementation of a queue using a linear (1D) array is discussed. A queue may have the following operations.

- ***Enqueue***: inserts an element into a queue.
- ***Dequeue***: removes an element from a queue.
- ***isEmpty:*** checks if the queue is empty.
- ***isFull:*** checks if the queue is full.
- ***headElement***: returns the head element.
- ***tailElement:*** returns the tail element.

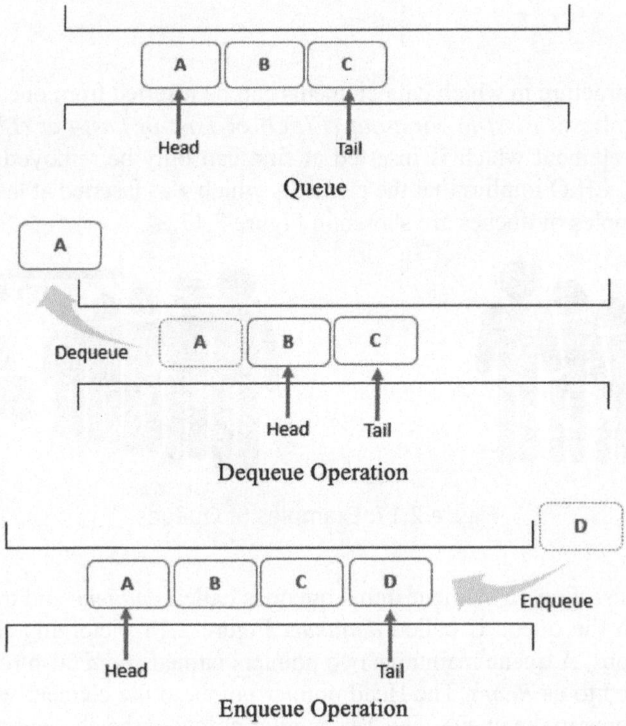

Figure 2.18: Enqueue and Dequeue operations on a Queue

2.3.1 Implementation of Queues

As mentioned above, this unit discusses the implementation of queues using array data structure. The enqueue and dequeue operations of a queue may be implemented in different ways. Depending on the ways these operations are implemented, the conditions of the queue being empty, full, and the number of elements that can be accommodated in the queue will be different. This section illustrates different scenarios. Let us assume that the data elements in the queue are stored in an array named `storage`, and the size of the array is `MAX` i.e., `int storage[MAX];`.

Scenario 1: Let us consider the following assumptions.

- When an element is enqueue, $Tail$ is incremented by 1.
- When an element is dequeue, $Head$ is incremented by 1.
- In the initial state of the queue, i.e., before performing any enqueue or dequeue operations, both the $Head$ and Tail are initialized to -1. $Head = -1;$ and $Tail = -1;$.
- When $Head == Tail;$, then the queue is empty.
- When $Tail = MAX - 1;$ then the queue is full.
- $Tail$ points to the last enqueue element, and $Head$ +1 points to the first enqueue element.

With the above assumptions, the following C program segment can be used to implement queue.

```
#include<stdio.h>
#define MAX 10
int storage[MAX];
int Head=-1, Tail=-1; //initially, queue is empty

int isEmpty(){   // check if the queue is empty
         if(Head==Tail){
             return 1;
         }
         else{
             return 0;
         }
}

int isFull(){   // check if the queue is full
         if(Tail==MAX-1){
             return 1;
         }
         else{
             return 0;
         }
}

void enQueue(int ele){
         if(isFull()!=1){
             storage[++Tail]= ele;
             printf("Enqueue successfully");
         }
         else printf("Queue Full");
}

int deQueue(void){
         if(isEmpty()!=1){
             Head++;
             return storage[Head];
         }
         else{
             printf("Queue Empty");
             return -1; // Assuming -1 is an invalid queue
                   // element. Any value representing
                   //invalid queue element can be returned.
         }
}
```

With the above function, it can be easily realized that the queue can accommodate upto MAX number of elements. That is, in the initial state of the queue, perform MAX numbers of enqueue operations, without performing any dequeue operations. After performing the last enqueue operation, $Head$ has the value -1, and $Tail$ has the value $MAX - 1$. From this statement, the above program seems to be an efficient implementation. However, the following issues will be experienced with the above implementation.

- If we dequeue all the elements in the queue, then $Tail = Head = MAX - 1$. Even if there is not element in the `storage` array, we cannot enqueue any more element as the $Tail$ is equal to $MAX - 1$.
- At the most, the above program will support only upto MAX number of enqueue operations.

Scenario 2: Practically, one should be able to perform any number of enqueue and dequeue operations (the number of successful dequeues should be always less than or equal to the number of enqueue operations) as long as there are free spaces in the `storage` array. To resolve the problem reported in Scenario 1, let us change the assumptions as follows.

- In the initial state of the queue, i.e., before performing any enqueue or dequeue operations, both the $Head$ and Tail are initialized to -1. $Head = -1;$ and $Tail = -1;$.
- When an element is enqueue, $Tail$ is incremented by 1.
- When an element is dequeue, move all the elements in the queue by one position forward, and decrement $Tail$ by 1.
- When $Tail == -1;$, then the queue is empty.
- When $Tail = MAX - 1;$ then the queue is full.
- $Tail$ points to the last enqueued element, and $Head$ +1 points to the first enqueued element.

Accordingly, the implementation of the queue is updated as follows, particularly the `isEmpty()` and `deQueue()` functions.

```
#include<stdio.h>
#define MAX 10
int storage[MAX];
int Head=-1, Tail=-1; //initially, queue is empty

int isEmpty(){    // check if the queue is empty
          if(Tail==-1){
              return 1;
          }
          else{
              return 0;
          }
}

int isFull(){    // check if the queue is full
          if(Tail==MAX-1){
```

```
                return 1;
            }
            else{
                return 0;
            }
    }

    void enQueue(int ele){
            if(isFull()!=1){
                storage[++Tail]= ele;
                printf("Enqueue successfully");
            }
            else printf("Queue Full");
    }

    int deQueue(void){
            int i, tmp=storage[Head+1];
            if(isEmpty()!=1){
                for(i=0; i<Tail; i++){
                        storage[i]=storage[i+1];
                }
                Tail--;
                return tmp;
            }
            else{
                printf("Queue Empty");
                return -1; // Assuming -1 is an invalid queue
                        // element. Any value representing
                        //invalid queue element can be returned.
            }
    }
```

In the above program, $Head$ always has the value -1. While all the operations in the Scenario 1 have time complexity $O(1)$, the time complexity of performing a dequeue operation will be $O(n)$, where n is the size of the array.

2.3.2 Circular Queue

Implementation in the Scenario 1 is space inefficient, though operations are of $O(1)$ time complexity. Scenario 2 is time inefficient, though space utilization is efficient. To take care of these observations; space utilization and time complexity, one can consider *circular queue*. Pictorially, a circular queue with example enqueue and dequeue operations is illustrated in Figure 2.19. As illustrated in the figure, the storage locations are organized in a circular manner, so that the elements are enqueued in a circular manner to consumption of free space available before the Head pointer.

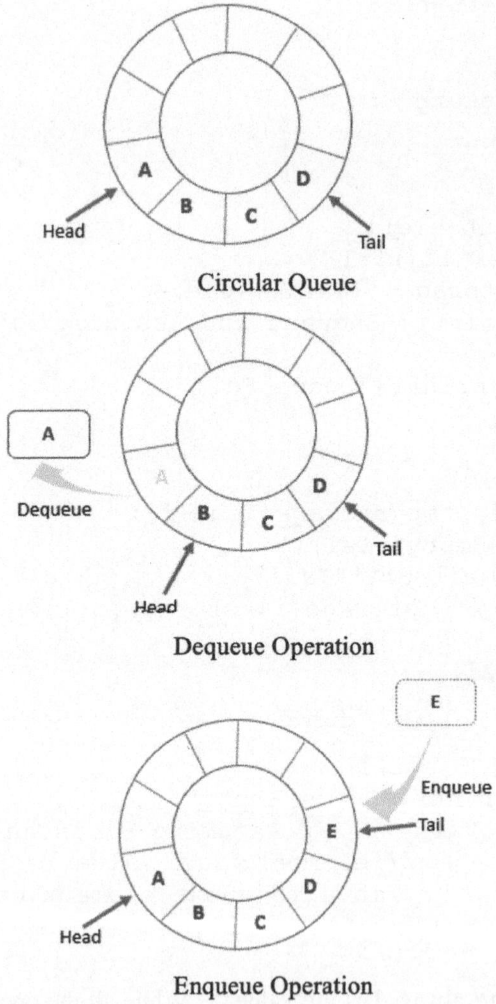

Figure 2.19: Enqueue and Dequeue operations on a Queue

Implementation of Circular Queue: A linear 1D array can be used for implementing a circular queue. Unlike in the Scenario 1 of the section 2.3.1, if an enqueue operation is performed, when the $Tail$ pointer is equal to $MAX - 1$ and there are free spaces before $Head$, the $Tail$ pointer will be assigned to 0 as illustrated below. Similarly, if a dequeue operation is performed when $Head = MAX - 1$, the $Head$ will move to index 0. Thus, circular movement of the storage location can be simulated over a 1D array as illustrated in Figure 2.20. From the figure, it can be seen clearly that whenever an element is enqueued, the $Tail$ pointer is updated as $Tail = (Tail + 1)\%MAX$. Similarly, the $Head$ pointer is updated as $Head = (Head + 1)\%MAX$ whenever an element is dequeued from the queue.

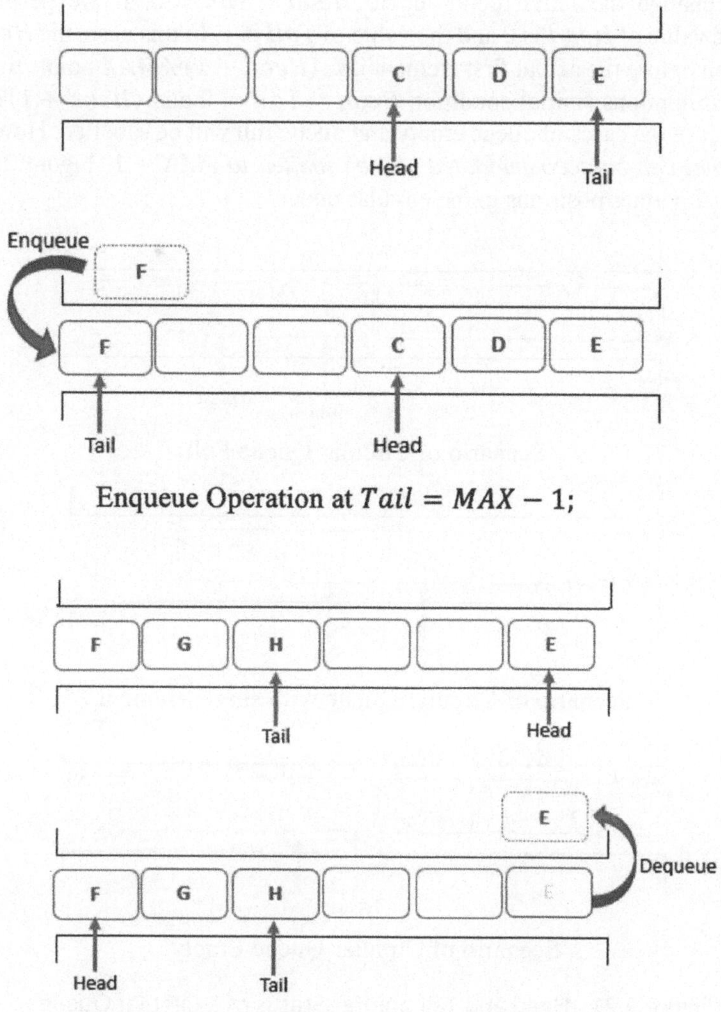

Figure 2.20: Enqueue and Dequeue operations on a Circular Queue

There is one issue that one need to take when implementing circular queue; *what will be the conditions of queue empty and full?* The following scenarios explain the cases.

Scenario 1: Queue is empty when $Head == Tail$, and Full when $(Tail + 1)\%MAX = Head.$

Initially, the $Head$ and $Tail$ are set to -1. Let us assume that MAX number of enqueue operations are performed. After performing MAX number of enqueue operations, $Tail$ is equal to $MAX - 1$, and all the available spaces are consumed. Now, $(Tail + 1)\%MAX = 0$, but $(Tail + 1)\%MAX \neq Head$. *The above queue full condition is not satisfied, and the algorithm fails*. Ideally, the $Head$ is expected to have the value 0 to satisfy the queue full condition

Now, let us change the initial condition to $Head = Tail = 0$. If we perform one enqueue operation, the value of $Head$ is 0 and the value of $Tail$ is 1. In this case, the $Head$ pointer points to one location before the actual first element i.e., $(Head + 1)\%MAX$ points to the first element. With these assumptions (initial condition $Head = Tail = 0$ and $(Head + 1)\%MAX)$ points to the first element), the cases of queue empty and queue full will be satisfied. However, *the number of elements that can be accommodated will be limited to* $MAX - 1$. Figure 2.21 illustrates the $Head$ and $Tail$ pointer positions in the circular queue.

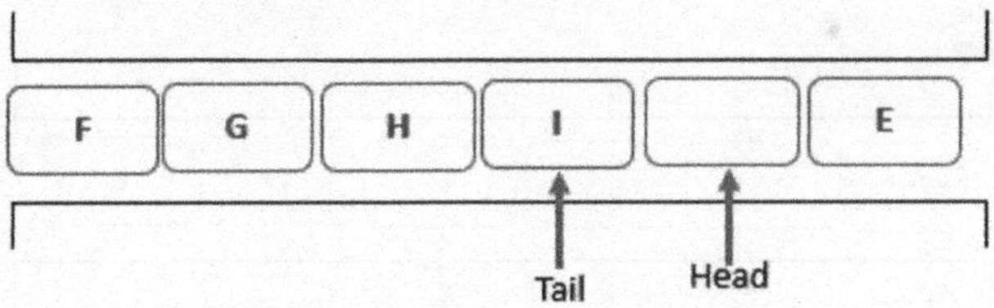

Scenario of Circular Queue Full

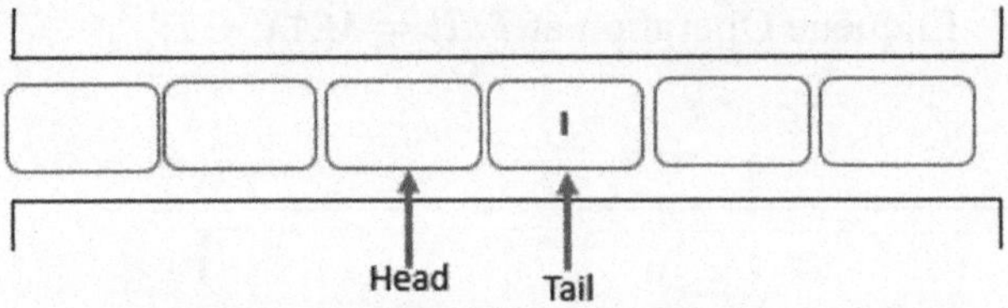

Scenario of Circular Queue with single element

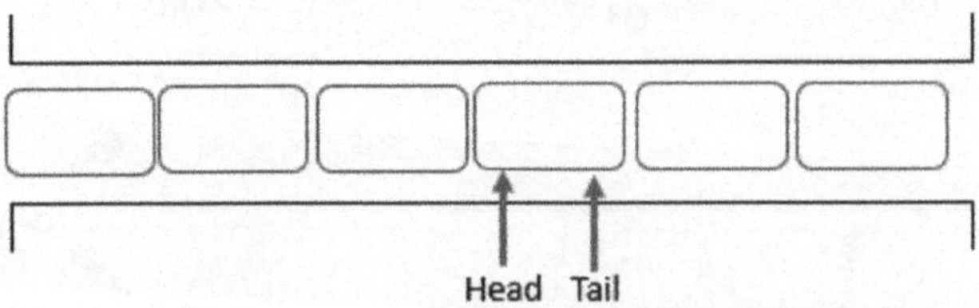

Scenario of Circular Queue Empty

Figure 2.21: Head and Tail pointer Status of a Circular Queue

The following program segment shows implementation of the above scenario in C programming language.

```
#include<stdio.h>
#define MAX 10

int storage[MAX];
int Head=0, Tail=0; //initially, queue is empty

int isEmpty(){    // check if the queue is empty
        if(Tail==Head){
            return 1;
        }
```

```
        else{
            return 0;
        }
}


int isFull(){    // check if the queue is full
        if((Tail+1)%MAX==Head){
            return 1;
        }
        else{
            return 0;
        }
}


void enQueue(int ele){
        if(isFull()!=1){
            Tail=(Tail+1)%MAX;
            storage[Tail]= ele;
            printf("Enqueue successfully");
        }
        else printf("Queue Full");
}


int deQueue(void){
        if(isEmpty()!=1){
            Head=(Head+1)%MAX;
            return storage[Head];
        }
        else{
            printf("Queue Empty");
            return -1; // Assuming -1 is an invalid queue
                  // element. Any value representing invalid
                  // queue element can be returned.
        }
}
```

Scenario 2: Queue is empty when $Num = 0$, and full when $Num = MAX$.

In scenario 1, the maximum number of elements that can be accommodated in the queue is one less than the actual space allocated for the queue. To take care of this, a new counter Num is introduced, which keeps track of the number of elements in the queue. $Head$ points to the first element and $Tail$ points to the last element. Whenever an enqueue operation is performed, the Num counter is incremented by one. Similarly, whenever a dequeue operation is performed, the Num counter is decremented by one. The queue will be empty when $Num == 0$, and the queue will be full when $Num == MAX$. Figure 2.22 illustrates $Head$ and $Tail$ pointers at different state of the queue. With the Num counter, complete allocated space can be utilized.

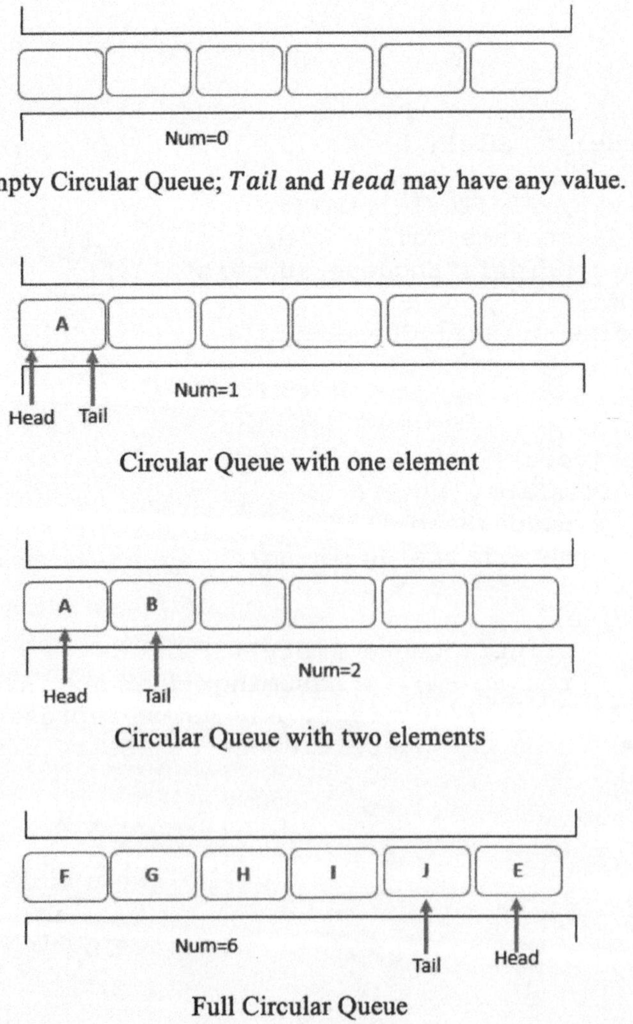

Figure 2.22: Head and Tail pointer Status of a Circular Queue

The following program segment shows implementation of the above scenario in C programming language.

```
#include<stdio.h>
#define MAX 10
int storage[MAX], Head, Tail, Num=0;

int isEmpty(){    // check if the queue is empty
        if(Num==0){
            return 1;
        }
        else{
            return 0;
        }
}


int isFull(){    // check if the queue is full
        if(Num==MAX){
            return 1;
        }
        else{
            return 0;
        }
}

void enQueue(int ele){
        if(isFull()!=1){
            if(isEmpty()==1){ // Num==0 condition can also be
                              // used
                Tail=0;       // Assuming that array index
                              // starts from 1
                Head=0;
                storage[Tail]= ele;
                printf("Enqueue successfully");
                Num++;
            }
            else{
                Tail=(Tail+1)%MAX;
                storage[Tail]= ele;
                printf("Enqueue successfully");
                Num++;
            }
        }
        else printf("Queue Full");
}
```

```
int deQueue(void){
            int tmp;
            if(isEmpty()!=1){
                tmp = storage[Head];
                Head=(Head+1)%MAX;
                Num--;
                Return tmp;
            }
            else{
                printf("Queue Empty");
                return -1; // Assuming -1 is an invalid queue
                       // element. Any value representing invalid
                       // queue element can be returned.
            }
}
```

For implementing circular queues, there could be other implementation scenarios to check whether queue is empty and queue is full. Other possible implementation cases are left as exercise.

2.3.3 Other Types of Queues

Double Ended Queue (Deque) is a generalized version of queue (with less restriction) which allows insert and removal of elements from both ends as shown in Figure 2.923 . It can be conceptualized as a data structure integration both stack and queue. By activating/using relevant operations, deque can be used either as a stack or a queue. Some of the basic operations on deque are listed below.

- Push_Front(): An element is inserted at the *Head* of the queue.
- Push_Back(): An element is inserted at the *Tail* of the queue.
- Pop_Front(): An element is removed from the *Head* of the queue.
- Pop_Back(): An element is removed from the *Tail* of the queue.
- isEmpty(): Check if the queue empty.
- isFull(): Check if the queue is full.
- Front(): Return the element at the head of the queue.
- Back(): Return the element at the tail of the queue.

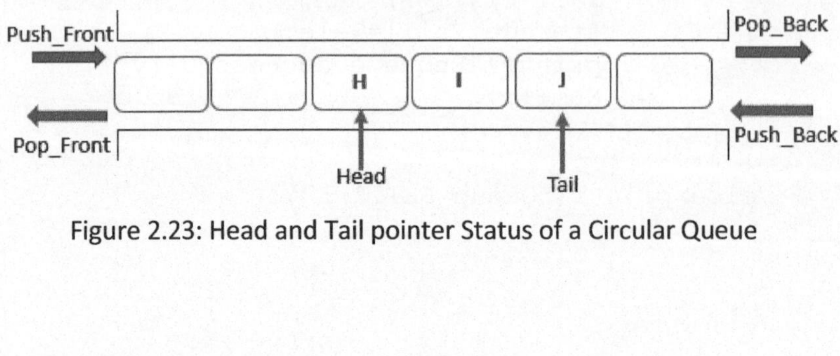

Figure 2.23: Head and Tail pointer Status of a Circular Queue

Further, a deque can be *input restricted deque,* where insertion is allowed only from one end, but removal is allowed from both the ends. Likewise, it can also be *output restricted deque*, where deletion is allowed only from one end, but insertion is allowed from both the ends. Queue implementation in the above sections can be modified to implement deque. However, it is left as an exercise to the readers. Though deque has been illustrated using array in this unit, it can be implemented using other data structures such as linked list.

Monotonic Queue: Monotonic queue is another type of queue where elements in the queue are kept in either increasing (increasing monotonic queue) or decreasing (decreasing monotonic queue) order of the values. Any element that violates the order is removed. As it involves the removal of elements from the tail of the queue to maintain ordering while inserting an element mid-value, deque data may be a preferred choice for implementing monotonic queue. Figure 2.24 illustrates insertion operation of an arbitrary element into an increasing monotonic queue. It shows that for inserting an element somewhere in the middle, elements larger than the new elements are removed.

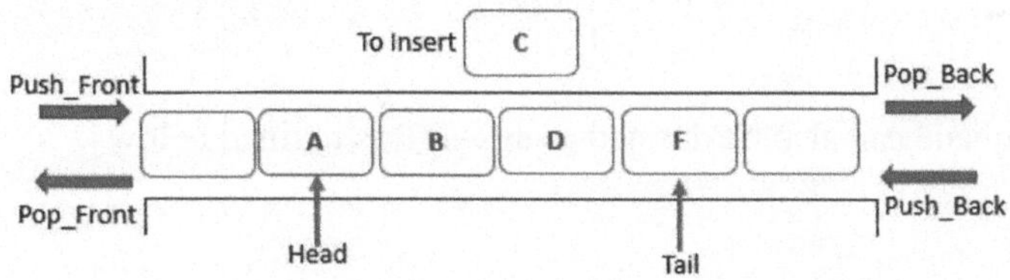

A Monotonic Queue

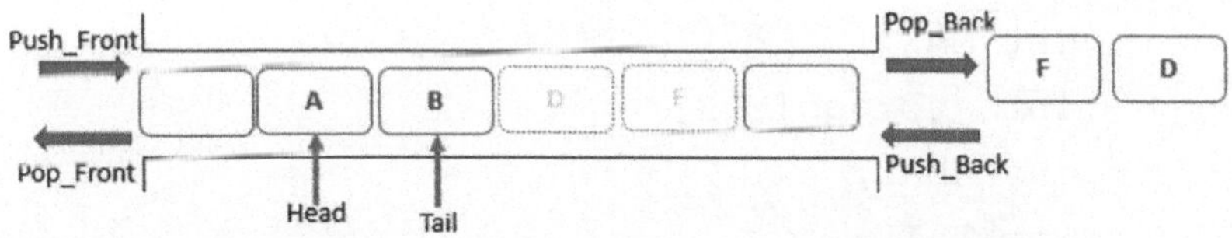

To Insert C, remove F and D using Pop_Back() function

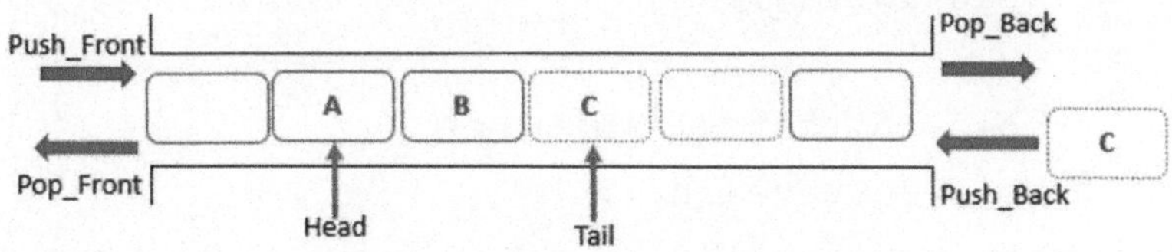

Insert C using Puch_Back() Function

Figure 2.24: Illustration of inserting an arbitrary element into increasing monotonic queue

Priority Queue: Priority queue is another type of queue where elements are removed based on their priority values. Each element in a priority queue has an associated priority value (which can be different from the data value). The elements can be inserted in any order, but element should be removed only in the order of their priority values. Priority queue can be implement using various data structures such as array, linked list, tree and so on. However, one should choose an appropriate implementation which can arrange the elements in the order of the priority values to support efficient dequeue operation. In practice, max heap ADT (discussed in Unit IV) implemented using array data structure is generally used. Priority queue can also be realised using the traditional queues discussed above by using layers of queues for different priority values as illustrated in the figure 2.25.

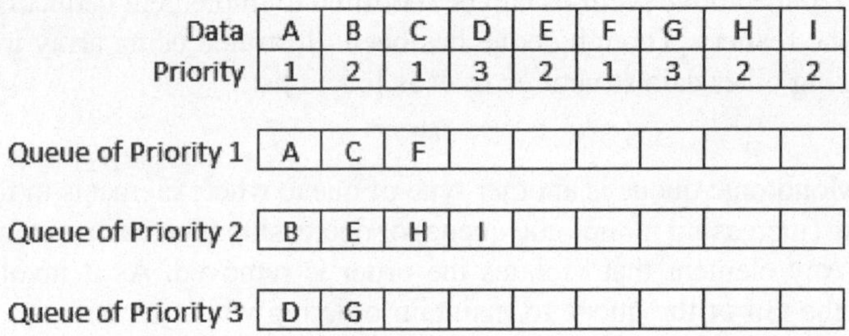

Figure 2.25: Priority Queue implementation using traditional queues

2.3.4 Queue ADT

Further, like in stack, queue can also be defined as an ADT as defined below.

```
<ADT> QUEUE{
        PRIVATE:
            int MAX;
            int storage[MAX];
            int HEAD;
            int TAIL;
            void init();
        PUBLIC:
            void initiate(){init();}
            void enQueue(int);
            int deQueue();
            int headElement();
            int tailElement();
            int isEmpty(void);
            int isFull(void);
};
```

2.4 Applications of Stack and Queue

A Stack data structure can be implemented using Queue data structure. Likewise, a Queue data structure can be implemented using Stack datastructure. Two such examples are listed below.

Case 1: Implement Stack Using two Queues

The idea here is to implement a data structure that follows Last-In First-Out (LIFO) - a Stack in this example, using data structures that follow First-In First-Out (FIFO) – two Queues in this example. We do not physically implement Stack, in the traditional manner. Instead, we mimic operations of a Stack, using physically implemented instances of two Queues and their operations. The target operations that we wish to mimic are push() and pop() of a Stack data structure, by actually performing enqueue() and dequeue() operations on the instances of the Queues.

Several approaches can be used to implement the above task. In this book, the following idea is used to realize the above task. Readers are encouraged to work out other alternatives.

a) Instantiate two Queues, namely Q_1 and Q_2.
b) Always place the last inserted element at the front of the Queue Q_1. A pop operation is realized by performing dequeue operation on Q_1.
c) Use Q_2 as auxiliary storage to ensure the above point b.

The following algorithm can be considered to realize the above operational idea.

Algorithm: PUSH

Assumption: Q2 is initially empty

Input: ele – the element to be pushed, Queue Q_1, Queue Q_2

```
BEGIN
Q2.enqueue(ele)   // ele is the only element in Q2
UNTIL (Q1.isEmpty()==False)  // Move all from Q1 to Q2. ele is at front of Q2
      Q2.enqueue(Q1.dequeue())
UNTIL (Q2.isEmpty()==False)  // Move all from Q2 to Q1
      Q1.enqueue(Q2.dequeue())
END
```

Algorithm: POP

Output: the popped element

Input: Queue Q_1

```
BEGIN
ele = Q1.dequeue()
RETURN ele
```

Time Complexity: The above algorithm has $\Theta(m)$ time complexity for POP operation, where m is the time complexity of dequeue operation on a Queue. Though m depends on the way the Queue is implemented, it can be as low as $\Theta(1)$. For instance, a circular Queue, or a Queue implementation using doubly linked list has $\Theta(1)$ dequeue time complexity. On the other hand, the above algorithm has $\Theta(nm)$ time complexity for PUSH operation, where n is the number of elements already stored in the Stack, and m is the time complexity of an enqueue/ dequeue operation on a Queue. If the $\Theta(1)$ is the time complexity of the underlying enqueue/dequeue operation, the time complexity of the PUSH operation is $\Theta(n)$. Space complexity is equivalent to that of the underlying Queue.

Case 2: Implement Queue using two Stacks.

The following idea can be used to realize the above task.

a) Instantiate two Stacks, namely S_1 and S_2.
b) Always place the oldest element at the top of the Stack S_1. A dequeue operation is realized by performing POP operation on S_1.
c) Use S_2 as auxiliary storage to ensure the above point b.

The following algorithm can be considered to realize the above operational idea. Note that, popping all the elements from a Stack and pushing the elements in another Stack in the order of popped sequence reverses the elements in the Stack.

```
Algorithm: enqueue
Assumption: S2 is initially empty
Input: ele - the element to be enqueued, Stack S1, Stack S2
BEGIN
// Move all from S1 to S2.
1. UNTIL (S1.isEmpty()==False)
2.          S2.push(S1.pop ())
3. S2.push(ele)

// Move all from S2 to S1
4. UNTIL (S2.isEmpty()==False)
5.          S1.push(S2.pop())
END
```

```
Algorithm: dequeue
Output: The dequeued element
Input: Stack S1
BEGIN
1.  ele = S1.pop()
2.  Return ele
END
```

If a PUSH or POP operation on a Stack can be done with $\Theta(1)$ time complexity, the above algorithm has $\Theta(n)$ for enqueue operation and $\Theta(1)$ for dequeue operation. Though the above example shows one specific approach of implementing the task, it can be implemented using different approaches. Readers are encouraged to work out other alternatives.

UNIT SUMMARY

This unit discussed three data structures – array, stack, and queue. Algorithms for different operations of these data structures are discussed and the complexities of these algorithms are also estimated. Working principles of these data structures, and their operations are explained with appropriate examples and diagrams.

EXERCISES

Many of these questions have been compiled from various sources including past GATE examinations.

Multiple Choice Questions

Q1. What is a stack data structure?

a) A linear data structure

b) A non-linear data structure

c) A hierarchical data structure

d) A tree data structure

Q2. If the index of the first element in an array is 0, What is the index of the 10th element in the array?

a. 10

b. 9

c. 11

d. 0

Q3. What is the time complexity of accessing an element in an array?

a. $\theta(1)$

b. $\theta(n)$

c. $\theta(n \log n)$

d. $\theta(\log n)$

Q4. What happens if you access an array element with an index that is out of bounds in C?

a. It will give an error

b. It will access the element at the last valid index

c. It will access the element at the first valid index

d. It depends on the size of the array

Q5. What is the characteristic feature of a stack data structure?

a) First In, First Out (FIFO)

b) Last In, Last Out (LILO)

c) Last In, First Out (LIFO)

d) First In, Last Out (FILO)

Q6. Which operation adds an element to the top of the stack?

a) Pop

b) Peek (top of Stack)

c) Push

d) Remove

Q7. What happens when a stack is full and a push operation is performed?

a) Stack becomes empty

b) Stack overflows

c) Stack remains unchanged

d) Stack underflows

Q8. What happens when a stack is empty and a pop operation is performed?

a) Stack becomes full

b) Stack underflows

c) Stack remains unchanged

d) Stack overflows

Q9. Which of the following data structures can be implemented using a stack?

a) Queue

b) Tree

c) Graph

d) All of the above

Q10. What is the time complexity of push and pop operations in a stack with a fixed size?

a) $\theta(1)$

b) $\theta(n)$

c) $\theta(2^n)$

d) $\theta(\log n)$

Q11. Which of the following is not a common application of a stack data structure?

a) Expression evaluation

b) Reverse a string

c) Binary tree traversal

d) Sorting elements

Q12. Which operation in a queue data structure removes the element from the front of the queue?

a) Dequeue

b) Peek (Front)

c) Enqueue

d) Remove

Q13. What is the time complexity of the dequeue operation in a queue implemented using a linked list? The head of the list points to the first element of the queue.

a) $\theta(1)$

b) $\theta(n)$

c) $\theta(2^n)$

d) $\theta(\log n)$

Q14. Which of the following operations can be used to add an element to the front of the queue?

a) Enqueue

b) Dequeue

c) Peek (Front)

d) Insert

Q15. Which of the following is not a disadvantage of using an array to implement a queue?

a) Fixed size

b) Inefficient insertion and deletion at the front

c) Requires shifting of elements after dequeue operation

d) High memory usage

Short and Long Answer Type Questions

Q1. What is the time complexity of the peek (top of the stack) operation in a stack?

Q2. What is the difference between a static stack and a dynamic stack?

Q3. What is the purpose of the "isEmpty" operation in a stack?

Q4. What is the time complexity of the "isEmpty" operation in a stack?

Q5. What is the purpose of the "isFull" operation in a stack?

Q6. What is the time complexity of the "isFull" operation in a stack?

Q9. Implement a function in C to reverse a string using a stack.

Q10. Implement a function in C to convert an infix expression to postfix expression using a stack.

Q11. Implement a function in C to find the size of a queue.

Q12. Implement a function in C to reverse the elements of a queue.

Q13. What is a circular queue?

Q14. How can you implement a circular queue using an array in C?

Q15. What is a priority queue?

Q16. How can you implement a priority queue using a heap in C? (Refer Unit III for details on Heap)

Q17. What is a double-ended queue or deque?

Q18. How can you implement a double-ended queue or deque using a doubly linked list in C?

Q19. Consider the sparse matrix implementation discussed in Section 2.1.3, determine the expression to estimate effective address of A[i][j] of a left upper triangular sparse matrix.

Q20. Consider the sparse matrix implementation discussed in Section 2.1.3, determine the expression to estimate effective address of A[i][j] of a right upper triangular sparse matrix.

Numerical Problems

Q1. What will be the output of the following C program?

```
#include <stdio.h>
#include <stdlib.h>

void push(int* arr, int* top, int x) {
    arr[++(*top)] = x;
}

int pop(int* arr, int* top) {
    return arr[(*top)--];
}

int main() {
    int stack[5];
    int top = -1;
    push(stack, &top, 10);
    push(stack, &top, 20);
    printf("%d\n", pop(stack, &top));
    return 0;
}
```

Q2. What will be the output of the following C program?

```
#include <stdio.h>
#include <stdlib.h>

void enqueue(int* arr, int* front, int* rear, int x) {
    if (*rear == 4) {
        printf("Queue is full.\n");
        return;
    }
    arr[++(*rear)] = x;
}
```

```
int dequeue(int* arr, int* front, int* rear) {
    if (*front == *rear) {
        printf("Queue is empty.\n");
        return -1;
    }
    return arr[++(*front)];
}

int main() {
    int queue[5];
    int front = -1, rear = -1;
    enqueue(queue, &front, &rear, 10);
    enqueue(queue, &front, &rear, 20);
    printf("%d\n", dequeue(queue, &front, &rear));
    return 0;
}
```

Q3. What will be the output of the following C program?

```
#include <stdio.h>
#include <stdlib.h>

void push(int* arr, int* top, int x) {
    if (*top == 4) {
        printf("Stack is full.\n");
        return;
    }
    arr[++(*top)] = x;
}

int pop(int* arr, int* top) {
    if (*top == -1) {
        printf("Stack is empty.\n");
```

```
        return -1;
    }
    return arr[(*top)--];
}

int main() {
    int stack[5];
    int top = -1;
    push(stack, &top, 10);
    push(stack, &top, 20);
    printf("%d\n", pop(stack, &top));
    return 0;
}
```

Q4. Implement a queue using two stacks.

Q5. Implement a stack using two queues.

Q6. Given an integer array A and an integer k, write a program to return the number of pairs (i, j) where $i < j$ such that $|A[i] - A[j]| == k$.

Q7. Given a sorted array A of n integers and an integer x, write a program to find the lower bound of x. The lower bound of x is the smallest index i such that $A[i] >= x$.

Q8. Given an array of integers A and an integer limit, return the size of the longest non-empty subarray such that the absolute difference between any two elements of this subarray is less than or equal to limit. . A subarray is a contiguous part of an array. Hints: Try to solve this problem using Double Ended Queue.

Q9. Given an integer array A and an integer k, return the size of the shortest non-empty subarray with a sum of at least k. If there is no such subarray, return -1. A subarray is a contiguous part of an array. Try to solve this in less than $O(n^2)$.

Q10. You are given an integer array A of length n that represents a permutation of the integers in the range $[0, n - 1]$. We split A into some number of chunks, and individually sort each chunk. After concatenating the sorted chunks, the result should equal the sorted array of A. Return the largest number of chunks we can make to sort the array.

KNOW MORE

Readers are encouraged to explore the following E-Books/E-Resources for additional examples, and discussions on related topics.

1. Stacks and Queues. Frank Pfenning, Andre Platzer, Rob Simmons (https://www.cs.cmu.edu/~rjsimmon/15122-s13/09-queuestack.pdf)
2. Queue. Chapter 6, Data Structures and Algorithms: Annotated Reference with Examples, Granville Barnett, and Luca Del Tongo,(https://www.mta.ca/~rrosebru/oldcourse/263114/Dsa.pdf)

REFERENCES AND SUGGESTED READINGS

- [Adamson, 1996] I. T. Adamson. (1996), Data structures and Algorithms: A first Course, Springer.
- [Aho, 1983] A. V. Aho, J. E. Hopcroft, and J D. Ullman. (1983), Data Structures and Algorithms, Addison-Wesley.
- [Cormen, 2001] Cormen, T. H.; Leiserson, C. E.; Rivest, R. L. & Stein, C. (2001), *Introduction to Algorithms* , The MIT Press .
- [Donald, 2009] Donald E. Knuth. (2009), The Art of Computer Programming: Fundamental Algorithms, Vol. 1, 3rd Edition, Pearson.
- [Greene, 1988] D. H. Greene and D. E Knuth. (1988) Mathematics for the analysis of Algorithms, Birkhauser.
- [Horowitz, 1983] E. Horowitz and S Sahni. (1983) Fundamentals of data Structure, Computer Science Press
- [Horowitz, 1993] E. Horowitz, S Sahni and A. Freed. (1993) Fundamentals of data Structure in C, Computer Science Press.
- [James, 2009] James A. Storer. (2009), An Introduction to Data Structures and Algorithms, 1st Edition, Birkhauser Springer.
- [Kingston, 1990] J. H. Kingston. (1990), Algorithms and data structures, Addison-Wesley.
- [Kozon, 1992] D. C. Kozen. (1992), The design and Analysis of Algorithms, Springer.
- [Lewis, 1991] H. R. Lewis and L. Denenberg. (1991) Data Structures and Their Algorithms, Harper Collins.
- [Mehlhorn, 1984] K. Mehlhorn, (1984), Data Structures and Algorithms, Vol. I, II, III Springer.
- [Nievergelt, 1993] J. Nievergelt and K. H. Hinrichs, (1993) Algorithms and Data Structures, Prentice Hall.
- [Reingold, 1983] E. M. Reingold and W. J. Hanson (1983), Data Structures, Little Brown and Co.

- [Standish, 1980] T. Standish, (1980) Data Sructures, Addison-Wesley.
- [Wirth, 1976] Wirth, N. (1976), *Algorithms + Data Structures = Programs* , Prentice-Hall.

Dynamic QR Code for Further Reading

Scan the following QR Code to navigate to an external page for know more, additional reading materials, and additional exercises.

3 Linked Lists and Trees

UNIT SPECIFICS

Broadly, this unit discusses two types of data structures, namely linked lists and trees. Different types of linked lists and different types of trees are presented with appropriate examples in details. To be specific, the following data structures are discussed:

- *Singly linked list;*
- *Doubly linked list;*
- *Circular linked list;*
- *Implementation of linked list using array and dynamic allocation;*
- *Operations on linked list and their algorithms*
- *Tree, Binary tree;*
- *Binary search tree, AVL tree, Red-Black Tree, Heap Tree, Threaded binary tree;*
- *Operations on different types of binary trees and their algorithms;*
- *B-tree and B++ Tree;*

The practical applications of some of these data structures are discussed with appropriate examples to further improve problem solving capacity.

A large number of exercise questions of different types - multiple choice, short and long answer typed questions, practice questions are also given. For additional questions and reading materials, a QR code has been provided which is linked to a web page, for further reading and exercises.

RATIONALE

Linked list and tree are two data structures with wide ranges of applications. While linked lists are considered to be linear data structures, trees on the other hand are non-linear data structures. Further, linked lists are used to implement other data structures such as stack, queue, B++ tree etc. While linked lists arrange data elements in linear order, trees order the data elements in a hierarchical manner. This unit will help the students to visualise linear and nonlinear ways of organising data, accessing data elements from such organization and usage of such data structures for different applications

PRE-REQUISITES

Programming: C programming language (Many of the examples are given in C like statements)
Computer System: Main Memory

UNIT OUTCOMES

List of outcomes of this unit is as follows:

U3-O1: Understanding the concepts of Linked list data structure and its types
U3-O2: Understanding operations on linked list and their implementation
U3-O3: Understanding tree data structure and its types
U3-O4: Understanding operations on trees and their implementation
U3-O5: Understanding special types of binary trees – AVL tree, Red Black Tree, B-tree, B++

Unit-3 Outcomes	EXPECTED MAPPING WITH COURSE OUTCOMES (1- Weak Correlation; 2- Medium Correlation; 3- Strong Correlation)					
	CO-1	CO-2	CO-3	CO-4	CO-5	CO-6
U3-O1	1	-	3	-	-	-
U3-O2	1	-	3	-	-	-
U3-O3	1	-	3	-	-	-
U3-O4	1	-	3	-	-	-
U3-O5	1	-	3	-	-	-

3.1 LINKED LIST

This unit focuses on two data structures namely *linked list* and *tree*. Linked list data structure is first discussed in this section, followed by tree data structure in the next section. Linked list is a *linear* data structure where its data elements are arranged sequentially. Unlike an array, data elements in a linked list are stored at *non-contiguous* memory locations. Therefore, the elements need to be linked to enable traversal across the data elements. Each data element of a linked list is generally called *node*. A node consists of two fields; *information* field which holds the values of the corresponding data element, and *address* field which holds the address of next node (Figure 3.1). A special pointer called *Head* stores the address of the first element. The address field of the first node holds the address of the second node. Similarly, the address field of the second node holds the address of the third node, and so on (Figure 3.2). The address field of the last node holds *null.* Unlike array, data elements in a linked list are stored at *non-contiguous* memory locations. As each node maintains the data and the address of the next data element, it is inherently a *heterogeneous* data structure. Further, information field can also maintain a set of heterogeneous data values. For example, a linked list of student records where information field consists of name, roll no, age, etc.

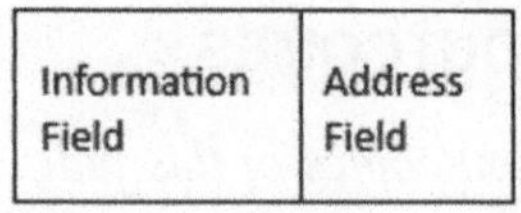

Figure 3.1: A node in a Linked List

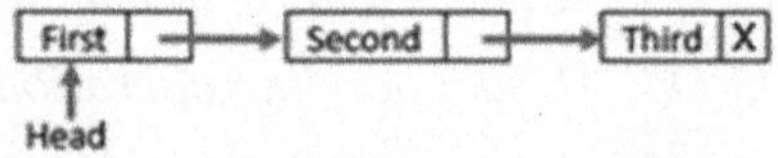

Figure 3.2: Connecting nodes in a Linked List.

Depending on whether a node in a linked list maintains the *address of the next node only* or the *addresses of both the previous node and the next node,* a linked list can be *Singly Linked List* or *Doubly Linked List.* The examples in the Figure 3.1 and Figure 3.2 are of singly linked list. If the type is not explicitly specified, the term *linked list* generally refers to as *singly linked list.* An example of doubly linked list is shown in Figure 3.3.

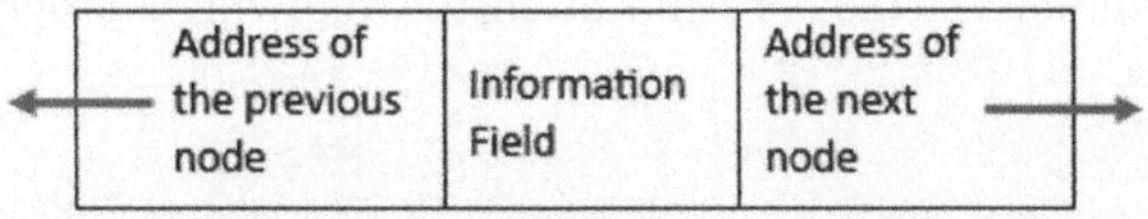

Node in a Doubly Linked List

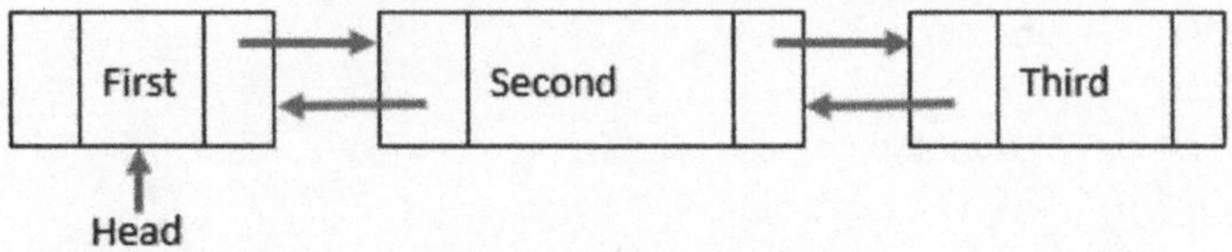

Figure 3.3: Connecting nodes in a Doubly Linked List.

3.1.1 Implementation of a Linked List in Memory

A linked list may be implemented using either *dynamic memory allocation* (allocate memory for each node separately) or *static memory allocation* (using arrays for storing data and address). In C programming language, the structure of a node for dynamic memory allocation can be defined as follows.

```
// Structure of a Singly Linked List
struct node{
        int info;
        struct node *next;
};

// Structure of a Doubly Linked List
struct node{
        int info;
        struct node *next;
        struct node *prev;
};
```

Once the structure is defined, memory for each node can be allocated dynamically as follows.

```
struct node *ptr;
ptr = (struct node *)malloc(sizeof(struct node));
```

Putting the above node definition and memory allocation, the following C program create a singly linked list of the elements 3 -> 1 -> 7.

```
#include <stdio.h>
#include<stdlib.h>
struct node{
    int info;
    struct node *next;
};

main(){
        struct node *head;

        // The First Node
        head = (struct node *)malloc(sizeof(struct node));
        head->info = 3;

        // The Second Node
        head->next= (struct node *)malloc(sizeof(struct node));
        head->next->info = 1;

        // The Third Node
        head->next->next = (struct node *)malloc(sizeof(struct
    node));
        head->next->next->info= 7;

        // Address field of the third node is assigned NULL
        head->next->next->next= NULL;

        printf("First element: %d\n",head->info);
        printf("Second element: %d\n",head->next->info);
        printf("Third element: %d\n",head->next->next->info);
}
```

The output of the above program is:

First element: 3

Second element: 1

Third element: 7

Pictorially, the above linked list can be visualized as follows.

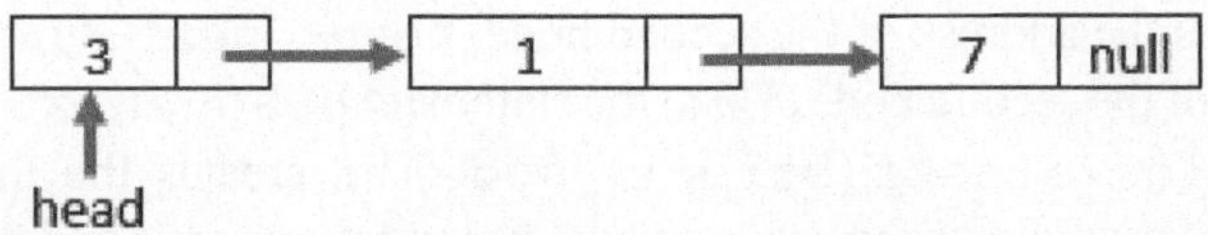

The statement `head = (struct node *)malloc(sizeof(struct node));` creates the first node, and the statement `head->info = 3;` assigns the value 3 in the information field of the first node.

The next statement `head->next = (struct node *)malloc(sizeof(struct node));` creates the second node and the address of the second node is assigned to the address field of the first node. If the address of the first node is stored at `head` pointer, `head->info` points to the information filed of the first node. Similarly, `head->next` points to the address field of the first node which can hold the address of another node as shown in figure 3.4. Therefore, `head->next = (struct node *)malloc(sizeof(struct node));` stores the address of the new node (i.e., second node) at the address field of the first node. Thus, the first and second nodes are sequentially connected.

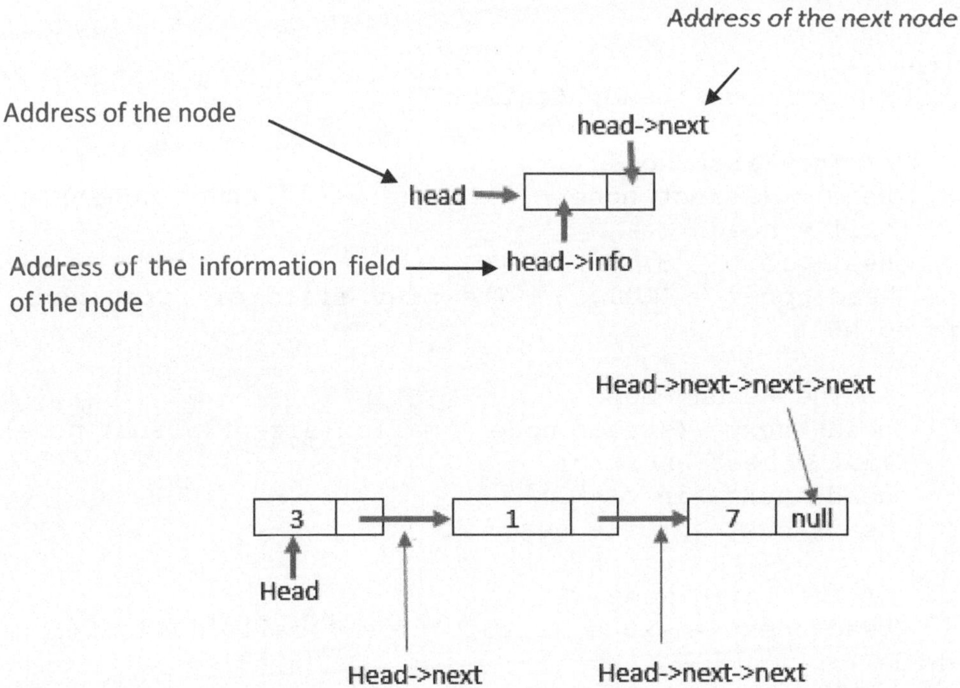

Figure 3.4: An example of headed linked list

As head->next stores the address of the second node, head->next->next stores the address of the address field of the second node. Thus, the statement head->next->next = (struct node *)malloc(sizeof(struct node)); creates the third node and stores its address to the address field of the second node, linking the second and third nodes sequentially.

In the similar manner, following C program creates a doubly linked list version of the above singly linked list. In a doubly linked list, each node has addresses of its next and previous nodes, linking the node to its next node as well as its previous node. Therefore, we can perform both forward movements, as well as backward movements. In order to support backward movement from the last node of the list, we also maintain a tail pointer in the following program, in addition to the head pointer. The head pointer stores the address of the first node, and the tail pointer stores the address of the last node.

```
#include <stdio.h>
#include<stdlib.h>
struct node{
    int info;
    struct node *next;
    struct node *prev;
};

main(){
        struct node *head, *tail;

        // The First Node
        head = (struct node *)malloc(sizeof(struct node));
        tail = head;
        head->info = 3;
        head->prev = NULL; // The prev field of first node is
assigned NULL

        // The Second Node
        head->next= (struct node *)malloc(sizeof(struct node));
        tail = head->next;
        head->next->info = 1;
        head->next->prev = head;

        // The Third Node
        head->next->next = (struct node *)malloc(sizeof(struct
    node));
        tail = head->next->next;
        head->next->next->info = 7;
        head->next->next->prev = head->next;
        head->next->next->next= NULL;

        // Print First to Last : 3 1 7
```

```
        printf("First element: %d\n",head->info);
        printf("Second element: %d\n",head->next->info);
        printf("Third element: %d\n",head->next->next->info);

        // Print Last to First : 7 1 3
        printf("First element: %d\n",tail->info);
        printf("Second element: %d\n",tail->prev->info);
        printf("Third element: %d\n",tail->prev->prev->info);
}
```

The output of the above program is:

First element: 3
Second element: 1
Third element: 7
First element: 7
Second element: 1
Third element: 3

The following figure illustrates the doubly linked list created by the above program.

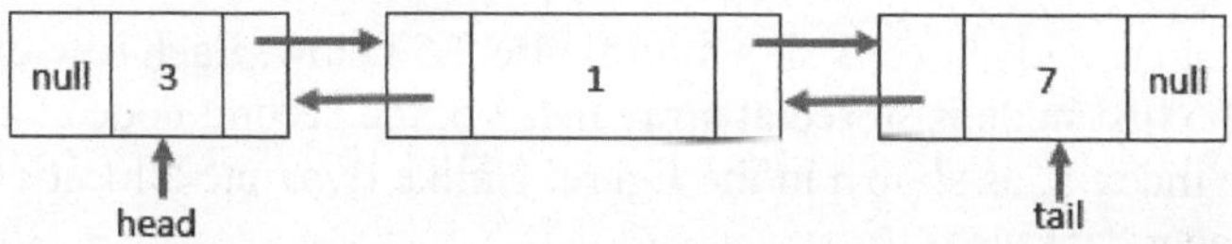

Linked List Implementation using Array: As mentioned above, a linked list can also be implemented using an array. A typical implementation using array is shown below. Another form of implementation is also presented in Unit I.

```
#include <stdio.h>
struct node{
   int info;
   int next;
};

main(){
   int a[10][2], head=5;
   struct node list[10];

   /* first node */
   list[head].info = 3; // data
   list[head].next = 2; // address of second node
```

```
    /* second node */
    list[list[head].next].info = 1; // data
    list[list[head].next].next = 8; // address of third node

    /* third node */
    list[list[list[head].next].next].info = 7;   // data
    list[list[list[head].next].next].next = -1; // last node

    printf("First element: %d\n",list[head].info);
    printf("Second element: %d\n", list[list[head].next].info
     );
    printf("Third element: %d\n", list[list[list[head].next
     ].next].info );
}
```

The output of the above program is:

First element: 3

Second element: 1

Third element: 7

Pictorially, the list created above is shown in figure 3.5 below. Each row of the array represents a *struct node*. The first node is stored at array index 5, the second node at array index 2, and the third node at the index 8, as shown in the figure. Unlike dynamic allocation, the `next` variable in node is an integer data type.

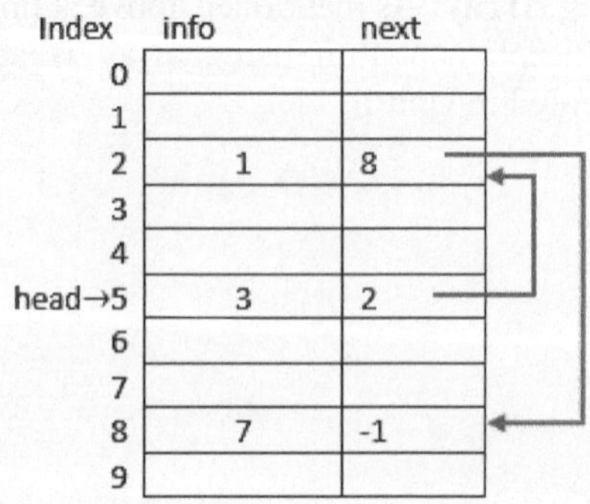

Figure 3.5: An example of array implementation of a linked list.

3.1.2 Operations on a Singly Linked List

Like any other data structure, a linked list data structure also needs to have operations like *insertion, deletion, search,* etc. Some of the common operations on linked list are listed below. Though the operation listed below are applicable for both singly as well as doubly linked list, the functions discussed in this section focus on singly linked list.

- **CREATE:** It creates an empty list. It is equivalent to declaring the `head` pointer, i.e., `struct node *head;`.

- **INSERTION:** It inserts an element into the list. Depending on the position of the insertion, the following suboperations may be defined.
  - insertFirst(): it inserts the new node before the current first node.
  - insertLast(): it inserts the new node after the current last node.
  - insertPosition(): it inserts the new node at a specified location.

- **DELETION:** It deletes an element from the list. Depending on the position of the deletion, the following suboperations may be defined.
  - deleteFirst(): it deletes the first node.
  - deleteLast(): it deletes the last node.
  - deletePosition(): it deletes a node at a specified location.

- **SEARCH:** It scans the list and checks for the occurrences of nodes with a specified data value.

- **TRAVERSAL:** It traverses the list from the first node till the last node and displays the data values. In case of a doubly linked list, traversal from first to last and last to first may be supported.

TRAVERSAL: Assume that a singly linked list is given and `head` points to the first node of the list. The following C function traverses the list from the first node till the last node.

```
void traverse(struct node *ptr){
        while(ptr != NULL){
                printf("%d ", ptr->info);
                ptr = ptr->next;
        }
}
```

The above function takes the address of the node from where the traversal will be started. If we want to start traversal from the first node, the address of the first node i.e., `head` should be passed as parameter while calling the function i.e., `traverse(head)`. Initially, when execution enters the `while` loop, `ptr = head`, as shown below and prints the value 3.

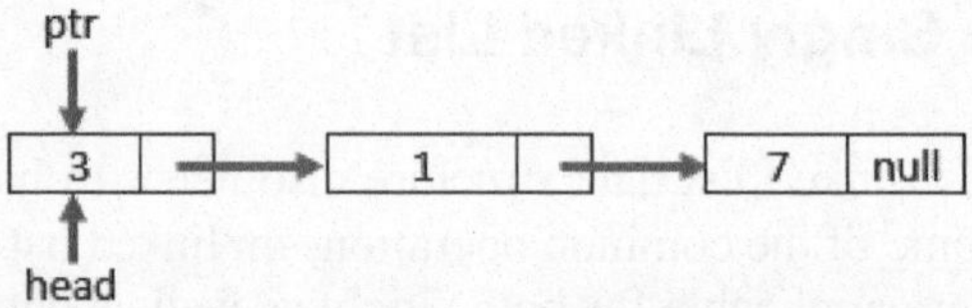

Then, the `ptr` variable is updated with the value stored at the address field of the node pointed by `ptr`, i.e., `ptr = ptr->next` inside the `while` loop. After this statement, `ptr` points to the second node as shown below.

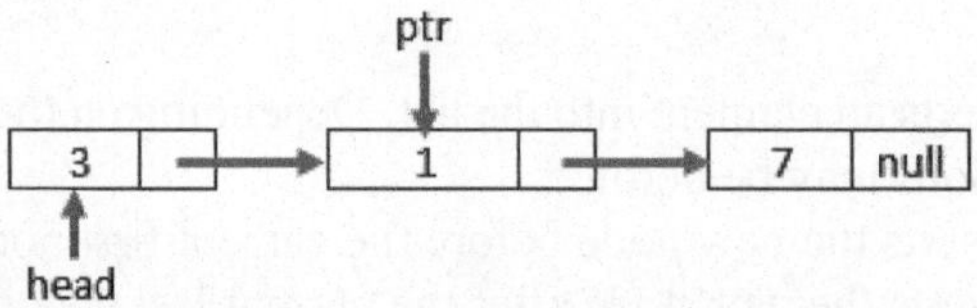

Likewise, after printing the value 1, `ptr` is updated with the address of the next node in the next iteration as shown below.

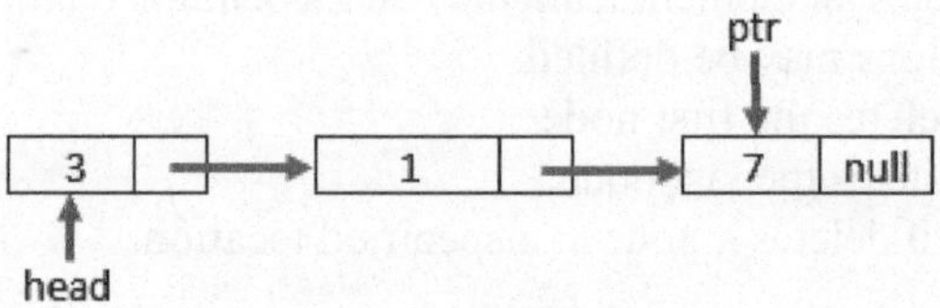

In the similar manner, the loop continues till `ptr = NULL`. The `traverse()` function mandatorily visits all the nodes in the list from the first node till the last node exactly once. Therefore, the time complexity of the function is $\theta(n)$. That means, $O(n)$ and $\Omega(n)$ also hold.

Instead of a singly linked list, if a doubly linked list is given, traversal could be from first to last or last to first. The following function traverses the list either from the first node or the last node based on the parameter `direction`. If the `direction` is 1, it traverses forward, otherwise backward. It takes addresses of the first node and last node as parameters.

```
void traverse(struct node *hPtr, struct node *tPtr, int
    direction){

    if(direction == 1){   // From first to last
        ptr = hPtr;
        while(ptr != NULL){
            printf("%d ", ptr->info);
            ptr = ptr->next;
        }
    }
    else{    // From last to first
```

```
            ptr = tPtr;
            while(ptr != NULL){
                printf("%d ", ptr->info);
                ptr = ptr->prev;
            }
        }
}
```

As the above function performs either a forward traversal or a backward traversal, its time complexity is still $\theta(n)$.

SEARCH: Search operation scans the list from the first node till the last node and checks the presence of the element to be searched. The following function takes the address of the first node `ptr` and the element to be searched `ele` as parameters. If the element `ele` is found, it returns 1, otherwise 0.

```
int search(struct node *ptr, int ele){
        while(ptr != NULL){
                if(ptr->info == ele){
                        printf("Found");
                        return 1;
                }
                ptr = ptr->next;
        }
        printf("Not Found");
        return 0;
}
```

Unlike the `traverse` function, the `search` operation not necessarily visits all the nodes in the list. It terminates at the first occurrence of the searched element in the list. It scans the entire list only when the searched element is present at the last node or the searched element is not found. Depending on the scenario, its time complexity will be different. The *best case* happens when the search element is present at the first node. It requires visiting only the first node. Hence, the best case time complexity is $O(1)$. The worst case happens when the searched element is present at the last node or the searched element is not found. For this case, all the nodes are visited, with the worst-case time complexity of order $O(n)$, where *n* is the number of nodes in the list. On an average, the function will visit $n/2$ number of nodes, with average case time complexity of order $O(n)$.

In a list, an element may occur repeatedly. However, the above `search` function terminates at the first occurrence of the searched element. Instead of just checking the presence or absence of the searched element, the above function may be modified to count the number of occurrences of the searched element as follows. If the count is 0, then the searched element is not found. Otherwise, it is found.

```
int count(struct node *ptr, int ele){
        int cnt=0;
        while(ptr != NULL){
              if(ptr->info == ele){
                    cnt++;
              }
              ptr = ptr->next;
        }
        return cnt;
}
```

As the count function mandatorily visits all the nodes in the list once, its time complexity is $O(n)$.

INSERTION: Depending on the position of the insertion, the scenario will be different. Given a singly linked list, *insertion at the first position* can be illustrated as follows.

Step 1: Create a new node and store the element to be inserted at the information field

```
nPtr = (struct node *)malloc(sizeof(struct node));
nPtr->info = 4;
```

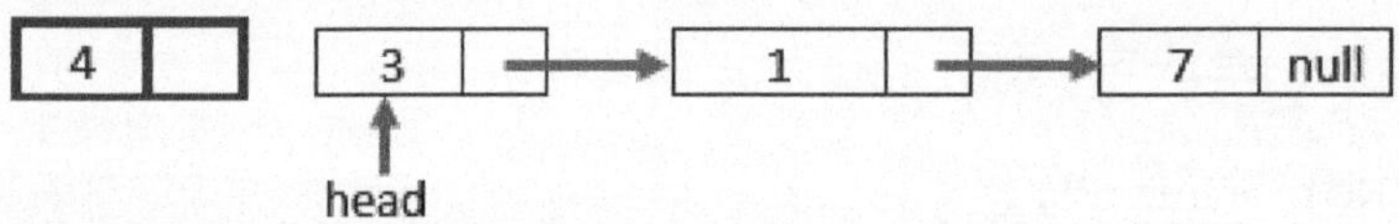

Step 2: Store the value of `head` at address field of the node

```
nPtr->next=head
```

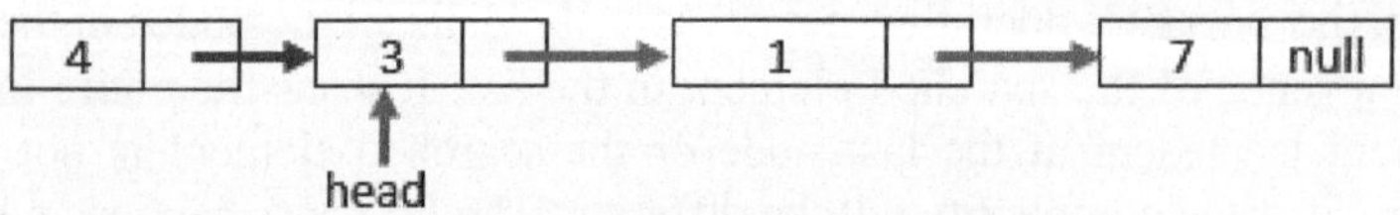

Step 3: Update `head` to the first node

```
head=nPtr;
```

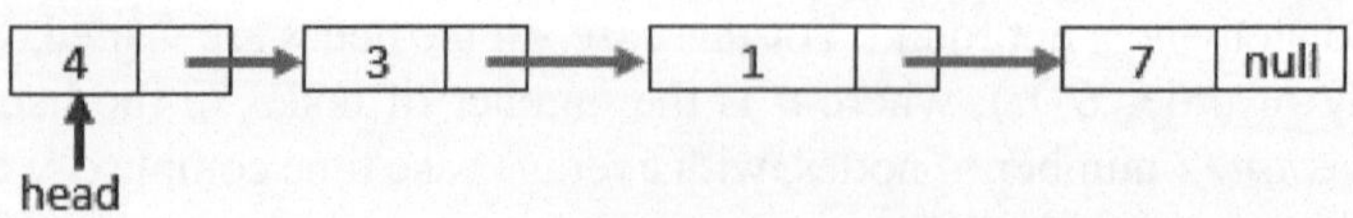

Following the above steps, the `insertFirst()` function below inserts a node before the existing first node. As it processes only one node, its time complexity is $O(1)$.

```
void insertFirst(struct node **hPtr, int ele){
    struct node *nPtr;

    // Step 1
    nPtr = (struct node *)malloc(sizeof(struct node));
    nPtr->info = ele;

    // Step 2
    nPtr->next = (*hPtr);

    // Step 3
    (*hPtr) = nPtr;
}
```

Insert at last operation traverse the list till the last node, and insert the new element as the last node of the list as illustrated below. As this operation scans the entire list, visiting each node once, its time complexity is $O(n)$.

Step 1: Create a new node and store the element to be inserted at the information field

```
nPtr = (struct node *)malloc(sizeof(struct node));
nPtr->info = 4;
nPtr->next = NULL;
```

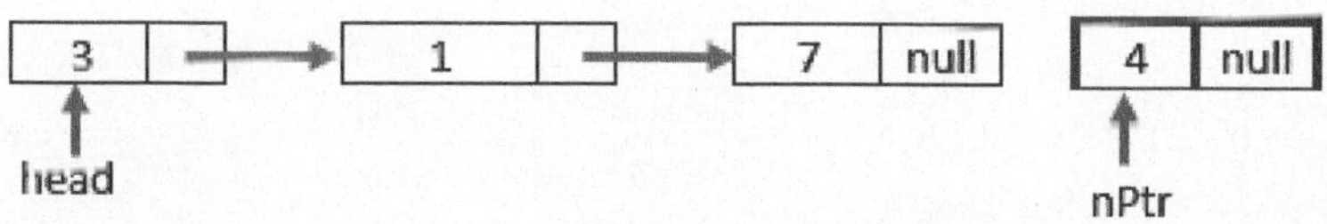

Step 2: Scan the list till the last node

```
ptr = hPtr;
while(ptr->next != NULL){
    ptr = ptr->next;
}
```

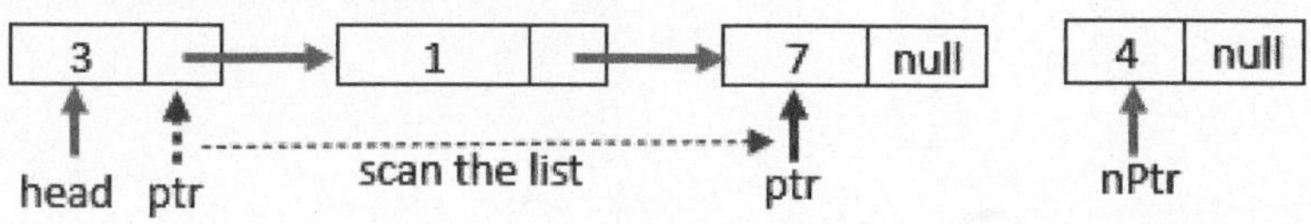

Step 3: Connect the last node to the new node

`ptr->next = nPtr;`

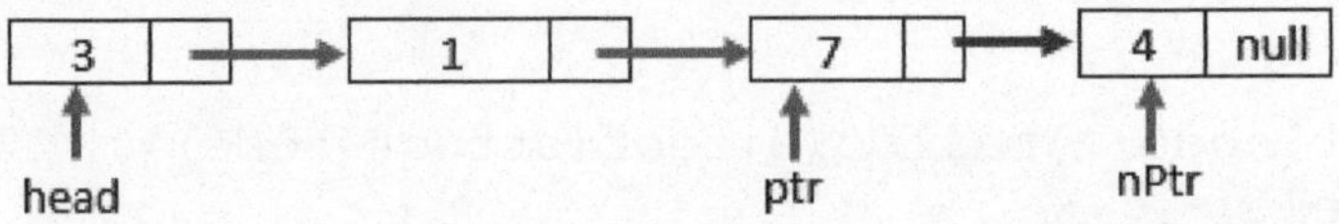

An implementation of `insertLast()` function is shown below.

```
void insertLast(struct node *hPtr, int ele){
     struct node *ptr, *nPtr;

     // Step 1
     nPtr =  (struct node *)malloc(sizeof(struct node));
     nPtr->info = ele;
     nPtr->next = NULL;

     // Step 2
     ptr = hPtr;
     while(ptr->next != NULL){
        ptr = ptr->next;
     }

     // Step 3
     ptr->next = nPtr;
}
```

Insert at a position: Instead of inserting a node at first or at last, it can also be inserted at any arbitrary position. In such a case, the list should be scanned from the head till the specified position and insert. Let us say, the position starts from 1, and position at 1 means *insert as first node*. Likewise, position 2 means insert as second node and so on. The function given below follows the following steps and inserts an element at the position `pos`.

Step 1: Create a new node and store the element to be inserted at the information field

```
nPtr = (struct node *)malloc(sizeof(struct node));
nPtr->info = 4;
nPtr->next = NULL;
```

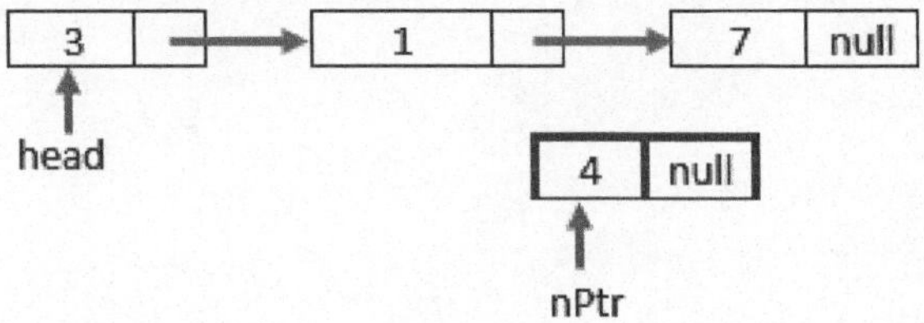

Step 2: Scan the list till the specified position

```
cnt = 1
ptr = hPtr;
while(cnt < pos-1){
     ptr = ptr->next;
     cnt++;
}
```

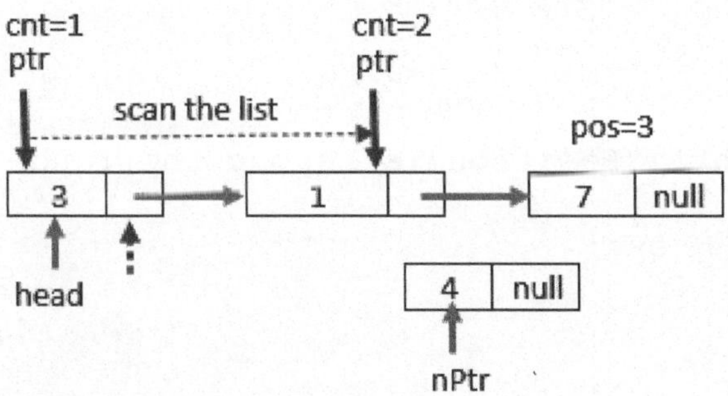

Step 3: Insert the new node

```
nPtr->next = ptr->next;
ptr->next = nPtr;
```

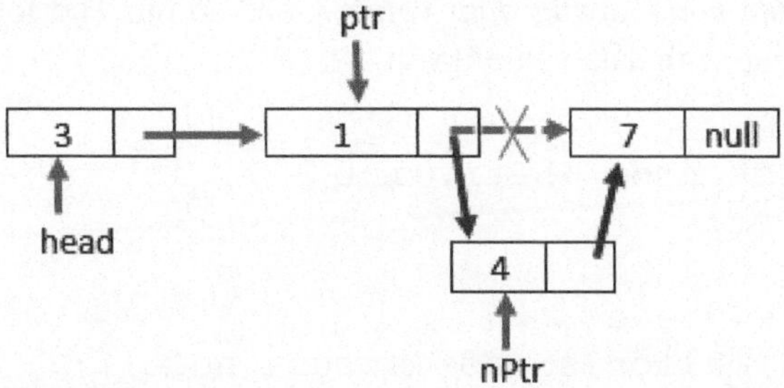


```
void insertPosition(struct node **hPtr, int ele, int pos){
```

```
    struct node *ptr, *nPtr;

    // Step 1
    nPtr = (struct node *)malloc(sizeof(struct node));
    nPtr->info = ele;
    nPtr->next = NULL;

    // Step 2
    if(pos == 1){
       // insert as first
       nPtr->next = (*hPtr);
       (*hPtr) = nPtr;
    }
    else{
       int cnt = 1;
       ptr = (*hPtr);
       while(cnt < pos-1 && ptr!=NULL){
             ptr = ptr->next;
             cnt++;
       }
    }

    // Step 3
    if(ptr == NULL) printf("Position is beyond the range");
    else{
       nPtr->next = ptr->next;
       ptr->next = nPtr;
    }
}
```

In the above program, the location of the insertion is defined by the sequential index position such as 1st , 2nd, 3rd and so on. Instead of defining the location of insertion by index, the location of the insertion may also be defined by the data present in the list. For example, *insert after the node having data value 1* or *insert before the node having data value 7*, and so on. The following function inserts a new node after the node with data value `data`.

```
void insertAfterData(struct node *hPtr, int ele, int data){
    struct node *ptr, *nPtr;

    // Step 1: Create a new node
    nPtr = (struct node *)malloc(sizeof(struct node));
    nPtr->info = ele;
    nPtr->next = NULL;
```

```
    // Step 2: Scan the list upto the node having data
    ptr = hPtr;
    while(ptr->info != data && ptr!=NULL){
            ptr = ptr->next;
    }

    // Step 3: Insert the new node after the node having data
    if(ptr == NULL) printf("Data not found");
    else{
       nPtr->next = ptr->next;
       ptr->next = nPtr;
    }
}
```

DELETION: Like insertion, deletion operation can be at first, last or any arbitrary node. The following function *deletes the first node*. It can be achieved by updating `head` pointer with the `head->next` i.e., `head=head->next;` with time complexity $O(1)$ as shown in the figure below.

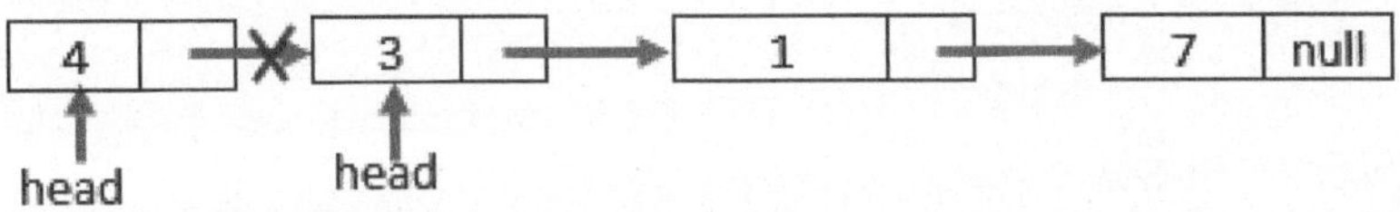

head = head->next

The function below implements the process of deleting the first node as illustrated above. In the function below, the *address of the memory location of the* `head` *pointer* is passed as the parameter (i.e., `struct node **hPtr`), instead of the content of the `head` pointer (i.e., `struct node *hPtr`). It is because, a new head address needs to be assigned at the memory location holding `head` pointer address.

```
int deleteFirst(struct node **hPtr){
     int data =(*hPtr)->info;
     (*hPtr) = (*hPtr)->next;
     return data;
}
```

Delete at Last: The following function deletes the *last node*. It scans the list till the last node. As we need to set the address field of the second last node to *NULL*, another pointer keeps track of the previous node of the currently visited node. As the function visits every node in the list once, its time complexity is $O(n)$. To simplify the implementation, the following implementation assumes that there are at least two nodes in the list. If there is only one node in the list, this function will conceptually delete the node, and the value of `head` pointer needs to be changed. In such a case, the *address of the memory location of the `head` pointer* needs to be passed as done in the previous function, instead of the content of the `head` pointer. Reader may refer to `insertPosition()` function or `deletePosition()` function for the same.

```
// We assume that the list has at list two elements
int deleteLast(struct node *hPtr){
    struct node *cur, *prev;
    int data;

    // Step 1: Scan till the last node, and maintain the
    // address of the previous node
    cur = hPtr;
    while(cur->next != NULL){
        prev = cur;
        cur = cur->next;
    }


    // Step 3: Delete the last node by setting cur->next=NULL
    prev->next = NULL;
    data = cur->info;
    free(cur);
    return data;
}
```

The above function follows the procedure given below.

Step 1: Define the `cur` and `prev` pointers. The `cur` pointer is initialized to head pointer.

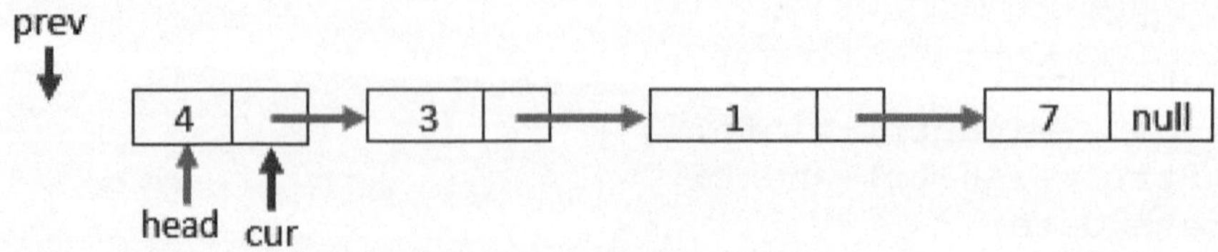

Step 2: Scan the list till the last node using cur pointer. The `prev` pointers points to the node before the `cur` pointer

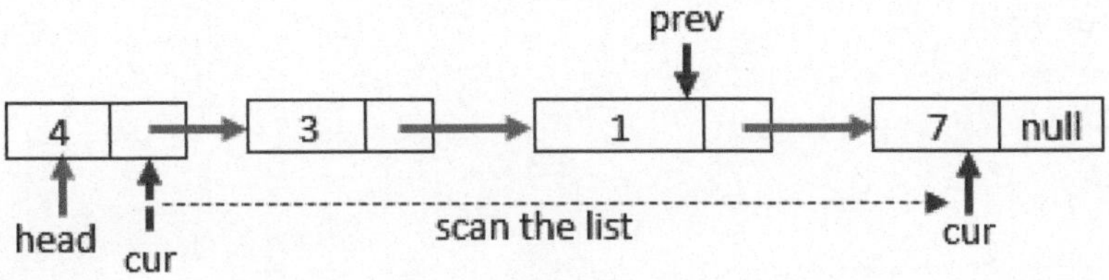

Step3: Delete the last node by assigning address field of `prev` to NULL.

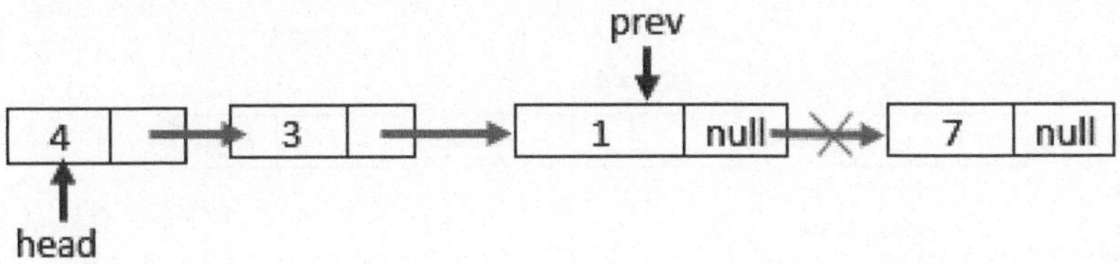

Delete at a Position: For deleting a node at a random location, the list needs to be scanned from the beginning till the position. At the same time, the address of the previous node also needs to be maintained, as done in `deleteLast()` function. Unlike `deleteLast()` function, the following function supports deleting the first node.

```
int deletePosition(struct node **hPtr, int pos){
    struct node *cur=NULL, *prev;
    int cnt=1, data;

    // Step 1: Scan the list till pos, and maintain the
    // address of the previous node
    if(pos == 1){ // if first node to be deleted, update head
       data = (*hPtr)->info;
       (*hPtr) = (*hPtr)->next;
    }
    else{
       cur = (*hPtr);
       while(cnt < pos && cur != NULL){
             prev = cur;
             cur = cur->next;
             cnt++;
       }
    }

    // Step 2: Delete the node at the position
    if(cur == NULL) printf("Position out of range.");
    else{
       prev->next = cur->next;
       data = cur->info;
```

```
            free(cur);
        }
        return data;
    }
```

Initial: Set the parameters.

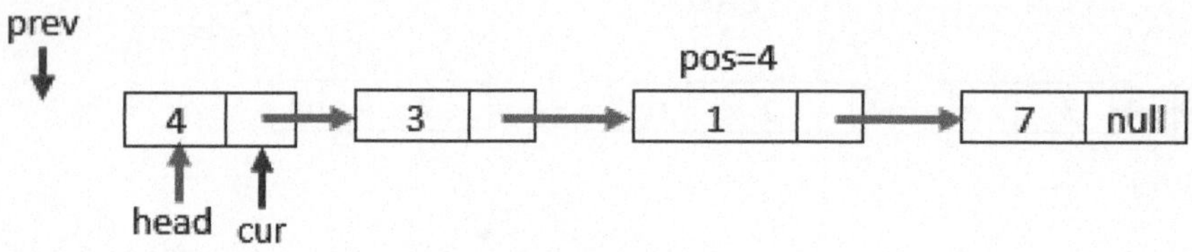

Step 1: Scan the list till the specified position

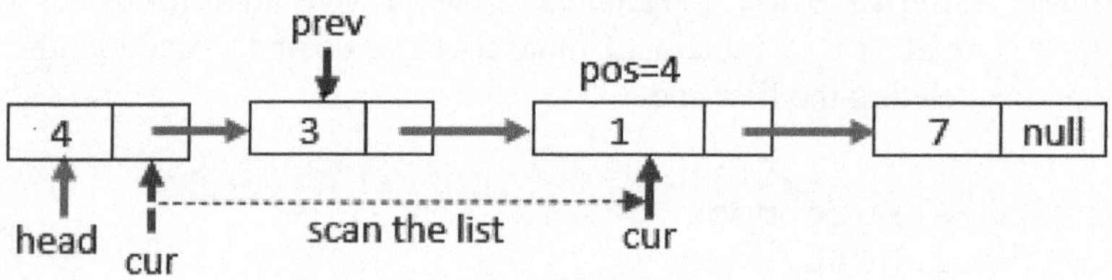

Step 2: Delete the node.

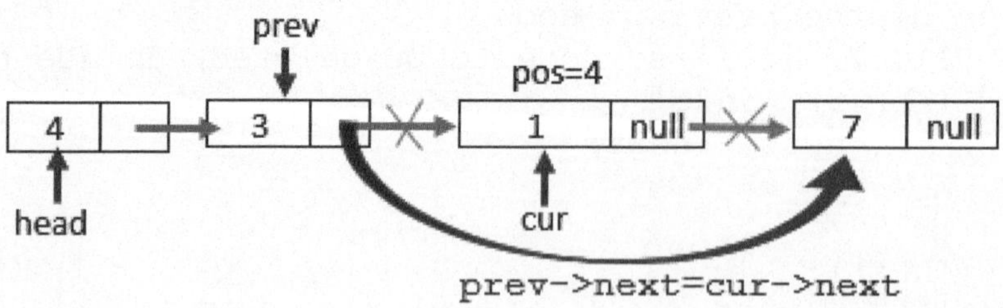

The number of nodes visited by the above function is equal to the value of the position. Therefore, best case time complexity $O(1)$ holds while deleting first node. Worst case time complexity $O(n)$ holds while deleting the last node. On an average, $n/2$ number of nodes may be visited while deleting at an arbitrary position, with a time complexity of $O(n)$.

3.1.3 Doubly Linked List

As mentioned above, unlike a singly linked list, each node in a doubly linked list has addresses of both the previous node and the next node in the sequence. Therefore, it can move in both forward and backward directions. It also maintains the addresses of both the first node and the last node. Due to its ability to move forward and backward, and also availability of both the first and last nodes, it has advantages over singly linked list specially for insertion at last.

Insertion at last: While the operation for the insertion at first can be kept the same as the one discussed in section 3.1.2, the insertion at last can be modified as follows. It directly goes to the last node of the list through `tail` pointer, update the next field of the tail pointer, update the previous field of the new node, and update the `tail` pointer to the new node. As it visits only one node, its time complexity is $O(1)$. Pictorially the process has been illustrated below.

Step 1: Create a new node and assign necessary values in the node

```
nPtr = (struct node *)malloc(sizeof(struct node));
nPtr->info = ele;
nPtr->next = NULL;
nPtr->prev = NULL;
```

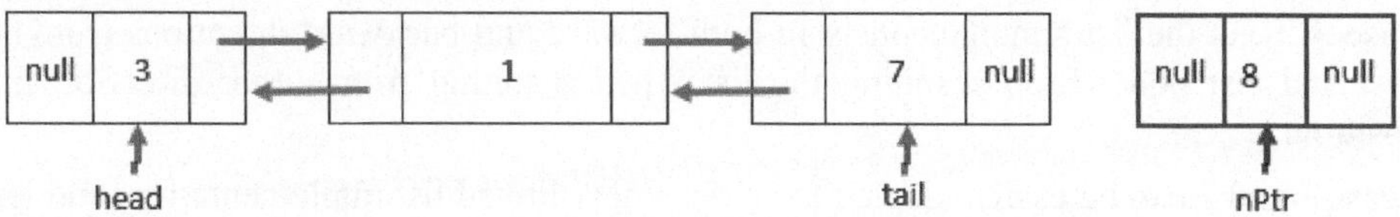

Step 2: Update next field of `tail` to the address of the new node `nPtr`, and change tail pointer to the new node

```
nPtr->prev - tail;
tail->next = nPtr;
```

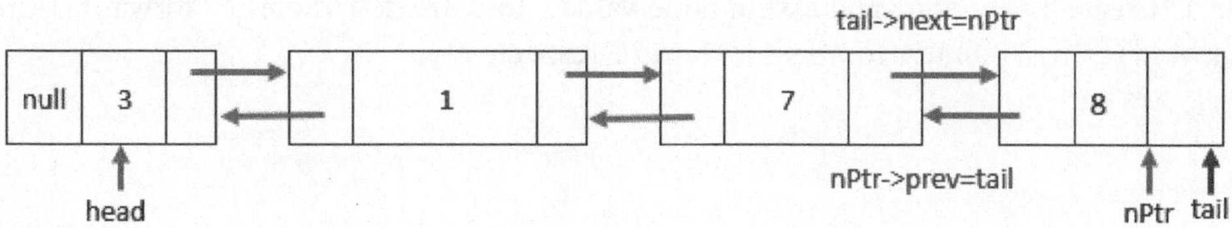

The above process is implemented as follows. Note that the `tail` parameter pointer reference (address of the `tail` pointer variable, instead of the pointer content). It is required to update the content of the `tail` pointer on the caller functer.

```
void insertLast(struct node **tPtr, int ele){
    struct node *nPtr;

    // Step 1
    nPtr = (struct node *)malloc(sizeof(struct node));
    nPtr->info = ele;
```

```
        nPtr->next = NULL;
        nPtr->prev = NULL;

        // Step 2
        nPtr->prev = (*tPtr);
        (*tPtr)->next = nPtr;
        (*tPtr) = nPtr;
    }
```

Insertion at any position: Like insertion of a node at last, as discussed above, *insertion of a node at any position* can also be benefited. Such an operation can be implemented in different ways as listed below.

- Case 1: If the position is less than or equal to the half of the number of nodes in the list, scan the list forward from the first node.
- Case 2: If the position is greater than or equal to the half of the number of nodes in the list, scan the list backward from the last node.
- Case 3: Scan the list simultaneously in both forward and backward directions from both the first and last node. Stop scanning the list when scanning from either direction finds the position.

The case 1 and 2 can be easily adapted from the singly linked list implementation, and left as an exercise. This section discusses the implementation of Case 3. All three cases will scan the list at the most upto $n/2$ number of nodes in the list, with a time complexity of $O(n)$. For simplicity, it is assume that the list has at least two nodes, insertion does not happen as first or last node, and the number of nodes in the list is known. Reader can modify the program to support without any restriction.

Step 1: Create a new node and assign node values. Initialise the values of forward (`hCur`) and backward (`tCur`) pointers to `head` and `tail` respectively.

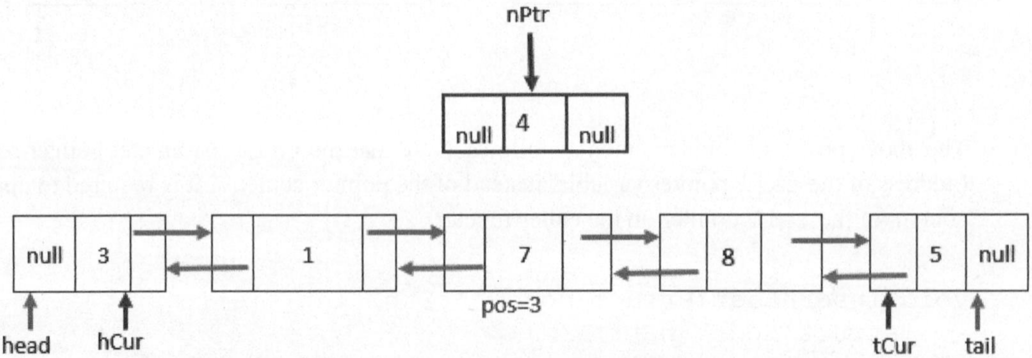

Step 2: Scan the list forward and backward simultaneously using `hCur` and `tCur` pointers till it finds the position or scanning reaches middle node. In this example, scanning stop one position before the actual position, so that insertion happens after the last scanned node.

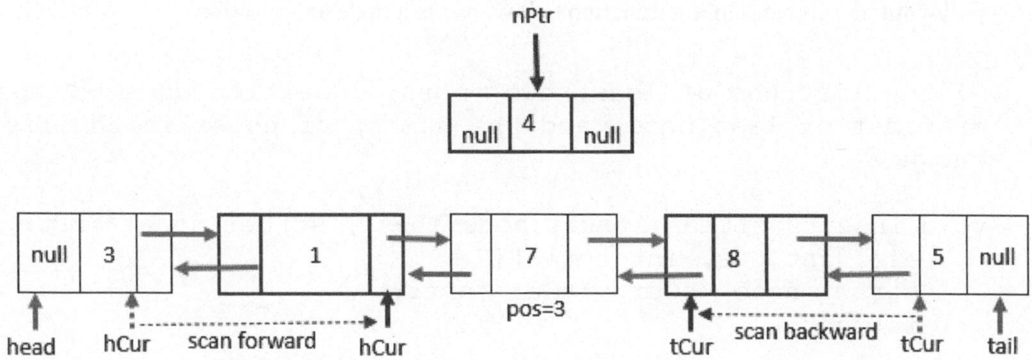

Step 3: Connect the new node with the node at the position. The pointers used in this connection depends on, whether the position lies in the first half or second half of the list. In this example, the position lies in the first half.

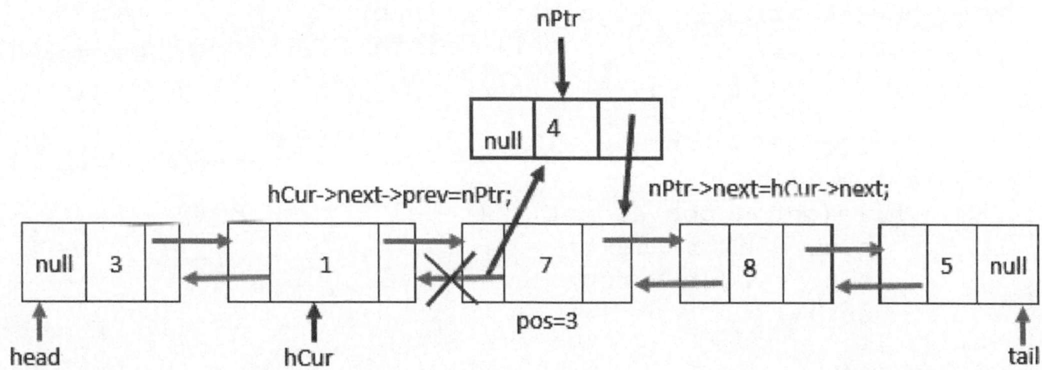

Step 4: Connect the previous node with the new node. Like in step 3, the pointers used in this connection depends on, whether the position lies in the first half or second half of the list. In this example, the position lies in the first half.

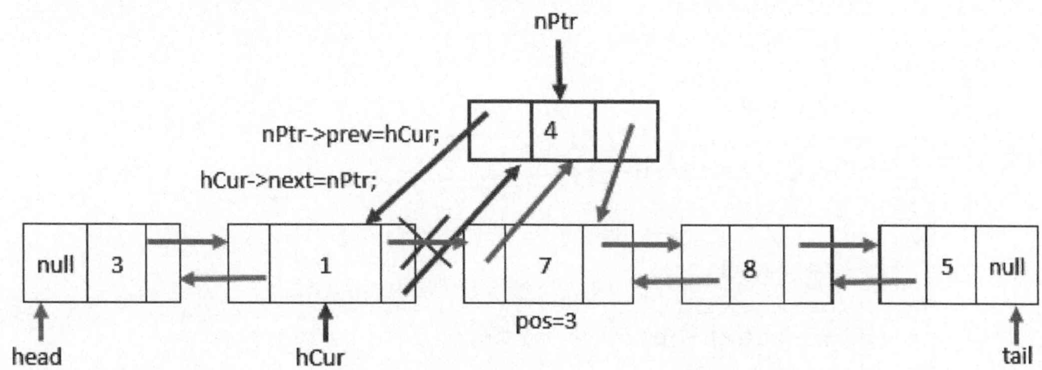

Following the above step, the function below inserts a node at a position.

```
// the list has at least two nodes, insertion does not happen
as first or last node, and the number of nodes in the list is
known

void insertPosition(struct node *hPtr, struct node **tPtr, int
    ele, int pos, int total){
    struct node *hCur, *tCur *nPtr;
    int cnt;


    // Step 1
    nPtr = (struct node *)malloc(sizeof(struct node));
    nPtr->info = ele;
    nPtr->next = NULL;
    nPtr->prev = NULL;
    hCur=hPtr; // assign head pointer
    tCur=tPtr; // assign tail pointer


    // Step 2
    cnt = 1;
    while(cnt < pos && cnt < (total - pos) ){
       hCur = hCur->next;
       tCur = tCur->prev;
       cnt++;
    }

    // Step 3 and 4
    if(cnt == (total - pos)){  // Found second half
       // Step 3
       nPtr->prev = tCur->prev;
       tCur->prev->next = nPtr;

       //Step 4
       nPtr->next = tCur;
       tCur->prev = nPtr;
    }
    else{   // Found in the first half
       // Step 3
       nPtr->next hCur->next;
       hCur->next->prev = nPtr;
```

```
        //Step 4
        hCur->next = nPtr;
        nPtr->prev = hCur;
    }
}
```

Delete at last: The operation of *delete at last* can also be done in $O(1)$ using `tail` pointer. The process of deleting at last is illustrated below.

Step 1: Go directly to the last node

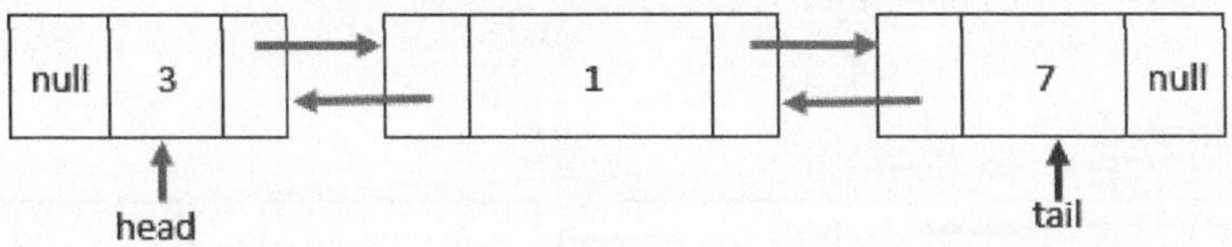

Step 2: Update the tail pointer to the second last node, and assign next address field to NULL

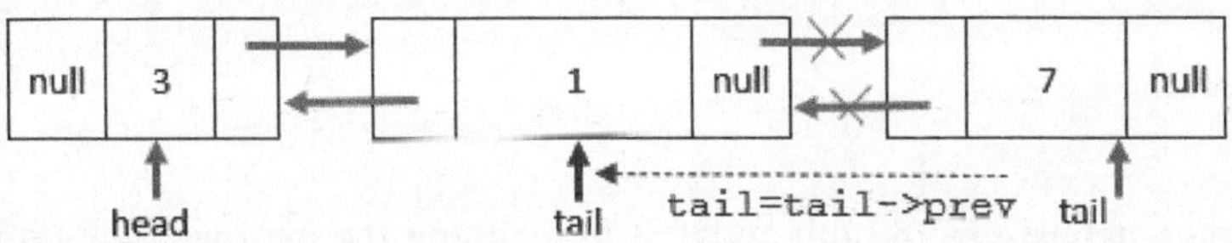

The function for delete at last can be implemented as below.

```
int deleteLast(struct node **tPtr){
    struct node *ptr;

    // Step 1
    ptr = (*tPtr);
    int data = ptr->info;

    // Step 2
    (*tPtr) = (*tPtr)->prev;
    (*tPtr)->next = NULL;
    free(ptr);
    return data;
}
```

Delete a node at a position: Like in insertion of a node at a position discussed above, *deletion of a node at a position* can also be implemented by scanning the list simultaneously from both ends, and reducing the number of iterations by half the number of nodes in the list, with time complexity $O(n)$. Depending on whether the position is in the first half or second half of the list, it can also have three cases.

- Case 1: If the position is less than or equal to half of the number of nodes in the list, scan the list forward from the first node.
- Case 2: If the position is greater than or equal to half of the number of nodes in the list, scan the list backward from the last node.
- Case 3: Scan the list simultaneously in both forward and backward directions from both the first and last node. Stop scanning the list when scanning from either direction finds the position.

The example given below scans the list from both the ends simultaneously, and locate the position to delete the node. It follows the following steps.

Step 1: Initialize the parameters.

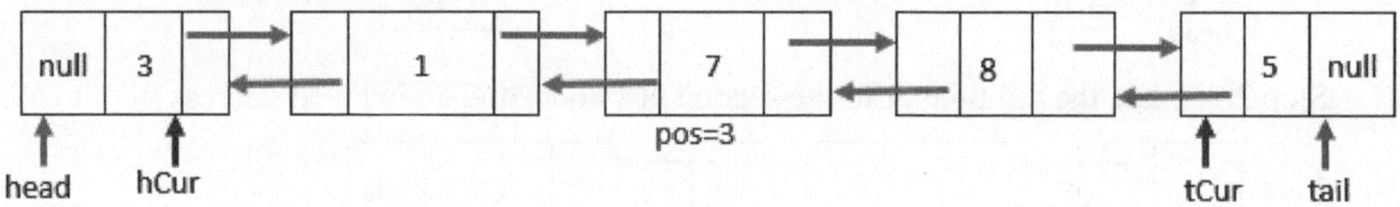

Step 2: Scan the list simultaneously from both ends. Stop scanning the list one position before the actual node to be deleted.

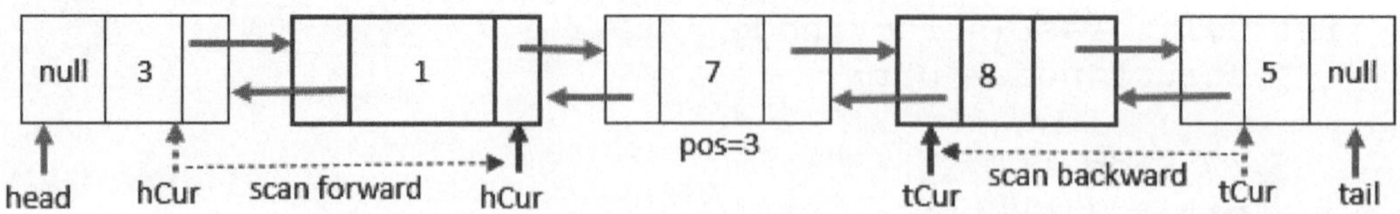

Step 3: Delete the target node by connecting the nodes one position before and one position after. Depending on whether the position is found in first half or second half, pointer manipulation will be different. Following example delete the node from the forward scan.

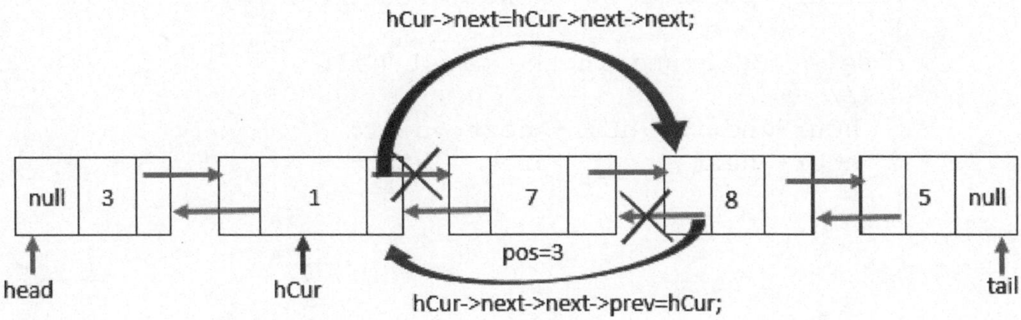

Implementation of the above operation is shown below.

```
// the list has at least two nodes, deletion does not happen
at first or last node, and the number of nodes in the list is
known

void deletePosition(struct node *hPtr, struct node **tPtr, int
    pos, int total){
    struct node *hCur, *tCur *nPtr;
    int cnt;


    // Step 1
    hCur=hPtr; // assign head pointer
    tCur=tPtr; // assign tail pointer
    // Step 2
    cnt = 1;
    while(cnt < (pos - 1) && cnt < (total - pos)-1 ){
       hCur = hCur->next;
       tCur = tCur->prev;
       cnt++;
    }

    // Step 3
    if(cnt == (total - pos)-1){  // Found second half
       tCur->prev = tCur->prev->prev;
```

```
        tCur->prev->prev->next = tCur;
    }
    else{    // Found in the first half
        //
        hCur->next = hCur->next->next;
        hCur->next->next->prev = hCur;
    }
}
```

3.1.4 Circular Linked List

A linked list could be circular as shown in Figure 3.6. In a circular singly linked list, the next field of the last node further points to the first node. Similarly, in a doubly linked list, the next field of the last node points to the first node, and previous field of the first node points to the last node. An advantage of circular linked list is that insertion or deletion operation in a list can be done by scanning the list only in one direction.

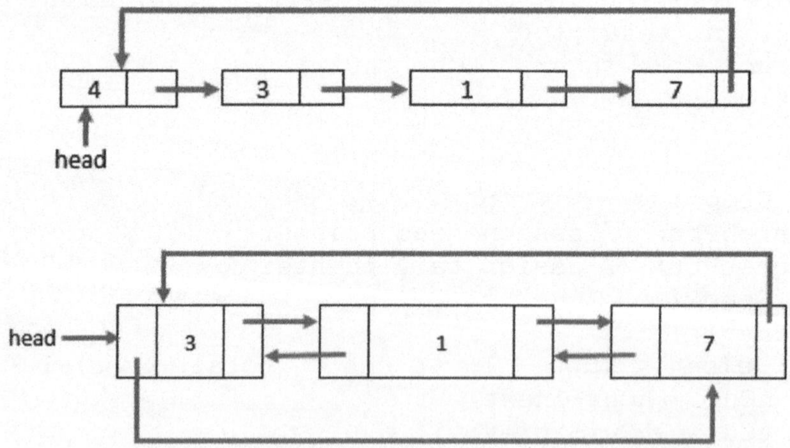

Figure 3.6: Examples of singly circular linked list and doubly circular linked list.

3.1.5 Linked List with Dedicated Headed Node

In the discussions above, we do not have a dedicated head node. Instead, we maintain a `head` pointer variable which points to the first node of the list. Maintaining a dedicated *header node* which always points to the first node of the list has advantages while implementing various operations on a list. As for example, in the `insertFirst()` or `deleteFirst()` function discussed above, the value of the `head` pointer changes inside the function. To support this, we need to pass the memory address of the pointer variable (`struct node **hPtr`), instead of the contain of the pointer variable (`struct node *hPtr`). Likewise, whenever a new first node is deleted or inserted (last node as well in the case of doubly linked list) in the list, special care should be taken to handle this issue. Further, when the list is empty, in the implementation above, the `head` pointer will not have a valid address, as there is no first node. So, to simplify the implementation in such a scenario, the above implementations have imposed some restrictions such as at least two elements, node insertion or deletion at first position, and so on. Maintaining a dedicated header node will take care of all the above issues, except that there will be one additional node in the list.

When we create a new linked list, we always assume that an empty linked list is first created as shown below (create header node).

```
head = (struct node *)malloc(sizeof(struct node));
head->next = NULL;
```

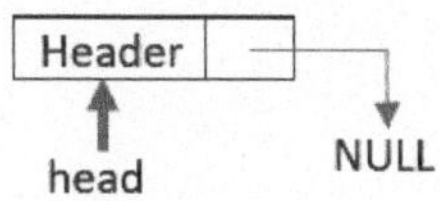

The above code creates a header node with its address field assigned to NULL to create an empty list. Figure 3.5 illustrates an example of a singly linked list with a dedicated header node.

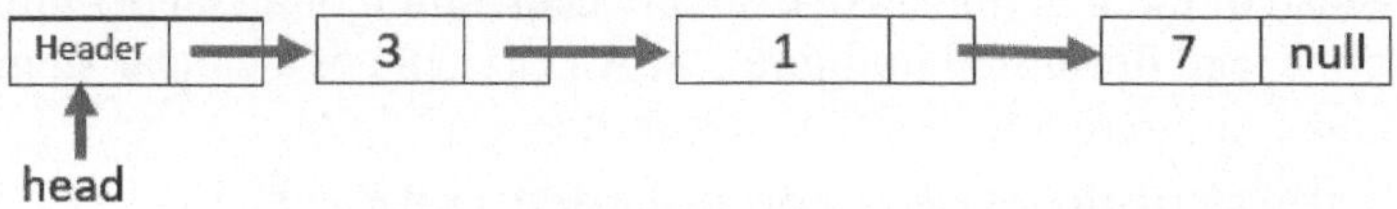

Figure 3.7: Example of a singly linked list with a dedicated header node.

We now modify `insertFirst()` function discussed above as follows. The function takes the address of the header node. Node that the parameter is `struct node *hPtr,` instead of `struct node **hPtr.` Pictorially, the insertion steps are illustrated below.

Step 1: link the new node with the first node

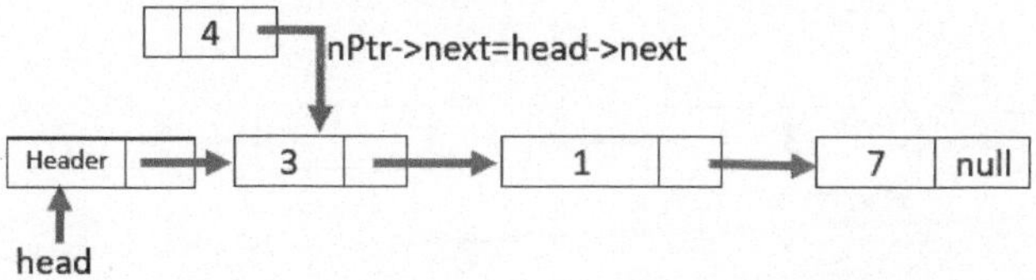

Step 2: Link the header node with the new node.

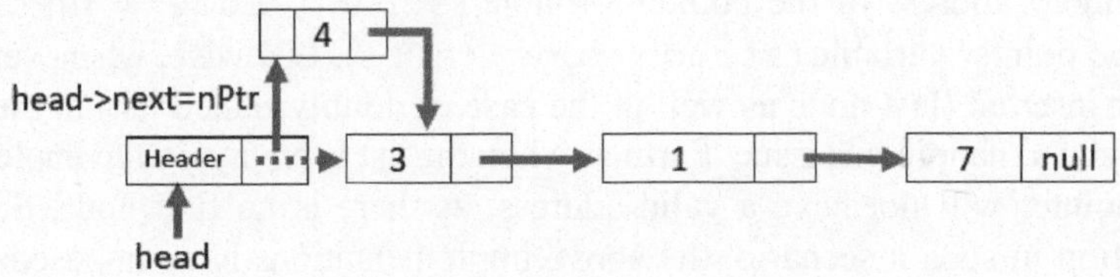

Following function shows implementation of the above steps.

```
void insertFirst(struct node *hPtr, int ele){
     struct node *nPtr;

     nPtr = (struct node *)malloc(sizeof(struct node));
     nPtr->info = ele;
     nPtr->next = hPtr->next;
     hPtr->next = nPtr;
}
```

In the similar manner, a circular singly linked list can also be created, where the last node points to the header node instead of the first node. An example declaration of an empty circular singly linked list is shown below, and illustrated in figure 3.8. An example of a cicular singly linked list with head node is shown in figure 3.9.

```
head = (struct node *)malloc(sizeof(struct node));
head->next = head;
```

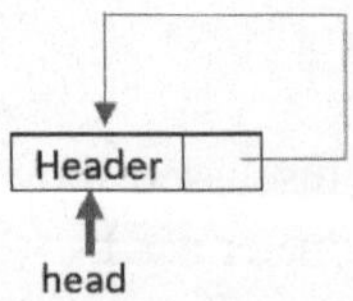

Figure 3.8: Head node of an empty circular linked list

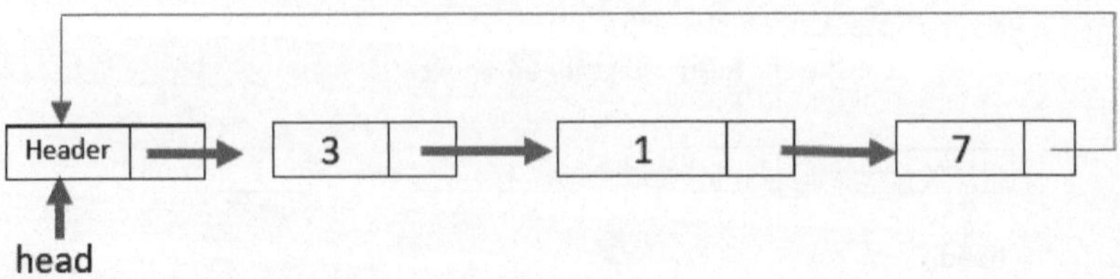

Figure 3.9: An example of a circular linked list.

3.1.6 Linked List ADT and its Applications

Like in Stack and Queue, linked list can also be defined as an ADT. The example below defines the declaration of a singly linked list ADT.

```
<ADT> List{
        PRIVATE:
            struct node {
                  int info;
                  struct node *next;
            };
            struct node *head;
            void init(){
             head=(struct node *)malloc(sizeof(struct node));
            }
        PUBLIC:
            void initiate(){init();}
            void insertFirst(int);
            void insertLast(int);
            void insertPosition(int, int);
            int deleteFirst(void);
            int deleteLast(void);
            int deletePosition(int);
            int isEmpty(void);
            int isFull(void);
};
```

The `isFull()` function may not be relevant, if the list is implemented using dynamic memory allocation. List will be full only when memory space in the system is exhausted/overflow. However, if the list is implemented using array (static memory allocation), `isFull()` function is applicable.

Implementation of Stack using a Singly Linked List: Assume that we have the above singly linked list ADT. Using the `insertFirst()` and `deleteFirst()` functions, we can implement a stack ADT as shown below.

```
<ADT> Stack{
    PRIVATE:
        <ADT> List stack;
        init(){ stack.initiate();}
    PUBLIC:
        void push(int ele){ stack.insertFirst(ele);}
```

```
            int pop(){
                    if(isEmpty()!=1){
                            return stack.deleteFirst();
                    }
            }
}
```

In the similar manner, stack operations can also be implemented using `insertLast()` and `deleteLast()` functions.

Implementation of Queue using a Singly Linked List: For queue implementation, we can use insertFirst() function for enqueue operation, and deleteLast() function for dequeue operation. An example queue ADT is defined below.

```
<ADT> Queue{
      PRIVATE:
            <ADT> List stack;
            init(){ stack.initiate();}
      PUBLIC:
            void enqueue(int ele){ stack.insertFirst(ele);}
            int dequeue(){
                    if(isEmpty()!=1){
                            return stack.deleteLast();
                    }
            }
}
```

3.2 TREES

So far, we have been discussing linear data structure. In this section, we will discuss a *non-linear* data structure called *Tree.* Many of the real-world data are inherently non-linear in nature. For example, organizational structure in an institution which may have different campuses, different departments under each campus, faculty members, staffs and students under each department, and so on. Linear data structure may not be suitable for storing information for such hierarchical data.

A tree consists of *nodes/vertices* and *arcs/edges.* Nodes are connected by arcs in a specific manner following *parent-child* relationships. Every tree has a special type of node called the *root* of the tree. A root node has no parent (only children). There are nodes with no children, but only parent. Such nodes are called *leaf* nodes or *terminal* nodes. All other nodes have both parent node as well as child nodes, and are called *internal/interior nodes*. A tree structure T can be recursively defined as the following.

1. *An empty structure is an empty tree, i.e., a tree with no root.*
2. *If $T_1, T_2, T_3, \ldots, T_k$ are disjoint trees, then T is also a tree given that the root of the T has the roots of the $T_1, T_2, T_3, \ldots, T_k$ as child nodes. In such a case, $T_1, T_2, T_3, \ldots, T_k$ are called subtrees of the tree T. If $k = 0$, then the tree has only root.*
3. *Only structures generated using the rule 1 and rule 2 above are trees.*

The figure below (Figure 3.10) illustrates a tree and also defines different terminologies associated with as tree (the same figure is also given in Unit I (Figure 1.4)).

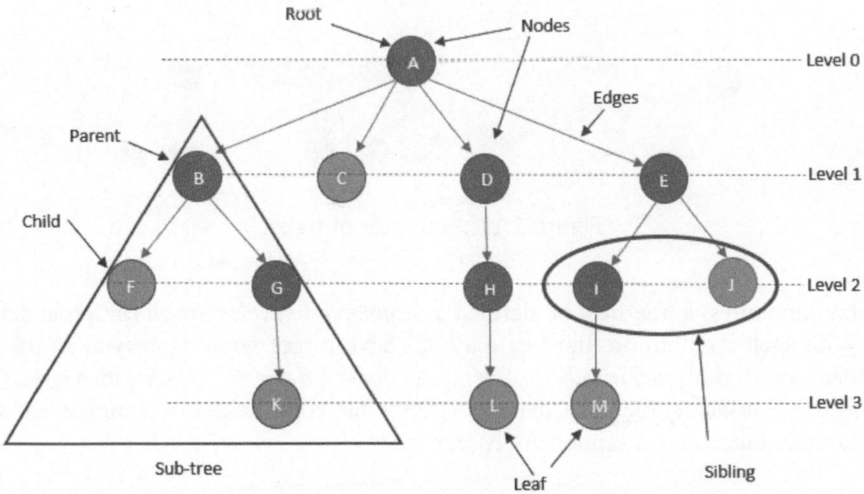

Figure 3.10: A brief description of a tree.

As shown in figure 3.6, all the child nodes of a node are placed at the same level. The root node is placed at level 0. The child nodes of the root node are placed at level 1. If a node B is a child node of another node A, then A is the parent node of the node B. The child nodes of the nodes at level i are placed at level $i + 1$ and so on. Likewise, a tree has a height. The height of a leaf node is assigned 0. The parents of the node with height 0 is assigned height 1, and so on. In some literatures, the level and height may be started from 1. The child nodes of a node are called *siblings*. Every node in a tree defines a subtree with the node as its root. Unlike natural tree, a tree data structure is generally depicted upside down with the root node at the top.

The number of child nodes of a node is known as *degree of the node*. The *degree of a tree* is defined by the *maximum degree* of any of its nodes. A *path* from a node n_1 to another node n_k is a sequence of node $(n_1, n_2, n_3, \ldots, n_{i-1}, n_i, n_{i+1}, \ldots n_k)$ such that n_i is the parent of node n_{i+1}. The *length of a path* is defined by the number of arcs in the path (i.e., $k-1$). Therefore, *height of a node* can be defined by the longest path length from the node to any leaf node. *Height of a tree* is the height of the root node. Similarly, *depth of a node* can be defined as the *path length from the root to the node*. In the above figure, depth of a node is defined by level. If there is a path from a node n_i to node n_j, then n_i is an ancestor of the node n_j , and n_j is the descendent of the node n_i. Few examples of trees are shown in figure 3.11.

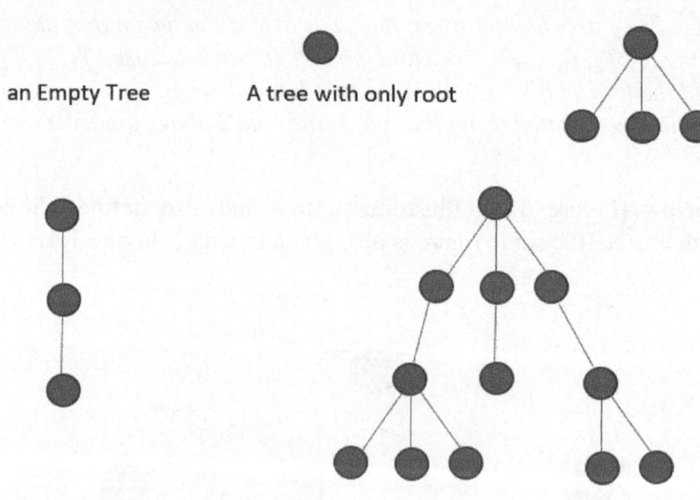

Figure 3.11: Examples of trees.

Note: In some literatures, a tree may be defined as *connected acyclic graph* (graph is defined in Unit IV). With such a definition, the tree may not have a root node. However, in this section, we consider *rooted connected acyclic graph* i.e., a *connected acyclic graph* with a special node called *root* as tree. Further, some book may also define the edges with direction (parent to child). All the examples taken in this section are ***rooted trees***.

3.2.1 Some Properties of Rooted Trees

Theorem 1: A tree with n nodes has exactly $n-1$ number of arcs.

Proof: (General Statement) Every node in a tree, except root node has exactly one parent node. And, every arc in a tree connects a node to its parent. Hence, for n number of nodes, there are $n-1$ number of arcs.

(By induction on n) A tree with $n = 1$ has 0 arc. So, the statement is true for $n = 1$. Let us assume that the statement is true for $n = k$ i.e., $k-1$ number of arcs. If we add one more node i.e., $n = k+1$, this will add one more arc and the number of arcs for $k+1$ number of nodes will be k. That means, it is also true for $k+1$ number of nodes. Hence proved.

Corollary: A tree with $n-1$ arcs has n nodes.

Theorem 2: If n is the sum of the degrees of the nodes in a tree, then there are $n+1$ number of nodes in the tree.

Proof: (By induction on n) If $n = 1$, there will be two nodes in the tree i.e., root node and a leaf node as the child of the root. So, the statement is true for $n = 1$. Let us assume that it is true for $n = k$. That means, there are $k+1$ number of nodes in the tree. If we increase the sum of the degrees of the nodes in the tree by 1, it means that a leaf node is added to one of the nodes in the tree. Therefore, with *k*+1 as the sum of the degrees of the nodes, there will *k*+2 number of nodes in the tree. Hence, the statement is also true for $n = k+1$ degree sum.

Corollary: A tree with n nodes has $n-1$ degree sum.

Theorem 3: Consider a tree with degree $k \geq 1$, and height $h \geq 0$. The maximum number of nodes that this tree can accommodate is $\frac{k^{h+1}-1}{k-1}$.

Proof: (By exact estimate) Since we are estimating the maximum number of nodes that can be accommodated in the tree, the following conditions are satisfied.

1. All the leaf nodes are at the level h.
2. Except for the leaf node, all other nodes have degree k. That means, every level has the maximum possible number of nodes.

Therefore, at level 0, there is one node i.e., root node. It can be represented as k^0.

At level 1, there are k number of nodes because the root node has k number of child nodes. It can be represented as k^1.

At level 2, there are k^2 number of nodes, because every node at level 1 has k child nodes.

Continuing the sequence, at level h, there are k^h number of nodes. Since the tree has height h, the nodes at the level h are leaf nodes. Now, the total number of nodes in the tree is $k^0 + k^1 + k^2 + k^3 + \cdots + k^{h-1} + k^h$. It is a GP (geometric progression) series. Hence, the sum is $\frac{k^{h+1}-1}{k-1}$.

Theorem 4: If a tree with degree $k \geq 1$ has n number of nodes, then the minimum possible height of the tree is $\lfloor \log_k n \rfloor$. The height of the leaf node is 0.

Proof: Left as an exercise.

Similarly, reader can also attempt to answer the following questions.

Question 1: If a tree with degree $k \geq 1$ has n number of nodes, what will be the maximum possible height of a tree?

Question 2: If a tree with degree $k \geq 1$ has n number of nodes, what will be the maximum possible number of leaf nodes?

Question 3: If a tree with degree $k \geq 1$ has n number of nodes, what will be the minimum possible number of leaf nodes?

Question 4: If a tree (rooted tree) has $n \geq 2$ number of nodes, what are the maximum and minimum possible number of leaf nodes?

3.2.2 Representation of a Tree

One way of representing a tree is to create a node consisting of an information field and a set of address fields, as done in the linked list, and connect the nodes to form the necessary structure. We can define a generalized node using `struct` to define a node of a tree with degree $k \geq 1$ as follows.

```
struct node {
            int info;
            struct node *child_1;
            struct node *child_2;
            struct node *child_3;
            .
            .
            .
            struct node *child_k;
};
```

The above declaration of a node has natural ways of visualizing a tree. However, it has the following disadvantages.

1. For a generalized declaration of a tree, we may not have the information about the degree of the tree. Therefore, the value of *k* has to be large enough at the time of declaration to cover all the expected cases.
2. Every node has to have children close to *k*, otherwise lots of pointer space will be wasted.
3. As there is no ordering of the child nodes of a node, any child node can take any of the available child pointers. Therefore, while processing a node, we need to scan all the *k* child pointers to check which ones are taken. Even for a node with degree 1, all the k child pointers should be checked, as any one of the *k* pointers can be used.

One way of solving the above issues is to use *first-child* and *next-sibling* representation as shown in the figure below. Every node has two pointers – (i) *pointer to its first child*, and (ii) *pointer to its sibling*.

```
struct node {
```

```
        int info;
        struct node *firstChild;
        struct node *sibling;
};
```

If a node has child nodes, one of its child nodes is considered as the first child and connect it to the `firstChild` pointer. If the node has its siblings, the sibling nodes form a linked list and its first node is connected to the `sibling` pointer. In the figure 3.12, the root node A has four child nodes (B, C, D, E) and no sibling. Considering B as its first child, `firstChild` pointer of root node connects to B and NULL to its `sibling` pointer. Similarly, node B has two child nodes (F, G) and three sibling nodes (C, D, E). Therefore, node B connects F as its first child node and C, D, and E as sibling nodes through a linked list. In the similar manner, all the nodes in the tree are connected.

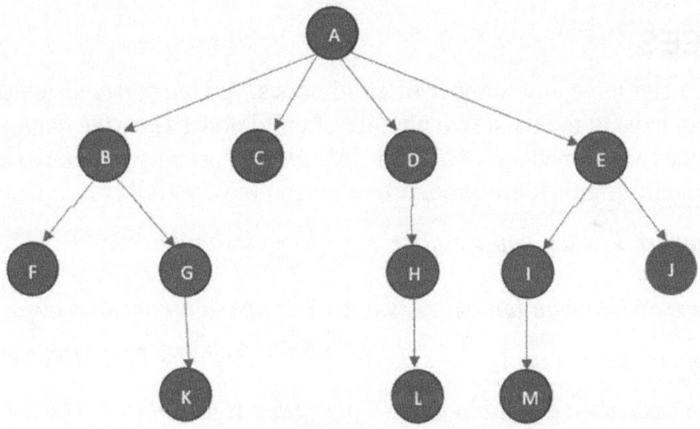

Example Tree

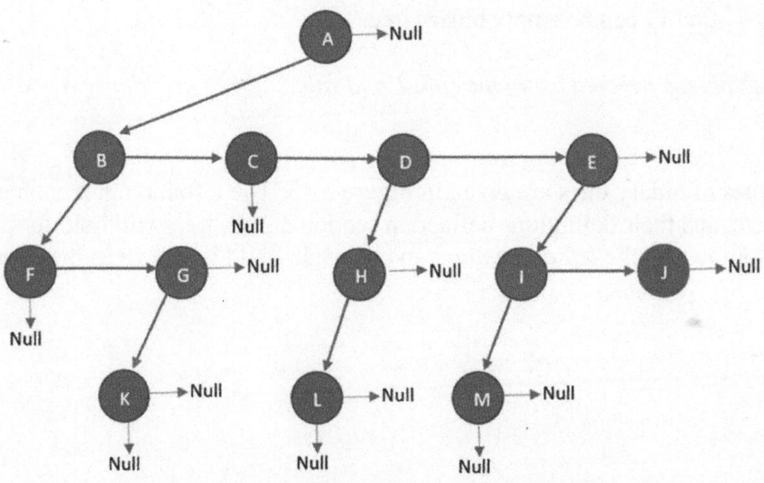

First Child Next Sibling representation

Figure 3.12: First Child Next Sibling representation of a tree.

This form of representation of a tree has the following advantages over the multi-child pointer representation.

- A tree with any degree can be represented.
- Every node has only two pointers. The number of NULL pointers is likely to be lesser as compared to multi-child pointer representation. In multi-child pointer representation, if the degrees of the nodes are closed to the number of child pointers, lots of NULL pointer will be present.
- It can traverse the tree level wise, just by following the links associated with the nodes of the tree.
- Both *breadth first search*, as well as *depth first search* (defined in Unit IV) of the tree can be supported.

3.3 BINARY TREES

The tree defined above can have any number of child nodes. A *binary tree* is a special type of tree in which a node can have at the most two number of child nodes (i.e., *the degree of the tree is two*), and the child nodes are named *left child* and *right child.* Formally, a binary tree *T* can be defined recursively by modifying the definition of tree given above as follows.

1. *An empty structure T is an empty binary tree (no nodes in the tree).*
2. *If T_1 and T_2 are two disjoint binary trees, then T is also a binary tree given that the root of the T has the roots of the T_1 and T_2 trees as its child nodes. The T_1 and T_2 are called subtrees of the tree T. If T_1 is called left subtree, the T_2 is called right subtree. The root of T_1 is called the left child of the root node of T, and the root of T_2 is called the right child of the root node of T. Note that T_1 and T_2* can be empty binary tree.
3. *Only structures generated using the rule 1 and rule 2 above are binary trees.*

Few examples of binary trees are given in Figure 3.13. The terminologies such as *height, depth, leaf node*, etc. and their definitions defined in section 3.2 for trees still hold for binary trees. The left child is known as the *left descendant* and the right child is known as the *right descendant* of a node.

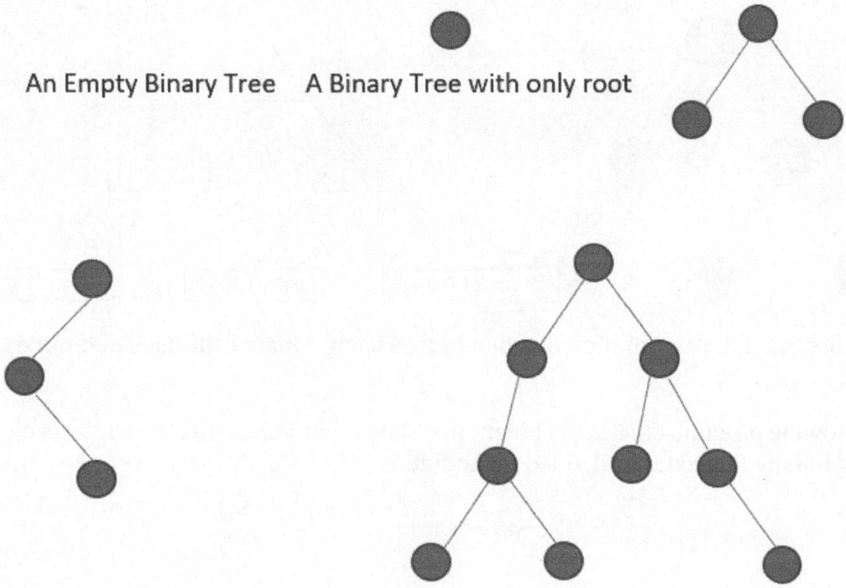

Figure 3.13: Few examples of binary trees.

3.3.1 Representation of Binary Trees

Using Dynamically Allocated Nodes, and Left Child and Right Child Linking: A binary tree may be implemented in various ways, using array, linked list or by allocating dynamic space for each node and connecting the allocated memory spaces. Using dynamically allocated nodes, we can form a binary tree in a natural way of visualizing a binary tree. Each node consists of three types of information; *data, address of the left child node* and *address of the right child node*. A typical example of a binary tree node is shown below, where the data is of `char` type. Based on the underlying application, the data type of the data element may be changed.

```
struct node {
        char info;
        struct node *lChild; // left child pointer
        struct node *rChild; // right child pointer
};
```

Figure 3.14 shows a representation of a binary tree using the dynamically allocated nodes defined above. Left child pointer of node A points to node B i.e., the address of node B is stored at `lChild` pointer of node A. Likewise, right child pointer of node A points to node C i.e., the address of node C is stored at `rChild` pointer of node A. In the similar manner, nodes D and E are stored as the left child and right child nodes of node B. Node F is stored as the right child of node C. As there is no left child of node C, it is assigned NULL. The left child and right child pointers of all the leaf nodes, i.e., D, E and F, are assigned NULL.

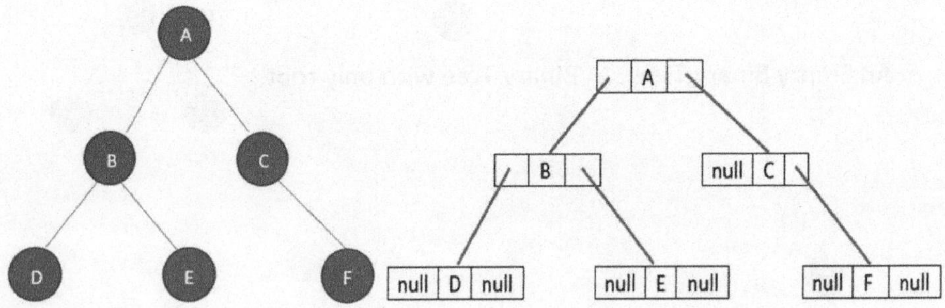

Figure 3.14: Representation of a binary tree using dynamically allocated nodes.

The following program creates the binary tree shown in figure 3.10 by creating each node one by one and linking the nodes as defined in the figure.

```
#include <stdio.h>
struct node{
   char info;
   struct node *lChild;
   struct node *rChild;
};
main(){
          struct node *root;

          // Node A
          root = (struct node *)malloc(sizeof(struct node));
          root->info = 'A';

          // Node B
          root->lChild = (struct node *)malloc(sizeof(struct
      node));
          root->lChild->info = 'B';

          // Node C
          root->rChild = (struct node *)malloc(sizeof(struct
      node));
          root->rChild->info = 'C';
          root->rChild->lChild = NULL;

          // Node D
          root->lChild->lChild = (struct node *)malloc (sizeof
      (struct node));
```

```
        root->lChild->lChild->info = 'D';
        root->lChild->lChild->lChild = NULL;
        root->lChild->lChild->rChild = NULL;

        // Node E
        root->lChild->rChild = (struct node *)malloc(sizeof
    (struct node));
        root->lChild->rChild->info = 'E';
        root->lChild->rChild->lChild = NULL;
        root->lChild->rChild->rChild = NULL;

        // Node F
        root->rChild->rChild = (struct node *)malloc(sizeof
    (struct node));
        root->rChild->rChild->info = 'F';
        root->rChild->rChild->lChild = NULL;
        root->rChild->rChild->rChild = NULL;
}
```

Non-linear representation of a binary tree in an array: The above example shows how a binary tree can be created by allocating memory space of the nodes in the tree at non-contiguous memory locations. A similar structure can also be created using array, where a block of contiguous memory locations is allocated to store the node information within the allocated space, but arranged in a non-linear manner. The example below shows an implementation of a binary tree over a contiguous block memory location. The number of nodes in such implementation will be limited to the number of nodes that can be accommodated within the block. The structure of a node is defined below, where `lChild` stores the array index of the left child node, and `rChild` stores the array index of the right child node.

```
struct node{
    char info;
    int lChild;
    int rChild;
};
```

Figure 3.15 illustrates the storage structure of the nodes in a non-linear manner in an array. It creates an array of `struct node`. In the figure, root node A is stored at the index 2. The `lChild` field of node A has the value 4 which is the index value of the left child node B in the array. The `rChild` value of node A is 0 which means that the right child C is stored at the index 0. Likewise, the `lChild` and `rChild` values of node B (i.e., index values 8 and

6 respectively) are the array indexes of the left child and right child nodes of B. In the similar manner, all other nodes in the tree are stored. The -1 value in the array denotes NULL.

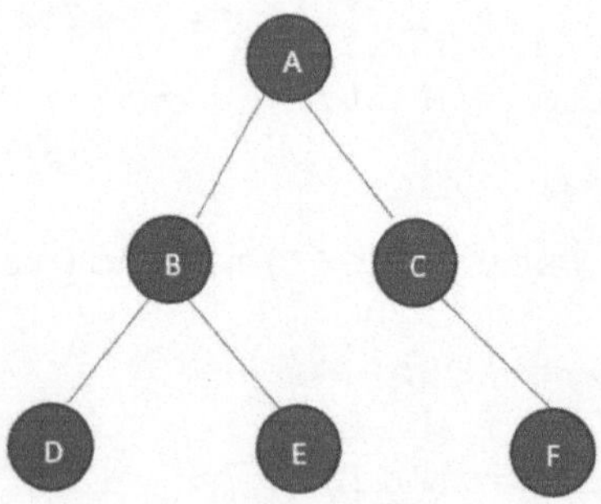

Binary Tree

index	info	lChild	rChild
0	C	-1	10
1			
root → 2	A	4	0
3			
4	B	8	6
5			
6	E	-1	-1
7			
8	D	-1	-1
9			
10	F	-1	-1
11			
12			

Implementation non-linearly over an array

Figure 3.15: Representation of a binary tree using an array in non-linear manner.

The following program shows the implementation of the above example.

```
#include <stdio.h>
struct node{
   char info;
   int lChild;
   int rChild;
};

main(){
          struct node BT[12];

          // Node A
          BT[2].info = 'A';
          BT[2].lChild = 4;
          BT[2].rChild = 0;

          // Node B
          BT[4].info = 'B';
          BT[4].lChild = 8;
          BT[4].rChild = 6;
```

```
    // Node C
    BT[0].info  = 'C';
    BT[0].lChild = -1;
    BT[0].rChild = 10;

    // Node D
    BT[8].info = 'D';
    BT[8].lChild = -1;
    BT[8].rChild = -1;

    // Node E
    BT[6].info = 'E';
    BT[6].lChild = -1;
    BT[6].rChild = -1;

    // Node F
    BT[10].info = 'F';
    BT[10].lChild = -1;
    BT[10].rChild = -1;
}
```

Linear representation of a binary tree in an array: A binary tree can also be implemented using a linear array. Let `BT[MAX]` be a 1D array to store the elements in the binary tree. In array representation of a binary tree, the following storage policies can be followed to store the elements in the tree.

1. *The root node is stored at the first index of the array. Let us say the index starts from 0.*
2. *If* i *is the index of a node in the array, its left child is stored at the index* $2i + 1$, *and its right child is stored at* $2i + 2$.

The figure 3.16 below shows storage of the nodes of a binary tree in an array following the above rules linearly.

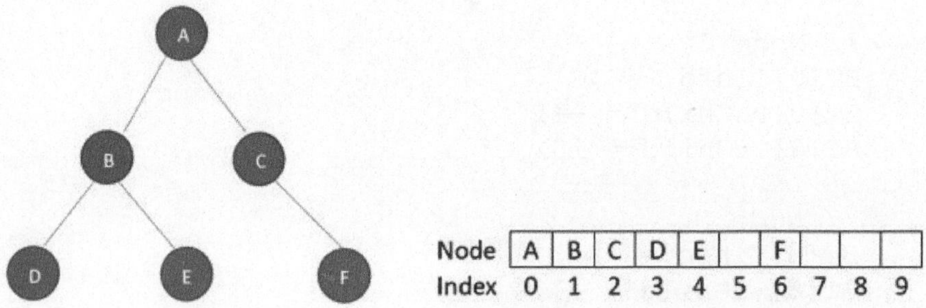

Binary Tree Implementation linearly over an array

Figure 3.16: Linear representation of binary tree using array.

If the index starts from 1, the left child of a node store at index i will be stored at $2i$ and right child will be store at $2i + 1$.

3.3.2 Binary Tree Traversal

Tree traversal is the process of visiting nodes in a tree. For a binary tree, there are three standard ways of traversing the tree – *inorder, preorder* and *postorder*. Given a binary tree T, the algorithms for these traversals are defined recursively as below.

Inorder Traversal Algorithm:

1. *Traverse the left subtree of T in inorder*
2. *Process the root of T*
3. *Traverse the right subtree of T in inorder*

Explanation:

1. Before visiting the root node, algorithm visits its left subtree (Rule 1).

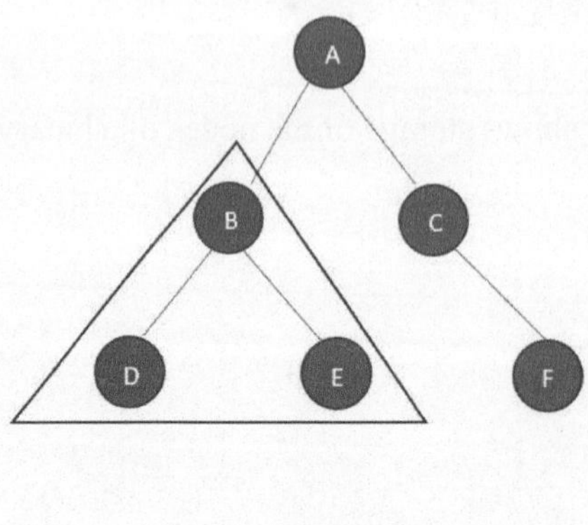

2. Before visiting node B, visit its left subtree (Rule 1).

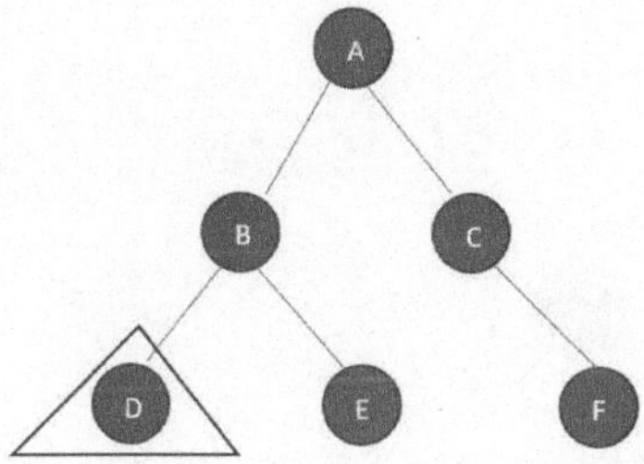

3. Before visiting node D, visit its left subtree (Rule 1). However, node D has no left subtree. So, apply rule 2 i.e., process root. As D is the root of this subtree, *D is printed.*

   Inorder Sequence: D

4. Apply rule 3. However, as there is no right child, algorithm returns to B rooted subtree. With this, processing of the left subtree of B is over, and it apply rule 2 to process root node. As B is the root node of this subtree, *B is printed.*

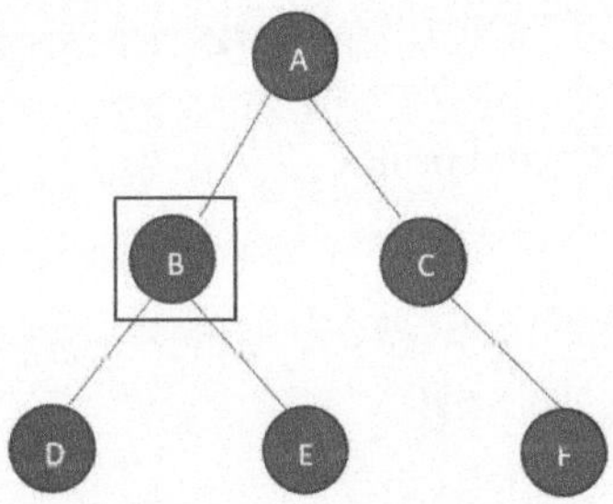

Inorder Sequence: D B

5. Apply rule 3 to go to the right subtree of B.

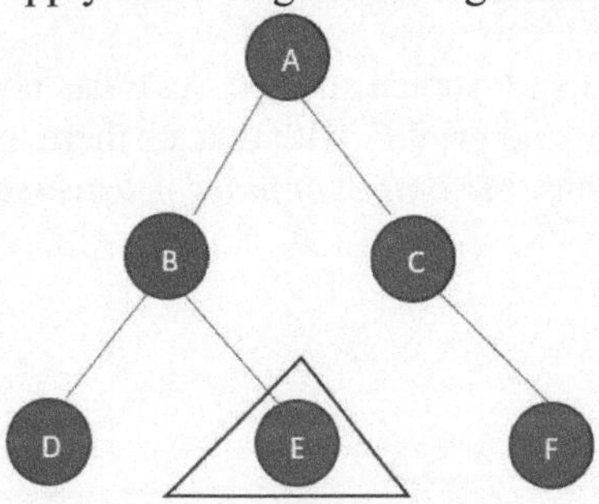

6. As E has no left child and no right child, apply rule 2 to print E.
   Inorder Sequence: D B E

7. With this processing of the left subtree of node A is over, and returns to node A. It then applies rule 2 to process node A, and print A.

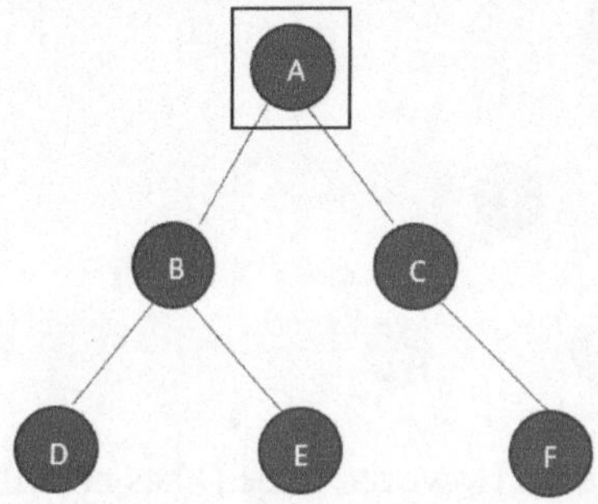

Inorder Sequence: D B E A

8. Apply rule 3 to go to the right subtree of A i.e., C rooted subtree.

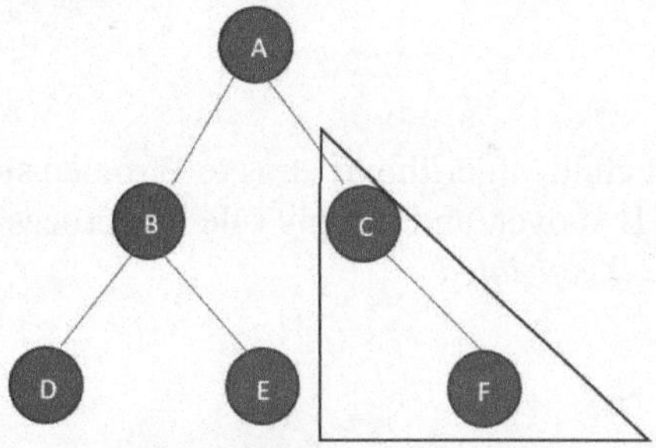

9. As C has no left child, apply rule 2 to process node C, and print C

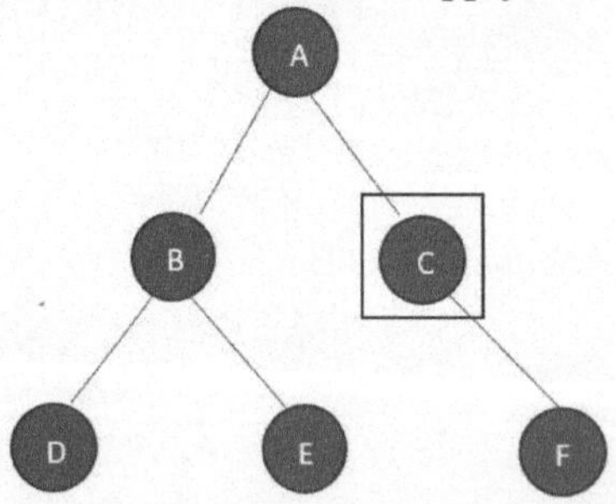

Inorder Sequence: D B E A C

10. Apply rule 3 to visit the right subtree of node C i.e., F rooted subtree. As F has no left child and no right child, apply rule 2 to process node F and print F. with this, as there is no more nodes to be visited, the algorithm terminates. Thus, *the output of inorder traversal is D B E A C F.*

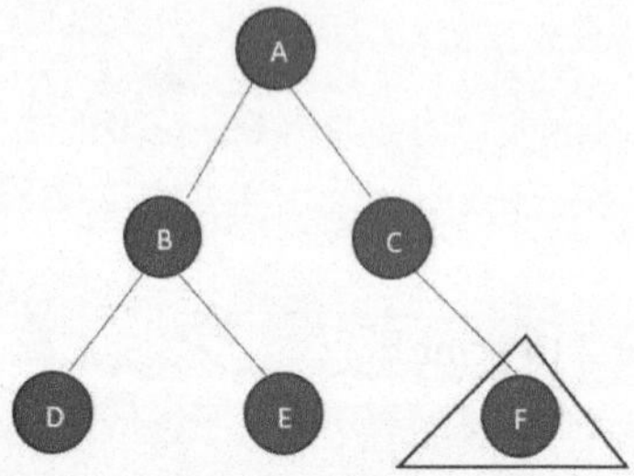

Inorder Sequence: D B E A C F

The sequence in which the algorithm visits the nodes in the tree is illustrated in the figure below.

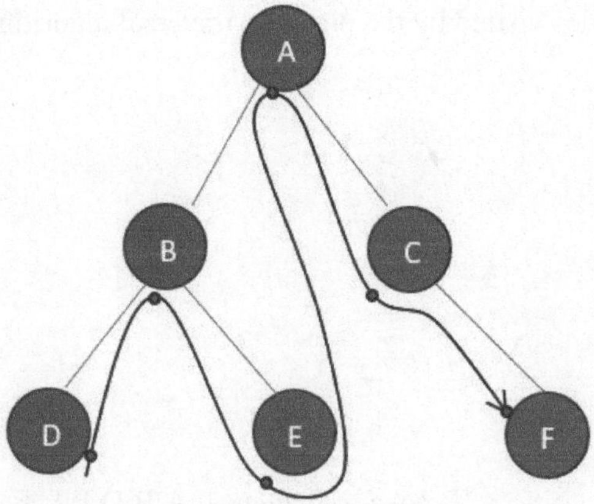

Inorder Sequence: D B E A C F

The recursive function for inorder traversal is given below.

```
void inorder(struct node* node)
{
        if (node != NULL){
                inorder(node->lChild);
                printf("%c ", node->info);
                inorder(node->rChild);
        }
}
```

The recurrence equation of the above function is $T(n) - 2T\left(\frac{n}{2}\right) + 1, T(1) = 1$. If we expand the expression, we get $T(n) = n + 1 = O(n)$.

Preorder Traversal Algorithm:

1. *Process the root of T*
2. *Traverse the left subtree of T in preorder*
3. *Traverse the right subtree of T in preorder*

The recursive function for preorder traversal is given below.

```
void preorder(struct node* node)
{
        if (node != NULL){
                printf("%c ", node->info);
                preorder(node->lChild);
                preorder(node->rChild);
        }
}
```

The figure below illustrates the sequence of nodes visited by the preorder traversal algorithm.

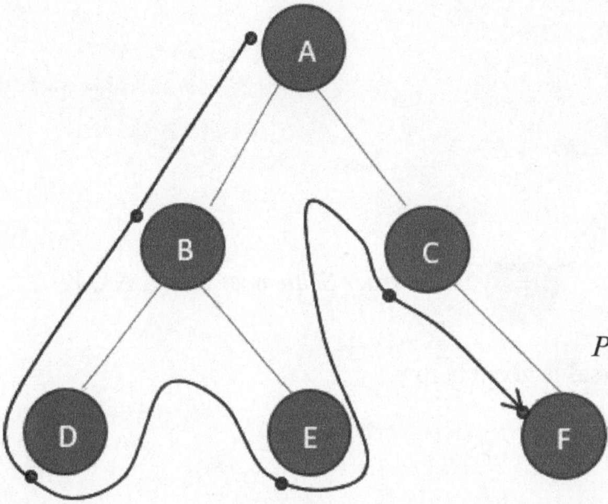

Preorder Sequence: A B D E C F

Postorder Traversal Algorithm:

1. *Traverse the left subtree of T in postorder*
2. *Traverse the right subtree of T in postorder*
3. *Process the root of T*

The recursive function for postorder traversal is given below.

```
void postorder(struct node* node)
{
        if (node != NULL){
              postorder(node->lChild);
              postorder(node->rChild);
              printf("%c ", node->info);
        }
}
```

The figure below illustrates the sequence of nodes visited by the postorder traversal algorithm.

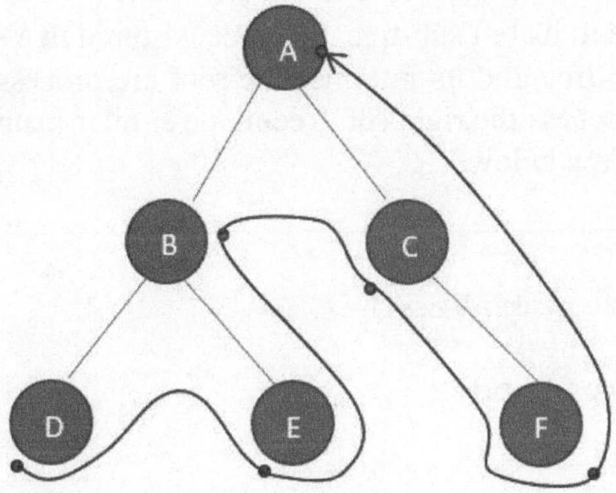


```
Postorder: D E B F C A
```

The inorder, preorder and postorder traversal of the tree is shown below.

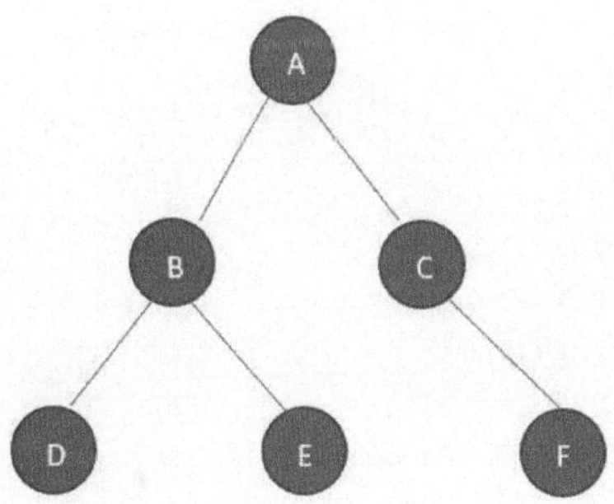


```
Inorder: D B E A C F

Preorder: A B D E C F

Postorder: D E B F C A
```

3.3.3 Iterative algorithms of Inorder, Preorder, and Postorder traversals

The above section presents recursive algorithms of inorder, preorder and postorder traversals. Recursive algorithms, specially for binary tree traversal, are natural and easy to visualized. Every recursive algorithm can be converted to an iterative counterpart. This section discusses iterative algorithms of inorder, preorder and postorder traversals of a binary tree.

Iterative Algorithm for Inorder: The idea in inorder traversal is that, given a node, process its left sub-tree before processing the tree. Once the given node is processed, process its right sub-tree. A pointer (named as current pointer `cur`) traverses from a node to another while processing the tree. While `cur` pointer moves from one node to its left sub-tree, the node is stored in a stack to enable to return to it latter. Once the left sub-tree and its intermediate root are processed, the current pointer jumps to its right sub-tree to process the right sub-tree in the similar manner. An iterative inorder traversal of a binary tree is given below.

```
Algorithm: Iterative Inorder Travesal
Input: Root of the binary tree
Output: Inorder Traversal of nodes
BEGIN
   // Initialize
1. Create an empty stack S
2. cur= root

   /* Loop terminating condition - If current is NULL and
   stack is empty then terminate. */
3. WHILE((S.isEmpty()== FALSE) OR (cur ≠ NULL))
       /* Search for leftmost child node. Store the
          parent in the stack as the current pointer
          moves to next left child */
4.     WHILE(cur ≠ NULL)
5.               S.push(cur)
6.               cur = cur->lChild
7.     END WHILE

       // The left most child is found
8.     IF (S.isEmpty()== FALSE)THEN
9.               popped_element=S.pop()
10.              Print popped_elemet->info
11.              cur = popped_element->rChild
12.    END IF
13. END WHILE
END
```

The execution of the above algorithm is illustrated with an example binary tree below.

Action	Stack	Inorder	Operations	Illustration after the operations
			Initially $cur = root$, and `Stack` is empty.	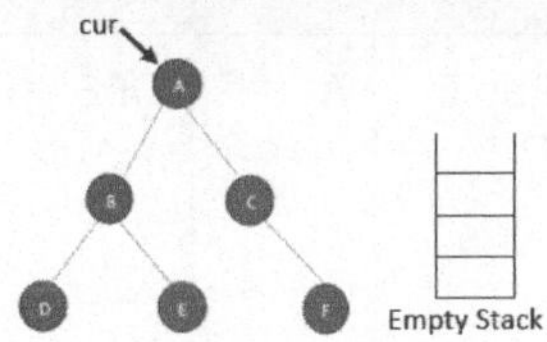
Push A	A		As $cur \neq NULL$, push `cur` to `Stack`. Then, $cur = cur\text{->}$ $lChild$.	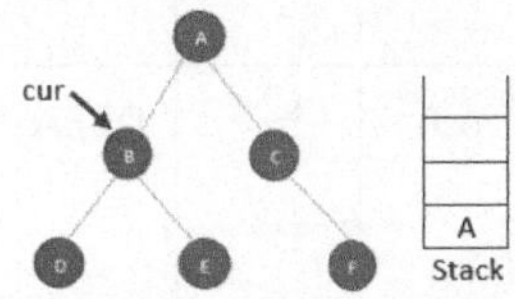
Push B	AB		As $cur \neq NULL$, push `cur` to `Stack`. Then, $cur = cur\text{->}$ $lChild$.	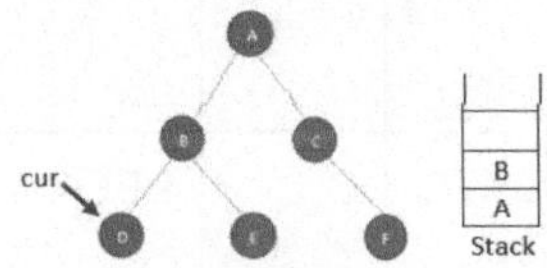
Push D	ABD		As $cur \neq NULL$, push `cur` to `Stack`. Then, $cur = cur\text{->}$ $lChild$.	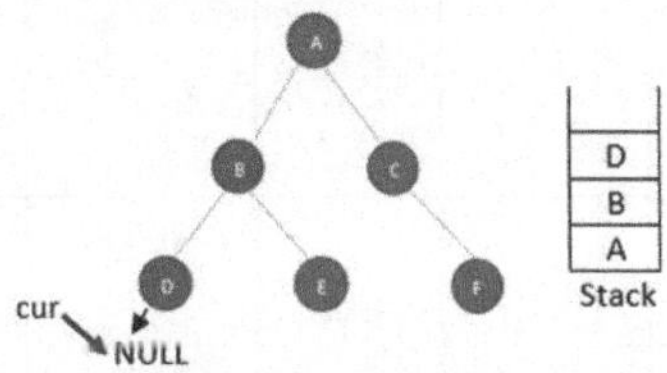
Pop D	AB	D	As $cur = NULL$, pop top of the stack and print the popped element as inorder. Then, assign it to $cur =$ $popped\ item \rightarrow rChild$..	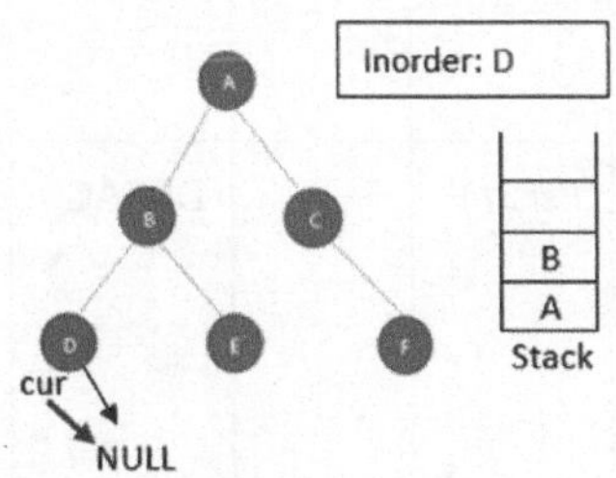
Pop B	A	DB	As $cur = NULL$, pop top of the stack and print the popped element as inorder. Then, assign it to $cur =$ $popped\ item \rightarrow rChild$.	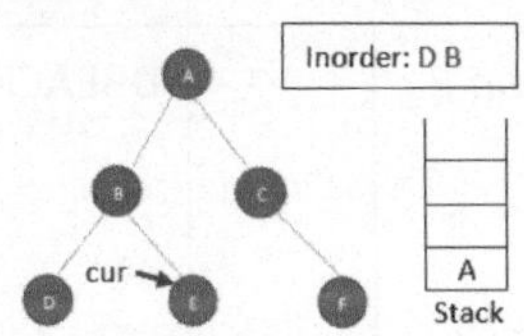
Push E	AE	DB	As $cur \neq NULL$, push `cur` to `Stack`. Then, $cur = cur\text{->}$ $lChild$.	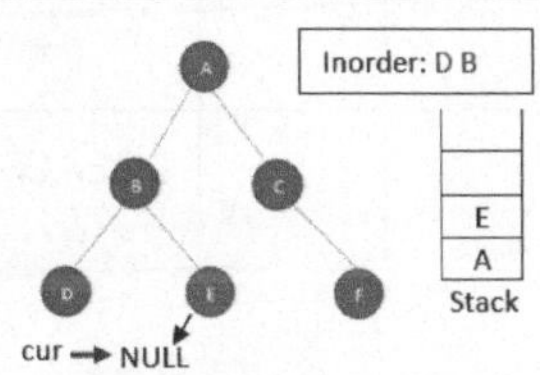

Action	Stack	Inorder	Operations	Illustration after the operations
Pop E	A	DBE	As $cur = NULL$, pop top of the stack and print the popped element as inorder. Then, assign it to $cur = popped\ item \rightarrow rChild$.	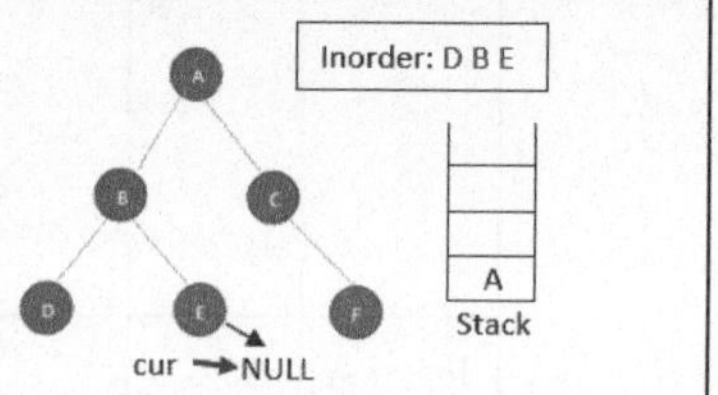
Pop A	-	DBEA	As $cur = NULL$, pop top of the stack and print the popped element as inorder. Then, assign it to $cur = popped\ item \rightarrow rChild$.	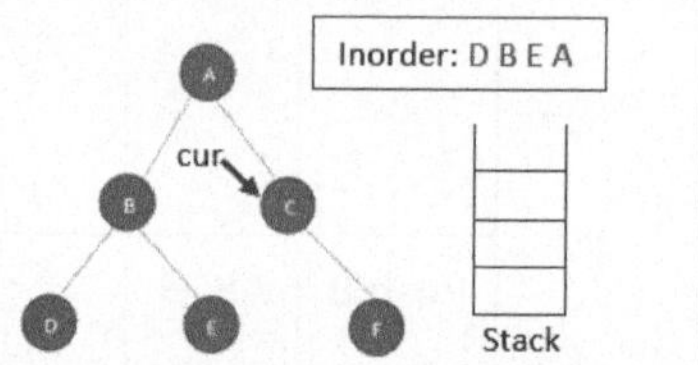
Push C	C	DBEA	As $cur \neq NULL$, push `cur` to `Stack`. Then, $cur = cur\text{->}\ lChild$.	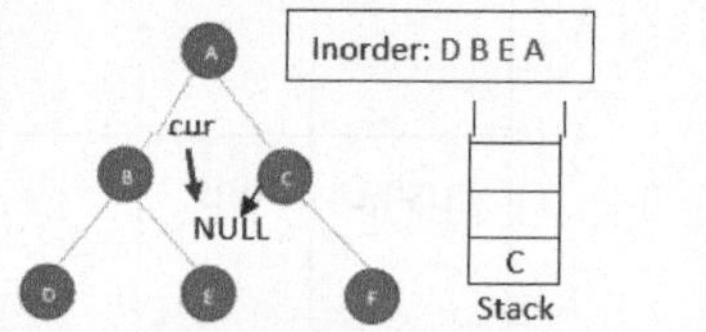
Pop	-	DBEAC	As $cur = NULL$, pop top of the stack and print the popped element as inorder. Then, assign it to $cur = popped\ item \rightarrow rChild$.	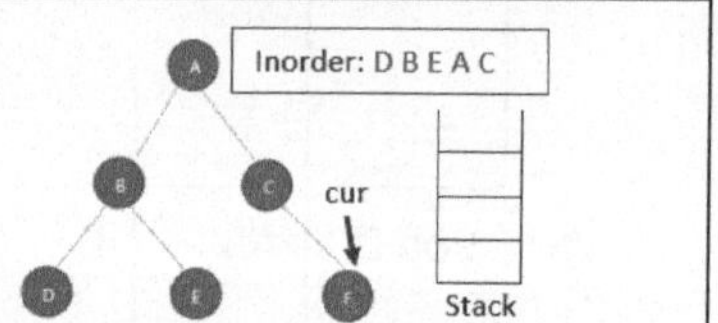
Push F	F	DBEAC	As $cur \neq NULL$, push `cur` to `Stack`. Then, $cur = cur\text{->}\ lChild$.	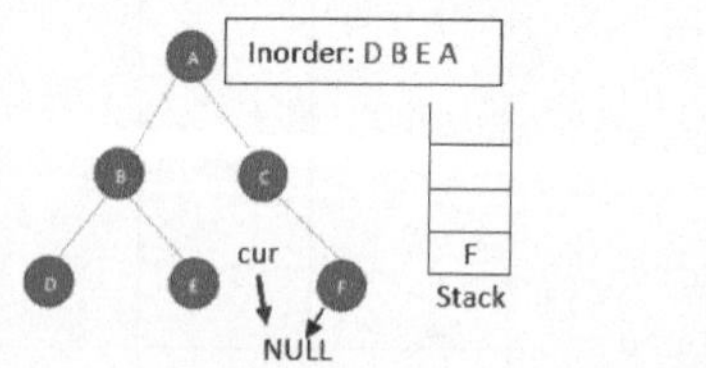
Pop F	-	DBEACF	As $cur = NULL$, pop top of the stack and print the popped element as inorder. Then, assign it to $cur = popped\ item \rightarrow rChild$.	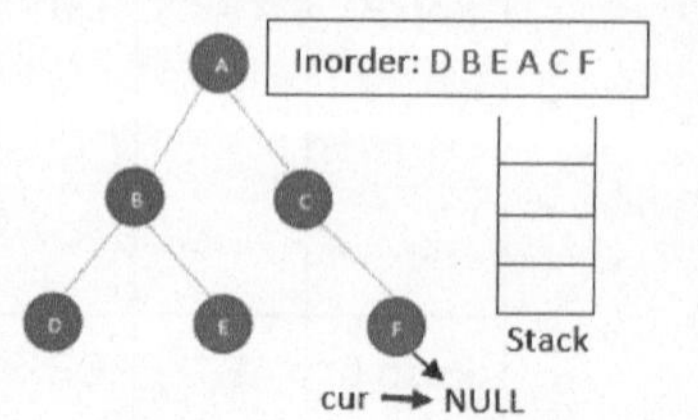
	-	DBEACF	As $cur = NULL$ and the Stack is empty, algorithm terminates	-

Iterative Algorithm for Preorder: Like in inorder traversal, iterative preorder traversal also uses a stack to keep track of its right child and left child of a node. A popped node from the stack is visited as preorder, and push its right child and left child. An iterative preorder traversal algorithm is given below.

```
Algorithm: Iterative Preorder Traversal
Input: Root node of the binary tree
Output: Preorder Traversal
BEGIN
1. Create an empty stack S
2. S.push(root)

   // Repeat till all the nodes are visited
3. WHILE (S.isEmpty() == FALSE)

        // Visit the node at the top of the stack
4.      popped_element = S.pop()
5.      Print popped_element-> info

        /* after printing the preorder, save its right child
           and left child */
6.      If(popped_element-> rChild ≠ NULL) THEN
7.              S.push(popped_element-> rChild)
8.      END IF
9.      If(popped_element-> lChild ≠ NULL) THEN
10.             S.push(popped_element-> lChild)
11.     END IF
12. END WHILE
END
```

Action	Stack	Preorder	Operations	Illustration after the operations
	A		Create Stack S and $S.push(root)$	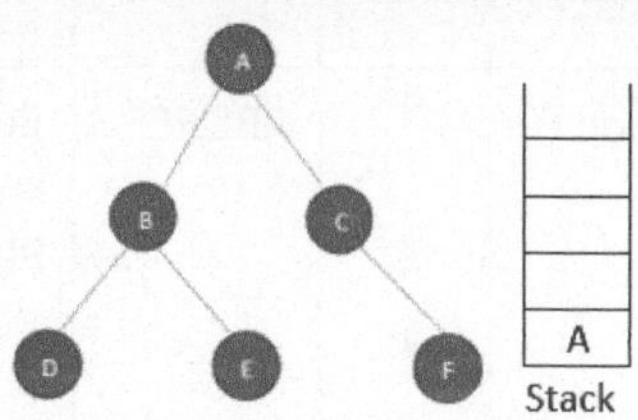
Pop A Push C Push B	BC	A	Pop top element A and push its right child C and left child node B	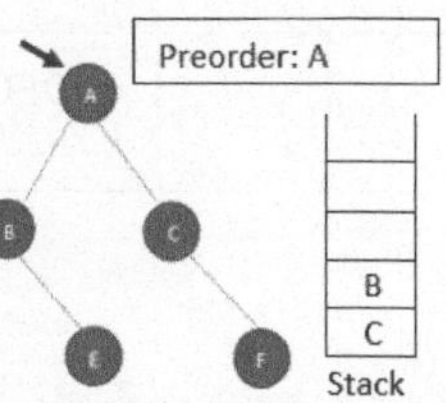

Action	Stack	Preorder	Operations	Illustration after the operations
Pop B Push E Push D	CED	AB	Pop top element B and push its right child E and left child node D	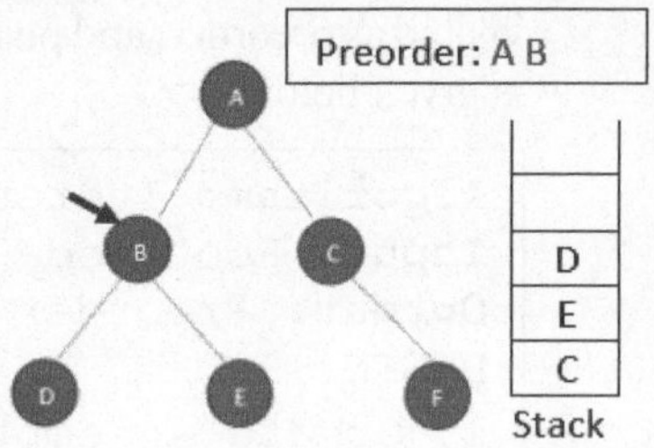
Pop D	CE	ABD	Pop top element D. As its right child and left child are NULL, no node is pushed into Stack.	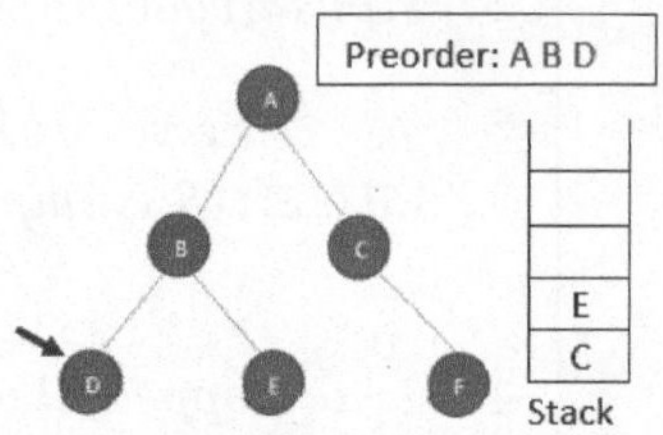
Pop E	C	ABDE	Pop top element E. As its right child and left child are NULL, no node is pushed into Stack.	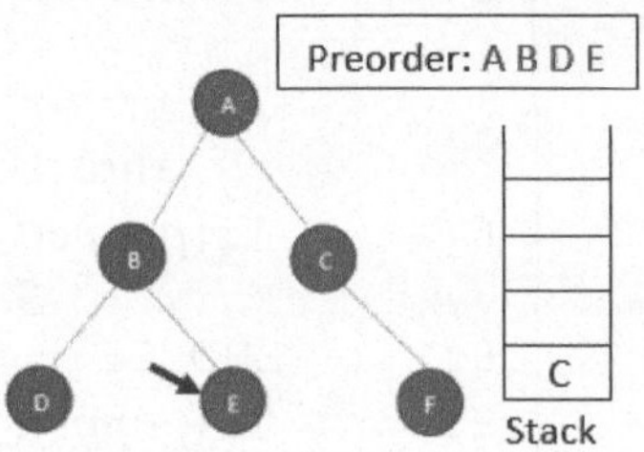
Pop C Push F	C	ABDEC	Pop top element C. As it has only right child, only the right child F is pushed into Stack.	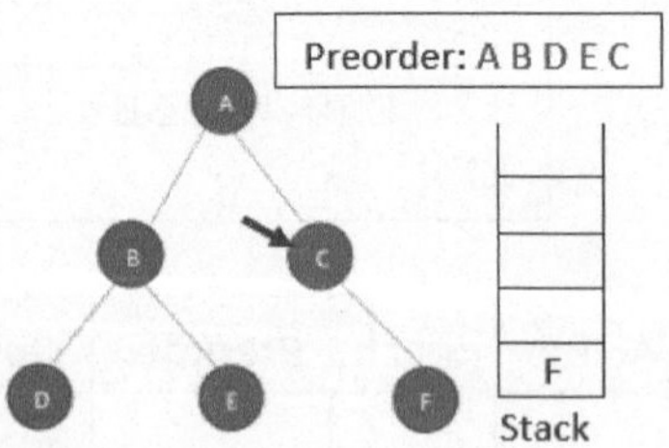
Pop F	-	ABDECF	Pop top element F. As its right child and left child are NULL, no node is pushed into Stack.	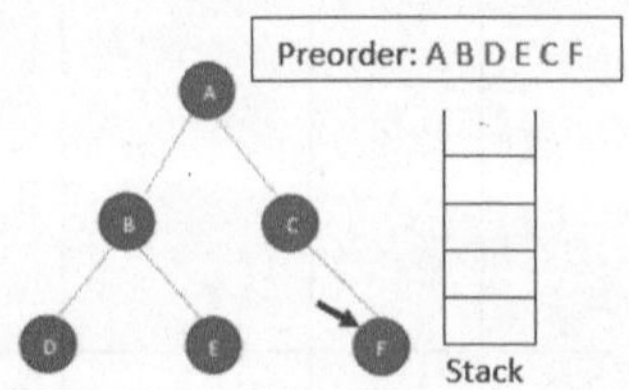
-	-	ABDECF	As the stack is empty, the algorithm terminates.	

Iterative Algorithm for Postorder: Compare to the iterative algorithm of inorder and preorder traversal, iterative algorithm of postorder is a bit more complex to visualize. The idea in this algorithm is that whenever a node with non-NULL right child node is visited, its right child node and the node are stored in the stack and it moves to its left child node. Whenever it visits a NULL left child node, it pops the top elements of the stack. If the popped node has no right child node or its right child node is different from top of the stack, a postorder node is found.

```
Algorithm: Iterative Postorder Traversal
    Input: Root of the binary tree
    Output: Postorder Traversal
    BEGIN
       // Initialize
    Create an empty stack S
    cur = root

       // Do the following until the stack is empty
    DO
        WHILE (cur ≠ NULL)
            IF (cur-> rChild ≠ NULL) THEN
                    S.push(cur-> right)
            END IF
            S.push(cur)
            cur = cur-> lChild
        END WHILE
        cur = S.pop()
       IF ((cur-> rChild ≠ NULL)AND (cur → rChild-> info == S.topElement()))
             S.pop()
             S.push(cur)
             cur = cur-> rChild
        Else
             Print cur-> info
             cur = NULL
        END IF
    WHILE(S.isEmpty()==FALSE)
    END
```

Let us illustrate the algorithm with an example tree. When the algorithm starts, the `cur` pointer points to the root of the tree as shown below.

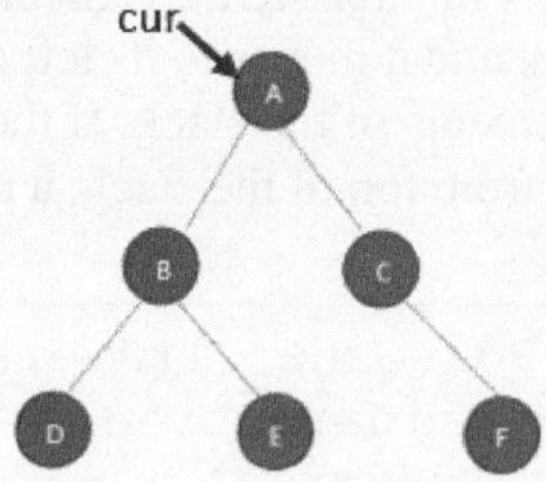

Since $cur \neq NULL$, and also $cur{-}{>}\,rChild \neq NULL$, the steps 6 – 9 will be executed. Then the following stack and tree status are obtained.

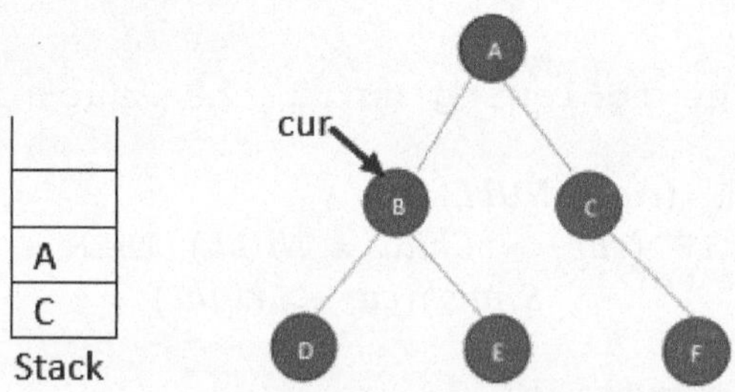

Since $cur \neq NULL$, and $cur{-}{>}\,rChild \neq NULL$ are further satisfied, the steps 6 – 9 in the loop will be executed. Then, the following stack and tree status are obtained.

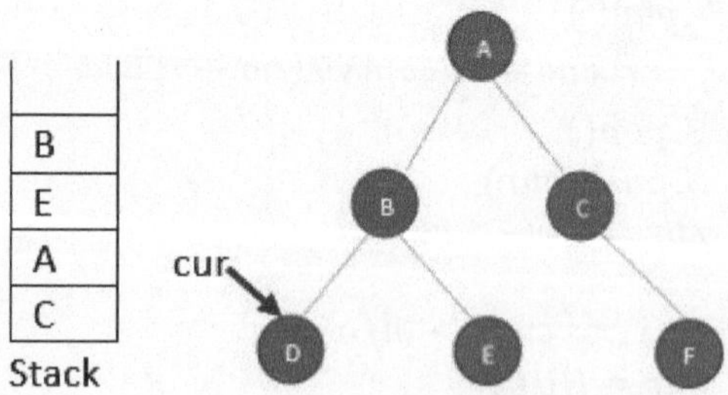

As $cur{-}{>}\,rChild == NULL$, only the steps 8 and 9 in the loop will be executed, and obtained the following stack and tree status.

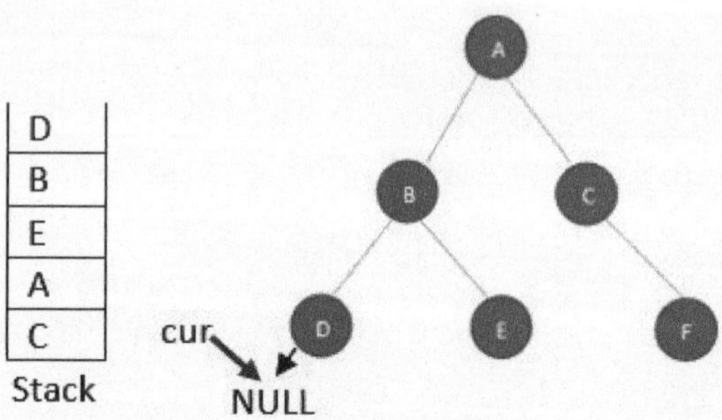

As $cur == NULL$, the loop terminates. Now, the top element is popped (step 11). Since the condition in step 12 fails, the steps 16-18 are executed, and we get the first postorder node i.e., `Postorder: D`. After printing the postorder, the step 11 is executed to obtained the following stack and tree status.

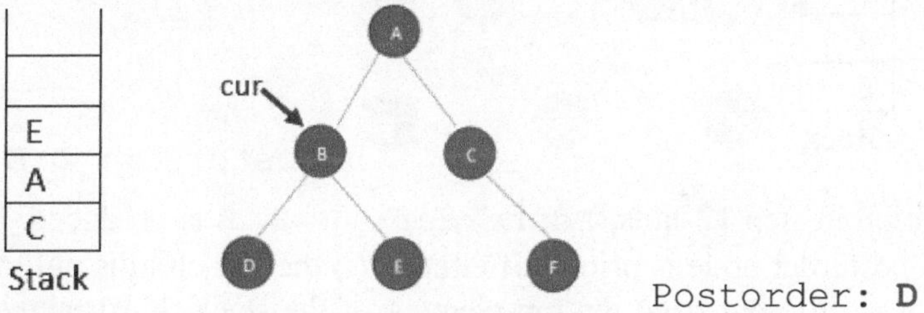

Now, the condition in step 12 is satisfied, and execute the steps 13-15 to obtain the following status.

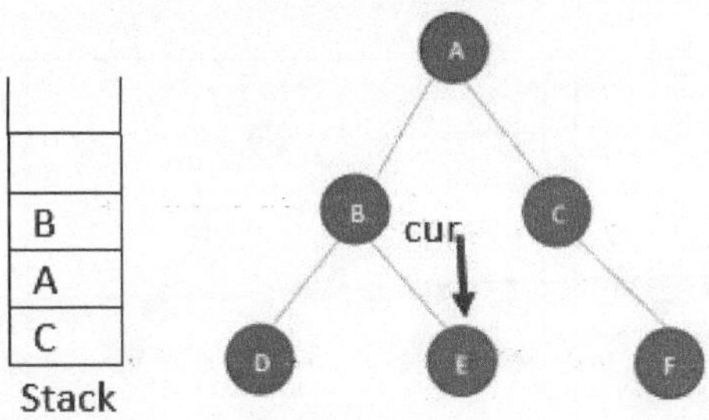

As $cur{-}{>}rChild == NULL$, only the steps 8 and 9 in the loop will be executed, and obtained the following stack and tree status.

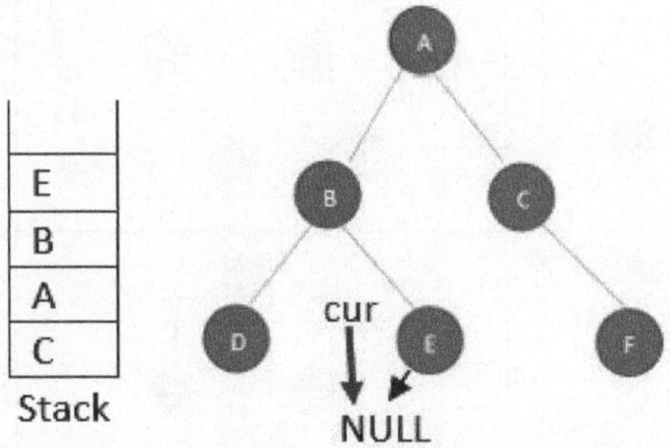

As $cur == NULL$, the loop terminates. Now, the top element is popped (step 11). Since the condition in step 12 fails, the steps 16-18 are executed, and we get the next postorder node i.e., `Postorder: D E`. After printing the postorder, the step 11 is executed to obtained the following stack and tree status.

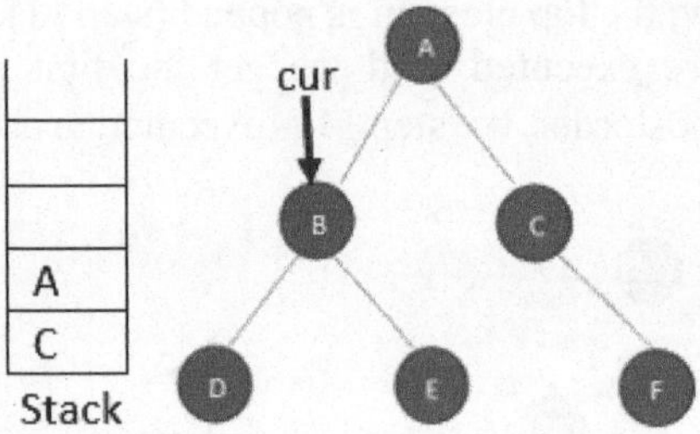

Postorder: **D E**

Now, as the condition in step 12 fails, `Postorder:` **D E B** is produced. By now, it may be noted that a postorder node is printed if either - (i) the left child is null or (ii) right child is present but it is different from the top element of the stack. Further, the algorithm iterates through the following sequence to produce postorder traversal of the given tree.

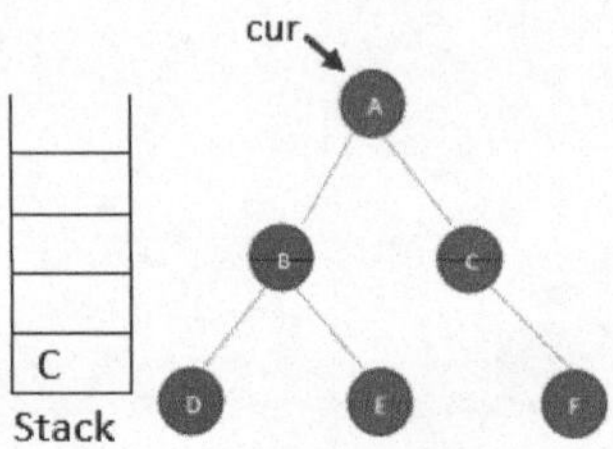	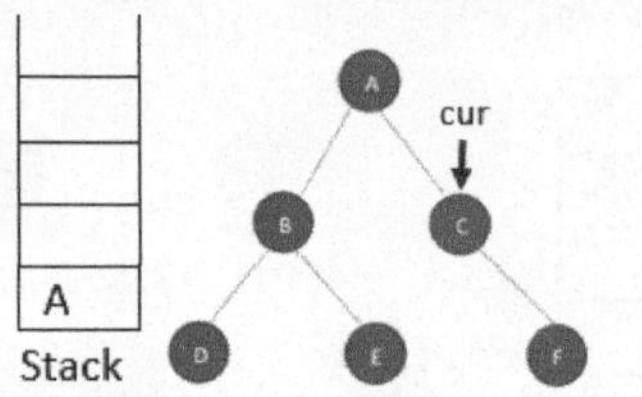	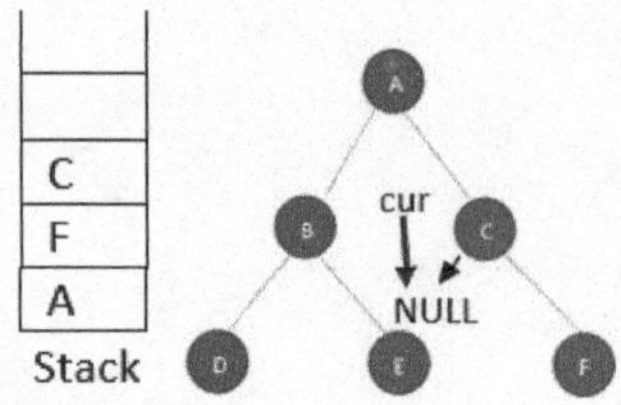
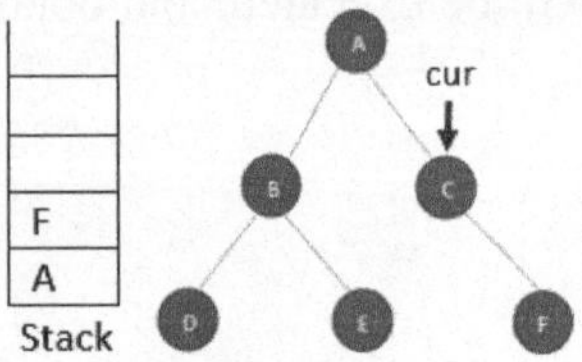	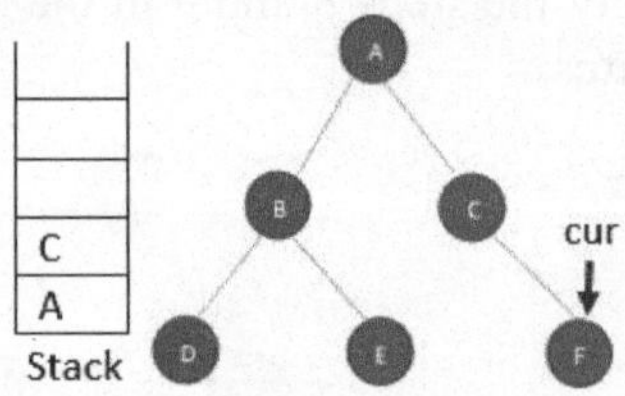	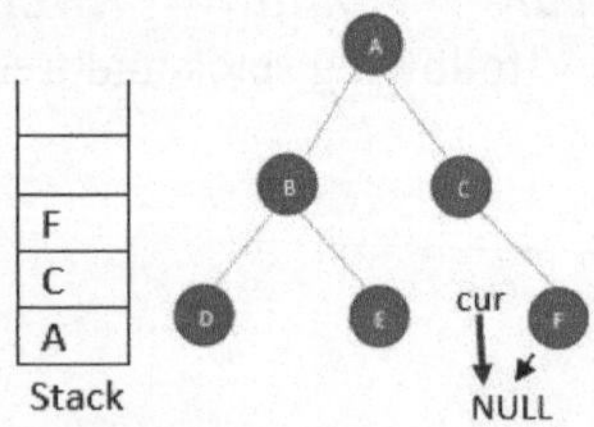
Postorder: **D E B F**	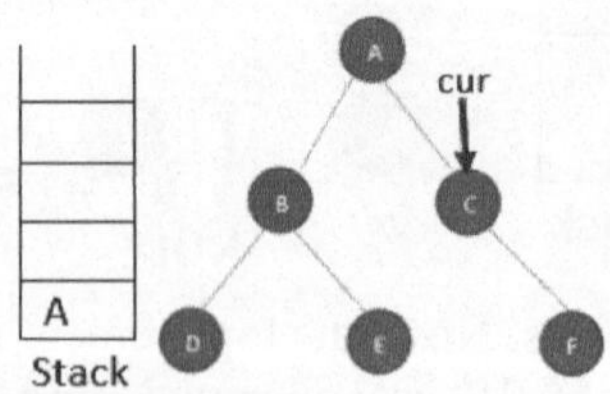	Postorder: **D E B F C**
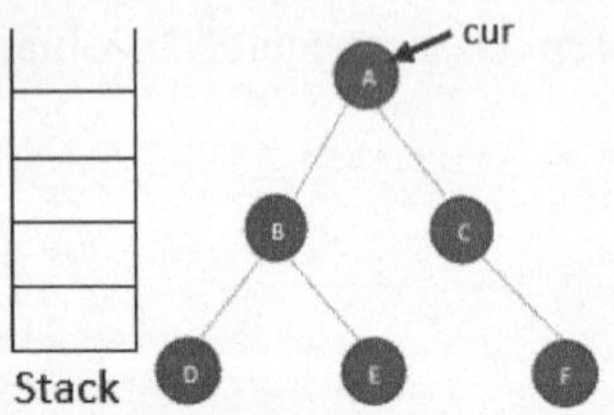	Postorder: **D E B F C A**	Algorithm Terminates as Stack becomes empty

3.3.4 Some properties of Binary Trees

Theorem 5: The maximum number of nodes at level $l \geq 0$ of a binary tree is 2^l.

Theorem 6: The maximum number of nodes in a binary tree of height $h \geq 0$ is $2^{h+1} - 1$.

Theorem 7: The minimum possible height of a binary tree with n nodes is $\lfloor \log_2 n \rfloor$, if the height of leaf is 0.

Theorem 8: The maximum possible height of a binary tree with n nodes is $n - 1$, if the height of leaf is 0.

Theorem 9: In a binary tree where every node has 0 or 2 child nodes, the number of leaf nodes is always one more than the number of nodes with 2 child nodes.

Theorem 10: In a non-empty binary tree, the number of arcs is always one less than the number of nodes in the tree.

Full Binary Tree: A binary tree is said to be full, if and only if every level of the tree has its maximum possible number of nodes. Every level $l \geq 0$ has 2^l number of nodes. Figure 3.17 illustrates an example of a full binary tree.

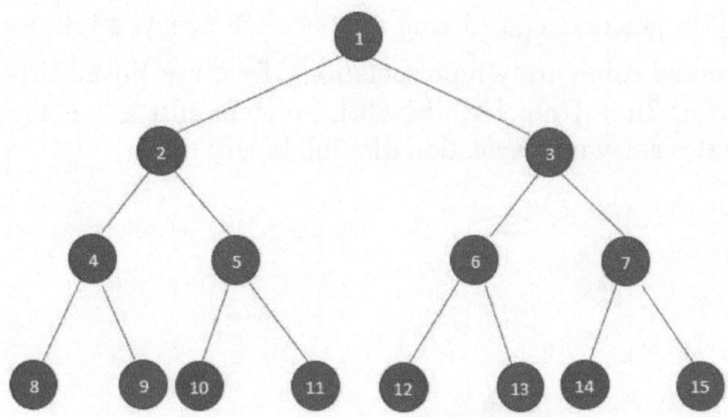

Figure 3.17: An example of Full Binary Tree

Complete Binary Tree: A binary tree is complete, if and only if every level is full except possibly the last level, and the nodes in the last level are arranged as far left as possible. Figure 3.18 illustrates an example of a full binary tree.

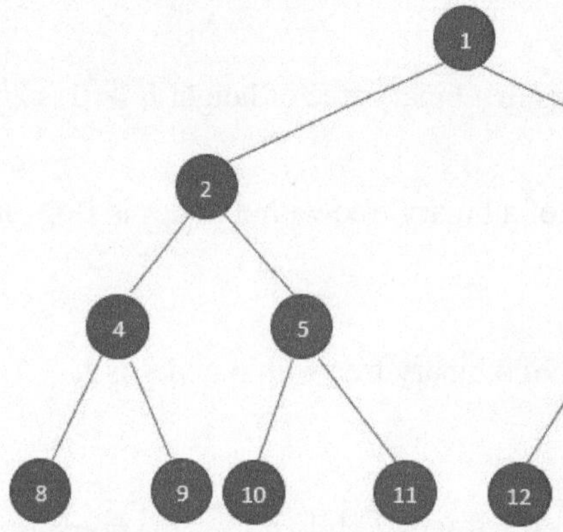

Figure 3.18: An example of Complete Binary Tree

The nodes in the above examples of full tree or complete tree are purposefully numbered level wise from left to right. It can be seen that the left child node of a node numbered with i is numbered as $2i$, and its right child node as $2i + 1$, if the numbering starts from 1. If the numbering starts from 0, the left child node of a node i will be numbered as $2i + 1$ and right child node as $2i + 2$. If we consider this numbering as the indexes in a linear array, the nodes in a full or complete binary tree can be effectively stored in an array without any in-between unoccupied indexes. From an arbitrary node (index in the tree), its left and right child nodes can be visited using the above expression. Similarly, if a node is assigned an index number $i \geq 0$, the index of its parent node will be $\left\lfloor \frac{i-1}{2} \right\rfloor$. In practice, considering its space efficiency, a full or complete binary tree is generally implemented using array representation. If we use linked list-based implementation, there will exist $2n$ or $2n + 1$ number of NULL pointers, if $n \geq 1$ is the number of leaf nodes. Figure 3.19 illustrates array representation of a full binary tree.

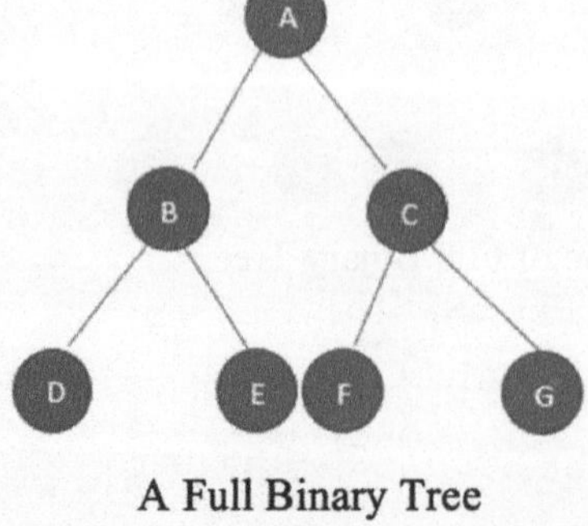

Node	A	B	C	D	E	F	G			
Index	0	1	2	3	4	5	6	7	8	9

A Full Binary Tree **Array Representation**

Figure 3.19: A full binary tree and its array representation

3.3.5 Binary Search Tree

Binary search tree is a special type of binary tree, in which the nodes are arranged satisfying the following properties.

1. The value of a node is larger than the value of its left child node, and
2. The value of a node is smaller than the value of its right child node.

The above properties assume that no node has the same value. In case duplicate values are allowed, the condition in one of the above two rules may include *equal to* condition i.e., *larger than or equal to* in rule 1, *smaller than or equal to* in rule 2. Few examples of binary search trees are shown in figure 3.20.

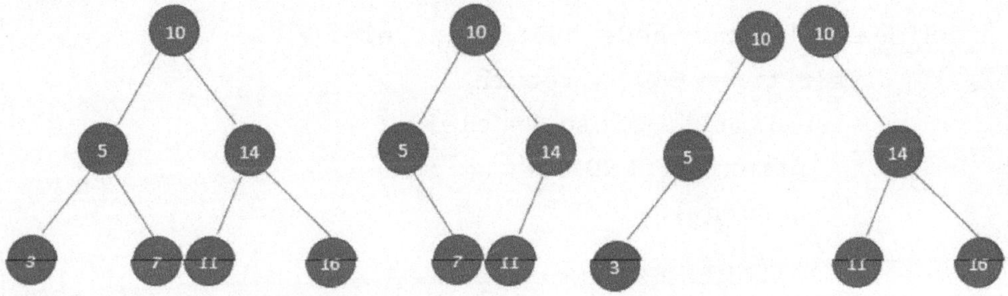

Figure 3.20: Examples of Binary Search Tree

From the above example, the followings are observed.

1. Given a node N, the values of the nodes in the left subtree of N are smaller than the value of N.
2. Given a node N, the values of the nodes in the right subtree of N are larger than the value of N.
3. Inorder traversal of a binary search tree will produce a sorted sequence in ascending order.

Search operation on Binary Search Tree: While a normal binary tree takes $O(n)$ time complexity for searching an element (all the nodes in the tree needs to be visited), searching time complexity is reduced to $O(h)$, where h is the height of the tree. However, the minimum height $h \geq 0$ of a binary search tree with n number of nodes is $\lfloor \log_2 n \rfloor$ and the maximum height is $n - 1$. Given a binary search tree T, the following algorithm finds an element in the tree

```
Algorithm: BST Search
Input: root- Root of BST and ele - search element
Output: Found or not
BEGIN
cur = root
IF (cur == NULL) THEN
        PRINT "The element is not found"
ELSE IF (cur-> info == ele) THEN
        PRINT "The element is found"
```

```
6. ELSE IF (cur−> info > ele) THEN
7.          cur = cur−> lChild
8.          Go to Step 2
9. ELSE IF (cur−> info < ele) THEN
10.         cur = cur−> rChild
11.         Go to Step 2
12. END IF
END
```

The above algorithm may be implemented recursively as follows in C language.

```c
int BSTSearch(struct node *rPtr, int ele){
        if(rPtr == NULL) return 0;
        else if(rPtr->info == ele){
            printf("FOUND");
            return 1;
        }
        else if(rPtr->info > ele)
            BSTSearch(rPtr->lChild, ele);
        else
            BSTSearch(rPtr->rChild, ele);
}
```

The following figures illustrate traversal of a binary search tree for searching nodes with the values 6, and 11. From the figures, it can be seen that the search operation traverse a particular path from the root node towards a leaf node, which could be any of the lead node depending on the searched value. Hence, worst case time complexity is defined by the height of the tree.

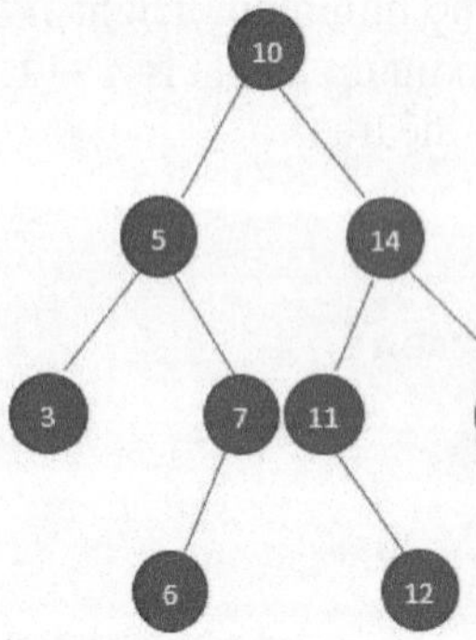

Binary Search Tree

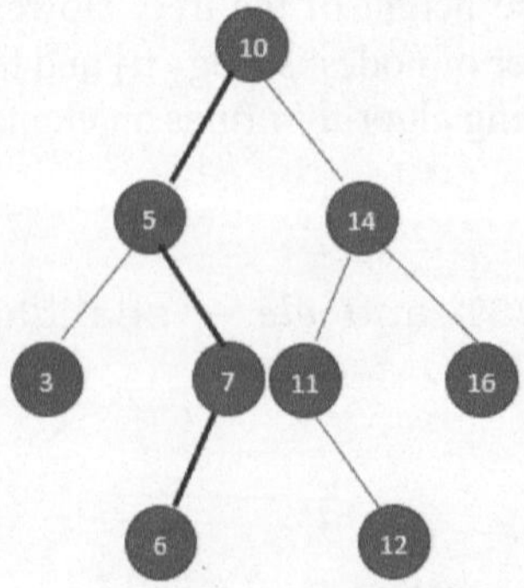

Search 6

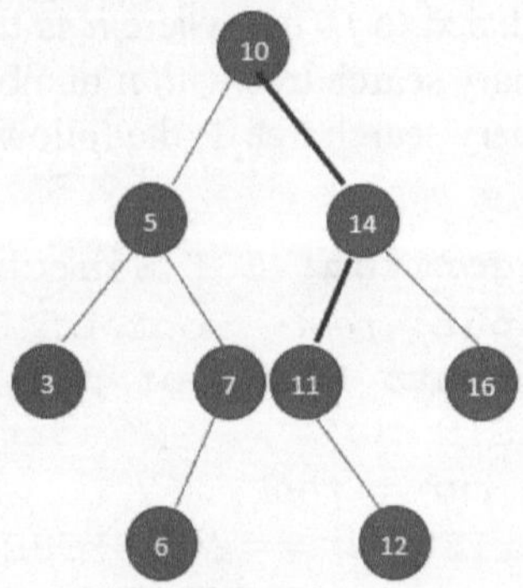

Search 11

The above search function returns either 0 for NOT FOUND or 1 for FOUND. This function can be modified to return the address of the node if FOUND, or NULL if NOT FOUND.

```
struct node * BSTSearch(struct node *rPtr, int ele){
        if(rPtr == NULL) return NULL;
        else if(rPtr->info == ele){
            return rPtr;
        }
        else if(rPtr->info == ele)
            return( BSTSearch(rPtr->lChild, ele));
        else
            return( BSTSearch(rPtr->rChild, ele));
}
```

Iterative Search Function of Binary Search Tree: The binary search tree can also be implemented using an iterative approach, as below.

```
int BSTSearch(struct node *rPtr, int ele){
        while(rPtr!=NULL){
            if(rPtr->info == ele){
                printf("FOUND");
                return 1;
            }
            else if(rPtr->info >= ele)
                rPtr = rPtr->lChild;
            else
                rPtr = rPtr->rChild;
        }
        return 0;
}
```

Insert a node in a Binary Search Tree: In a binary search tree, a node is always inserted as a leaf node, satisfying the binary search tree condition. Therefore, the main task of inserting a node in a binary search tree is to locate the anchored node which will connect the new node as its left child or right child depending on the value of the anchored node and the new node. The anchored node will always be either a node with one child or a leaf node. The following provides the algorithm for inserting a node in a binary search tree. Depending on the value of the node to be inserted, the algorithm explores a particular path looking for the anchored node. The anchored node could be any node in the tree, and the number of comparisons is the number of nodes in the path from the root to the anchor node (including the root and the anchored node). Therefore, time complexity of inserting a node in a binary search tree is defined by the height of the tree i.e., $O(h)$.

```
Algorithm: BST Insert
Input: root - of BST and ele - the element to be inserted
Output: New element inserted BST
BEGIN
1. new = Node(ele) //Create a new BST node and assign value to it
2. cur = root
3. prev = NULL
4. IF (cur == NULL) THEN
5.          IF (prev == NULL)
6.              root = new
7.          ELSE
8.              IF (prev-> info < ele) THEN
9.                      prev-> rChild = new
10.             ELSE
11.                     prev-> lChild = new
12.             END IF
13.         END IF
14. ELSE IF (cur-> info > ele) THEN
15.         prev = cur
16.         cur = cur-> lChild
17.         Go to Step 4
18. ELSE
19.         prev = cur
20.         cur = cur-> rChild
21.         Go to Step 4
22. END IF
END
```

The above algorithm may be implemented as the following function in C language.

```
struct node *insert(struct node *rPtr, int ele){
    struct node *nPtr = (struct node *)malloc(sizeof(struct
    node));
    nPtr->info = ele;
    nPtr->lChild = NULL;
    nPtr->rChild = NULL;
    struct node *cur = rPtr;
    struct node *prev = NULL;
```

```
        while(cur!=NULL){
            if(cur->info >= ele){
                prev = cur;
                cur = cur->lChild;
            }
            else{
                prev = cur;
                cur = cur->rChild;
            }
        }
        if(prev == NULL) return nPtr;
        else{
            if(prev->info >= ele)
                prev->lChild = nPtr;
            else
                prev->rChild = nPtr;
            return rPtr;
        }
    }
```

Recursive: The above iterative function for inserting a node in a binary search tree can also be implemented recursively as follows.

```
struct node *insert(struct node *cur, struct node *prev, int ele){
    if(cur == NULL){
        struct node *nPtr = (struct node *)malloc(sizeof(struct
    node));
        nPtr->info = ele;
        nPtr->lChild = NULL;
        nPtr->rChild = NULL;

        if(prev == NULL)
            return nPtr;
        else{
            if(prev->info >= ele)
                prev->lChild = nPtr;
            else
                prev->rChild = nPtr;
        }
    }
    else{
        if(cur->info >= ele)
            return insert(cur->lChild, cur, ele);
```

```
            else
                    return insert(cur->rChild, cur, ele);
        }
    }
```

The following figure illustrates insertion of a node with value 8.

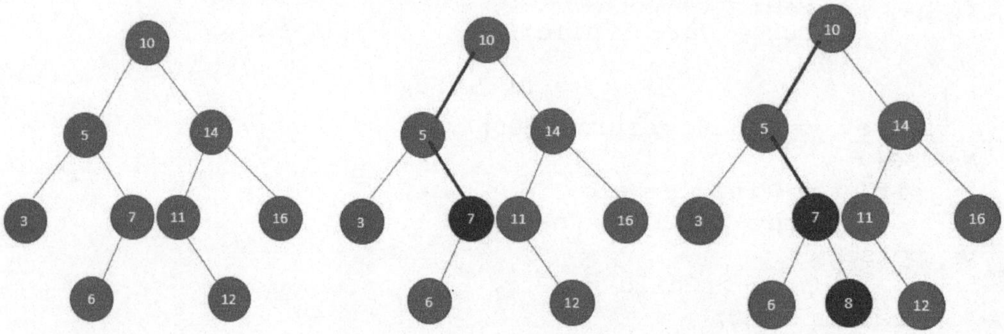

Given Binary search tree　　Find the anchored node　　Insert the node as the right child of the anchored node.

Deletion of a node from a Binary Search Tree: Unlike insertion, deletion of a node from a binary search tree may experience three different scenarios as defined below.

Case-1: The node to be deleted is a leaf node.

In this scenario, the node to be deleted is a leaf node. We first search for the node to be deleted. After locating the node, we simply disconnect the node from its parent as shown in the figure.

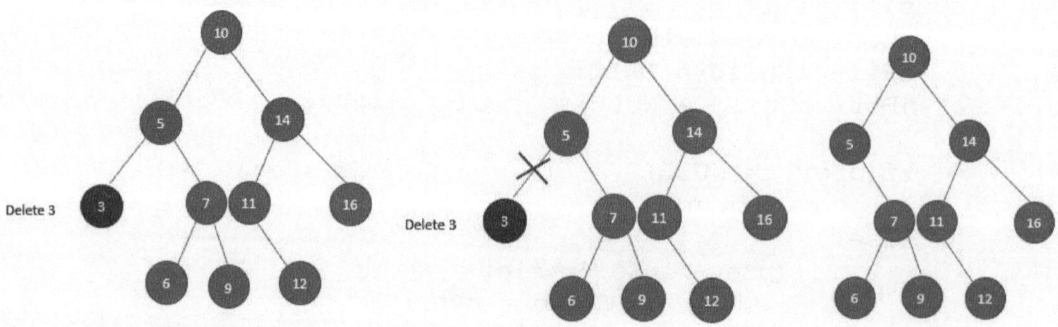

Find the node to be deleted　　Delete the node　　After deleting the node

Case-2: The node to be deleted has 1 child.

In this scenario, the node to be deleted has only one child. Depending on whether the node to be deleted is a left child or the right child, the child of the deleted node is connected as either as left child or the right child to the parent of the delete node. If the node to be deleted is the left child of its parent, after deleting the node, the child of the deleted node is connected as the left child of the parent of the deleted node. Likewise, if the node to be deleted is the right child of its parent, after deleting the node, the child of the deleted node is connected as the right child of the parent of the deleted node. The figures below illustrate the deletion process.

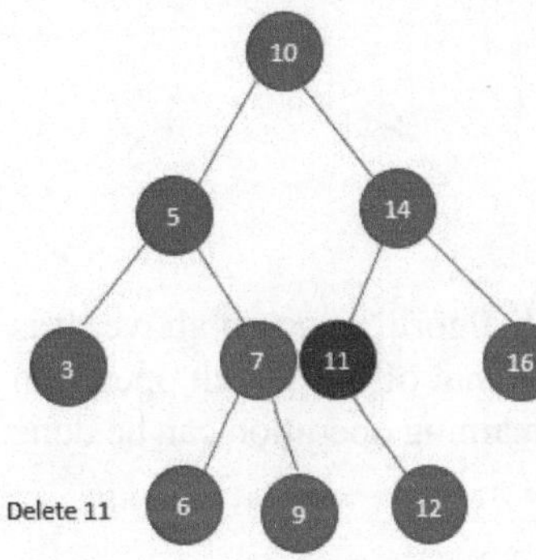

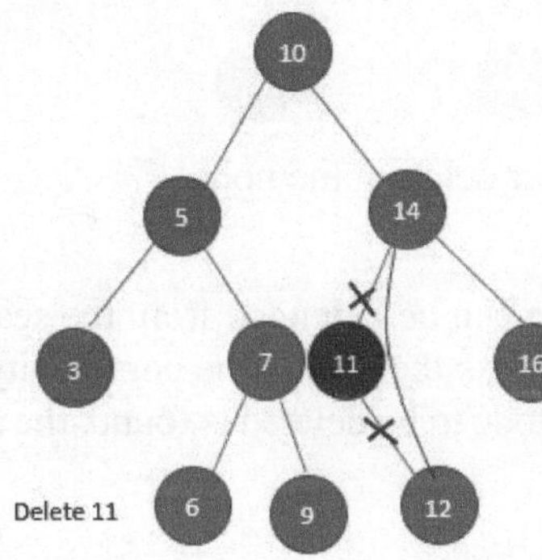

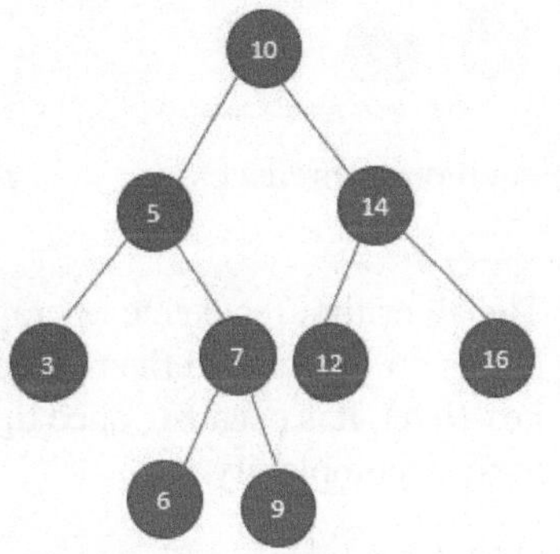

Find the node to be deleted | Link the parent node to the child node | After deleting the node

Case-3: The node to be deleted has 2 child nodes.

In this scenario, the node to be deleted has both the left child and the right child. In such a case, we can proceed in two ways.

1. Replace the node to be deleted by the largest node of its left subtree (i.e., inorder predecessor), or
2. Replace the node to be deleted by the smallest node of its right subtree (inorder successor), or

The following figures illustrate step by step procedure of deleting a node with two child nodes using the first approach.

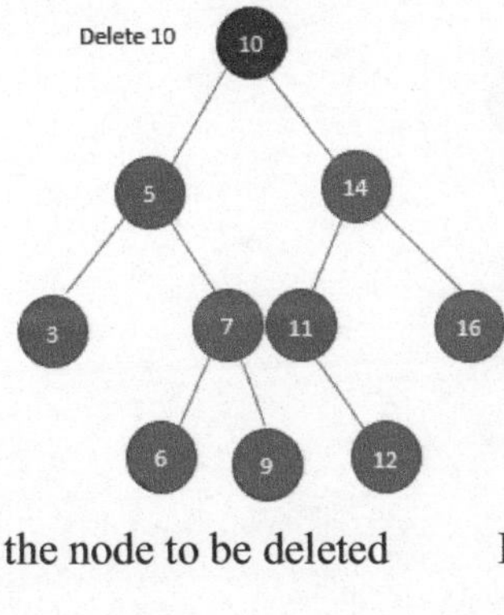

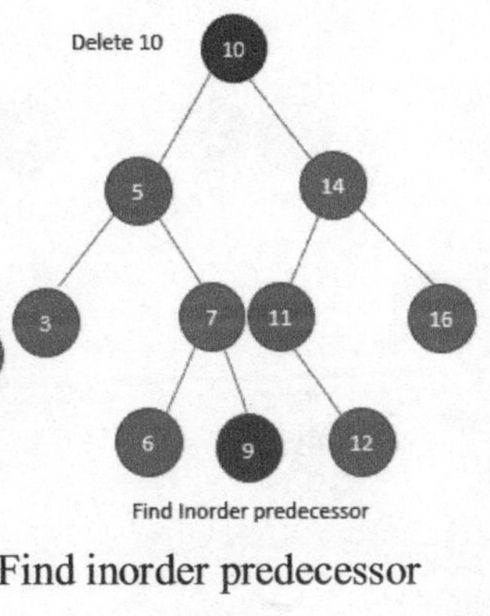

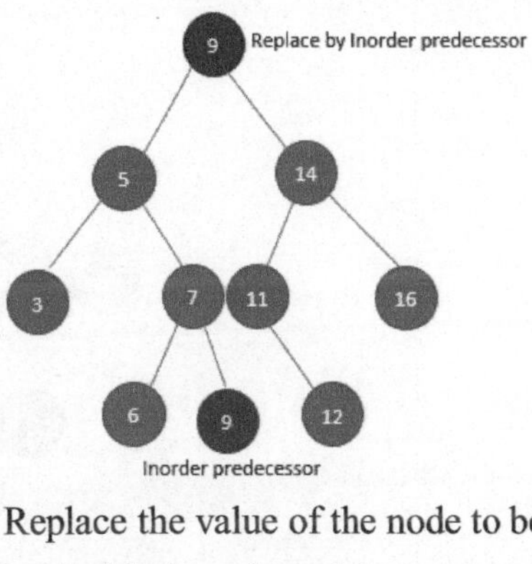

Find the node to be deleted | Find inorder predecessor | Replace the value of the node to be deleted with the value of the predecessor

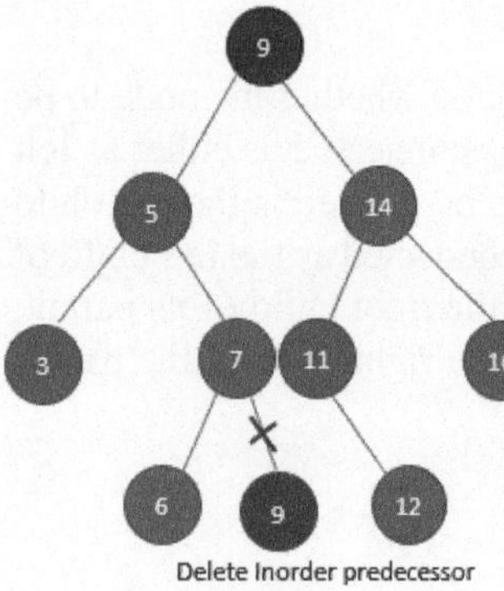

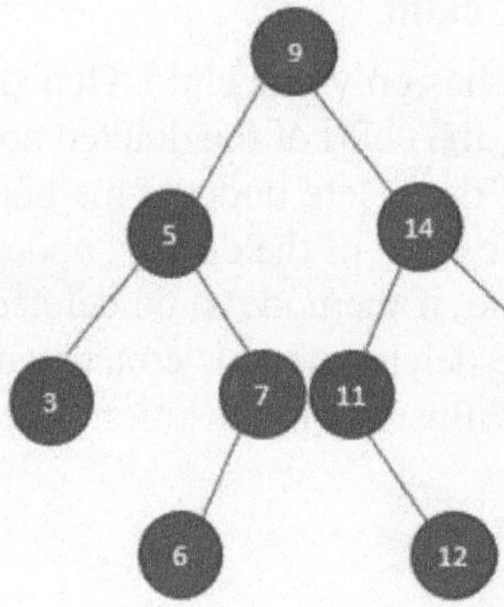

Delete inorder predecessor After deleting the node

The algorithm for delete operation can be extended from the search algorithm given above. It is left as an exercise to the reader. It has the same time complexity as that of the search operation i.e., $O(h)$. It is because, once the node to be deleted is found, the remaining operation can be done in $\theta(1)$ complexity.

3.3.6 Expression Tree

Given an infix expression, an expression tree is a special binary tree in which internal nodes represent operator, and leaf nodes represent operand of their parent node. The binary tree given below shows the expression tree of the infix expression $2 * (3 + 4)/2 + (4 - 3)$. Inorder traversal of an infix expression gives *infix expression*. Postorder traversal will provide *postfix expression.* Similarly, preorder traversal will provide the *prefix expression*.

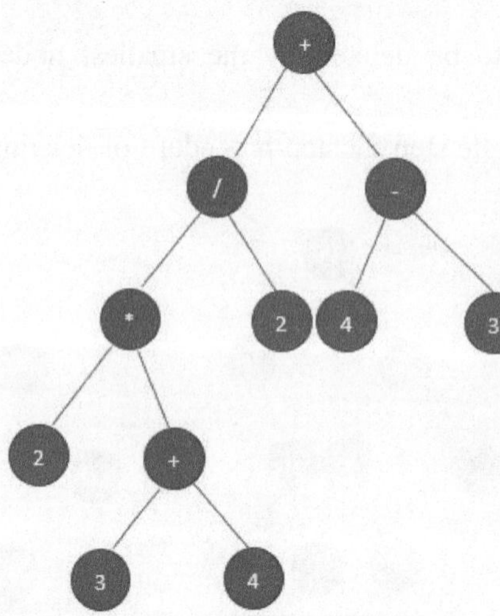

Construction of an expression tree is generally done using postfix expression, as it simplifies parsing the expression and identifies the operators and their corresponding operands. In the simplest approach, it can be two steps process.

1. Convert the infix expression to its corresponding postfix expression.
2. Construct expression tree from the postfix expression.

The algorithm for converting an infix expression to its postfix expression is discussed in Unit II. It is based on the *Shunting Yard Algorithm* proposed by *Edsger Dijkstra*. Given a postfix expression of an infix expression, the following algorithm constructs the corresponding expression tree.

```
Algorithm: Construct Expression Tree
Input: Postfix Expression
Output: Expression tree
Stack S //Create an empty Stack

//Scan the postfix expression
token = nextToken(postfix expression)
WHILE(token! = EoF) // token not equal to end of the expression
        new = newNode() // Create a new node
        new-> info = token
        new-> lChild = NULL
        new-> rChild = NULL

        // if the token is an operand
        IF (isOperand(token) == TRUE) THEN
            S.push(new)
        ELSE // if the token is an operator
            popped_elemet = S.pop()
            new-> rChild = popped_element
            popped_elemet = S.pop()
            new-> lChild = popped_element
            S.push(new)
        END IF
END WHILE
root = S.pop() // Only the root will be present in the stack
return(root)
END
```

The executon of the above algorithm is illustrated using an example postfix extression 234+*2/43-+.

Postfix	Token	Stack	Step	Expression tree
234+*2/43-+				
34+*2/43-+	2	2	7	
4+*2/43-+	3	23	7	
+*2/43-+	4	234	7	
*2/43-+	+	2 +	9	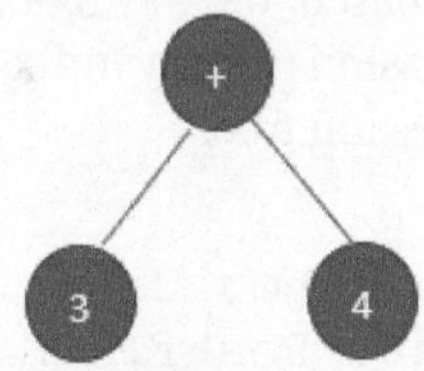
2/43-+	*	*	9	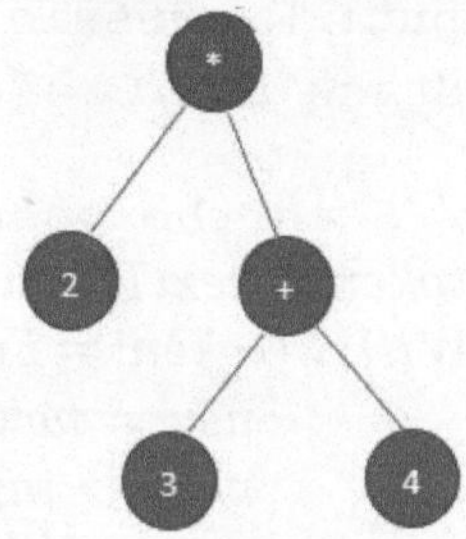
/43-+	2	*2	7	
43-+	/	/	9	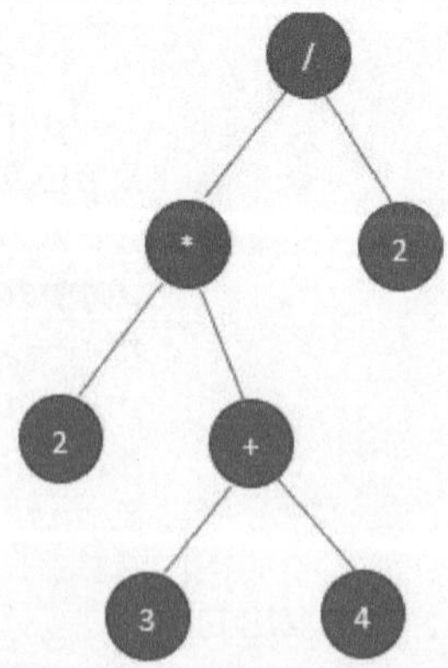
3-+	4	/4	7	
-+	3	/43	7	

Postfix	Token	Stack	Step	Expression tree
+	-	/-	9	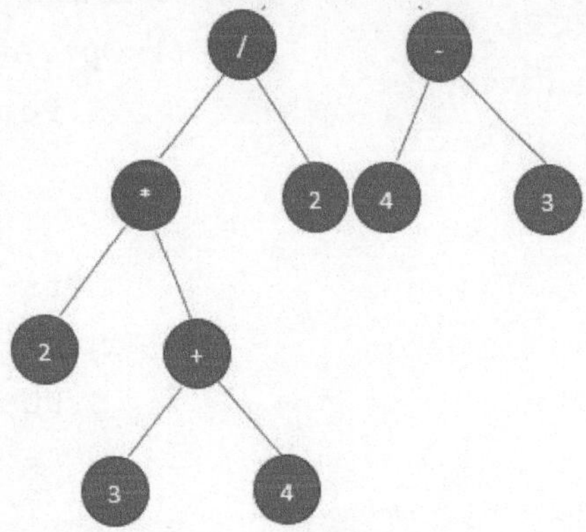
	+		9	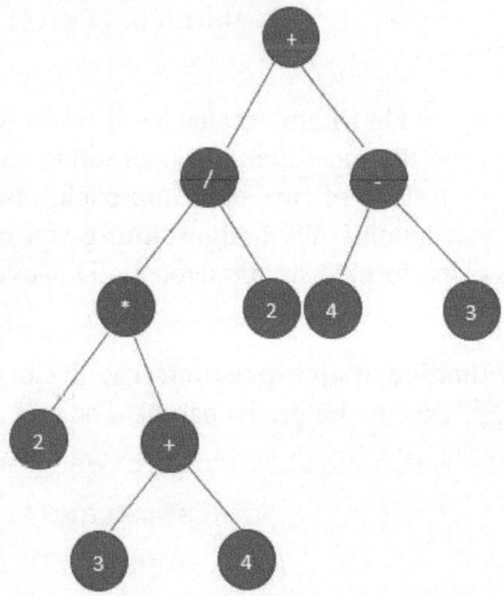

The program for the above algorithm can be defined as follows.

```
struct node * expreesionTree(char postfix[], int n){
        int i;
        <ADT > STACK S; //Appropriate Stack ADT should be used
        struct node *nPtr, *r, *l;
        for(i=0; i<n; i++){
           nPtr = (struct node *)malloc(sizeof(struct node))
           nPtr->info=postfix[i];
           nPtr->lChild=NULL;
           nPtr->rChild=NULL;
```

```
            // Assume that isOperand() exists
            if(isOperand(postfix[i])==1){
                  S.Push(nPtr);
            }
            else{
                  nPtr->rChild = S.Pop();
                  nPtr->lChild = S.Pop();
                  S.Push(nPtr);
            }
      }
      return(S.Pop());
}
```

Since the algorithm iterates for n times where n is the number of tokens in the postfix expression and at the most two pop operations (constant time), the time complexity of the algorithm is $O(n)$. Instead of two steps approach, reader can modify the *infix to postfix conversion algorithm* (or Shunting Yard Algorithm) given in Unit II so that postfix conversion and tree construction are performed simultaneously. However, it is left as an exercise to the reader.

Evaluation of an expression tree: It can be noted from the figure that a child operator node will always execute before its parent. The root node executes at the last.

```
int evaluationExpressionTree(struct node *rPtr){
      if(isOperand(rPtr->info))
            return rPtr->info;
      else
            return   evaluate(   evaluationExpressionTree(rPtr-
>lChild), evaluationExpressionTree(rPtr->lChild),rPtr->info);
}
```

The recurrence equation of the above function can be defined as $T(n) = 2T\left(\frac{n}{2}\right) + 1, T(1) = 1$. If we expand the expression, we get $T(n) = n + 1 = O(n)$. The figures below illustrate step by step execution of the above algorithm over an expression tree.

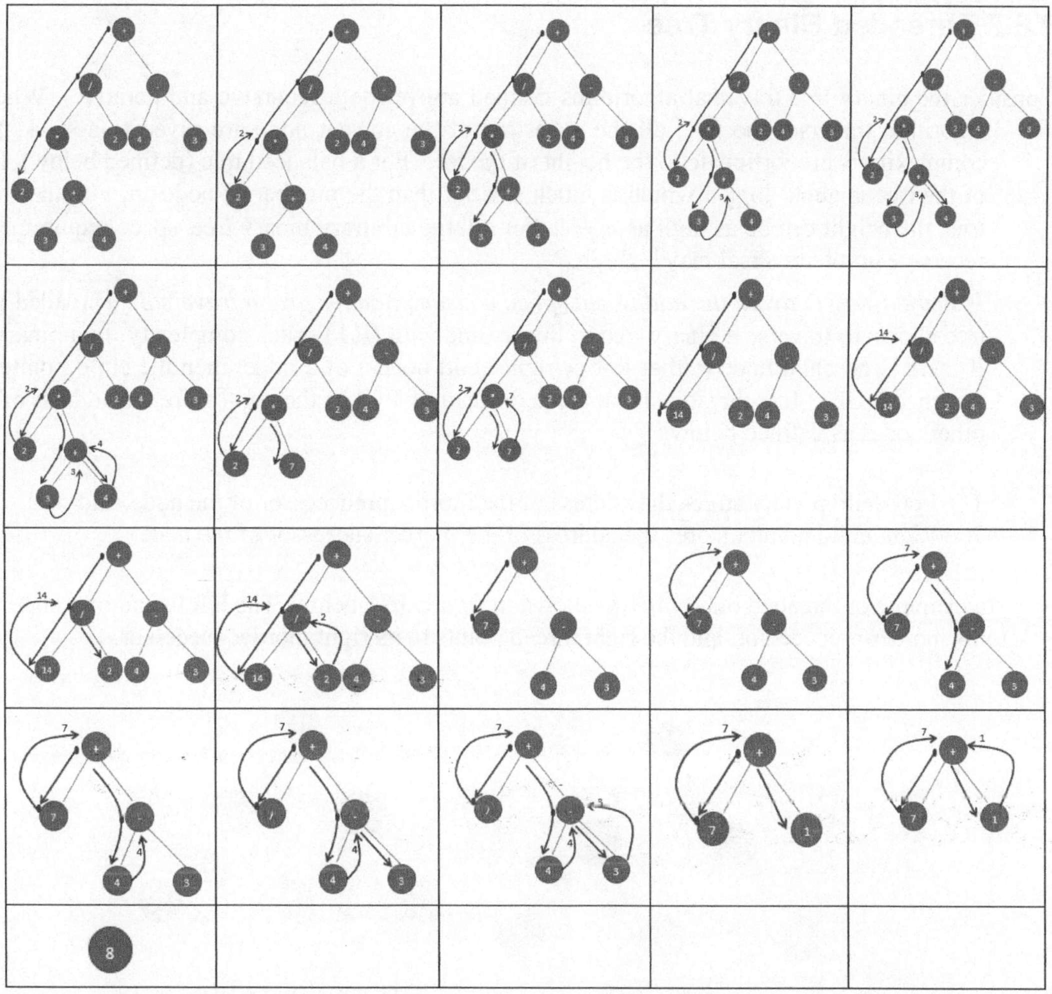

A tree may be implemented in various ways, using array, linked list or by allocating dynamic space for each node and connecting the allocated memory spaces.

3.3.7 Threaded Binary Tree

Consider the binary tree traversal algorithms defined above (both recursive and iterative). When the algorithm traverses the tree, all the ancestors of the current node are saved to a stack. Space complexity is proportionate to the height of the tree. For a balanced tree (defined below), height of the tree is about $\log_2 n$ which is much smaller than the number of nodes n. For an arbitrary tree, the height can be as high as $n - 1$. For a large arbitrary binary tree, space requirement for recursive graph traversal may be high.

Is there a way to avoid the additional space consumption for graph traversal? Threaded binary tree allows to traverse a binary tree in linear time with $O(1)$ space complexity. In a binary tree, if there is no child node (either left or right child nodes) of a node, then the child pointers are assigned NULL. In a threaded binary tree, instead of NULL, they will store the address of some other nodes as defined below.

1. Left child pointer stores the address of the inorder predecessor of the node, and
2. Right child pointer stores the address of the inorder successor of the node.

An example of threaded binary tree is shown in figure 3.21 below. The left thread of a node points to its inorder predecessor, and the right thread points to its right inorder successor.

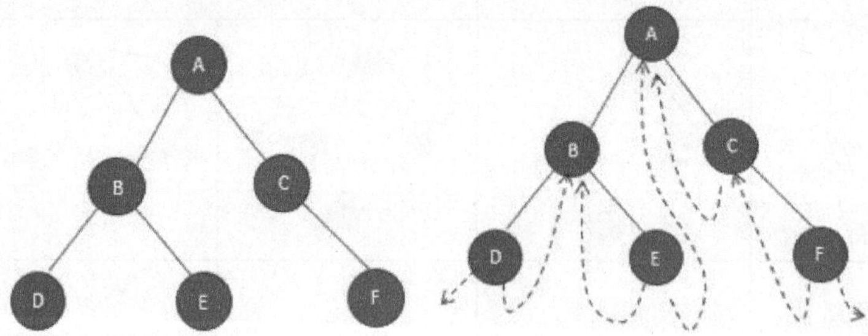

Binary Tree Threaded Binary Tree

Figure 3.21: An example of a threaded binary tree

While implementing a threaded binary tree, there should be a way to distinguish a thread pointer from its child pointer. Generally, every node will maintain two thread flags (one for left child and another for right child). If the left child pointer is a thread, then the flag is set to true, otherwise false. Similarly, if the right child pointer is a thread, then the flag is set to true, otherwise false. A typical node structure looks like the following.

```
struct node{
        char info;
        struct node *lChild;
        bool lChildThread; // set to true if it is a thread
        struct node *rChild;
        bool rChildThread; // set to true if it is a thread
};
```

From a node in a threaded binary tree, for an inorder traversal, it simply follows the inorder successor node. Given a node in a threaded binary tree, the following function returns its inorder successor.

```
struct node *inorderSuccessor(struct node *ptr){
        if(ptr->rChildThread==True)
            return ptr->rChild;
        else{
            ptr = ptr->rChild;
            while(ptr->lChildThread != True){
                    ptr = ptr->lChild;
            }
            return ptr;
        }
}
```

We can call the above function n times starting from leftmost node i.e., D to generate inorder traversal of the tree. However, there is one problem. To start calling the above function, we should first go to the leftmost node of the tree. To generalize the above function, we add one more node known as *thread head*. This head node connects the root of the tree as its left child, and its right pointer as thread pointing to itself as shown in the figure 3.22. The left child thread of the leftmost node points to the head node. And, the right child thread of the right most node points to the head node. With this head node, if we call the above inorder successor function $n + 1$ times from the head, we will get inorder traversal of the tree. It basically means, starting from head, find inorder successor till the successor is the head node itself.

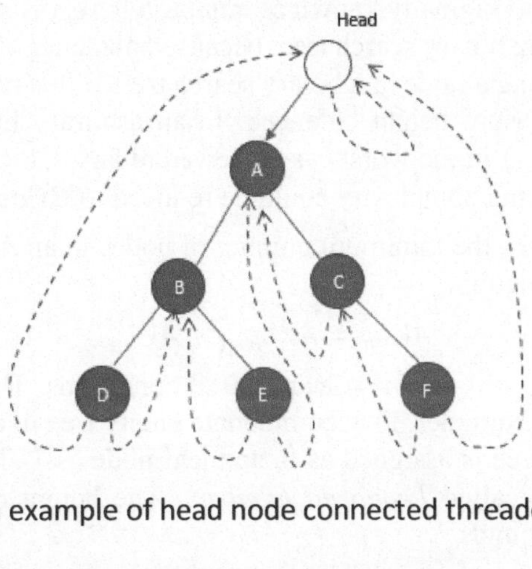

Figure 3.22: An example of head node connected threaded binary tree

In the similar manner, by exploiting the threads, we can also perform pre-order and post-order traversals. The detail is left as an exercise.

3.4 HEIGHT BALANCED TREE

A binary tree is said to be height balanced tree, if all the nodes in the tree are height balanced. A node is height balanced, if the height of its left child and right child differs not more than 1. Following figures show example of height balanced binary tree and height unbalanced binary tree. The difference between the height of the left child and right child is referred to as *balancing factor (BF)*. Figure 3.23 shows examples of height balanced and height unbalanced trees.

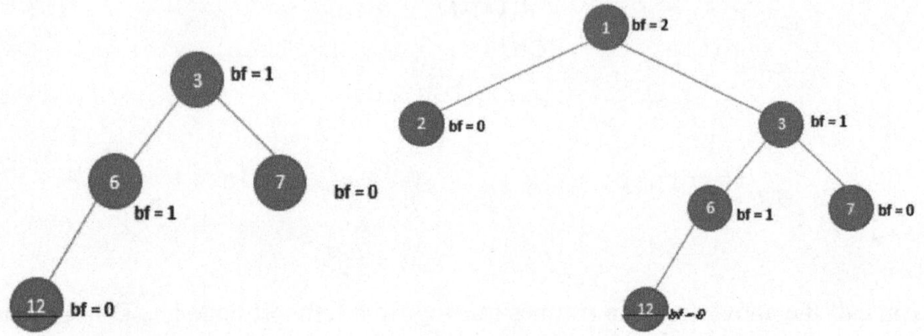

Height Balanced Height Unbalanced

Figure 3.23: Examples of height balanced and height unbalanced trees.

3.4.1 AVL Tree

AVL (Adelson Velsky Landis), originally known as *admissible tree*, is a height balanced binary search tree. It is a self-balancing binary search tree, because balancing of the tree is ensured at the time of creation. Upon inserting a node in a binary search tree, if it is not balanced, the affected nodes will be rearranged to ensure height balanced. In an arbitrary binary search tree, search time complexity could be $O(n)$ in the worst case (skewed binary search tree). By maintaining height balance, its worst-case time complexity could be reduced to $O(\log_2 n)$.

As the definition suggests, the minimum number of nodes in an AVL tree can be defined by the following recurrence equation.

$$AVL_h = AVL_{h-1} + AVL_{h-2} + 1$$

where $h \geq 0$, and $AVL_0 = 0$, $AVL_1 = 1$ are initial conditions. Though height of a leaf node is assigned 0 in the above examples, to accommodate empty tree in the recurrence equation above, the height of an empty tree is assigned as 0, and leaf node as 1. The numbers generated by this recurrence equation are called *Leonardo numbers*. The height of an AVL tree with n nodes satisfies the following bounds.

$$\log_2(n+1) \leq h \leq 1.44 \log_2(n+2) - 0.328$$

From the above bound, it can be seen that the height of an AVL tree is bound by $O(\log_2 n)$. Further, the percentage difference between the lower bound and upper bound is about 44%. That means, its worst case search scenario will need 44% more number of comparisons than that of its best-case search scenario.

Insertion and Construction of AVL Tree: To understand the self-balancing concept in AVL tree, let us consider construction of a binary search tree considering the following data sequence – 1, 2, 3. The following sequence of trees shows the resultant binary search tree after inserting them.

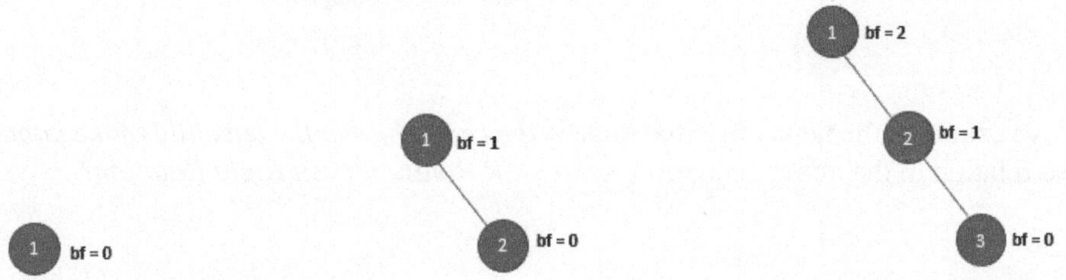

(a) Insert 1. It is balanced. (b) Insert 2. It is balanced. (c) Insert 3. It is unbalanced.

The (c) tree is unbalanced after inserting the node 3. We can make this tree balanced by rotating the nodes such that node 1 becomes the left child of the node 2 as shown below.

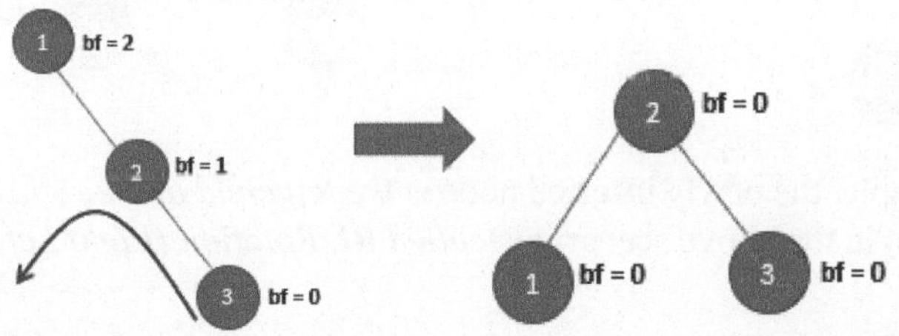

In the above example, the newly inserted node is *the right child of the right child of the unbalanced node*. The rotation in the above scenario is *called RR Rotation (Right Right Rotation)*.

Like above, let us now assume that a binary search tree is constructed from the sequence – 3, 2, 1, and obtained the below skewed binary tree.

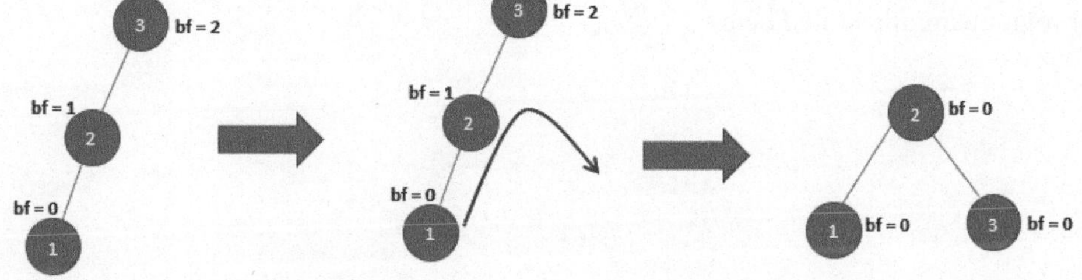

In the above example, the newly inserted node is *the left child of the left child of the unbalanced node*. The rotation in the above scenario is *called LL Rotation (Left Left Rotation).*

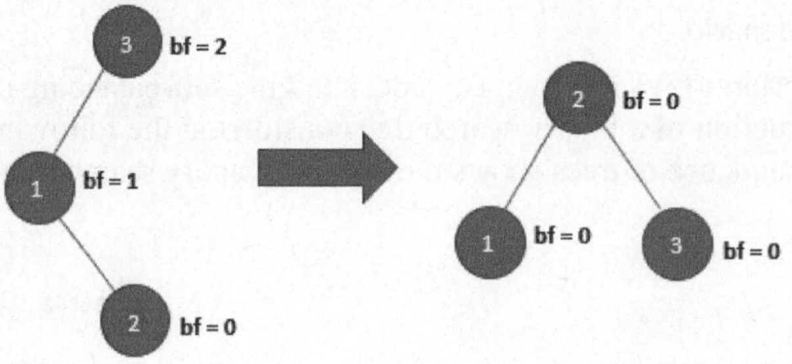

In the above example, the newly inserted node is *the right child of the left child of the unbalanced node*. The rotation in the above scenario is *called LR Rotation (Left Right Rotation).*

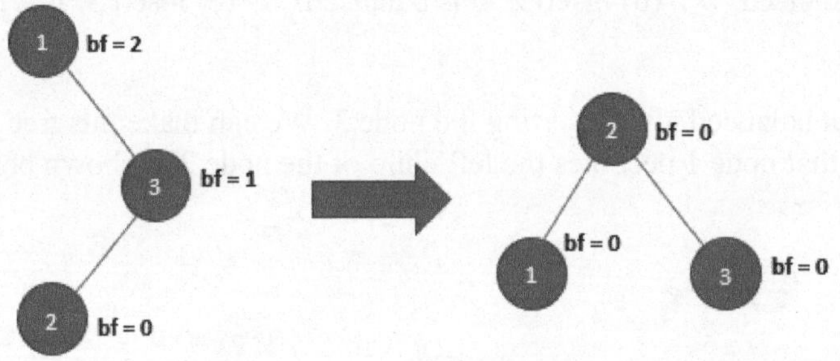

In the above example, the newly inserted node is *the left child of the right child of the unbalanced node*. The rotation in the above scenario is *called RL Rotation (Right Left Rotation).*

Generalization: After understanding the above four cases, the four rotations described above are formally defined below. Let T be an AVL tree. Let T_A be the A rooted balanced subtree.

Right Right Rotation (RR Rotation): It is also referred to a *left rotation.* Let B be the right child of the node A. The T_A subtree is initially balanced. The case of RR rotation happens when the node A is unbalanced after inserting a new node in the right subtree of B. The scenario and the output after rotation are illustrated below.

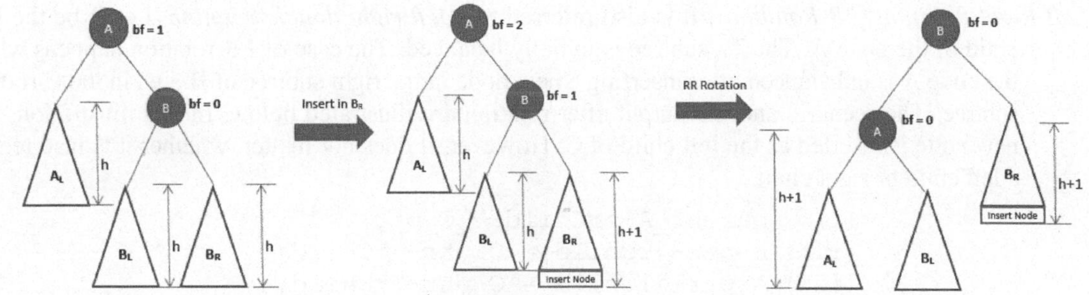

Balanced AVL subtree Unbalanced after insertion in B_R Perform RR Rotation

Let `parent_A` denotes the address of the parent node of the node A. Let `A_ptr` and `B_ptr` be the addresses of the nodes A and B. Assuming that node A is the right child of its parent, the sequence of operations to be performed in RR rotation is shown as follows.

```
1. parent_A->rChild = B_ptr;
2. A_ptr->rChild = B_pr->lChild;
3. B_ptr->lChild = A_ptr;
```

If node A is the left child of its parent, the step 1 should be changed to `parent_A->lChild = B_ptr;`.

Left Left Rotation (LL Rotation): It is also referred to a *right rotation.* Let B be the left child of the node A. The T_A subtree is initially balanced. The case of LL rotation happens when the node A is unbalanced after inserting a new node in the left subtree of B. The scenario and the output after rotation are illustrated below.

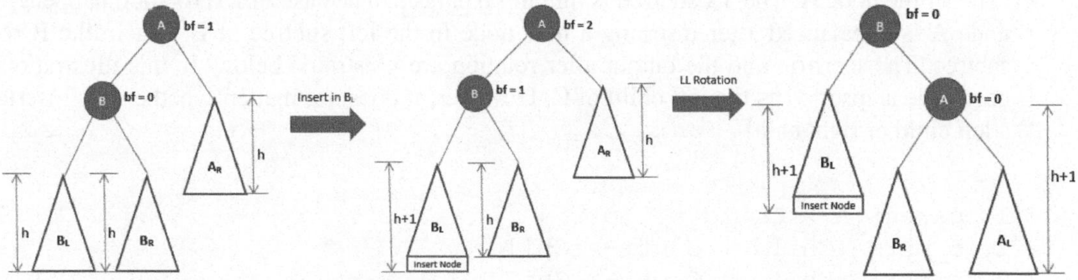

Balanced AVL subtree Unbalanced after insertion in B_L Perform LL Rotation

Assuming that node A is the right child of its parent, the sequence of operations to be performed in RR rotation is shown as follows.

```
1. parent_A->rChild = B_ptr;
2. A_ptr->lChild = B_pr->rChild;
3. B_ptr->rChild = A_ptr;
```

Left Right Rotation (LR Rotation): It is also referred to a *left right double rotation.* Let B be the left child of the node A. The T_A subtree is initially balanced. The case of LR rotation happens when the node A is unbalanced after inserting a new node in the right subtree of B, i.e., in the C rooted subtree. The scenario and the output after rotation are illustrated below. In this illustration, the new node is inserted as the left child of C. However, it does not matter, whether it is inserted as a left child or right child.

```
(i)   parent_A->rChild = C_ptr;
(ii)  B_ptr->rChild = C_ptr->lChild;
(iii) A_ptr->lChild = C_ptr->rChild;
(iv)  C_ptr->lChild = B_ptr;
(v)   C_ptr->rChild = A_ptr;
```

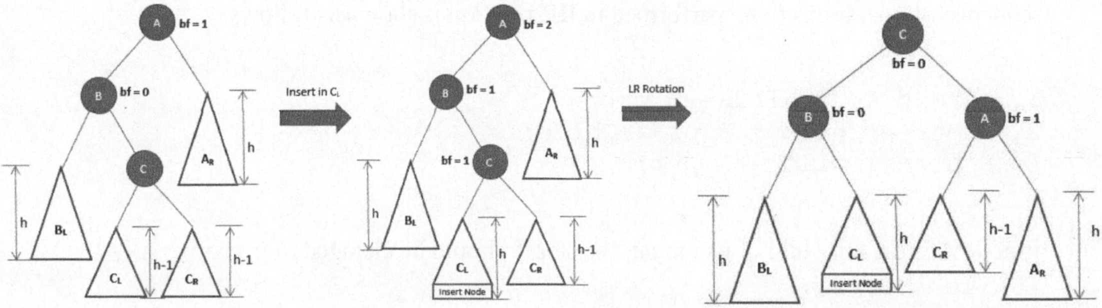

Balanced AVL subtree Unbalanced after insertion in B_R Perform LR Rotation

Right Left Rotation (RL Rotation): It is also referred to a *right left double rotation.* Let B be the right child of the node A. The T_A subtree is initially balanced. The case of RL rotation happens when node A is unbalanced after inserting a new node in the left subtree of B, i.e., in the B rooted subtree. The scenario and the output after rotation are illustrated below. In this illustration, the new node is inserted as the left child of C. However, it does not matter, whether it is inserted as a left child or right child.

```
1. parent_A->rChild = C_ptr;
2. B_ptr->lChild = C_ptr->rChild;
3. A_ptr->rChild = C_ptr->lChild;
4. C_ptr->lChild = A_ptr;
5. C_ptr->rChild = B_ptr;
```

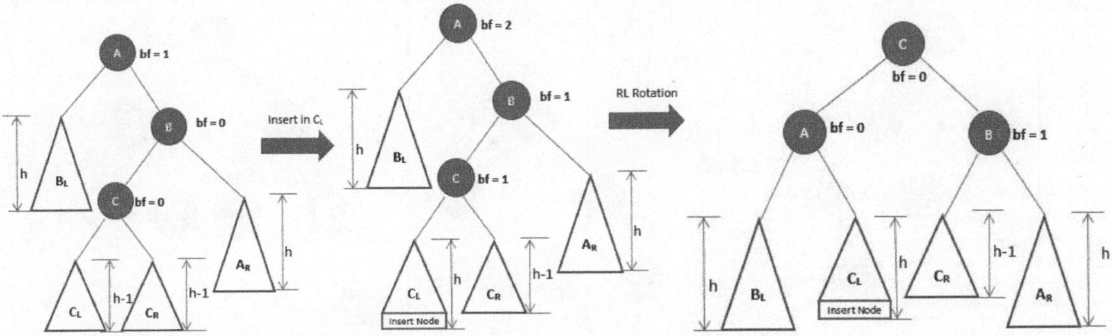

Balanced AVL subtree   Unbalanced after insertion in B_L Perform RL Rotation

Construct AVL tree of the sequence - 3 5 4 7 9 8 2 1

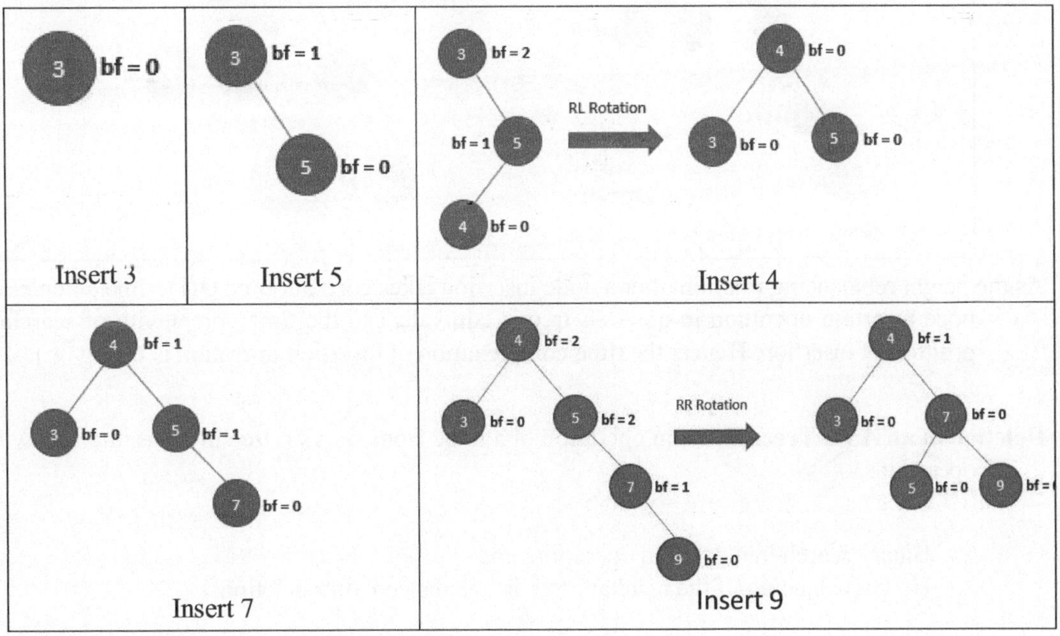

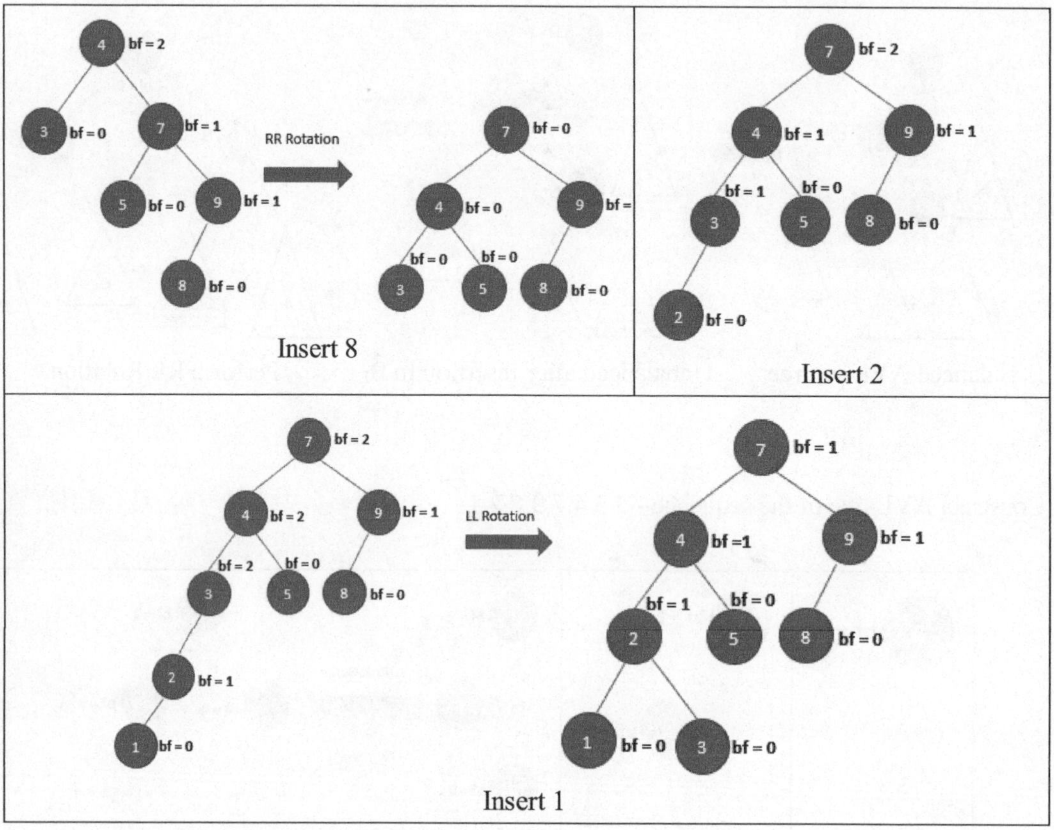

As the height rebalancing rotation after a node insertion takes constant time $O(i)$, time complexity of a node insertion operation in an AVL tree is equivalent to the time complexity of searching the position of insertion. Hence, the time complexation of insertion operation is $O(\log_2 n)$.

Deletion in an AVL Tree: Deletion operation of a node from an AVL tree involves the following two operations.

1. Binary search tree deletion operation, and
2. Height balancing, if the resultant tree is unbalanced after deletion.

As seen in binary search tree deletion, there may be three cases – *deleting a leaf node*, *deleting a node with single child node*, and *deleting a node with two child nodes*.

Case 1: Delete a leaf node

Consider the following AVL tree shown in (i) and delete the leaf node with value 20. After applying binary search tree delete operation, we get the tree shown in (ii) which is an unbalanced tree.

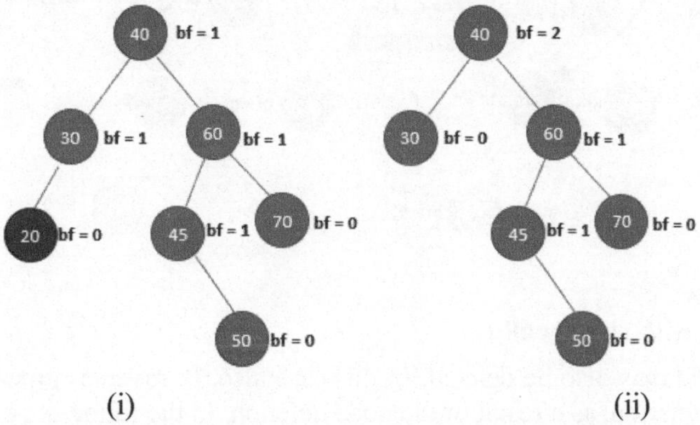

After deleting the node, check the balance factor of the nodes starting from its parent node up till the root. If a node violating the height policy is found, stop traversing up at that node. It can be seen that node 40 does not satisfy the balance policy. Since the parent node of the deleted node lies in the left subtree of the violated node, it goes to the right subtree and locate the grandchild node with larger height. If both the grandchild nodes have same height, then select one of the grandchild nodes. However, to make the algorithm deterministic, select the right grandchild as it explores the right subtree of the violating node. In the given example, consider node 45, as it has a larger height than the node 70. Considering the violating node (40), its right child (60), and its grandchild (45), perform RL rotation to balance the height, as shown below.

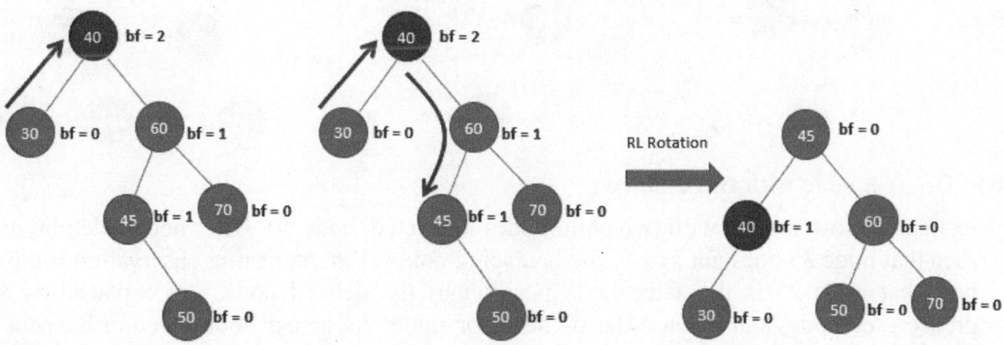

In the above example, the height of the left grandchild (45) is larger than the right grandchild (70). In case, heights are same, consider the right grandchild as shown below. Assume that node 70 has its child nodes.

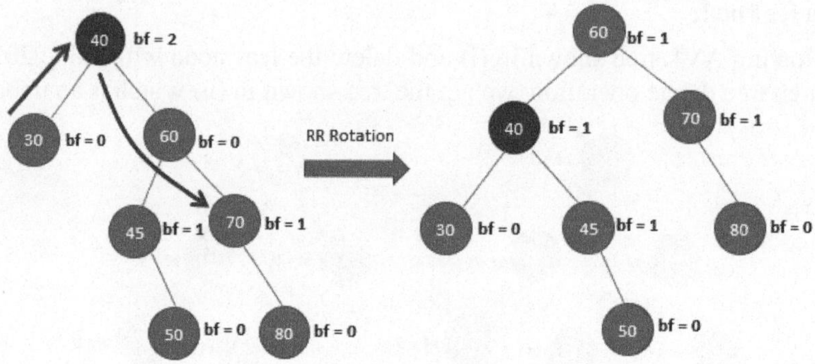

Case 2: Delete a node with single child

A node with single child may also be deleted. In this case also, It traverses upward to find nodes with balance policy violation, as a result of the node deletion. In the following example, after deleting node 30, it can be seen that node 40 does not satisfy the balance policy. It then finds the appropriate child and grandchild nodes in the right subtree, and perform appropriate rotation (RL rotation in this example).

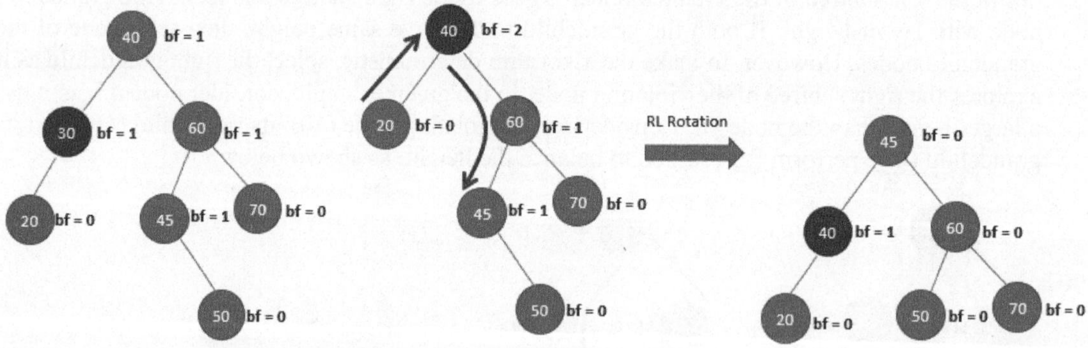

Case 3: Delete a node with two children

In the example below, a node with two child nodes is deleted, node 40. After node deletion, it can be seen that node 35 does not satisfy the balancing policy. An interesting observation can be made here that node 35 is the same node position of the deleted node, i.e., replaced by inorder predecessor node, and deleted the predecessor node. As actual node deletion happens at the predecessor node, the height of the left subtree of the intended node for deleting (node 40) may be reduced by 1, resulting in balance violation at the same node position. Therefore, checking for the balance violating node should start from the same position i.e., node 35. It may be noted in the case 1 and 2 that checking may start from the parent node.

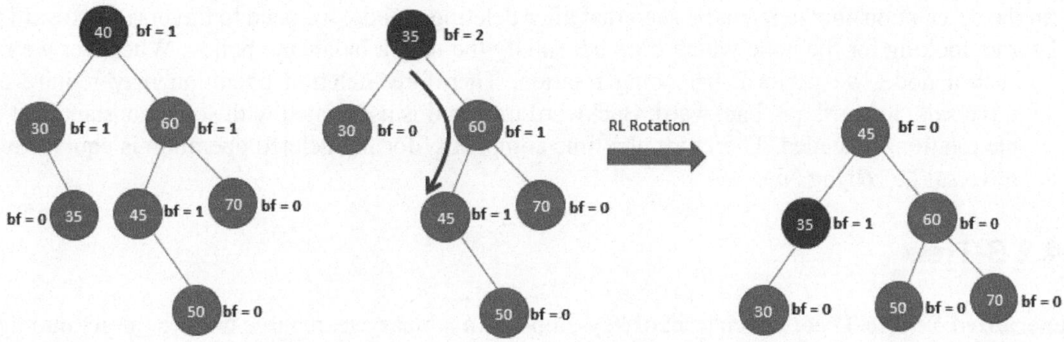

Multiple rotations: From the examples above, it is evident that deletion of a node in an AVL tree may result in reducing the height of its parent node, grandparent node and so on up to the root. It may have cascading effects and in turn causes some upward nodes to root in violating the height policy. As a result, we could need to perform more than one height balancing rotations. Every rotation may result in another balance violation. Therefore, after deleting a node, we would need to check the balance factor of upward nodes. An example of such a situation is illustrated below. Deletion of node 30 results in two rotations.

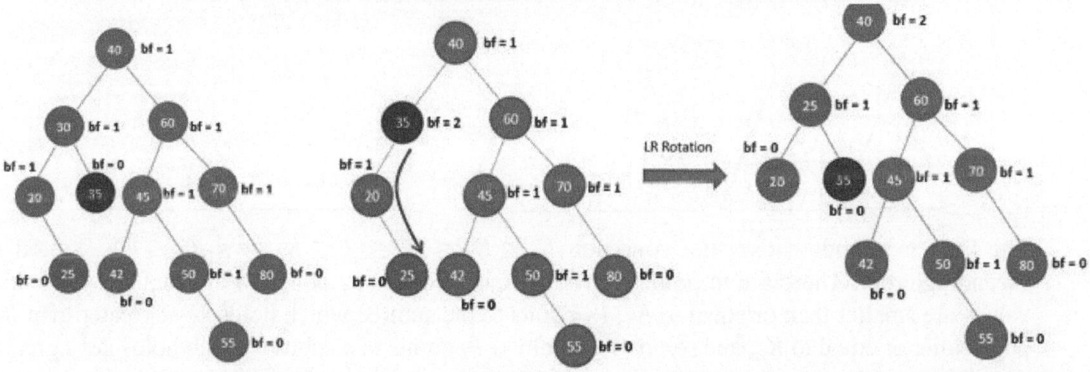

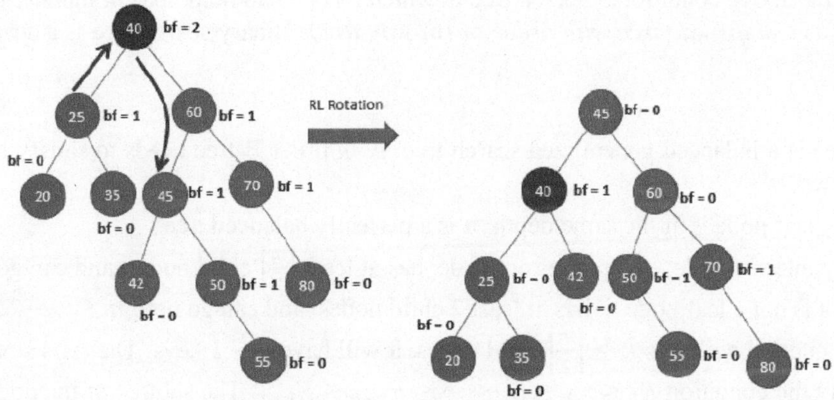

From the description above, it can be seen that after deleting a node, we need to traverse up toward the root looking for the node which does not satisfy the height balancing policy. Whenever we find such a node, we perform balancing rotation. Therefore, deletion operation may require two traversals, forward and backward. Backward traversal is associated with some constant cost for the rotation, if needed. Therefore, the time complexity for the deleted operation is equivalent to traversal i.e., $O(\log_2 n)$.

3.4.2 B-Tree

Generalized Search Tree: Given a set of keys, a node in a binary search tree divides the set into three subsets – *the key in the dividing node, the keys which are less than or equal to the dividing key,* and *the keys which are greater than the dividing key*. In other word, binary search tree is a 2-way search tree, because a node in the tree splits a key space into two – a *lesser half* and a *greater half.*

Let us generalized the above condition and allows a node to hold upto $m-1$ number of keys in sorted order and upto m number of pointers as defined below.

$$K_1 \le K_2 \le K_3 \le \cdots \le K_{m-2} \le K_{m-1}$$

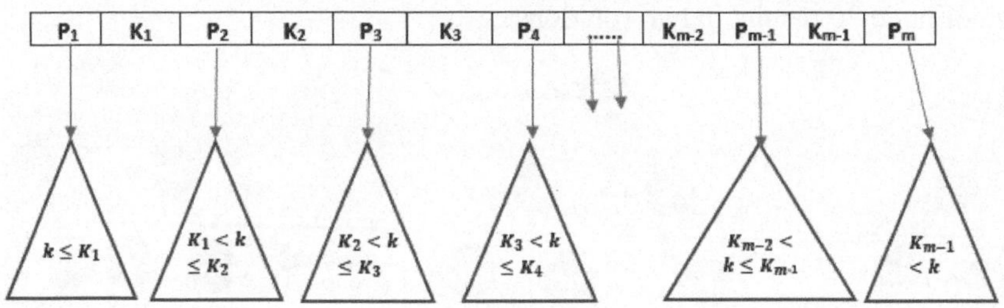

The keys in a node satisfy the condition $K_1 \le K_2 \le K_3 \le \cdots \le K_{m-2} \le K_{m-1}$ i.e., sorted in ascending order. There are m pointers. The leftmost pointer P_1 points to the subtree whose key values are smaller than or equal to K_1, P_2 points to the subtree which holds keys greater than K_1, but smaller or equal to K_2, and so on. So, a pointer P_i points to a subtree which holds keys greater than K_{i-1}, smaller than or equal to K_i, as shown above. All the nodes in a generalized search tree satisfy the above conditions. Such a tree in which a node can hold upto m number of subtrees is known as a *multi-way tree with order m (m-way tree).* Binary search tree is a search tree with order 2.

B-Tree: B-tree is a balanced generalized search tree. A m order B-tree needs to satisfy the following properties.

1. Every leaf node is at the same depth. It is a perfectly balanced tree.
2. Every internal node, except the root node, has at least $\left\lceil \frac{m}{2} \right\rceil$ child nodes, and can go upto m.
3. If root is not a leaf node, it has at least 2 child nodes, and can go upto m.
4. If an internal node has $k \ge \left\lceil \frac{m}{2} \right\rceil$ child nodes, it will have $k-1$ keys. The keys stored in a node satisfy the condition $K_1 \le K_2 \le K_3 \le \cdots \le K_{k-2} \le K_{k-1}$. The subtree of the node pointed by the pointer P_i between K_{i-1} and K_i holds the keys larger than K_{i-1} and smaller than or equal to

K_i. Though the equal to condition is associated with left subtree, it can be associated with left or right subtree.

5. Every node, except the root node, has at least $\left\lceil \frac{m}{2} \right\rceil - 1$ key elements, and can go upto $m - 1$.

An example of B-tree with order 5 is shown below for the elements 10, 15, 20, 30, 35, 40, 45, 46, 50, 50, 53, 55, 60, 60, 64, 68, 70, 72, 75, 80, 80, 86, 87, 90, 95. It can be seen that every node, except root, has at least 2 keys (i.e., minimum $\left\lceil \frac{5}{2} \right\rceil - 1 = 2$ keys). All the keys are arranged in ascending order. All the leaf nodes are at the same level. All the internal nodes have minimum $\left\lceil \frac{5}{2} \right\rceil = 3$ child nodes. The root has two child nodes (it is allowed as a special case).

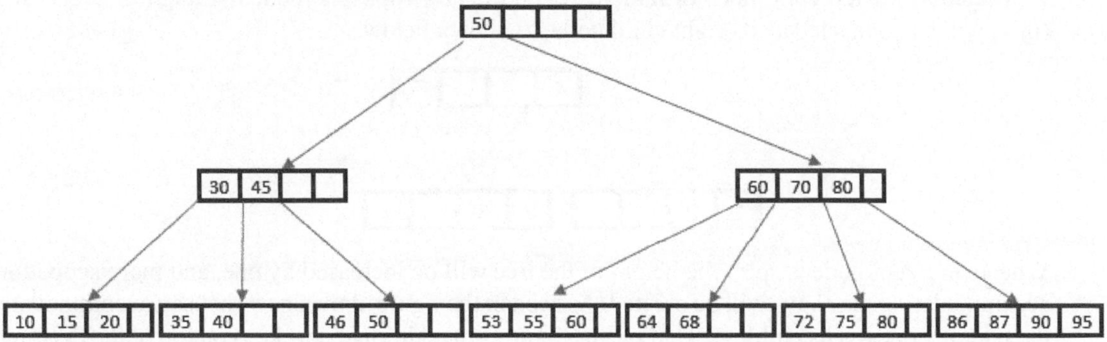

From the definition of a B-tree, the following theorems can be derived.

Theorem 11: The maximum number of keys that can be accommodated in a m-way B-tree of height $h \geq 0$ is $m^{h+1} - 1$.

Theorem 12: The minimum number of keys that can be accommodated in a m-way B-tree of height $h \geq 0$ is $2\left(\left\lceil \frac{m}{2} \right\rceil^{h} - 1\right) + 1$.

Theorem 13: The minimum height $h \geq 0$ of a m-way B-tree with n nodes is $\lfloor \log_m n \rfloor$.

Theorem 14: The maximum height $h \geq 0$ of a m-way B-tree with n nodes is $\left\lfloor \log_{\left\lceil \frac{m}{2} \right\rceil} \left(\frac{n-1}{2}\right) \right\rfloor + 1$.

Construction of B-tree: Given a sequence of keys – 4 1 6 8 2 7 2 9 10 3 4 11 18 15 20 17 16, let us try to construct a B-tree of order 5 to understand the process of constructing a B-tree. Initially, the tree is empty. When the first key is inserted, a new node is created, and inserted the first key element 4 as shown in figure below.

As there are three free spaces, the next three key elements 1, 6, and 8 are inserted maintaining the ascending order as shown below.

Now, if we try to insert the next key element 2, as there is no free space, *the node is overflown*.

To accommodate the new element, this node will be split in the middle of 1, 2, 4, 6, 8 and obtained the division (1, 2), 4, (6, 8). The middle key element 4 will be inserted to the parent node of the original node. As there is no parent node, a new parent node will be created, and the new parent node will act as the root of the tree. The smaller half will be stored in the existing node, and a new node will be created for the larger half. The node holding the small half (1, 2) will be connected as the left child node of middle key in the new root. The node holding the larger half (6, 8) will be connected as its right child node, as shown below.

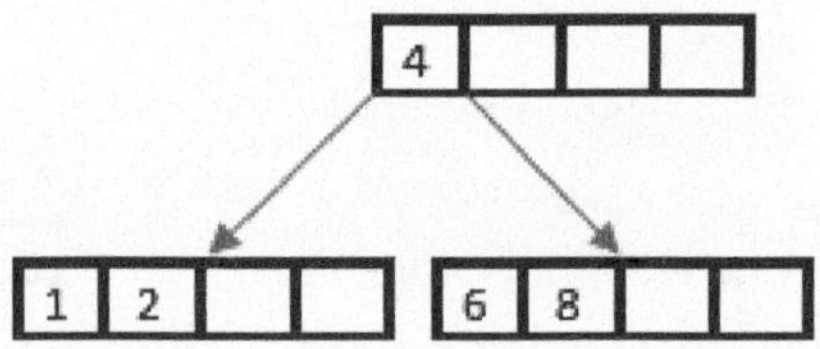

Whenever a root node is split, the height of the tree will be increased by one, and more scope for accommodating new keys will be created. As seen in the figure above, new root can accommodate three more nodes as its children. That means, $3(m-1)$ additional new keys on top of the existing free spaces. These three nodes will be created as a result of splits of the exiting nodes due to node *overflow*. This process can be seen in the subsequent insertions. For the next three elements 7, 2, and 9, there is no issue. They can be accommodated in the existing nodes as shown below.

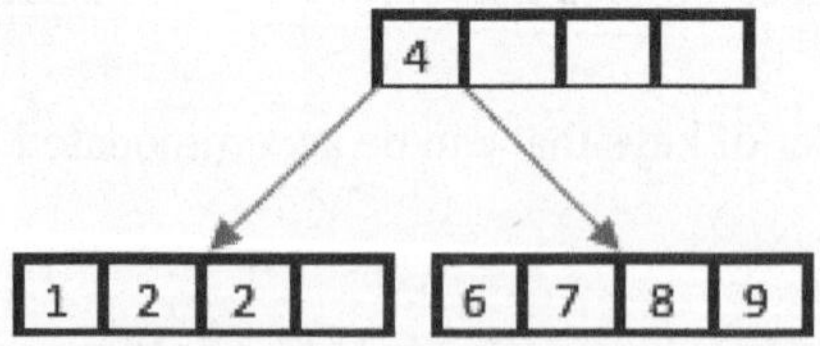

Now, if we attempt to insert the next element, then the second leaf node *overflows*.

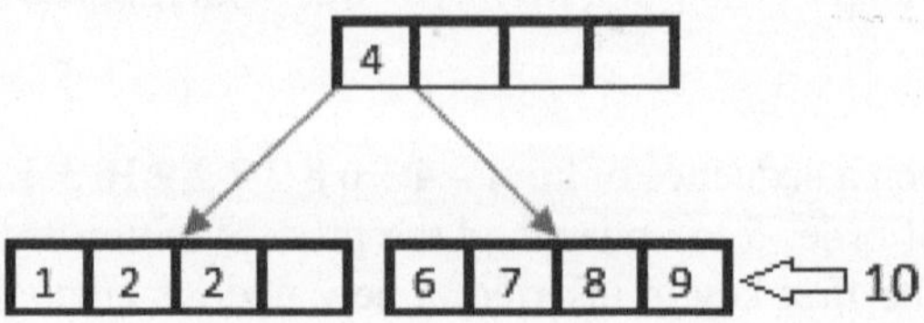

The keys in the overflowing node will be split in the middle as (6, 7), 8, (9, 10). As there is free space in the parent node, it will be inserted in the parent node. The smaller half will be stored in the existing node, and a new node will be created to hold the larger half keys. This new node will be connected as its right child node, as shown below.

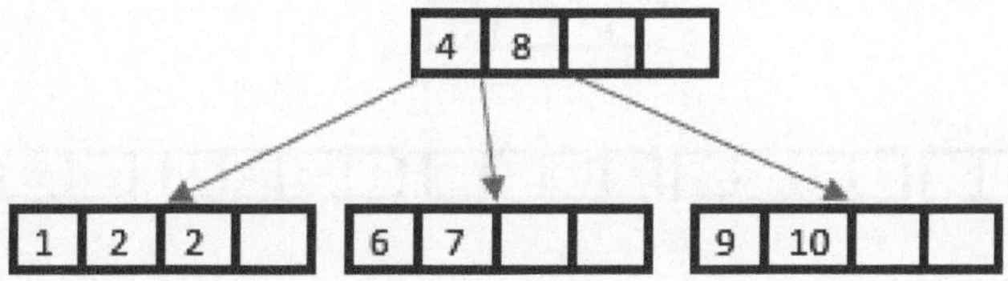

In the similar manner, the next key element 3 is inserted without any issue. But, there is overflow while attempting to insert the next element 4.

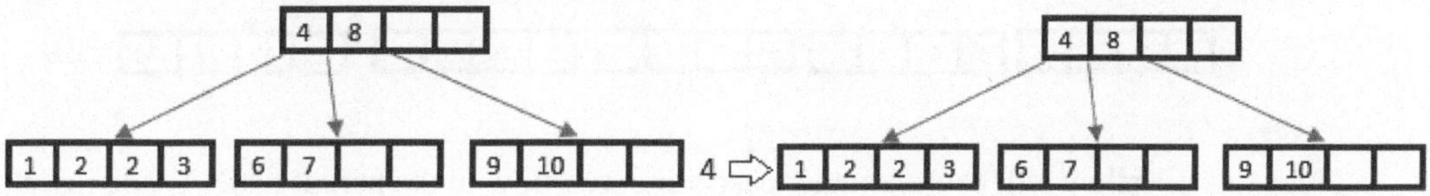

Insert 3 Overflow while inserting 4

Like above, the overflown node is split, and middle element is inserted in the parent node, as shown below.

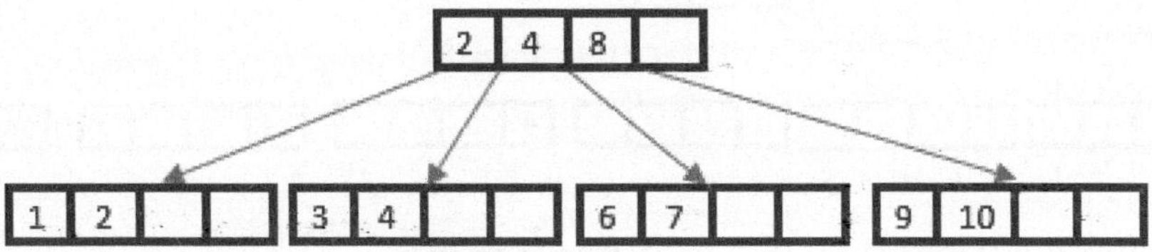

The next two key elements 11 and 18 are inserted without any issue. But, overflow happens while inserting 15.

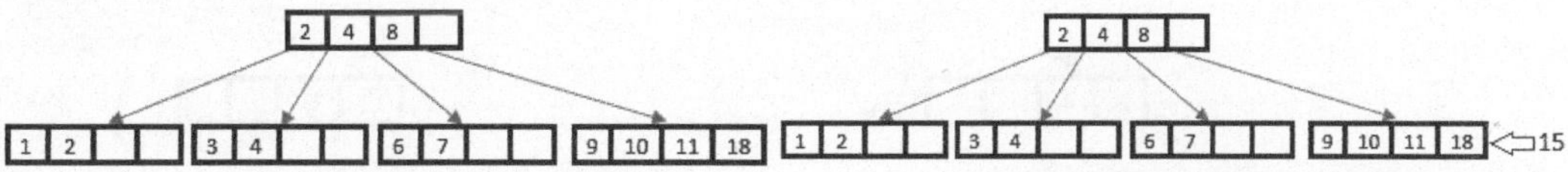

Insert 11 and 18 Overflow while inserting 15

Now, split the overflown node and insert the middle key element to the parent.

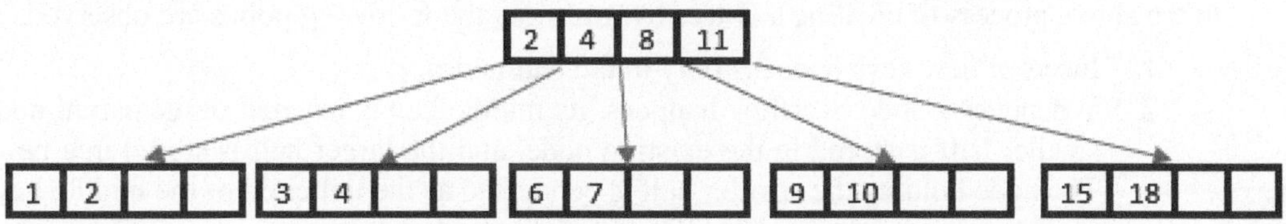

Next, insert 20 and 17 without any issue, but overflow while inserting 16.

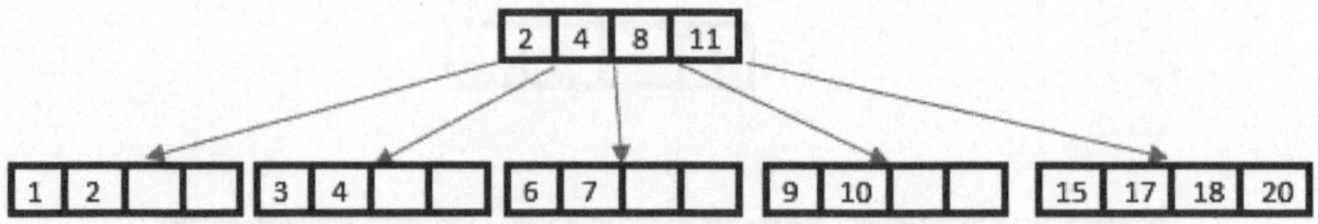

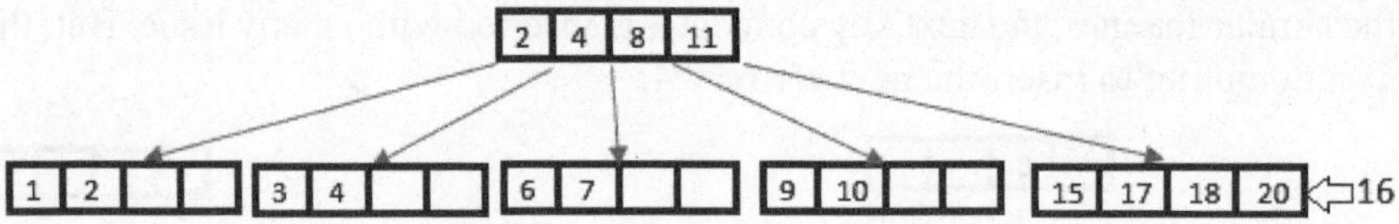

Now, this overflow will cause another cascading overflow in the parent node. While inserting 16, the keys in the node will be split into (15, 16), 17, (18, 20). The middle key 17 will be inserted in the parent node. However, the parent node is also full, and the parent node overflows. It will result in splitting of the parent node, and creating a new root node, as shown below. Whenever, a root node is split, the height of the tree will be increased by 1.

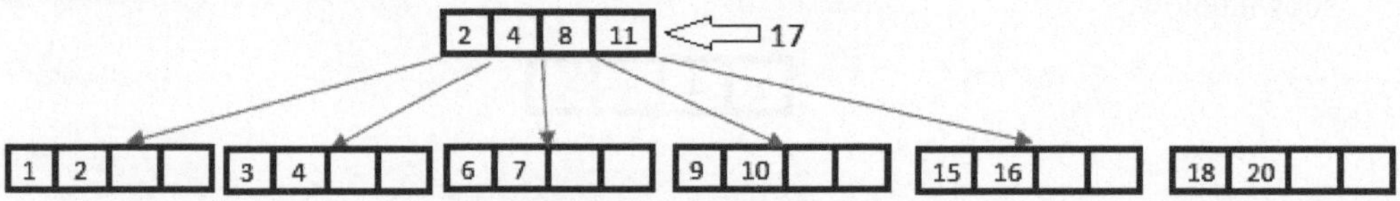

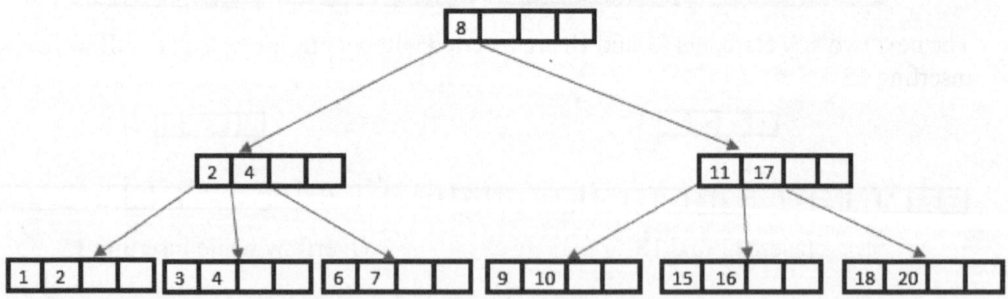

In the above process of creating a B-tree by insertion, the following points are observed.

1. Insert of new keys happens only in the leaf nodes.
2. Whenever a node overflow happens, its middle key is inserted in the parent node. The smaller half is stored in the existing node, and the larger half is stored in a new node. The node holding the smaller half is connected as the left child of the middle key in the parent node, and the larger half as the right child.
3. An overflow may cause subsequent cascading overflows to the parent nodes upto root node.
4. Whenever a root node is split, height of the tree will be increased by 1.

Deleting a node from a B-tree: While inserting a key in a B-tree, overflow of a node may happen. Likewise, while deleting a node from a B-tree, a node may experience underflow (number of keys lesser than the permissible numbers). Depending on the position of the key to be deleted, the following two cases may occur.

Case-1: Delete from a leaf node

If the key to be deleted is present in a leaf node, the key will be simply removed from the node. While removing the key, it may cause one of the following two scenarios.

Scenario -1: After removing the key, the node still has the minimum required number of keys. In such a scenario, there is no issue. It simply removes the key. No further action is needed.

Scenario -2: After removing the key, the node underflows i.e., the node has less than the required number of keys. In such a case, we will look at the preceding and succeeding siblings of the node, and perform one of the followings depending on the situation.

a) If one of the sibling nodes holds number of keys more than the required number, perform rotation of keys between the sibling node (smallest key of succeeding sibling is chosen, or largest key of preceding sibling is chosen), parent node (parent key of the deleting node and selected sibling node) and the deleting node, as shown below.

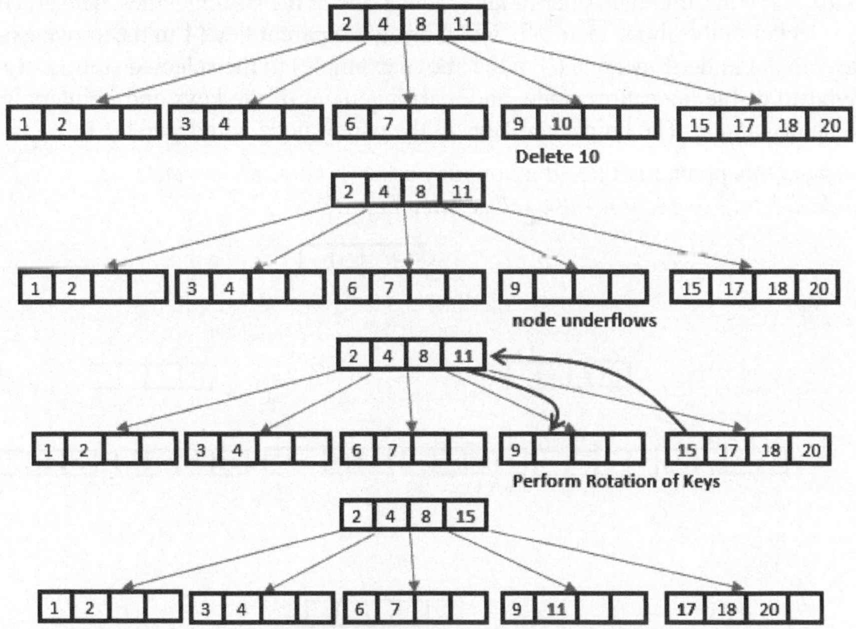

b) If both the sibling nodes hold minimum number of keys, perform merging of the deleting node, one of the sibling nodes, and the parent key, as shown below.

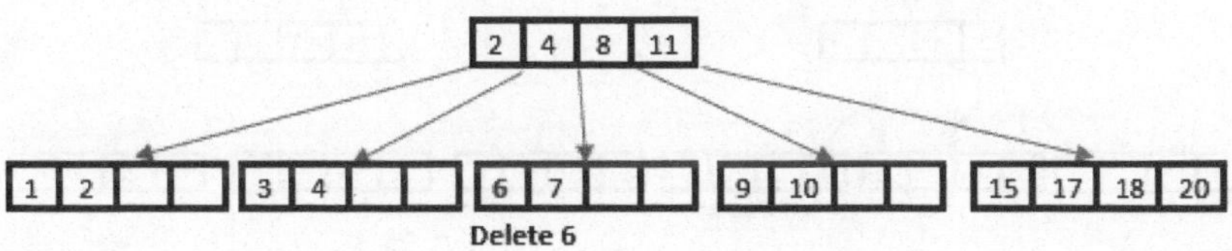

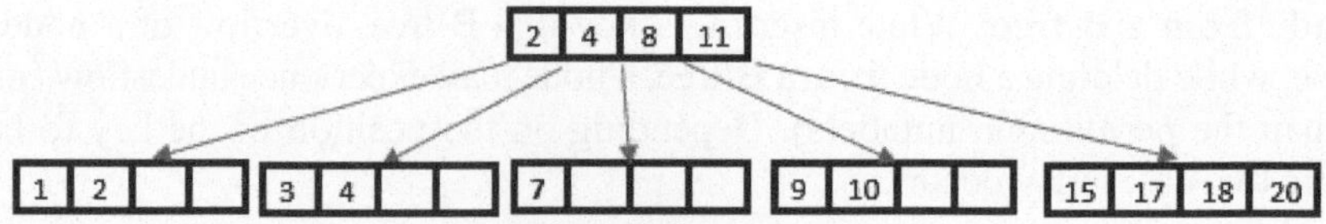

Node underflows

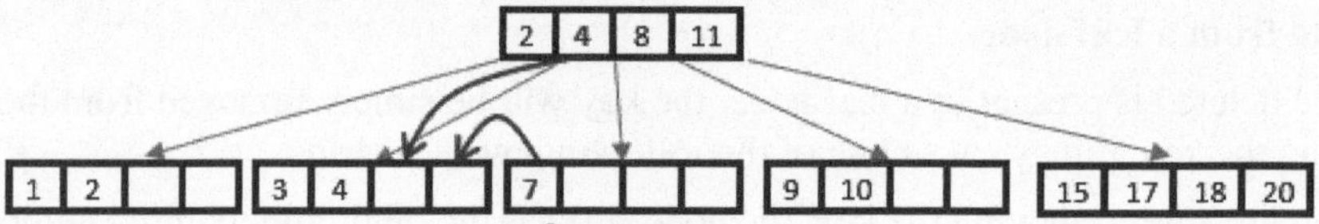

Perform merge

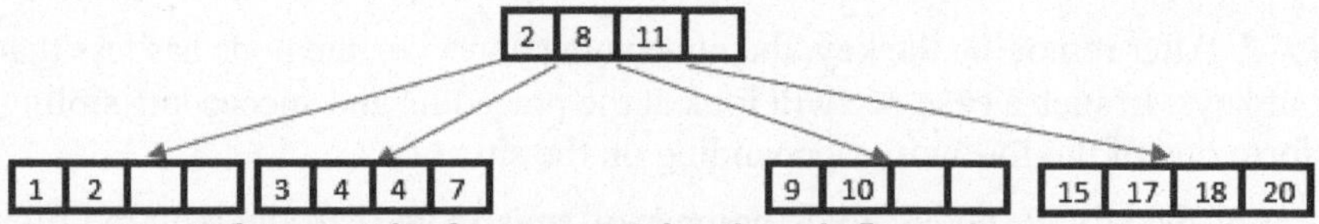

Delete parent key from parent, Delete the underflow node

It first deletes the node from the leaf node, and checks if underflow happens. If it underflows, check the number of keys in its preceding sibling and succeeding sibling nodes. If both the sibling nodes have minimum number of keys, select one of the sibling nodes. The preceding sibling node is selected in the above example. Now, bring the parent key (4 in the above example) and all the keys in the underflow node (7 in the above example) to the selected sibling. It results in physical removal of the underflow node, and rearrangement of the keys and pointers in the parent node, as shown above. The number of keys in the parent node is reduced by 1.

Now, at this point, another situation may arise. *What if the parent node underflows as a result of node deleting in a leaf node, as illustrated below?*

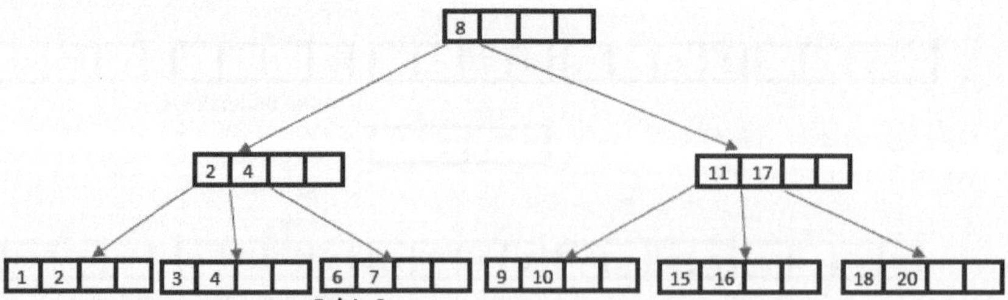

Delete 6

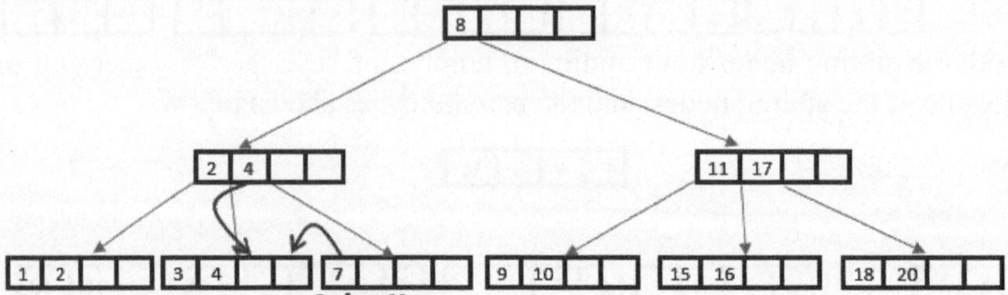

Perform Merge

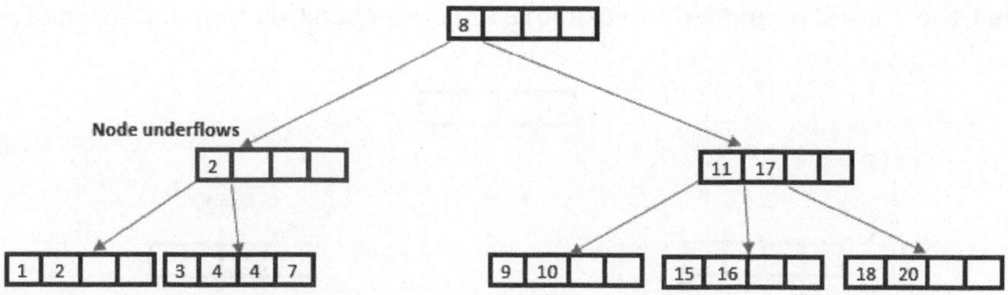

In the above example, the parent node underflows as a result of merging of keys. In this situation, we further perform rotation of keys like in situation 1 above, or merging of keys like in situation 2. In the above example, the sibling node also has minimum number of keys. Therefore, we perform merging of keys, and rearrangement of pointers. Such merging operation may further cause underflow in the parent node and subsequent underflows till its root node. If subsequent underflow reaches root node, it will result in a reduction in the height of the tree by 1, as shown below.

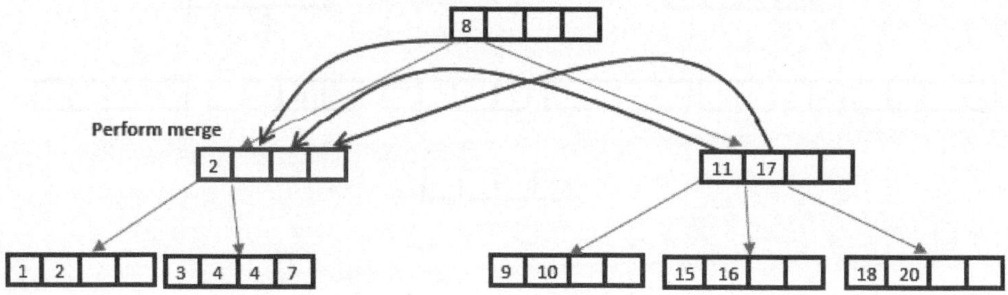

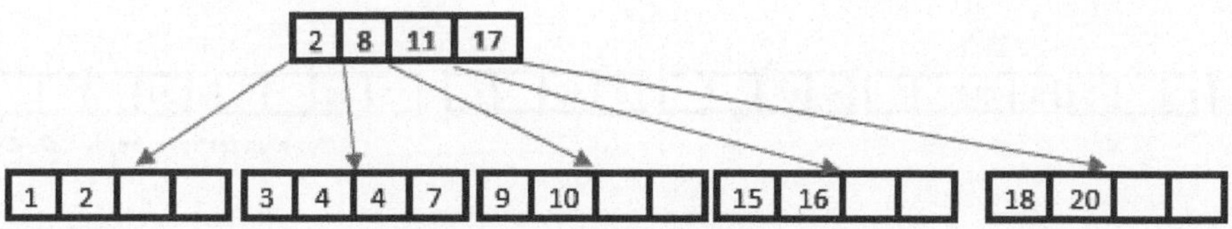

Height of the tree is reduced by 1.

Case -2: Delete from an internal node

Deletion of a key from an internal node is similar to deletion of a node with two child nodes in binary search tree. We will replace the key to be deleted by either its inorder predecessor or inorder successor key. Therefore, actual physical deletion happens in the deletion of its inorder predecessor or inorder successor key in the leaf node. Depending on which leaf node (inorder predecessor node or inorder successor node) holds larger number of keys, a replacement key will be selected. If both the leaf nodes hold minimum number of permissible keys, one of the nodes can be selected. Once the replacement key is deleted from the leaf node, the deletion process as given in Case – 1 will be applied. An example of delete operation from internal node is illustrated below.

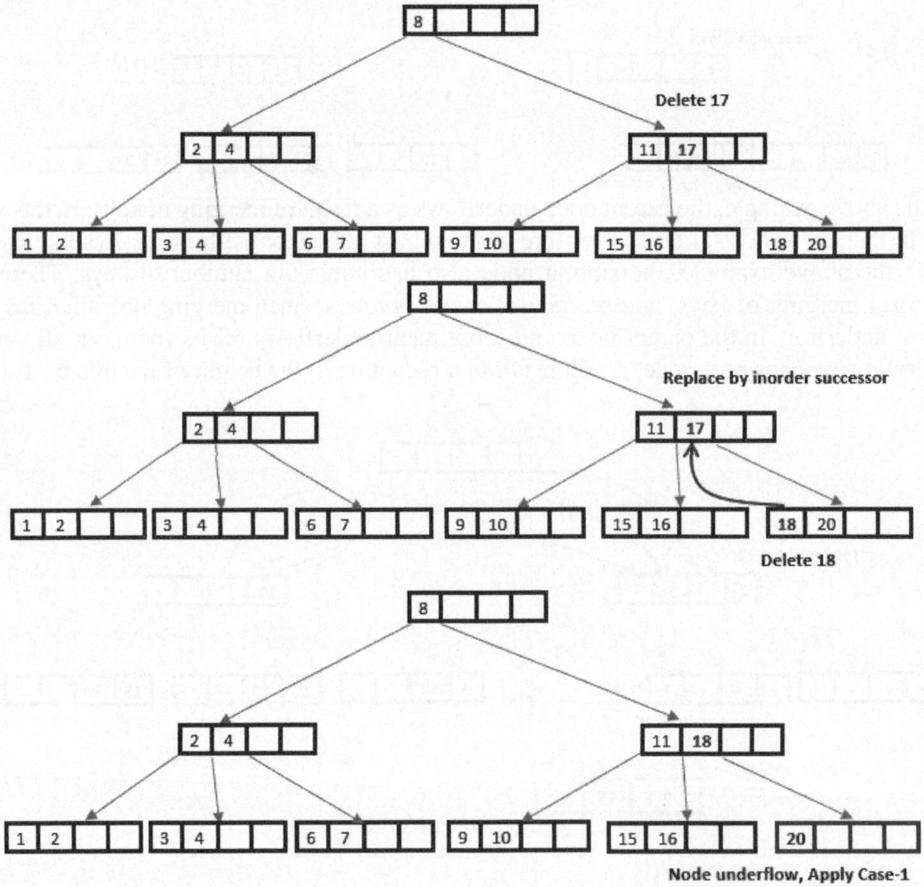

3.4.3 B+ Tree

In B-tree, the keys are distributed across all the nodes in the tree. However, in B+ tree, all the keys are stored in leaf node, and the index values (not the actual key) are stored in the non-leaf nodes. B+ tree has similar rode structural properties like that of the B-tree, plus additional properties. The node properties of a B+ tree of order m are defined below.

a) Every leaf node is at the same depth. It is a perfectly balanced tree.
b) Every internal node, except the root node, has at least $\left\lceil \frac{m}{2} \right\rceil$ child nodes, and can go upto m.
c) If root is not a leaf node, it has at least 2 child nodes, and can go upto m.
d) If an internal node has $k \geq \left\lceil \frac{m}{2} \right\rceil$ child nodes, it will have $k - 1$ index values. The index values stored in a node satisfy the condition $K_1 \leq K_2 \leq K_3 \leq \cdots \leq K_{k-2} \leq K_{k-1}$. The subtree of the node pointed by the pointer P_i between K_{i-1} and K_i holds the index/key values larger than K_{i-1} and smaller than or equal to K_i. Though the equal to condition is associated with left subtree, it can be associated with left or right subtree.
e) Every node, except the root node, has at least $\left\lceil \frac{m}{2} \right\rceil - 1$ key/index elements, and can go upto $m - 1$.
f) All the key elements are stored in the leaf nodes, and non-leaf nodes store the index elements.
g) All the leaf nodes are connected linearly (possibly through a doubly linked list.)

The figure below shows an example B+ tree of a key sequence 10, 15, 20, 35, 40, 46, 50, 53, 55, 60, 64, 68, 72, 75, 80, 86, 87, 90, 95. As shown in the figure, the leaf nodes hold the keys, and the internal nodes hold the index values. While the index values could be any valid values satisfying the generalized search tree properties, for simplicity, either the inorder predecessor or inorder successor can be considered. In the example below, inorder predecessor has been considered.

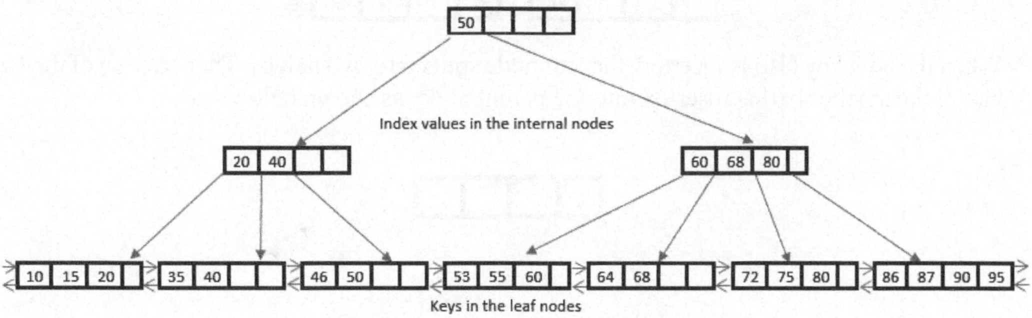

The process of inserting a node or deleting a node to/from a B+ tree is similar to that of the B-tree. Given a sequence of keys, the process of constructing a B+ tree is a sequence of insert operations. Following example shows the process of constructing a B+ tree from a given sequence of keys.

Construction of B+ tree: Given a sequence of keys – 4 1 6 8 2 7 2 9 10 3 11 18 15 20 17 16, let us construct B+ tree. Initially, the tree is empty, and the first keys are inserted without any problem by creating a leaf node, as shown below.

For the first four keys (4, 1, 6,8), there is no issues. They are simply inserted into the leaf node as shown below.

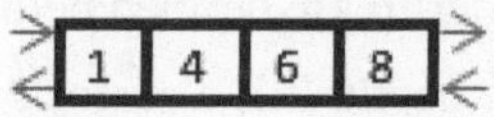

When the next key (2) is inserted, there is node overflow, and the leaf node is split into half. A new root node is created, and largest key of the left child is inserted into the root node, as shown below. The height of the tree is increased by 1. *Note that, a copy of the largest of the smaller half is inserted in the parent node as index value, without removing the key from the leaf node.*

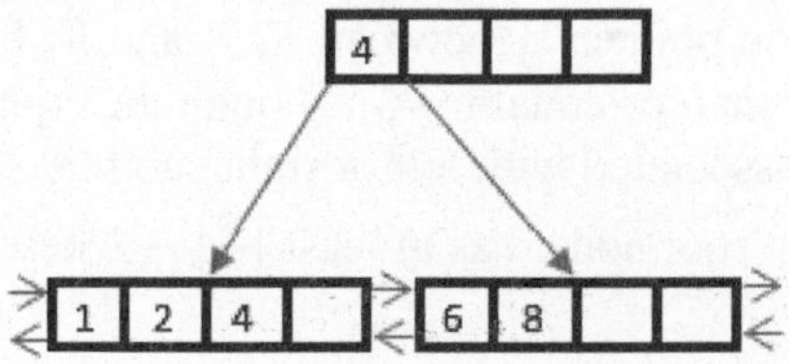

Then, the next three keys (7, 2, 9) are inserted without any split in the existing leaf nodes, as shown below.

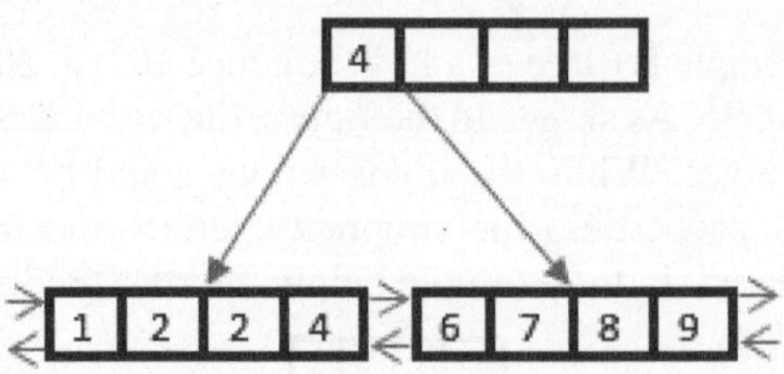

When the next key (10) is inserted, the leaf node splits into two halves. Then, a copy of the largest key of the smaller half is inserted into the parent node, as shown below.

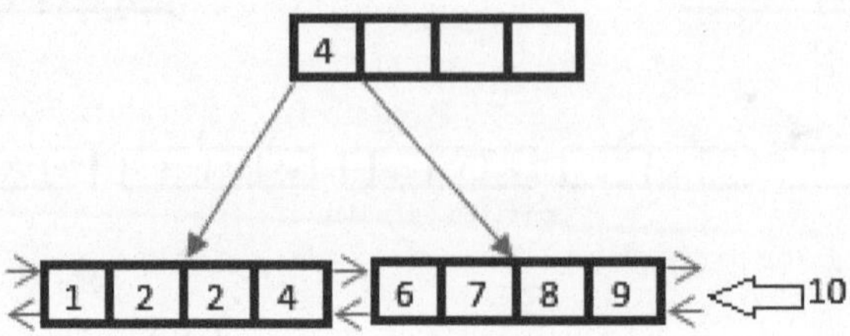

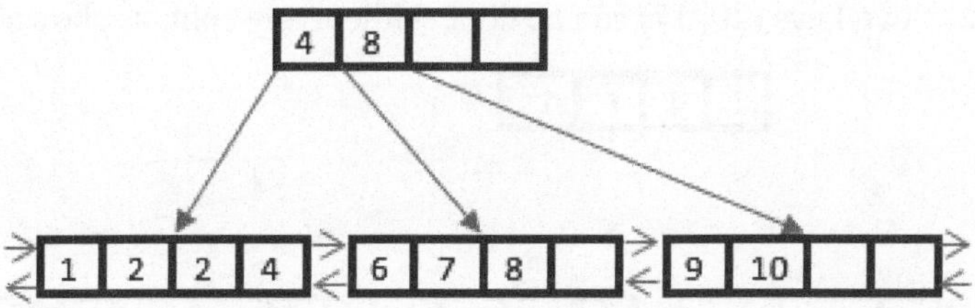

Insertion of the next key (3) causes split of the first leaf node into two halves. Then, a copy of the largest key of the smaller half is inserted into the parent.

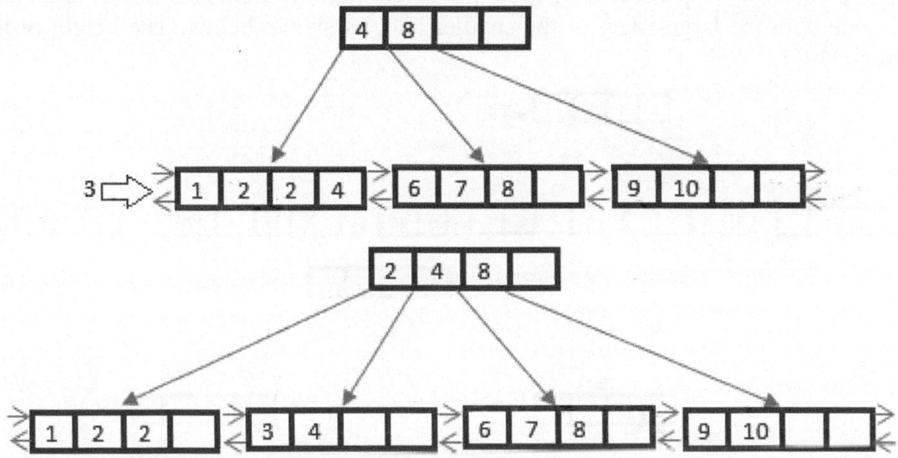

Then, the next two keys (11, 18) are inserted without any split.

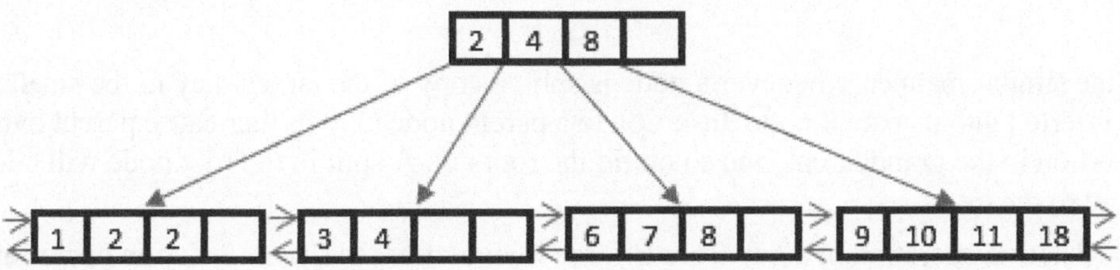

Now, insertion of the next key (15) will cause splitting of the last leaf node, and insertion of a copy of the largest key of the smaller half in the parent, as shown below.

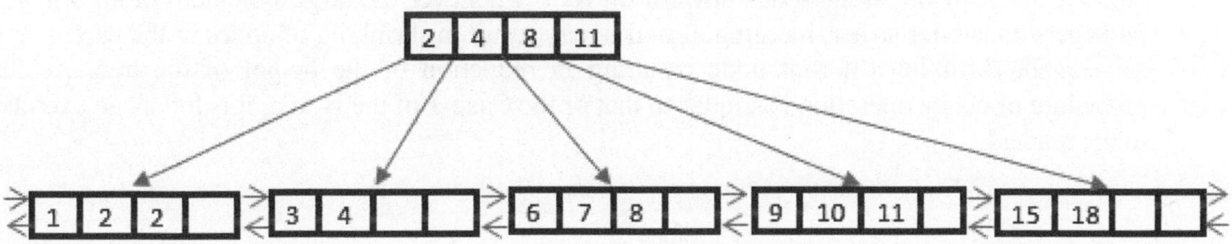

Insertion of next two keys (20, 17) can be done without any split, as shown below.

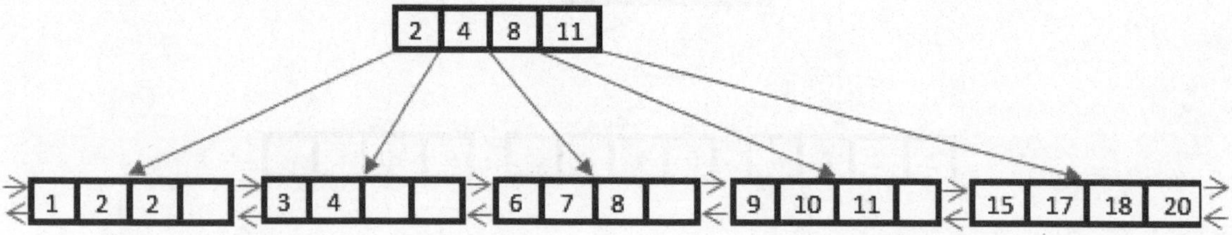

Next, the insertion of the next key (16) will cause splitting of the last leaf node into halves. A copy of the largest key in the smaller half will be inserted into the parent. However, the parent is full, and overflow happens. It then splits the parent note (present root node), and creates a new root node with the largest key of the smaller half, as shown below. The height of the node is increased by 1.

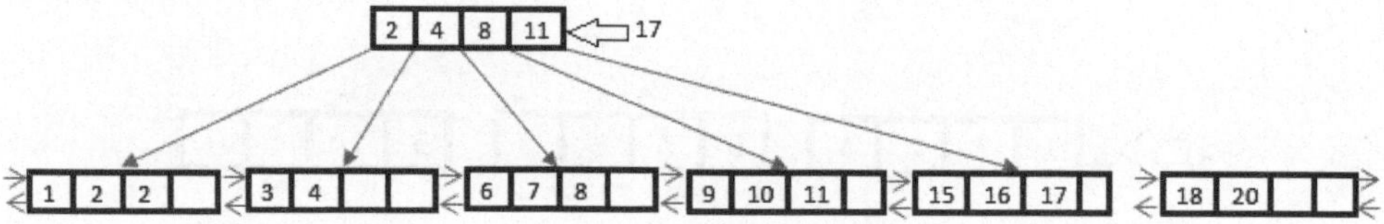

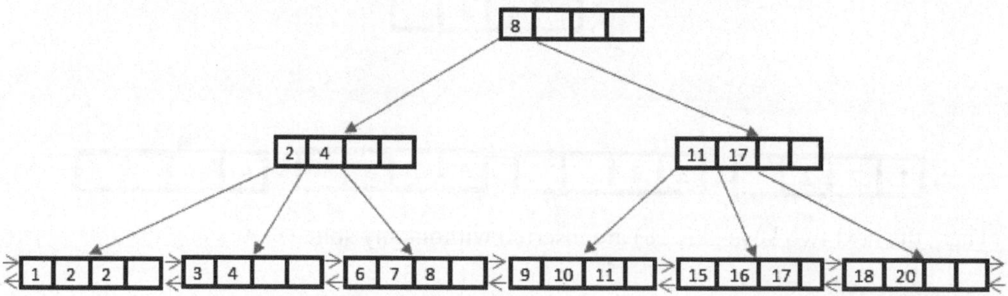

In the similar manner, whenever a node is split, a copy of the largest key in the smaller half will be inserted into its parent node. Insertion to a parent node may further cause parent overflow, and insertion in the grandparent, and so on till the root not. A split in the root node will add one level more to the tree.

The deletion operation of a key from B+ tree is similar to the Case-1 deletion operation of the B-tree, as all the insertion happens in the leaf node. However, instead of bringing key from the parent node, we only bring the key from the sibling node while merging. It then updates the index value to subsequent parent nodes upward till root, whenever the largest element of an affected node gets updated. Further, merging of nodes may result in shrinking of nodes in the parent, and subsequent shrinking till root node resulting in reduction of the height of the tree. As the procedure of delete operation is similar to that of the Case-1 of the B-tree, it is left as an exercise to the readers.

3.4.4 Other Balanced Trees

There are other types of balanced trees such as 2-3 tree, red-black tree, weight balanced tree, etc. These trees are briefly defined below with an example, without much details. Reader may find the details of these trees from the reference materials.

2-3 Tree: 2-3 tree is a B-tree with order 3. It has two types of internal nodes – (i) 2-Node: nodes with two child nodes and one data element, and (ii) 3-Node: nodes with three child nodes and two data elements. Leaf nodes have one or two data elements. All the leaf nodes are at the same level. Except for 2-node and 3-node condition, other properties of B-tree are also held for 2-3 tree. The search, insertion and deletion operations of a 2-3 tree are similar to that of the B-tree. While average and worst-case time complexities of a binary search tree are $O(\log n)$ and $O(n)$ respectively, 2-3 tree has $O(\log n)$ time complexity for both average and worst case. Figure 3.24 shows an example of 2-3 tree.

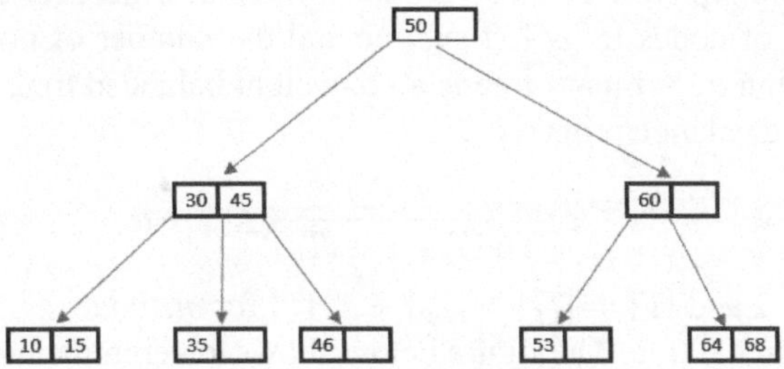

Figure 3.24: An example of 2-3 Tree

Red-Black Tree: Red-Black tree is a height balance binary search tree, where every node in the tree is coloured either red or black, and satisfies the following properties.

a) The colour of the root node is black.
b) Leaf nodes are coloured black, and are NULL.
c) All the leaf nodes (NULL nodes) have the same *black depth*. That means, every path from root to leaf has the same number of black nodes.
d) No two adjacent nodes (both parent and child) are coloured red.
e) The child nodes of a red node are coloured black.

Red-black trees are roughly balanced and its operations (insertion, deletion and search) have $O(\log n)$ time complexity for both average and worst case. It is because, the height of a red-black tree has a bound $O(\log n)$. Few examples of Red-Black trees are shown below. Figure 3.25 shows an example of red-black tree.

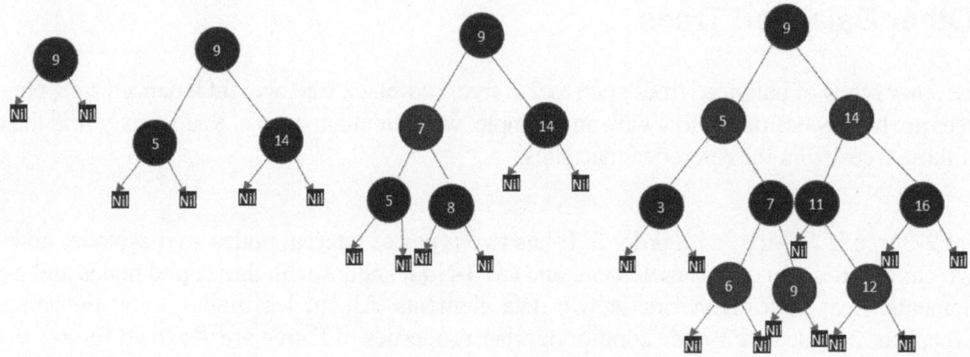

Figure 3.25: An example of Red-Black tree

Weight balanced tree: A *weight balanced tree* is a binary tree in which, for every node, the difference between the number of nodes in its left subtree and the number of nodes in its right subtree is controlled by a fraction α. A binary tree is an α-weight balanced tree, iff every node in the tree satisfies the following balance property.

$$\alpha \leq \frac{w(T_L)}{w(T_L) + w(T_L)} \leq 1 - \alpha$$

where $w(T) = |T| + 1$ and $|T| = |T_L| + |T_R| + 1$, $|T|$ for *nil-node* is 0. Therefore, $w|T|$ is the number of nil-nodes in the tree. The figure below shows a weight balanced tree in which, for every node in the tree, the weight of the left sub-tree is at least half or at most twice that of the of the right subtree. Figure 3.26 shows an example of weight balanced tree.

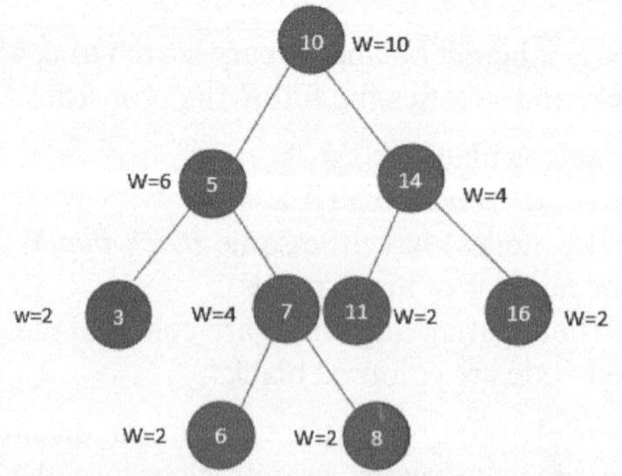

Figure 3.26: An example of weight balanced tree.

3.5 HEAP

A heap is a special type of binary tree which satisfies the following properties.

1. The tree is a complete binary tree (ref. 3.3.4).
2. A heap can be either a *max heap* or a *min heap*.
    a. In a max heap, for any given node in the tree, its value is smaller than or equal to the value of its parent.
    b. In a min heap, for any given node in the tree, its value is greater than or equal to the value of its parent.

Few examples of *max heap* are shown below (in figure 3.27). For any given node in the trees, its value is larger than or equal to the values of the nodes in its left subtree and right subtree, if exist.

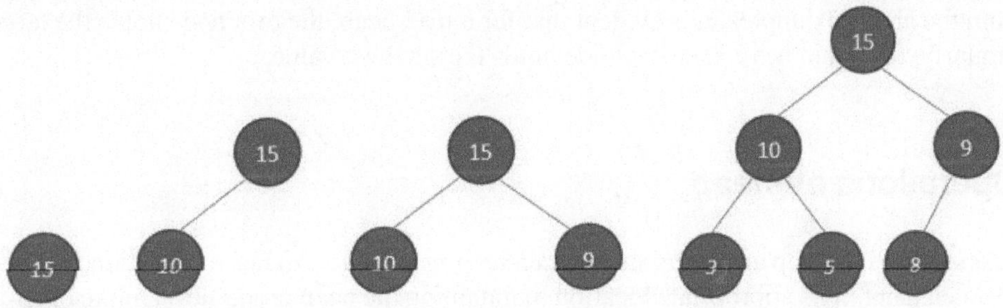

Figure 3.27: Examples of max heaps

The following trees are not *max heaps*, because they violate either one of the properties or both.

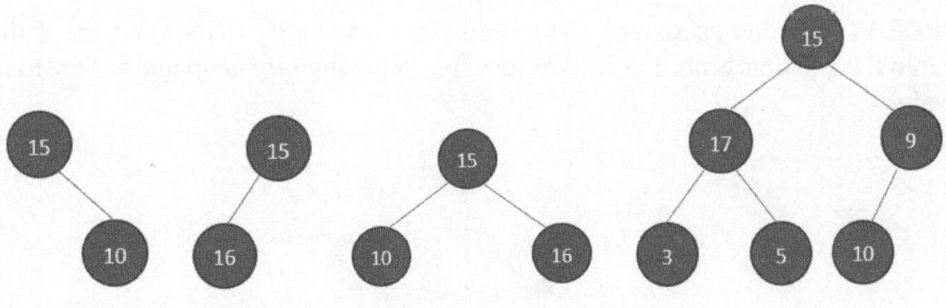

Similarly, following examples are *min heap* trees.

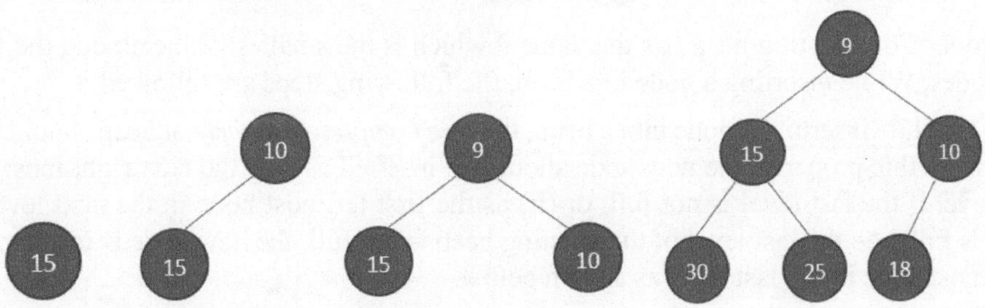

Likewise, the following examples are not *min heap.*

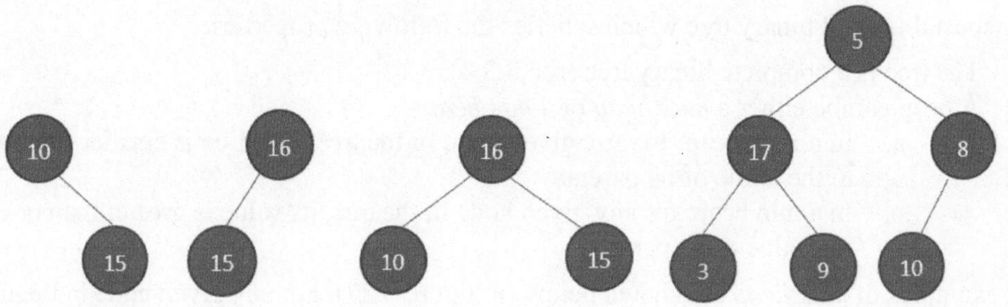

From the above examples, it is evident that for a max heap, the root node holds the largest value. Similarly, for a min heap, the root node holds the smallest value.

3.5.1 Operations on heap

The basic operations on heap are *insert* and *mindelete or maxdelete*. An insert operation on a heap inserts a data element in its appropriate location maintaining the heap properties. Unlike other tree, heap allows deletion of a node only at *root of the heap* i.e., *mindelete* if the heap is a min heap or *maxdelete* if the heap is a max heap. Before formally introducing the algorithm of insert and delete operations, we illustrate the operation with an example.

INSERT OPERATION: Let us assume that a heap exists and we try to insert a node with an arbitrary value into the existing heap. Let us consider the following *min heap* and we try to insert a node with value 8.

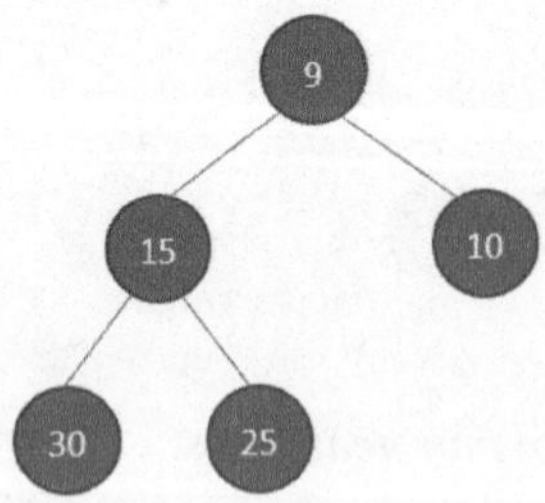

The root of the existing heap has the value 9 which is the smallest value among the values in all the nodes. While inserting a node in a heap, the following steps are followed.

Step 1: While inserting a node into a heap, the *tree complete property* of heap should be satisfied. To ensure this property, the new node should be inserted as - (i) the next right most node in the last level if the last level is not full, or (ii) as the first leftmost node in the next level if the last level is full). As the last level of the existing heap is not full, the new node is inserted as the next rightmost node in the last level as shown below.

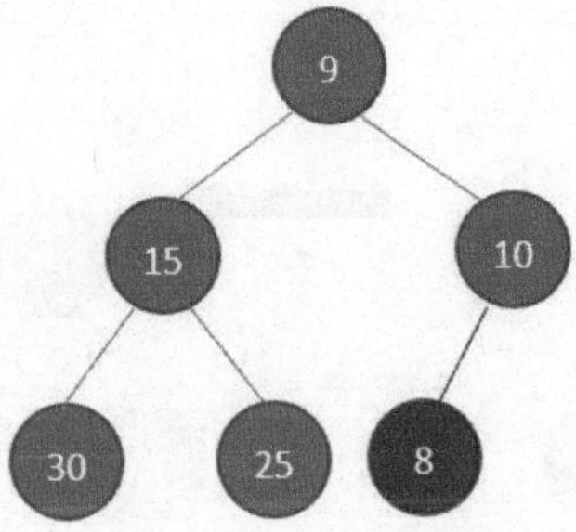

Suppose, the last level of the existing heap is full, the new node will be inserted as the leftmost node of the next level, as shown below.

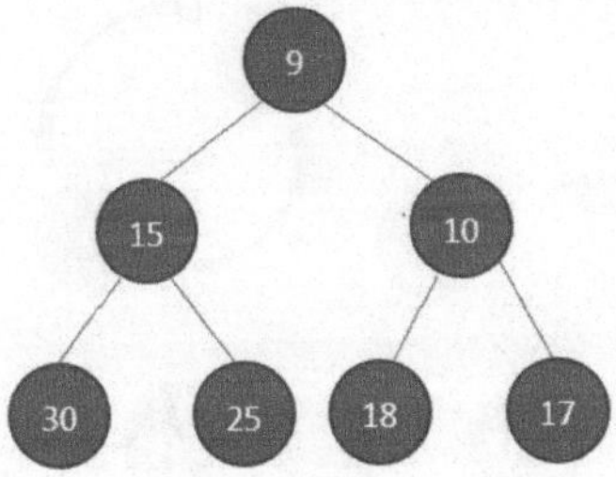

Existing Heap

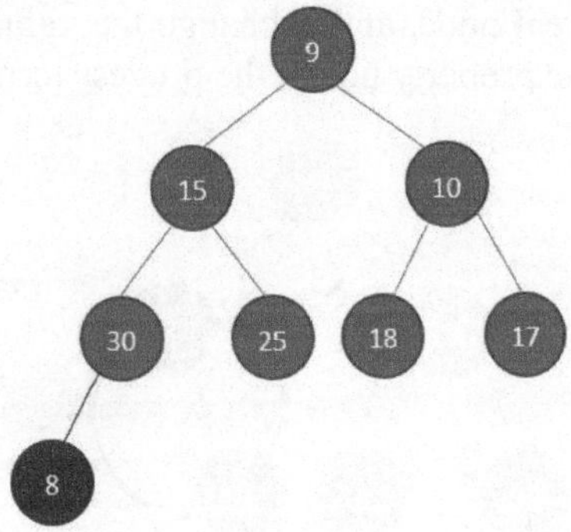

New node inserted as left most node

Step 2: The tree obtained after step 1 is a complete tree, satisfying the first property of heap. Now, we need to check the second property of heap i.e., *"for any given node in the tree, its value is greater than or equal to the value of its parent"*.

If this property is satisfied with the newly inserted node, then the node is in its right place and the process terminates.

If this property does not satisfy with the newly inserted node, we need to find its appropriate place by comparing its value with the values of the nodes along the upward path from the node till the root.

In this example, the value of the new node 8 is smaller than the value of its parent node i.e., 10. The second property does not hold. Then, we will exchange the value of the node with that of its parent as shown below.

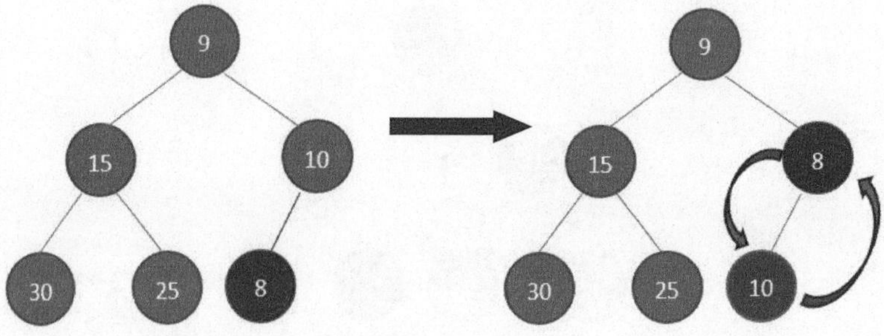

After this exchange operation, the affected node holding the new value (i.e., 8) will be compared with its parent node, and exchange the values if the min heap property does not hold, a shown below. If the property holds, the process terminates.

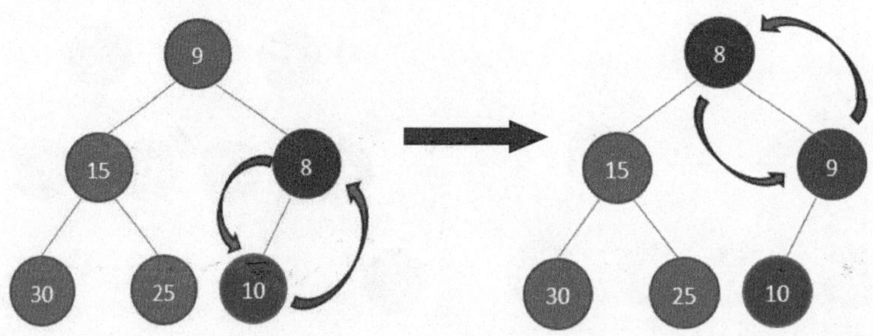

After this exchange operation, there is no further parent nodes to compare and the process terminates. The root of the min heap after inserting as node with value 8 has the minimum value i.e., 8. This operation of placing a newly inserted value to its right location is known as *heapify*. The algorithm for heapify operation is discussed in detail, while discussing implementation of heap in section 3.5.2.

Insertion operation in a max heap is also same as that of the min heap, except that max heap property will be checked at the time of heapify operation.

Construction of a min heap from a given set of values: Using the above insert operation, we can construct a min heap by performing repeated insertion of all the values into the subsequent heap. The following diagram shows construction of min heap from a given set of $\{4, 10, 3, 5, 1\}$. The values are processed in the order of the values in the set. Initially the tree is empty.

Insert the first value in the set i.e., 4	
Insert the value 10. It is inserted as the left child of 4. The new node holds the min heap property, no heapify operation is needed.	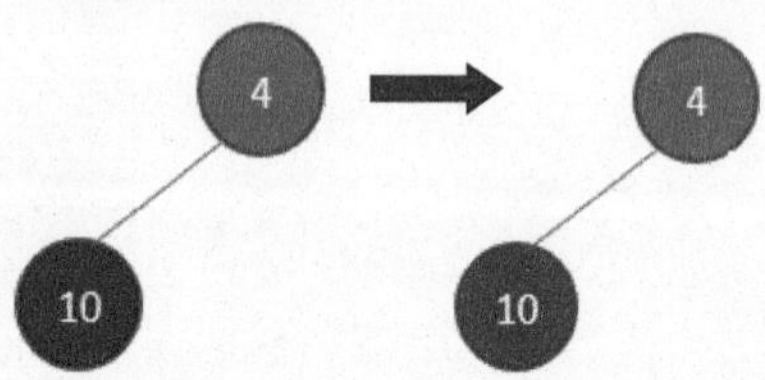

Insert the value 3. As the new node does not hold min heap property, perform heapify operation.	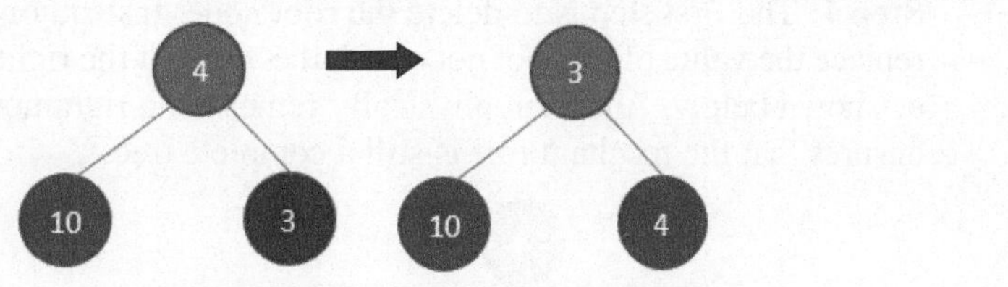
Insert the value 5. As the new node does not hold min heap property, perform heapify operation.	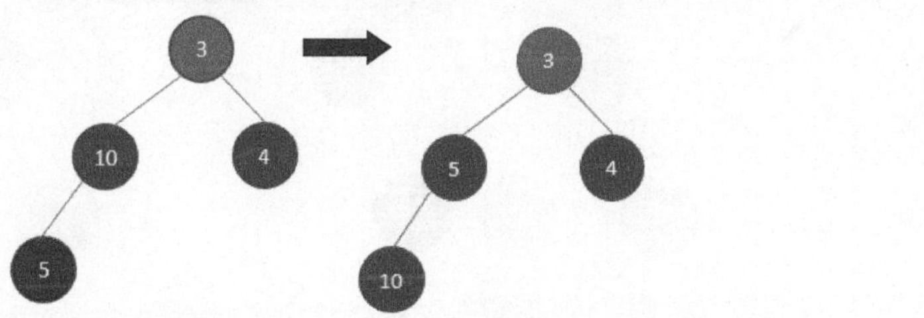
Insert the value 1. As the new node does not hold min heap property, perform heapify operation.	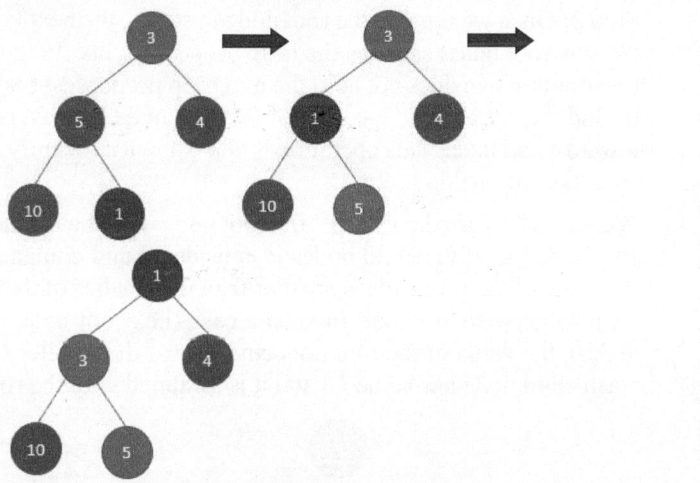

DELETE OPERATION: As mentioned above, deletion of a node from a heap is allowed only from the root. That means, only the root node is deleted. A delete operation on a min heap is referred to as *mindelete*, and that of the max heap is referred to as *maxdelete*. Like in insertion operation, delete operation is also done in two steps. Let us consider the following min heap to explain the process of deleting the root node.

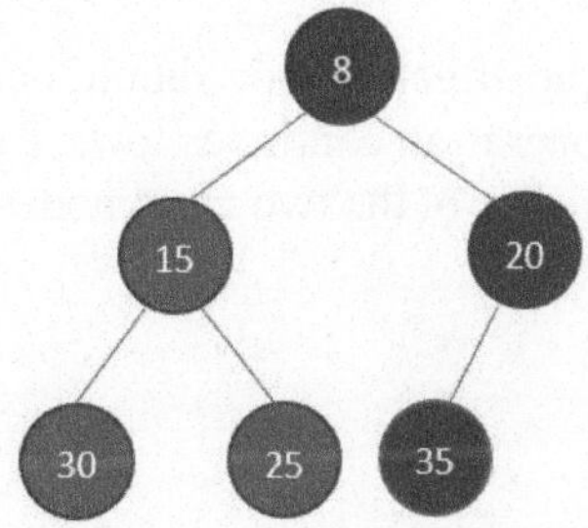

Step 1: The first step is to delete the root node. Instead of physically deleting the root node, we replace the value of the root node with the value of the rightmost node in the last level of the heap as shown below. And then physically remove the rightmost node in the last level. This process ensures that the resultant tree is still a complete tree.

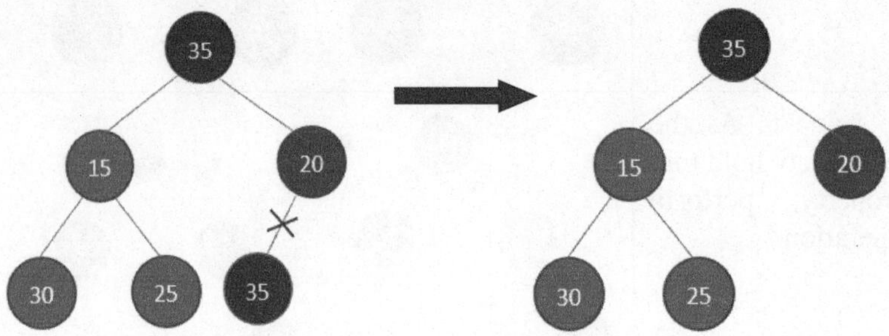

Step 2: Once we remove the root node in step 1, the next task is to check if the resultant tree (i.e., the new root node) satisfies the heap property or not. In the above example, the new root node in the resultant tree does not hold the min heap properties. Like in the insert operation, we now need to find the appropriate location of the root node by traversing the tree downward from the root toward a leaf node. This operation is also known as heapify, but in the reverse order of the heapify operation applied in insert.

We now, compare the value of the root node with that of the values of its child nodes, if any. The smaller value of the child nodes is considered and compared with the value of the root node. If the value of the root node is smaller than the smaller of the child node, then the resultant tree is a heap. Otherwise, it is not. In such a case (i.e., root node is larger than the smaller of the child nodes), the value of the root node and that of the smaller child node are exchanged. That is, the small child node has value 15 and it is swapped with the root node, as shown below.

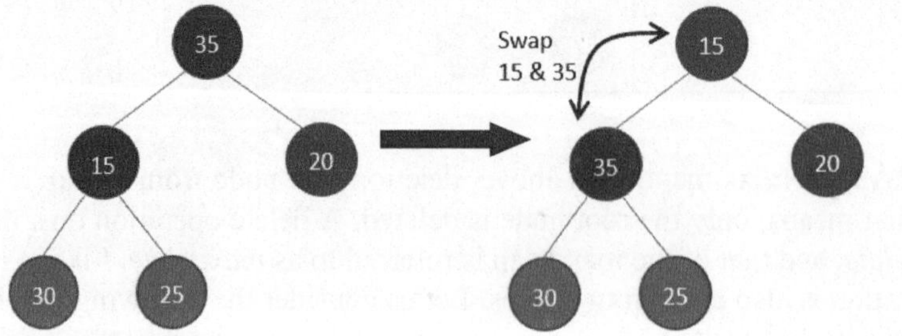

Now, the min heap property of the affected node should be checked. If it holds, then the process terminates. Otherwise, heapify operation continues toward a leaf node. The value of the affected node i.e., 35 is larger than the smaller of the two child nodes i.e., 25. Therefore, the values 35 and 25 are exchanged, as shown below.

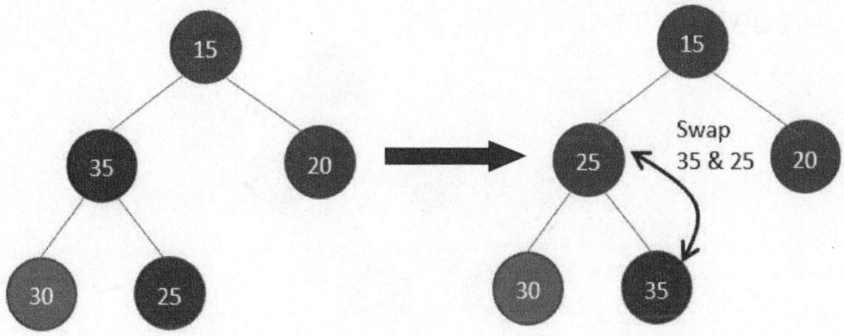

After this exchange operation, the node with value 35 is a leaf node, and thus the process terminates and obtained the following min heap.

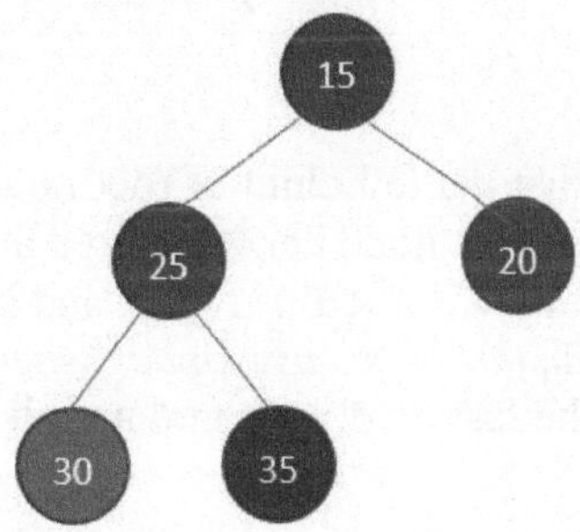

3.5.2 Implementation of Heap

Heap may be implemented either using dynamic memory allocation (like binary tree implementation discussed in section 3.3.1) or static memory allocation using array. As heap is a complete tree, it is simpler to implement a heap using array in terms of memory efficiency and accessing elements in the tree. Therefore, heap is generally implemented using array. This book discusses implementation of heap using array.

Let `A` be an array of size n which will store the elements in heap. Then, using `A`, we can store a heap consisting of upto n nodes. If the index of array A starts from 0, then nodes in the heap are stored as follows.

1. *The root node is stored at the first index of the array.*
2. *If* `i` *is the index of a node in the array, its left child is stored at the index* $2i + 1$, *and its right child is stored at* $2i + 2$.

Similarly, if the index of the array starts from 1, the nodes in the heap are stored as follows.

1. *The root node is stored at the first index of the array.*
2. *If* `i` *is the index of a node in the array, its left child is stored at the index* $2i$, *and its right child is stored at* $2i + 1$.

For the min heap given below,

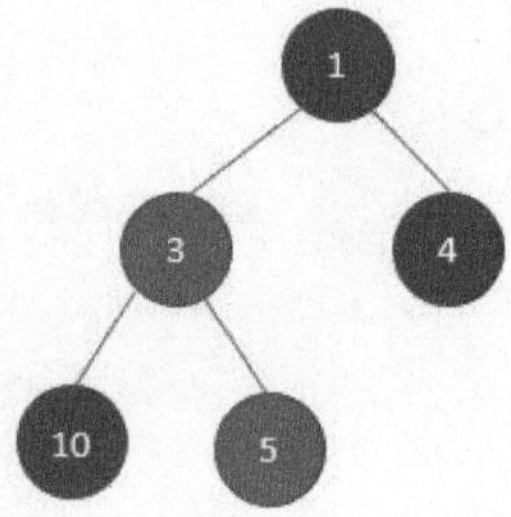

its array representation can be defined as follows. The index of the array starts from 0.

Array A	1	3	4	10	5					
Index	0	1	2	3	4	5	6	7	8	9

In this representation, we see that the left child of root node i.e 3 is stored at the index $2 \times 0 + 1 = 1$, and the right child of the root node i.e. 4 is stored at the index $2 \times 0 + 2 = 2$. Similarly, the left child of the node 3 is stored at $2 \times 1 + 1 = 3$, and its right child at $2 \times 1 + 2 = 4$. From the above array, it can be seen that from the array index where the root node is stored till the index where the rightmost node of the last level is stored are all occupied. It is because the tree is a complete tree.

To understand the characteristics of the array when we insert a node in the heap, and perform heapify operation, we insert a node, and explain characteristics of the subsequent state of the array. The following figure illustrates the state of the tree and its respective array after Step -1 of the insert process in the heap shown above. It inserts a node with value 2 into the heap.

Step - 1: The new node is inserted as the rightmost node in the last level of the tree. The new node is connected as the left child of the node 4. It is realized as storing the value 2 at the index 5 of the array. Note that index 5 is the next available index in the array (existing heap occupies only upto index 4, and new element is inserted at index 5).

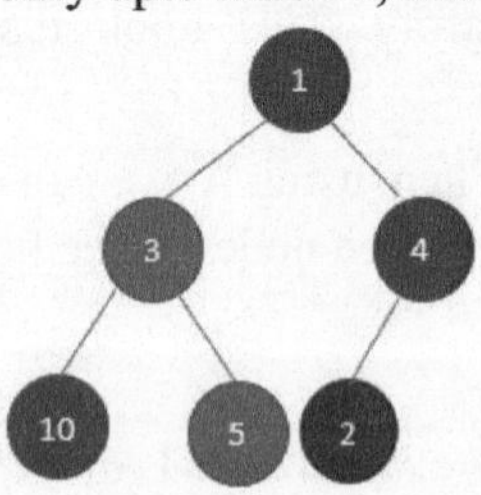

Array A	1	3	4	10	5	2				
Index	0	1	2	3	4	5	6	7	8	9

Step - 2 (Heapify): Check if min heap property holds with the parent of the newly added node. The newly inserted node is added at index 5, therefore its parent node is stored at the index $\left\lfloor \frac{i-1}{2} \right\rfloor = \left\lfloor \frac{5-1}{2} \right\rfloor = 2$. As the value of the newly added node is smaller than that of its parent node, the min heap property does not hold and the two nodes are exchanged, as shown below.

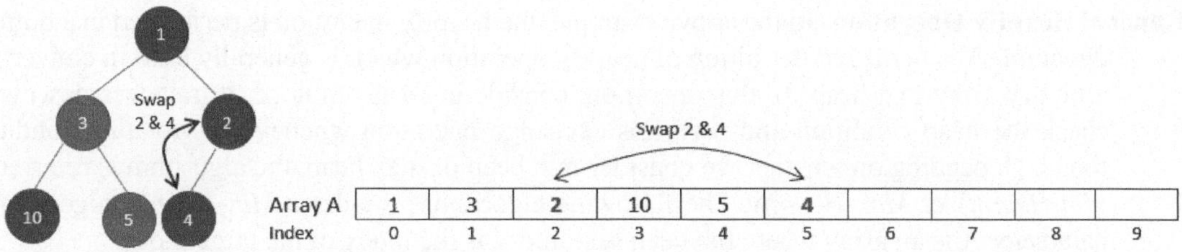

Now, the index of the newly added node becomes 2 and its parent index is $\left\lfloor\frac{2-1}{2}\right\rfloor = \left\lfloor\frac{2-1}{2}\right\rfloor = 0$. The values of the two nodes are compared. As the min heap property holds, the process terminates, as shown below.

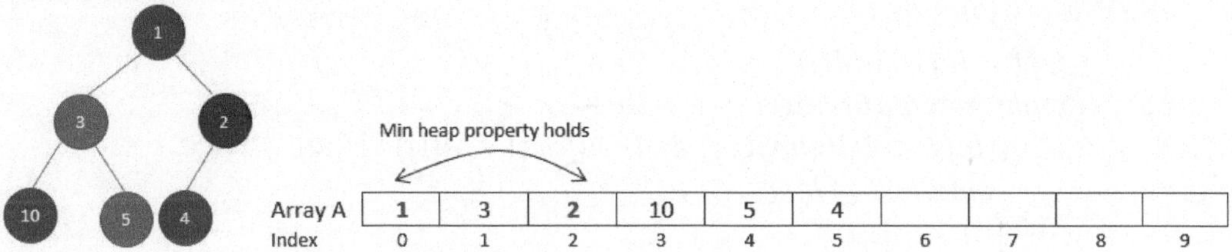

Heapify Operation for Insertion: The following algorithm performs the heapify operation of inserting a node in an existing min heap, as explained above. This algorithm assumes that the array index starts from 0, and i is the index of the newly added node in the array, at the time of calling the algorithm.

```
Min-Heapify-Insert(A,i)
/* A: array storing the min heap; i: index of the new element */
BEGIN
      parent = ⌊(i-1)/2⌋
      IF (parent ≥ 0) THEN
           IF (A[i] < A[parent]) THEN
                    Swap(A[i], A[parent])
                    Min - Heapify - Insert(A, parent)
           END IF
      END IF
END
```

As discussed above, the algorithm will traverse from the newly added leaf node towards root, until it finds the condition satisfying min heap property. As the maximum number of exchange operations is the height of the tree, its time complexity is $O(\log_2 n)$.

General Heapify Operation: In the above example, the heapify operation is performed in a bottom-up direction. A generalized definition of heapify operation which is generally used in converting an arbitrary array to a heap. In this operation, considering a given node, it traverses downward to check the heap condition and performs exchange operation whenever a violation condition is found. Depending on whether we consider min heap or max heap, the algorithm is referred to as *Min-Heapify* or *Max-Heapify*. The following algorithm provides a *Min-Heapify* algorithm. The parameter A is an array where the heap is stored, *i* is the index of the target node.

```
Min-Heapify(A,i)
/* A: array storing the min heap; i: index of the new element */
BEGIN
      left = leftChild(i)        // 2i + 1, i ≥ 0
      right = rightChild(i)      // 2i + 2, i ≥ 0
      IF ((left < A.HeapSize) AND(A[left] < A[i]) THEN
          smallest = left
      ELSE
          smallest = i
      END IF
      IF ((right < A.HeapSize) AND (A[right] < A[smallest])) THEN
          smallest = right
      ELSE
          smallest = i
      END IF
      IF (smallest ≠ i) THEN
          Swap(A[i], A[smallest])
          Min − Heapify(A, smallest)
      END IF
```

Given an arbitrary index i, Min-Heapify(A,i) traverses the tree downward with at most the number of exchange operations equal to the height of the tree i.e., $O(\log_2 n)$.

Delete Operation on Heap: Now, for deleting a node from the heap (root of the tree), we can apply `Min-Heapify(A,0)` i.e., heapify on the root of the tree after Step-1 of the delete operation discussed in section 3.5.1. That is, first the `A[0]` is replaced by `A[HeapSize -1]`, and `HeapSize` is reduced by 1. Therefore, the delete operation needs one Min-Heapify operation, and hence needs $O(\log_2 n)$ time complexity.

Converting an Array to a Heap: Once we define `Min-Heapify(A,i)`, converting an array to a min heap is simple. We just need to call `Min-Heapify(A,i)` function for all the elements in the array, from the last node in the array till the first node. Therefore, the time complexity of converting an array to a heap is $O(n \log_2 n)$ i.e., `Min-Heapify()` function is called n times.

As the nodes in the last level are all leaf nodes, the number of calls to `Min-Heapify()` function can be limited only for the elements in the array from the first index till the last index of the last but one level of the tree. Thus, the following function converts an arbitrary array to a min heap. The `build-Min-Heap()` runs on all the nodes in the heap, starting from the right most node of the last but one level of the tree. It is because we expect that the subtrees of the affected node are already heaps.

```
Build-Min-Heap(A)
     FOR i = ⌊(A.HeapSize−1)/2⌋ downward to 0
          Min-Heapify(A,i)
     END FOR
```

It may also be noted that the min-heapify operations in the higher level nodes (towards leaf nodes) take much lesser time than the $O(log\ n)$. The above $O(n\ log\ n)$ time complexity is not a tight bound complexity. A better bound complexity can be obtained. In the above algorithm, also known as Floyd's algorithm, starts heapify operations from the highest-level nodes i.e., leaf nodes with height equal to 0 upward to their parent nodes and so on upto root. The heapify operations need to be performed for all the nodes in the array, from the node in the last index till the first index. Therefore, we can define the complexity of converting the array to a heap $f(n)$ as follows.

$f(n) \leq \sum_{h=0}^{\lfloor \log n \rfloor} \frac{n}{2^h} O(h)$, note that number of nodes in heap at height h is less than $\frac{n}{2^h}$.

$$\Rightarrow f(n) \leq O\left(n \sum_{h=0}^{\lfloor \log n \rfloor} \frac{h}{2^h}\right)$$

$$\Rightarrow f(n) \leq O\left(n \sum_{h=0}^{\infty} \frac{h}{2^h}\right)$$

$$\Rightarrow f(n) = O(n)$$

3.5.3 Heapsort and Priority Queue

Heapsort is a sorting algorithm which sorts the elements in a given array by applying `Build-Min-Heap()`, repeated application of `Min-Heapify()` operations. Given an array A with n elements, we first convert the array into a min heap using `Build-Min-Heap()` operation. Once min-heap is constructed, we then exchange the smallest element of the heap (i.e., A[0]) with the right most node of the last level of the heap. After exchange, the effective size of the heap is reduced by one and `Min-Heapify()` function is applied on the new root node. Thus, the exchange and heapify operations are performed till heap has only two nodes. Formally, algorithm for *heapsort* is given below.

```
Heapsort(A)
/* The array A stores the elements */
1.      Build-Min-Heap(A) // Build initial minheap
        // For all the index; higest to the least
2.      FOR i = A.Size − 1 downto 1
           // Store the smallest element to the last index in heap
3.         Swap(A[i],A[0])
           // reduce the effective heap size by one
4.         A.HeapSize = A.HeapSize - 1
5.         Min-Heapify(A,0) // from root to leave within A.HeapSize
6.      END FOR
```

The algorithm sorts the array in descending order (for ascending order, one can apply `Build-Max-Heap` and `Max-Heapify`, which is left as an exercise). For an array of size *n*, one `Build-Min-Heap()` operation is required with a time complexity of $O(n\log_2 n)$ for converting the array to heap. And, $n-2$ number of Min-Heapify operations, each operation requires $O(\log_2 n)$ time complexity. Therefore, the time complexity of heapsort algorithm is $O(n\log_2 n) + O(n\log_2 n) = O(n\log_2 n)$.

Priority Queue: As mentioned above, heaps are used to implement priority queues. Assume that each element in the queue has its associated priority (weight). As the elements of the queue arrive, each element is inserted into a heap which is constructed considering the priority weight of the elements. This operation is considered as the enqueue operation into the priority queue. The root of the heap will have the queue element with the highest priority. An enqueue operation needs one heapify operation with a time complexity of $O(\log_2 n)$.

For a dequeue operation, it performs a delete operation, i.e., deleting the root node needing one heapify operation on the root of the tree. It holds a time complexity of $O(\log_2 n)$.

UNIT SUMMARY

This unit discussed two data structures namely linked list and tree. Different types of linked lists such as singly linked list, doubly linked list, circular list are discussed along with their implementation algorithms. Implementations of stack and queue using linked list are also discussed. Further, tree data structure is introduced. Binary tree, a special type of tree, is discussed in details. Further, special types of binary tree namely binary search tree, AVL tree, B/B+ tree, Heap, threaded binary etc. are also discussed in details.

EXERCISES

Many of these questions have been compiled from various sources including past GATE examinations.

Multiple Choice Questions

Q1. What is the worst-case time complexity of inserting n elements into an empty linked list, if the linked list needs to be maintained in sorted order?

1. $\Theta(n^2)$
2. $\Theta(n)$
3. $\Theta(1)$
4. $\Theta(n \log n)$

Q2. N items are stored in a sorted doubly linked list. For a delete operation, a pointer is provided to the record to be deleted. For a decrease-key operation, a pointer is provided to the record on which the operation is to be performed.

An algorithm performs the following operation on the list in this order:

$\Theta(N)$ delete, $O(\log N)$ insert, $O(\log N)$ find, and $\Theta(N)$ decrease-key. What is the time complexity of all these operations put together ?

a) $O(\log^2 N)$
b) $O(N)$
c) $O(N^2)$
d) $\Theta(N^2 \log N)$

Q3. Let P be a singly linked list, Let Q be the pointer to an intermediate node x in the list. What is the worst-case time complexity of the best-known algorithm to delete the node x from the list?

1. $O(n)$
2. $O(\log^2 n)$
3. $O(\log n)$
4. $O(1)$

Q4. The following C function takes a simply-linked list as an input argument. It modifies the list by moving the last element to the front of the list and returns the modified list. Some part of the code is left blank.

```
typedef struct node {
    int value;
    struct node *next;
} Node;
```

```
Node *move_to_front(Node *head) {
    Node *p, *q;
    if ((head = = NULL: || (head->next = = NULL)) return head;
    q = NULL; p = head;
    while (p-> next !=NULL) {
      q=P;
      p=p->next;
    }
    ..............................

   return head;
}
```

Choose the correct alternative to replace the blank line.

1. q = NULL; p -> next = head; head = p
2. q -> next = NULL; head = p; p -> next = head
3. head = p; p -> next = q; q -> next = NULL
4. q -> next = NULL; p -> next = head; head = p

Q5. The following C function takes a single-linked list of integers as a parameter and rearranges the elements of the list. The function is called with the list containing the integers 1,2,3,4,5,6,7 in the given order. What will be the contents of the list after the function completes execution?

```
struct node {
    int value;
    struct node *next;
};
void rearrange (struct node *list ){
    struct node *p, * q;
    int temp;
    if( !list || !list-> next) return;
    p = list; q = list->next;
    while (q) {
      temp = p->value;
      p-> value = q ->value;
      q-> value = temp;
      p = q-> next;
      q = p ? p->next : 0;
    }
}
```

1. 1,2,3,4,5,6,7
2. 2,1,4,3,6,5,7
3. 1,3,2,5,4,7,6
4. 2,3,4,5,6,7,1

Q6. A circularly linked list is used to represent a Queue. A single variable p is used to access the Queue. To which node should p point such that both the operations enQueue and deQueue can be performed in constant time?

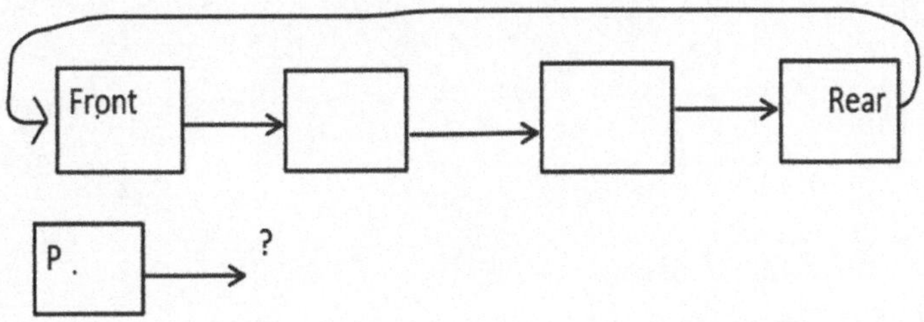

1. Rear node
2. Front node
3. Not possible with single pointer
4. Node next to front

Q7. Suppose a binary search tree with 1000 distinct elements is also a complete binary tree. The tree is stored using the array representation of binary heap trees. Assuming that the array indices start with 0, the 3rd largest element of the tree is stored at index __________.

a) 509
b) 590
c) 608
d) 950

Q8. The preorder traversal of a binary search tree is 15, 10, 12, 11, 20, 18, 16, 19. Which one of the following is the postorder traversal of the tree?

a) 20, 19, 18, 16, 15, 12, 11, 10
b) 10, 11, 12, 15, 16, 18, 19, 20
c) 11, 12, 10, 16, 19, 18, 20, 15
d) 19, 16, 18, 20, 11, 12, 10, 15

Q9. What is the worst-case time complexity of inserting n^2 elements into an AVL tree with n elements initially?

a) $\Theta(n^2)$
b) $\Theta(n^2 logn)$
c) $\Theta(n^4)$
d) $\Theta(n^3)$

Q10. The number of leaf nodes in a rooted tree of n nodes, with each node having 0 or 3 children is

a) n/2

b) (n-1)/3

c) (n-1)/2

d) (2n + 1)/3

Short and Long Answer Type Questions

Q1. In a binary tree, for every node the difference between the number of nodes in the left and right subtrees is at most 2. If the height of the tree is $h > 0$, then the minimum number of nodes in the tree is.......................

Q2. How many distinct binary search trees can be created out of 4 distinct keys?

Q3. Postorder traversal of a given binary search tree T produces the following sequence of keys 10, 9, 23, 22, 27, 25, 15, 50, 95, 60, 40, 29. Find out the sequence of keys which represents the inorder traversal of the tree T?

Q4. A binary search tree contains the numbers 1, 2, 3, 4, 5, 6, 7, and 8. When the tree is traversed in pre-order and the values in each node are printed out, the sequence of values obtained is 5, 3, 1, 2, 4, 6, 8, 7. If the tree is traversed in post-order, the sequence obtained would be....................

Q5. A Priority Queue is implemented as a Max-Heap. Initially, it has 5 elements. The level-order traversal of the heap is given below: 10, 8, 5, 3, 2 Two new elements "1‘ and "7‘ are inserted in the heap in that order. The level-order traversal of the heap after the insertion of the elements is.................

Q6. A binary search tree is generated by inserting in order the following integers: 50, 15, 62, 5, 20, 58, 91, 3, 8, 37, 60, 24. The number of nodes in the left subtree and right subtree of the root respectively is....................

Q7. A program takes as input a balanced binary search tree with n leaf nodes and computes the value of a function g(x) for each node x. If the cost of computing g(x) is min{ no. of leaf-nodes in left-subtree of x, no. of leaf-nodes in right-subtree of x } then the worst-case time complexity of the program is...................

Q8. While inserting the elements 71,65,84,69,67,83 in an empty binary search tree (BST) in the sequence shown, the element in the lowest level is......................

Q9. The postorder traversal of a binary tree is 8,9,6,7,4,5,2,3,1. The inorder traversal of the same tree is 8,6,9,4,7,2,5,1,3. The height of a tree is the length of the longest path from the root to any leaf. The height of the binary tree above is.........................

Q10. The following numbers are inserted into an empty binary search tree in the given order: 10, 1, 3, 5, 15, 12, 16. What is the height of the binary search tree (the height is the maximum distance of a leaf node from the root)?

Numerical Problems

Q1. A binary tree T has 20 leaves. The number of nodes in having two children is _____________.

Q2. The height of a tree is the length of the longest root-to-leaf path in it. The maximum and minimum number of nodes in a binary tree of height 5 are _____ and ______respectively

Q4. The height of a binary tree is the maximum number of edges in any root to leaf path. Find the maximum number of nodes in a binary tree of height h.

Q5. A scheme for storing binary trees in an array X is as follows. Indexing of X starts at 1 instead of 0. the root is stored at X[1]. For a node stored at X[i], the left child, if any, is stored in X[2i] and the right child, if any, in X[2i+1]. To be able to store any binary tree on n vertices the minimum size of X should be ___________.

Q6. The numbers 1, 2, ..., n are inserted in a binary search tree in some order. In the resulting tree, the right subtree of the root contains p nodes. The first number to be inserted in the tree must be ________________

Q7. Let T be a full binary tree with 8 leaves. (A full binary tree has every level full). Suppose two leaves a and b of T are chosen uniformly and independently at random. The expected value of the distance between a and b in T (i.e., the number of edges in the unique path between a and b) is (rounded off to 2 decimal places) _____.

Q8. The number of ways in which the numbers 1,2,3,4,5,6,7 can be inserted in an empty binary search tree, such that the resulting tree has height 6 is _____________. (Note: the height of a tree with a single node is 0)

Q9. Suppose we have a balanced binary search tree T holding n numbers. We are given two numbers L and H and wish to sum up all the numbers in T that lie between L and H. Suppose there are m such numbers in T. If the tightest upper bound on the time to compute the sum is O($n^a \log^b n + m^c \log^d n$), the value of a + 10b + 100c + 1000d is ______.

Q10. When searching for the key value 60 in a binary search tree, nodes containing the key values 10, 20, 40, 50, 70 80, 90 are traversed, not necessarily in the order given. How many different orders are possible in which these key values can occur on the search path from the root to the node containing the value 60?

Q11. A complete n-ary tree is a tree in which each node has n children or no children. Let I be the number of internal nodes and L be the number of leaves in a complete n-ary tree. If L = 41, and I = 10, what is the value of n?

Q12. In a complete k-ary tree, every internal node has exactly k children. The number of leaves in such a tree with n internal nodes is ____________

PRACTICAL

Q1. You are given an array of k linked-lists lists, each linked-list is sorted in ascending order. Merge all the linked-lists into one sorted linked-list and return it.

Q2. Given the head of a linked list, reverse the nodes of the list k at a time, and return the modified list. k is a positive integer and is less than or equal to the length of the linked list. If the number of nodes is not a multiple of k then left-out nodes, in the end, should remain as it is. You may not alter the values in the list's nodes, only the nodes themselves may be changed.

Q3. Given the root of a binary search tree (BST) and an integer target, split the tree into two subtrees where one subtree has nodes that are all smaller or equal to the target value, while the other subtree has all nodes that are greater than the target value. It is not necessarily the case that the tree contains a node with the value target. Additionally, most of the structure of the original tree should remain. Formally, for any child c with parent p in the original tree, if they are both in the same subtree after the split, then node c should still have the parent p. Return an array of the two roots of the two subtrees. The example below illustrates an input and expected outputs for a target value 2.

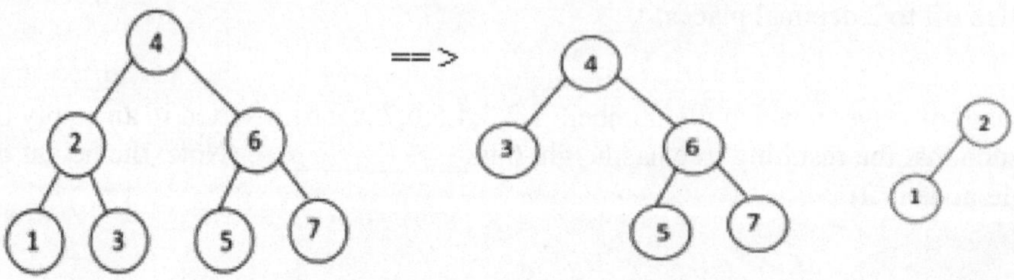

Q4. Given a binary tree, find its minimum depth. The minimum depth is the number of nodes along the shortest path from the root node down to the nearest leaf node. Note: A leaf is a node with no children.

Q5. You are given an array of *k* singly linked-lists, each linked-list is sorted in ascending order. Merge all the linked-lists into one sorted linked-list and return it.

Q6. Given a singly linked list, remove all the nodes which have a greater value on their right side.

Q7. Given the head of a linked list, return the node where the cycle begins. If there is no cycle, return null.

Q8. Given the root of a binary tree, return its maximum depth. A binary tree's maximum depth is the number of nodes along the longest path from the root node down to the farthest leaf node.

Q9. Consider all the leaves of a binary tree, from left to right order, the values of those leaves form a leaf value sequence. Two binary trees are considered leaf-similar if their leaf value sequence are the same. Given two binary trees, write a C program to find if the binary trees have the same leaf value sequences.

Q10. Given a binary tree root, a node X in the tree is named good if in the path from root to X there are no nodes with a value greater than X. Return the number of good nodes in the binary tree.

KNOW MORE

Readers are encouraged to explore the following E-Books/E-Resources for additional examples, and discussions on related topics.

1. List, Binary Trees, Balanced Trees, Priority Queue. Chapters 2, 4, 5, 6, Electronic Lecture Notes - DATA STRUCTURES AND ALGORITHMS, by Y. Narahari (https://gtl.csa.iisc.ac.in/hari/wp-content/uploads/2021/10/dsa.pdf)
2. Linked List and Binary Trees, Chapter 2 and 3, Data Structures and Algorithms: Annotated Reference with Examples, Granville Barnett, and Luca Del Tongo,(https://www.mta.ca/~rrosebru/oldcourse/263114/Dsa.pdf)
3. Trees, Chapter 4, Data Structures and Algorithm Analysis in C++, Weiss, Mark Allen, 4th Ed. (https://www.uoitc.edu.iq/images/documents/informatics-institute/Competitive_exam/DataStructures.pdf).
4. Dynamic Information Structures, Chapter 4, Data Structures and Algorithms, N. Wirth. (https://people.inf.ethz.ch/wirth/AD.pdf)

REFERENCES AND SUGGESTED READINGS

- [Adamson, 1996] I. T. Adamson. (1996), Data structures and Algorithms: A first Course, Springer.
- [Aho, 1983] A. V. Aho, J. E. Hopcroft, and J D. Ullman. (1983), Data Structures and Algorithms, Addison-Wesley.
- [Banachowski, 1991] Banachowski L. Kreczmar A. and Rytter W.,(1991) Analysis of Algorithms and Data Structures, Addison-Wesley.

- [Cormen, 2001] Cormen, T. H.; Leiserson, C. E.; Rivest, R. L. & Stein, C. (2001), *Introduction to Algorithms* , The MIT Press .
- [Donald, 2009] Donald E. Knuth. (2009), The Art of Computer Programming: Fundamental Algorithms, Vol. 1, 3rd Edition, Pearson.
- [Greene, 1988] D. H. Greene and D. E Knuth. (1988) Mathematics for the analysis of Algorithms, Birkhauser.
- [Gonnet, 1981] G. H. Gonnet and R. Baeza Yates, (1991) Handbook of Algorithms and Data Structures, Addison-Wesley
- [Horowitz, 1983] E. Horowitz and S Sahni. (1983) Fundamentals of data Structure, Computer Science Press
- [Horowitz, 1993] E. Horowitz, S Sahni and A. Freed. (1993) Fundamentals of data Structure in C, Computer Science Press.
- [James, 2009] James A. Storer. (2009), An Introduction to Data Structures and Algorithms, 1st Edition, Birkhauser Springer.
- [Kingston, 1990] J. H. Kingston. (1990), Algorithms and data structures, Addison-Wesley.
- [Kozon, 1992] D. C. Kozen. (1992), The design and Analysis of Algorithms, Springer.
- [Lewis, 1991] H. R. Lewis and L. Denenberg. (1991) Data Structures and Their Algorithms, Harper Collins.
- [Wirth, 1976] Wirth, N. (1976), *Algorithms + Data Structures = Programs* , Prentice-Hall.

Dynamic QR Code for Further Reading

Scan the following QR Code to navigate to an external page for know more, additional reading materials, and additional exercises.

4 Sorting, Hashing, Graph

UNIT SPECIFICS

This unit focuses on three broad topics of data structures and algorithms namely Sorting, Hashing and Graphs. Within these topics, the following aspects have been looked at:

- *Understanding the working principle of different types of sorting algorithms;*
- *Estimating the complexity of different sorting algorithms;*
- *Understanding different approaches of hashing and understanding their complexities;*
- *A brief introduction to Graph and traversal on Graph;*

While the topics on sorting and hashing are discussed in details, discussion on graph has been limited to an introductory level.

A collection of multiple-choice questions, short and long answer types question and practical exercise are also provided in the exercises section. A QR code which links to an external web page is also provided for additional questions and exercises, additional topics, additional reading materials. Readers are encouraged to check the external web page regularly to follow the updates.

RATIONALE

This unit covers three important topics of data structures and algorithms namely sorting, hashing and graph. In several computing applications, one often needs to arrange underlying data elements in a particular order – ascending or descending. Several types of sorting algorithms have been discussed in this unit – comparable/non-comparable, internal/external, stable/unstable sorting algorithms etc. Estimation of the complexities of these algorithms – best case, average case and worst case scenarios are also discussed in detail.

Like sorting, hashing is also a class of methods for indexing keys so that the data elements can be retrieved efficiently. Several hashing methods have been discussed in this unit and effectiveness of these methods are also discussed. While sorting and hashing topics have been discussed in great details, this unit only covers an introductory understanding of graphs in terms of representation and traversal. Other relevant algorithmic topics of graph such as shortest path, minimum spanning tree, maximum flow, matching etc. are beyond the scope of this book. Readers are encouraged to refer to external web page for additional topics beyond the scope of this book.

PRE-REQUISITES

Programming: C programming language (Many of the examples are given in C like statements)

Computer System: Main Memory

UNIT OUTCOMES

List of outcomes of this unit is as follows:

U4-O1: Different sorting algorithms and estimating their complexities

U4-O2: Different hashing methods and understanding their efficiently.

U4-O3: Introduction of Graph, representation and traversal.

Unit-4 Outcomes	EXPECTED MAPPING WITH COURSE OUTCOMES (1- Weak Correlation; 2- Medium Correlation; 3- Strong Correlation)					
	CO-1	CO-2	CO-3	CO-4	CO-5	CO-6
U4-O1	1	-	-	3	3	
U4-O2	1	-	-	3	3	
U4-O3	1	-	-	3	3	

4.1 SORTING

Given a collection of data elements, the task of sorting is to arrange the given data in a particular order – *either ascending or descending* (figure 4.1). In many of the real-world data handling situations, arranging data elements/objects in a particular order is often one of the essential tasks. Searching for an object in a large collection of random objects could be easier, if the objects are arranged in a particular order. For example, binary search operation, or binary search tree. This section discusses various sorting algorithms.

Given data:
5 8 1 3 7 9 6
Ascending Order:
1 3 5 6 7 8 9
Descending Order:
9 8 7 6 5 3 1

Figure 4.1: Sorting

4.1.1 Terminologies

Internal and External Memory Sorting Algorithms: Depending on whether an algorithm can handle data in secondary storage or not, a sorting algorithm can be internal memory or external memory. Internal memory sorting algorithms are the class of algorithms which need the entire data to be residing in the internal memory. Whereas, for external memory sorting algorithms, the entire data not necessarily should be in internal memory.

Stable Sorting Algorithm: A sorting algorithm is said to be stable, if two data elements with the same value appear in the same order in the sorted output, as they appear in the unsorted input.

In-placed Sorting Algorithm: Sorting algorithms which do not use auxiliary data structure for storing data elements other than the original input storage are known as in-placed algorithms. However, it may use auxiliary necessary variables like iterator or temporary storage of holding a data element, but not for storing chunks of data.

Let us consider the following sorting approach. Given an array with unsorted data elements, let us construct a binary search tree of the given data elements. We further perform inorder traversal on the binary search tree, and the traversal output is then stored in the original array. This algorithm is not an in-placed sorting algorithm. Likewise, we can construct a min heap tree from the given array, and then perform a sequence of delete root operations on the heap to get the sorted order. Or, we can scan the given array to find the first minimum, second minimum, and so on, and store the obtained minimums to another array to generate the sorted array. All these approaches use auxiliary data structures for data processing, not directly on the original input array. Such algorithms are known as *out-of-place* sorting algorithms. In an in-placed algorithm, operations are performed directly on the given input array, overwriting the elements in the array while processing the algorithm.

Adaptive and Non-adaptive: If time taken for sorting depends on the initial ordering of the elements in the input collection, the algorithm is known as adaptive. If initial ordering does not affect the sorting time, the algorithm is called non-adaptive.

Inversion Count: Given an array, inversion count denotes how far the given array is from its sorted order. If the elements in the input array is already in the target ordering, then its inversion count is 0. If the elements in the input array is in the reverse order of the target ordering, its inversion count is maximum.

Lower Bound Theory: It defines the minimum time complexity of a class of algorithms.

Comparison and non-comparison: Sorting algorithms which perform sorting by comparing the values of the data elements are referred to as comparison sorting algorithms, otherwise, non-comparison.

4.1.2 Bubble Sort

Given an array, bubble sort scans the array multiple times (referred to as *pass*) from the lower index to the highest applicable index. The idea is that, in each pass, depending on whether the algorithm attempts to arrange the data in ascending or descending order, the algorithm will bubble up the largest or smallest element. The algorithm can also scan the array from the largest index to the smallest applicable index, instead of smallest to higher. The process discussed in this section scans the array from the smallest to highest applicable index. We first illustrate the idea and procedure before presenting the algorithm/program.

Let A be the array to be sorted as shown below. Let the algorithm sorts the array in the descending order (*from largest to the smallest*).

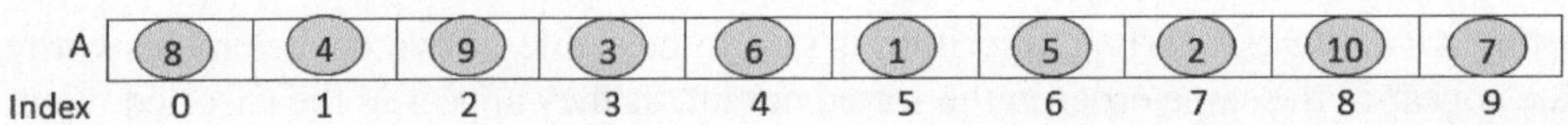

We will scan the array from the smallest index to the highest applicable index. When the scanner moves forward, the smallest element among the elements processed so far will be kept bubbling up along with the scanner. In the pass 1, the idea is to bubble up the smallest element to the end of the array. When the scanner is at the index 0, the algorithm has processed the array upto index 0, in this pass. As the scanner has processed only one element i.e., $A[0] = 8$, the smallest element is the element itself i.e., 8.

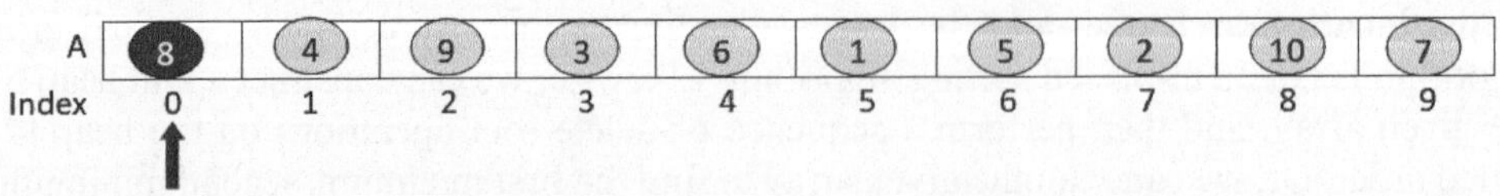

Then, the scanner moves to the second index, i.e., A[1] and compares the element at A[1] with the smallest element stored at A[0]. Since $A[1] < A[0]$, the elements are in order. No reordering is required. A[1] has the smallest element, as shown below.

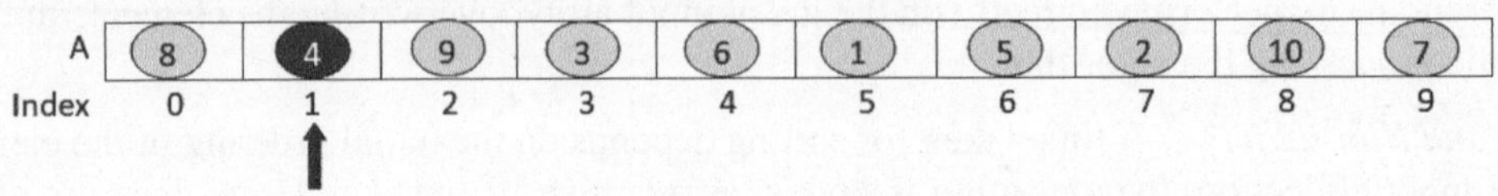

Now, the scanner moves to A[2] and compares with the smallest element found so far i.e., the previous element (A[1]). As $A[2] > A[1]$, the elements are not in order i.e., A[2] should have the smallest element. So, the elements at A[2] and A[1] are exchanged, as shown below. Now, A[2] has the smallest element.

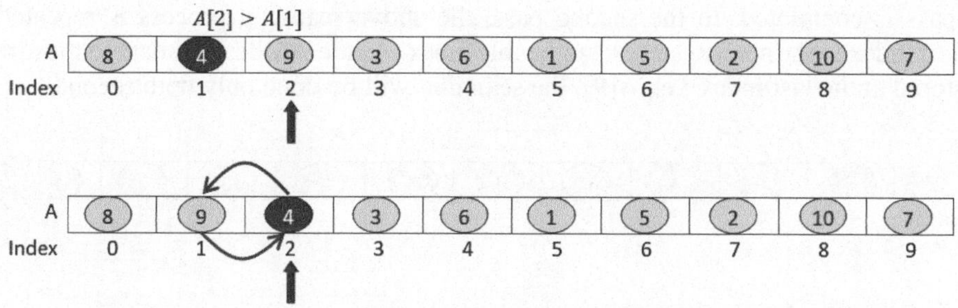

Likewise, scanning continues till the last element, as shown below.

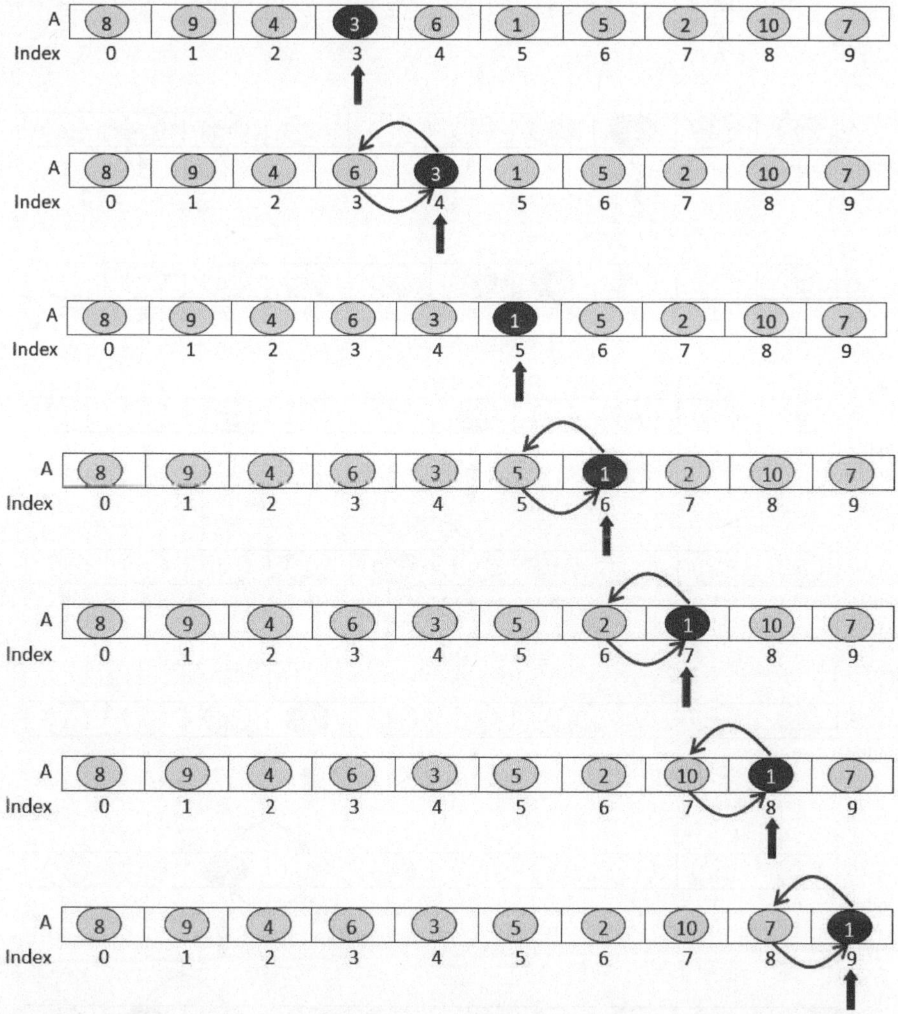

As illustrated above, when the scanner reaches the last index, the last index of the array has the smallest element. It can be noted that as the scanner moves forward, the smallest element is bubbled up along with the scanner. Hence, the algorithm is named as *bubble sort.* With this, the first pass is completed. In the second pass, the above scanning process is repeated from the smallest index to the second largest applicable index. As the smallest element in the array is found and stored at the last index i.e., A[9], the scanning will be done only upto second last index i.e., A[8].

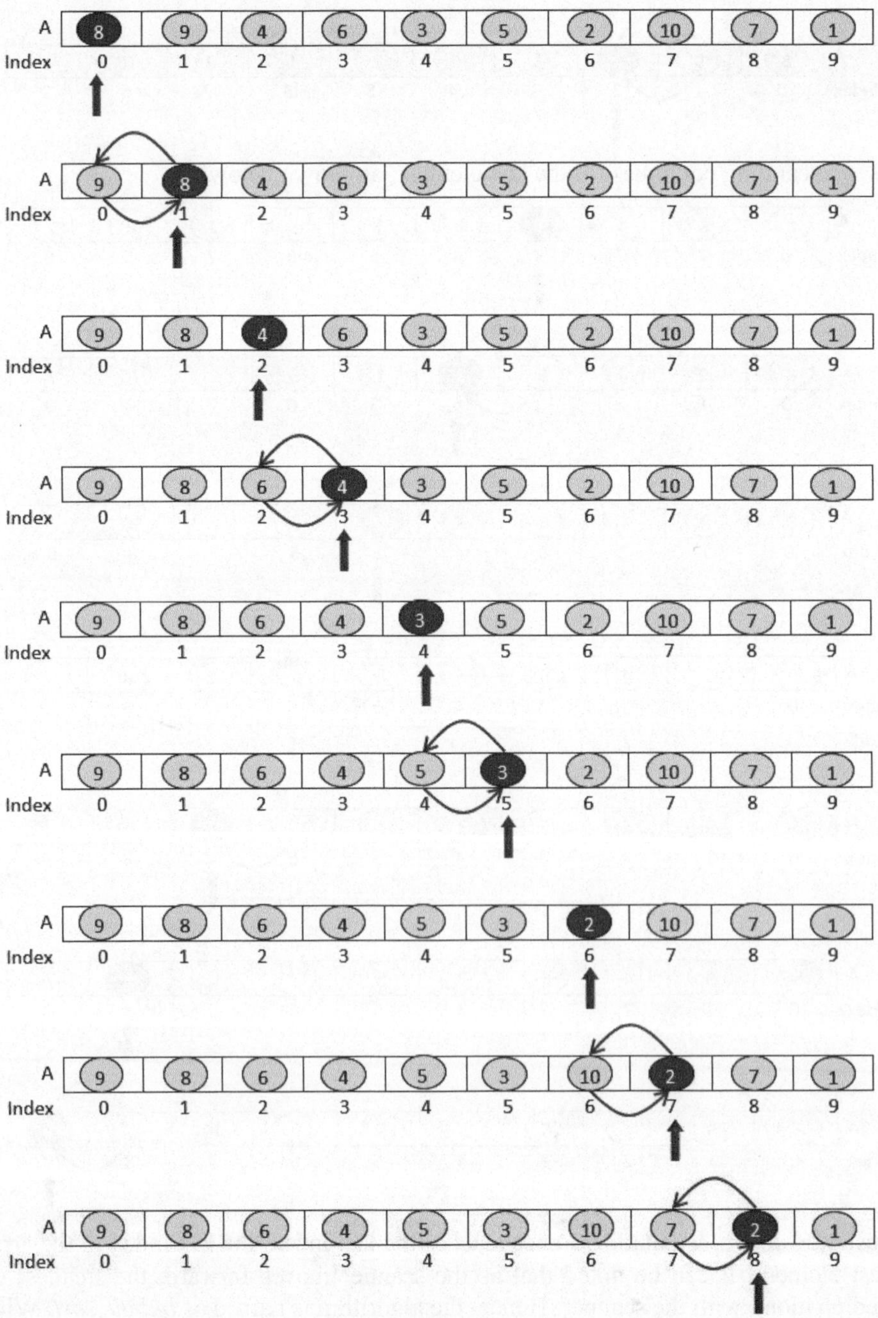

Likewise, the scanning continues for pass 2, 3, 4 and so on upto pass 10, and obtains the following pass-wise orderings.

PASS -3

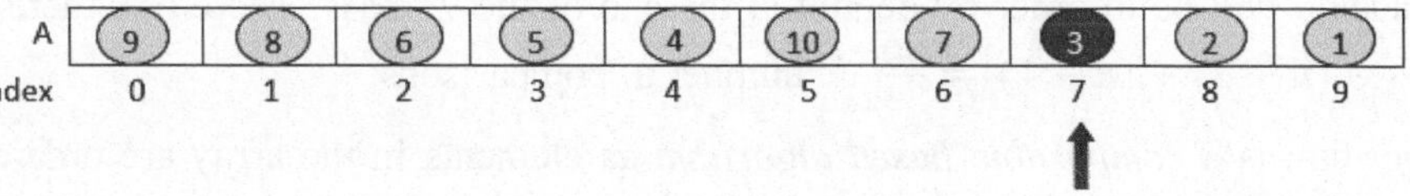

PASS -4

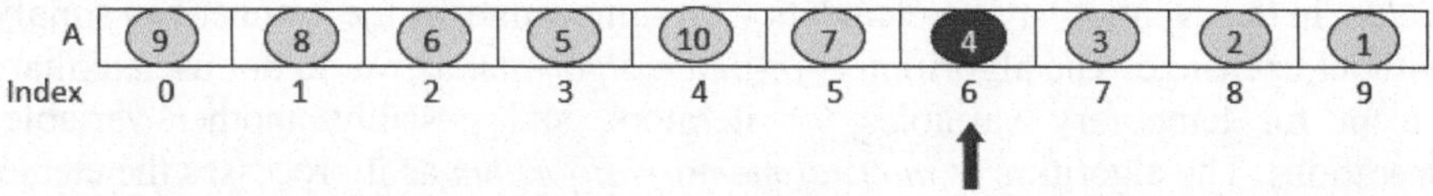

PASS -5

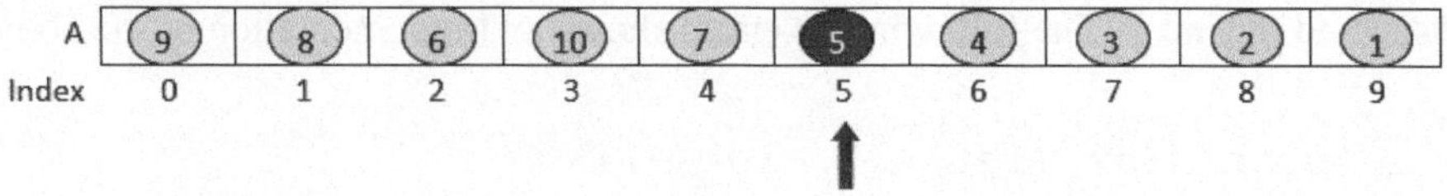

PASS -6

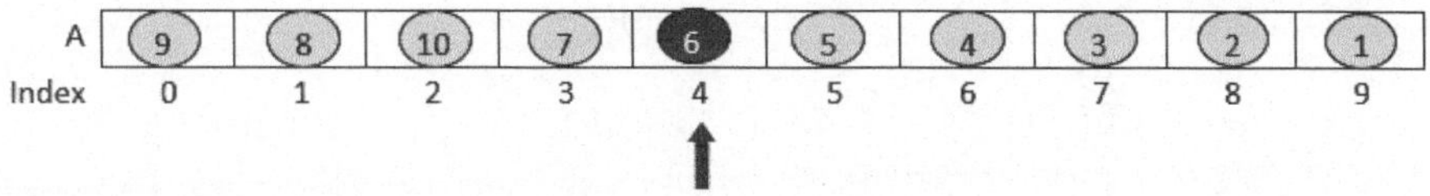

PASS -7

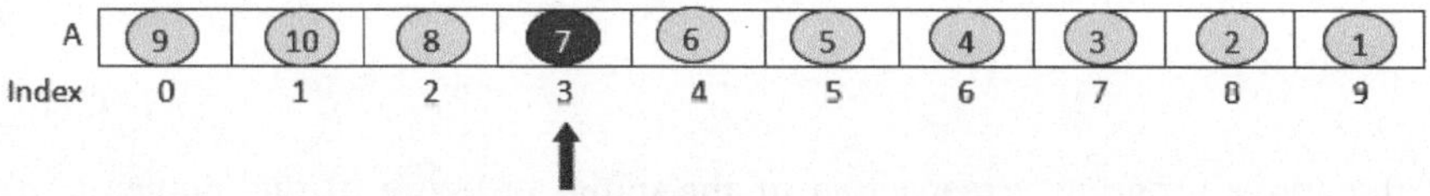

PASS -8

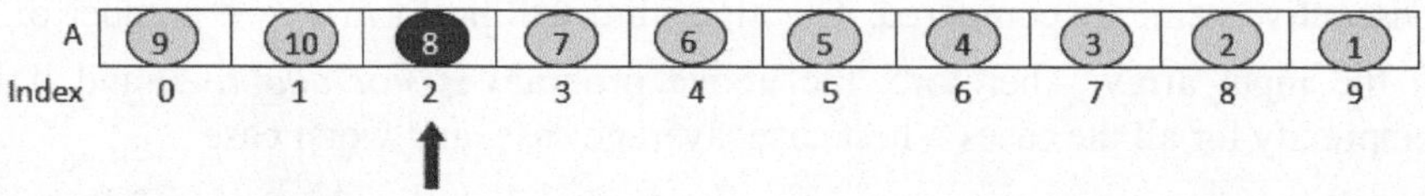

PASS -9

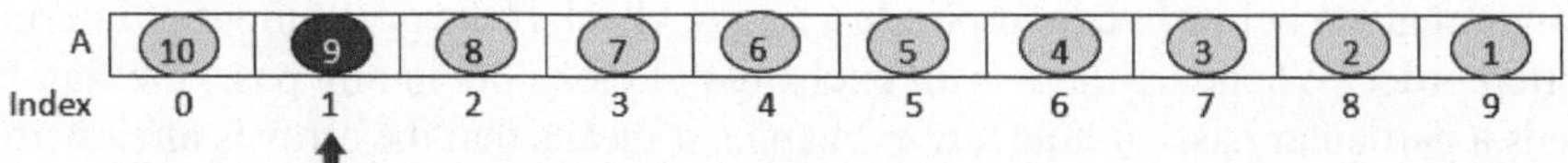

PASS -10

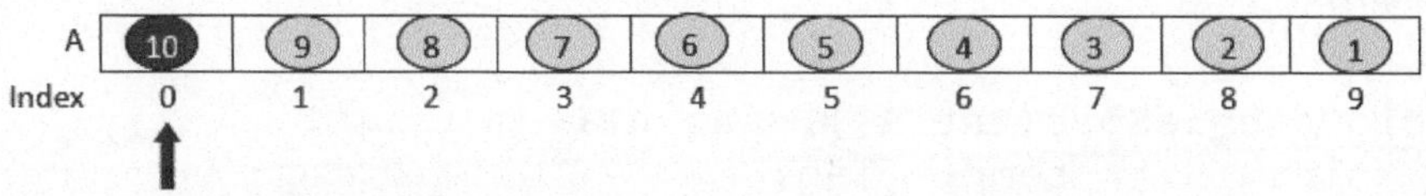

In the first pass, the algorithm performs $n - 1$ number of comparisons. When the scanner is at the index 0, no comparison requires. It can simply move forward. As such, when the scanner is at index 0, we can start comparison with the second element, reducing the scanning in the first pass only upto $n - 1$. In the second pass, the algorithm performs $n - 2$ number of comparisons.

Likewise, $n-3$ number of comparisons in 3rd pass, $n-4$ number of comparisons in 4th pass and so on. Though, there are 10 passes for 10 elements, the passes can stop at 9th pass, the element at index 0 will be in order by default at the end of the 9th pass. Therefore, there are $1+2+3+\cdots.+(n-2)+(n-1) = \frac{n(n-1)}{2}$ number of comparisons.

The algorithm is a *comparable based algorithm* as elements in the array are ordered by comparing between the values of the element and exchanging the unordered two elements. The algorithm is *stable*, in the event of having elements with same value, as the scanner can simply move forward without exchange. The algorithm is *in-place algorithm* as we do not use auxiliary data structure except for temporary variables for iterators, and possibly another variable for exchange operations. The algorithm is *internal memory algorithm* as it processes the elements in an array, and the entire array needs to be in RAM. An algorithm for bubble sort is given and briefly discussed in Unit 1. The following program shows an implementation of the above process.

```
void bubbleSort(int A[], int n){
    int i, j, temp;
    for (i = 0; i < n - 1; i++){
        for (j = 0; j < n - i - 1; j++){
            if (A[j] < A[j + 1]){
                  temp = A[j];
                  A[j] = A[j+1];
                  A[j+1] = temp;
            }
        }
    }
}
```

In the above program, irrespective of the initial ordering of the elements in the array, every consecutive pairs are compared. The algorithm will perform $\frac{n(n-1)}{2}$ number of comparisons for all the input array. Therefore, the above program is *not adaptive*, and it has $O(n^2)$ time complexity for all the cases – best case, average case, and worst case.

The above algorithm/program can be modified and made adaptive as follows. In the modified program given below, we incorporate a flag to check if the given input or intermediate array is in sorted order. Whenever there is an exchange of elements in any pass, the flag is set to true. If it finds a particular pass without any exchange, it means that the array is already in sorted order and the algorithm/program terminates. Hence, bubble sort algorithm can be modified to make it *adaptive*.

```
void bubbleSort(int A[], int n){
    int i, j, temp, flag;
    for (i = 0; i < n - 1; i++){
        flag=0;
        for (j = 0; j < n - i - 1; j++){
            if (A[j] < A[j + 1]){
                  temp = A[j];
```

```
                    A[j] = A[j+1];
                    A[j+1] = temp;
                    flag=1;
                }
            }
            if(flag==0) break;
        }
}
```

The above program terminates if the inner loop does not set the flag. It means, the underlying array processed by the inner loop is already in the sorted order. With this modification, if the given input array is already in the sorted order (i.e., inversion count of the input array equals to 0), the algorithm will scan only one time and terminate. Therefore, the time complexity of this situation (best case) could be enhanced to $O(n)$. A detailed analysis of best case, average case and worst case is provided in Unit 1.

4.1.3 Insertion Sort

The idea in the insertion sort is to insert an element in a sorted subarray. Like in bubble sort, the insertion sort will also scan the array multiple times through different passes. However, unlike bubble sort, it assumes to have an intermediate sorted subarray, and a new element is inserted in order to the sorted sub-array in subsequent pass, as described below. Let us consider the following array, and sort the array in ascending order.

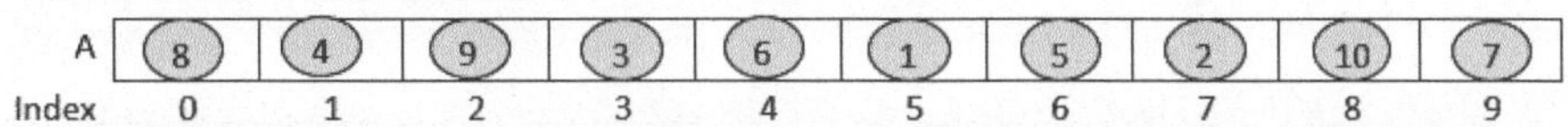

In the first pass, we assume to have an empty sorted array, and the scanner inserts the element at index 0 to the empty sorted array. Thus, it produces a sorted subarray of element 8.

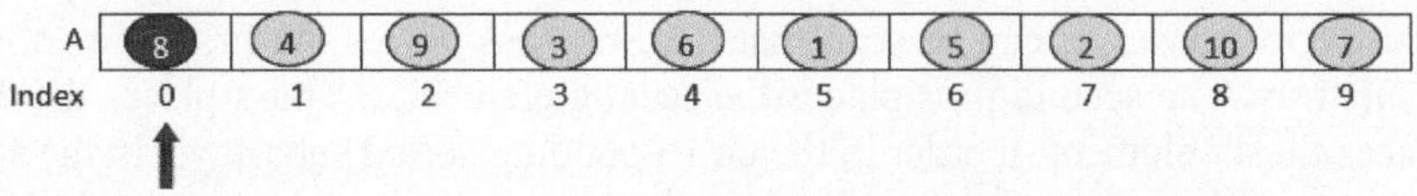

In the second pass, it considers the sorted subarray obtained from pass 1, and the scanner inserts the element at A[1] to the sorted subarray in order (ascending) by scanning backward, as shown below. As the element to be inserted 4 is smaller than the largest of the sorted subarray 8, 4 and 8 are exchanged.

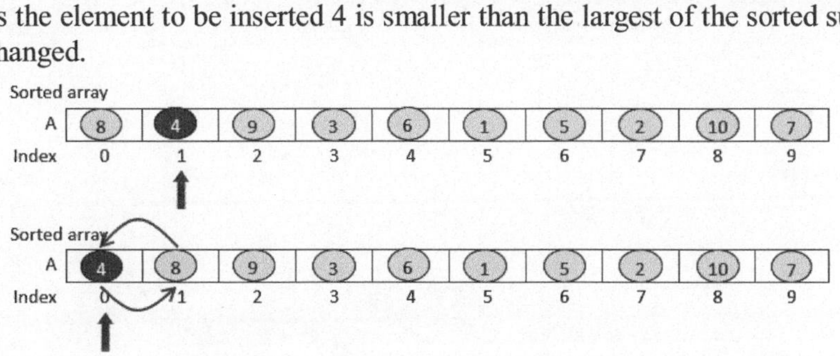

In the third pass, it considers the sorted subarray obtained from pass 2, and the scanner inserts the element at A[2] i.e., 9 to the sorted subarray (4, 8) in order (ascending) by scanning backward. However, 9 is larger than the largest element in the sorted sub array. Therefore, 9 is already placed in order, and terminate the pass.

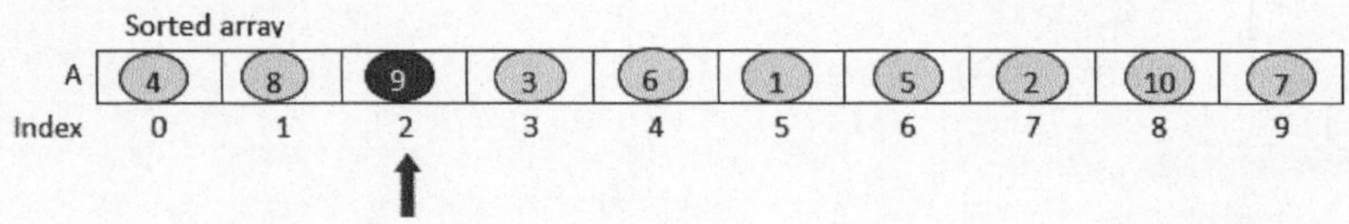

In the fourth pass, the scanner inserts the element at A[3] i.e., 3 to the sorted subarray (4, 8, 9) by scanning the array backward. 3 is smaller than 9, so 3 and 9 are swapped. Then, 3 and 8 are swapped. Lastly, 3 and 4 are swapped.

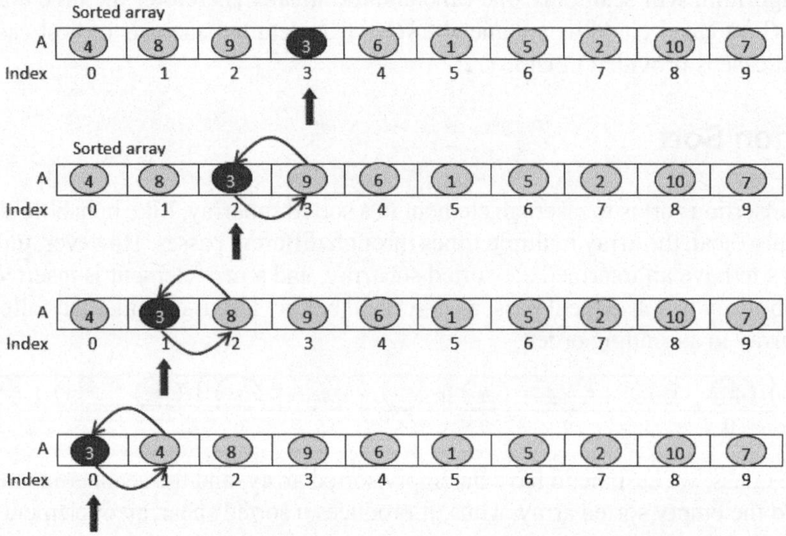

From the above passes, it can be seen that the first pass places the first element in order in the sorted subarray. The second pass places the second element, 3rd pass places the 3rd element, 4th pass places the 4th element in order in the corresponding sorted subarrays. In the similar manner, the remaining subsequent passes will place the corresponding element in the sorted subarray obtained from the previous pass, as shown below.

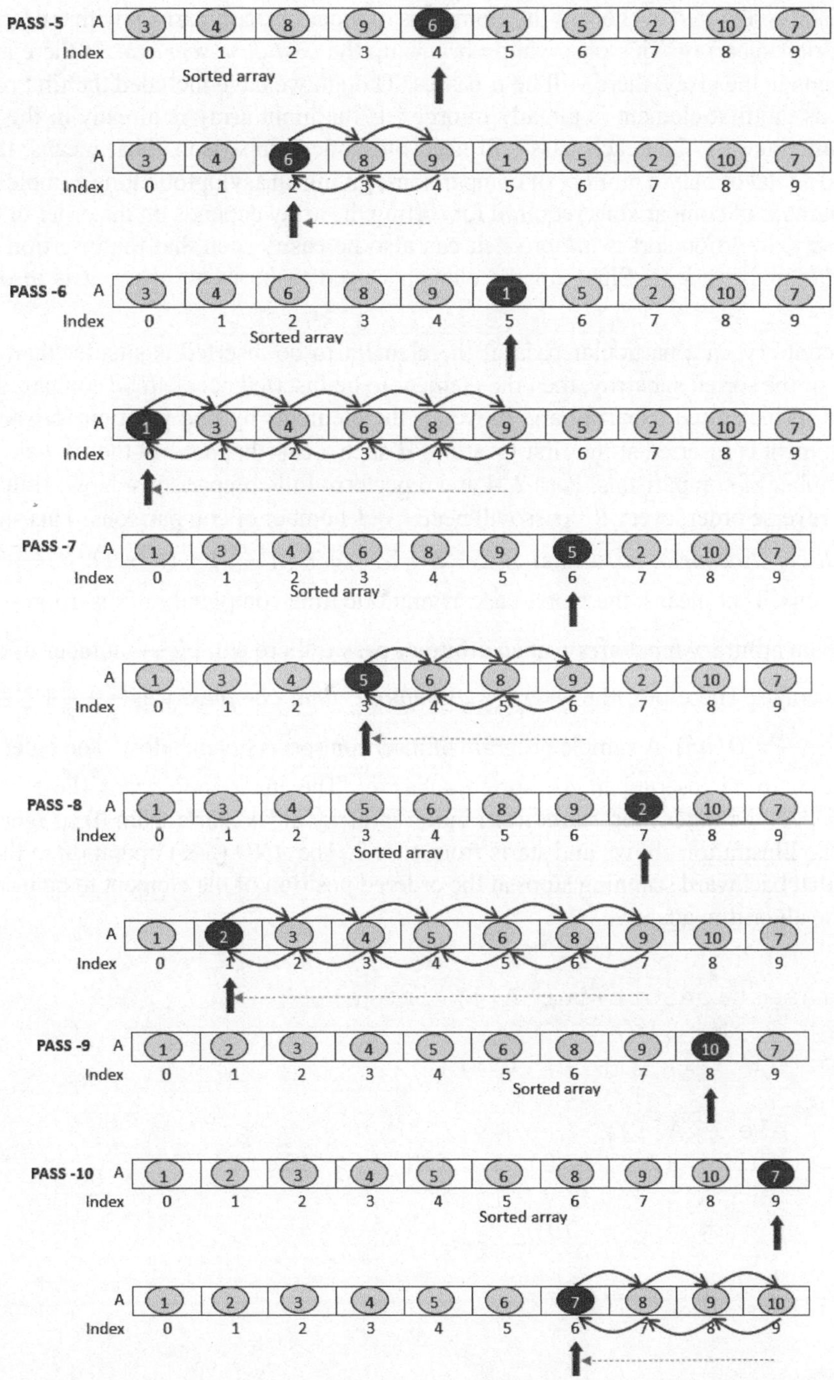

For the above example, it can be seen that in a particular pass, if the element to be inserted is larger than the largest element in the sorted subarray, that pass will perform only one comparison. Pass 3, 6 and 9 perform only one comparison as the target element is already in order. One comparison is required to check if the element is in order i.e., comparison with the largest element of the sorted subarray. This observation brings up the *best case scenario*. If there are n number of elements in the array, there will be n passes. Though we have included the first pass, it can be ignored as the first element is already in order. If the input array is already in the sorted order (inversion count 0), then each pass will need only one comparison. That means, the algorithm will need a total of only n number of comparisons, giving an asymptotic time complexity of $O(n)$. As the number of comparisons required for sorting the array depends on the order of the elements in the array, insertion sort is *adaptive*. It can also be easily seen that the insertion algorithm is also *stable* and *in-place*. Since all the elements need to be in an array, it is also an *internal* algorithm.

On the contrary, in a particular pass, if the element to be inserted is smaller than the smallest element of the sorted subarray, then the element to be inserted needs to be compared with all the elements in the sorted subarray and move all the elements by one position forward. Then, the target element is inserted at the first location. If such a case happens in the ith pass, it will need $i-1$ number of comparisons. Pass 2, 4 and 6 perform full comparisons. Now, if the input array is in the reverse order, every i^{th} pass will need $i-1$ number of comparisons. This situation gives the *worst-case scenario*. So, a total of $1+2+3+\cdots+(n-2)+(n-1)=\frac{n(n-1)}{2}$ number of comparisons. That means, the worst-case asymptotic time complexity of insertion sort is $O(n^2)$.

Now, for an arbitrary input array, at an arbitrary pass i, there will be $\frac{i-1}{2}$ number of comparisons on an average. Therefore, the *average asymptotic time complexity* is $\frac{1}{2}+\frac{2}{2}+\frac{3}{2}+\cdots+\frac{n-2}{2}+\frac{n-1}{2}=\frac{n(n-1)}{4}=O(n^2)$. A sample program of insertion sort is given below. The outer loop selects the element to be inserted in the sorted subarray. The inner loop scans the sorted subarray backward. As the outer loop starts from index 1 (array index starts from 0), it ignores the first pass of the illustration above, and starts from pass 2. The *AND* (&&) operation in the inner loop ensures that backward scanning stops at the ordered position of the element to be inserted, which makes the algorithm adaptive.

```
void insertionSort(int A[], int n){
    int i, j, ele;
    for (i = 1; i < n; i++){
        j = i - 1;
        ele = A[i];
        while ((j >= 0) && (A[j] > ele)){
            A[j + 1] = A[j];
            j = j - 1;
        }
        A[j + 1] = ele;
    }
}
```

Like bubble sort, insertion sort is stable, in-place, internal memory, and comparable based sorting algorithm. Further, it is adaptive, as the running time depends on the initial ordering of the input array.

4.1.4 Selection Sort

In the above bubble sort and insertion sort algorithms, whenever two successive elements are out of order in the inner loop, they are exchanged. Though asymptotic complexity is not affected, actual computational time will be affected by the $O(1)$ swap operations. *Can we reduce the number of swap operations while sorting an array?* Selection sort is motivated by this question. Unlike bubble or insertion sort, selection sort does not swap the element immediately. Instead, a pass in the selection sort algorithm selects a location and scans the unordered array to find the element to be placed in the selected location. It, then, swaps the elements at the selected location and the location *where the target element is found.* For ascending order, the minimum element will be considered. However, for descending order, the maximum element will be considered. Let us say, we are sorting the array in ascending order, and in the ith pass, the ith minimum element in the unsorted subarray is found at loc. Then, $A[i-1]$ and $A[loc]$ are swapped. We consider $A[i-1]$, because array index starts from 0, and pass numbering starts from 1, in our discussion below. Each pass performs at the most one swap operation.

Consider the following array and sort the elements in ascending order.

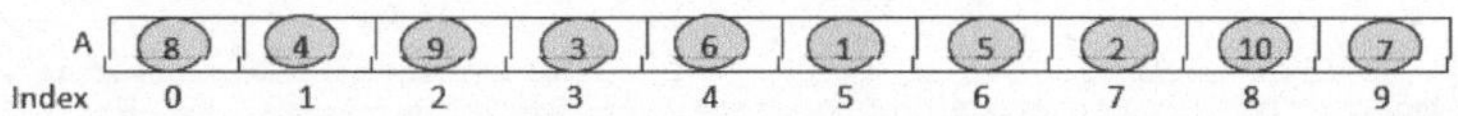

In the pass 1, scan the entire array and find the location of the smallest element loc. After finding the smallest element, swap the elements at $A[0]$ and $A[loc]$, as shown below. Each pass divides the array into two parts – *sorted subarray* and *unsorted subarray*.

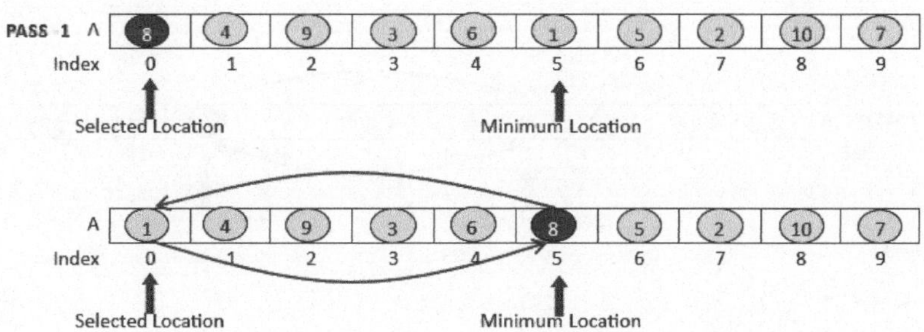

In the pass 2, scan the entire unsorted array and find the location of the smallest element loc. After finding the smallest element, swap the elements at $A[1]$ and $A[loc]$, as shown below. Pass 2 obtains the second element of the sorted subarray.

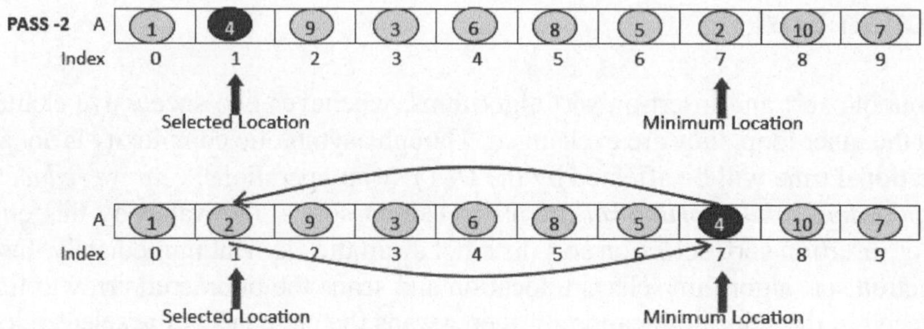

Like in pass 2, in pass 3, the scanner locates the location of the smallest element 3, and it is swapped with the element in the selected location, as shown below.

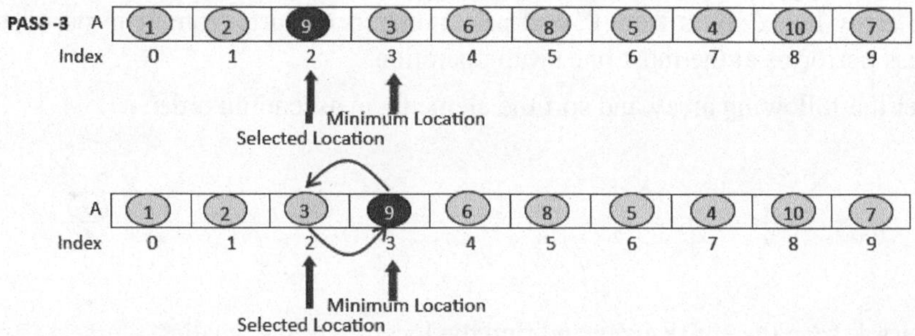

In the similar manner, in the subsequent passes, the minimum elements are located and placed in the corresponding selected locations, as shown below.

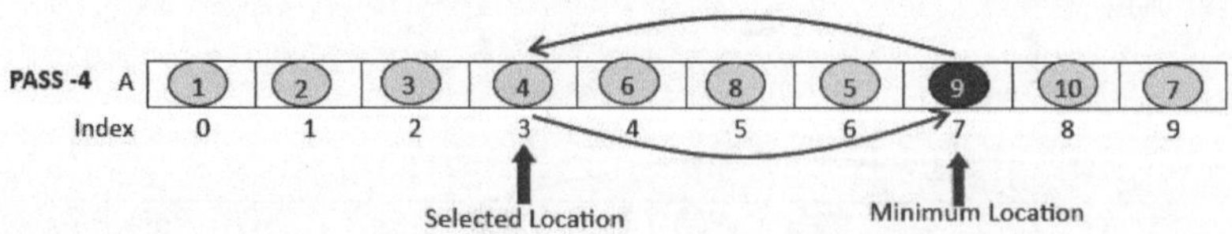

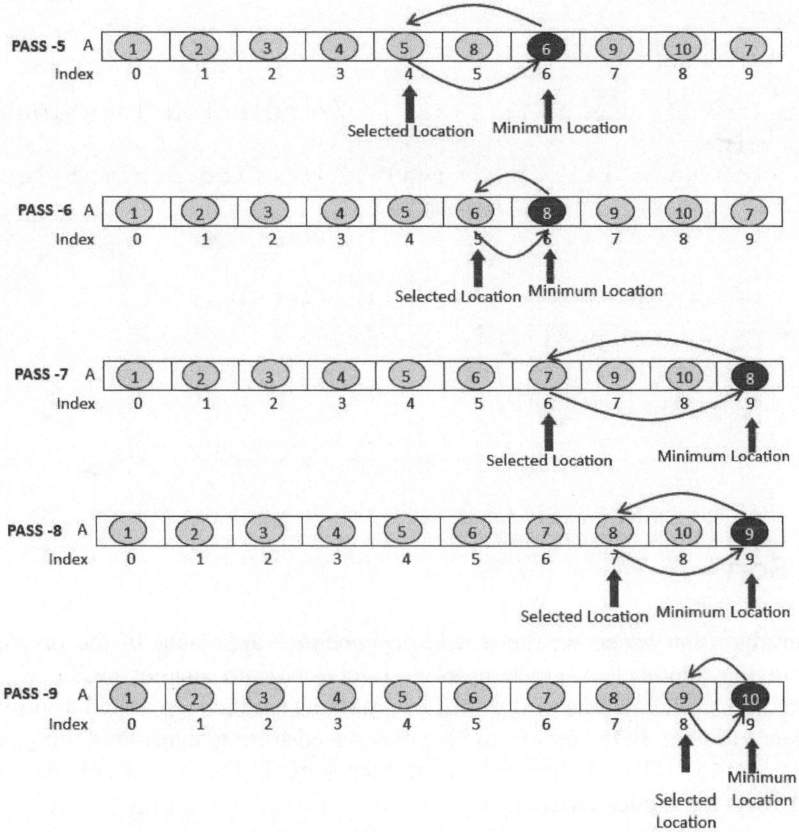

In the above example, pass 1 performs $n-1$ number of comparison operations to locate the minimum element. Likewise, pass 2 performs $n-2$ comparison operations, pass 3 performs $n-3$ comparison operations, and so on. The last pass (i.e., $n-1$ pass) performs one comparison operation to obtain the sorted array. Therefore, selection sort performs a total of $(n-1)+(n-2)+\cdots+3+2+1=\frac{n(n-1)}{2}$ number of comparison operations. It may also be noted that for a given n elements, finding minimum needs exactly $n-1$ number of comparisons irrespective of its initial ordering. Therefore, every i^{th} pass performs $n-i$ number of comparison operations. So, for all the cases (*best case, average case,* and *worst case*), selection sort will perform $\frac{n(n-1)}{2}$ number of comparisons, and has $O(n^2)$ asymptotic time complexity.

An implementation of the above process is given below. The outer loop acts as the pass, and selects the location for which an appropriate minimum element should be found. The inner loop scans the unsorted subarray and finds the minimum element. The if-condition swaps the element in the selected location and the minimum. Like bubble and insertion sort, selection sort is in-place, internal memory, comparable, but unstable and non-adaptive sorting algorithm.

```
void selectionSort(int A[], int n)
```

```
{
    int i, j, min, temp;

    for (i = 0; i < n-1; i++){     // selected location
        min = i;
        for (j = i+1; j < n; j++){ // find minimum location
            if (A[j] < A[min])
                min = j;
        }
        if(min != i){   // swap elements
            temp = A[min];
            A[min] = A[i];
            A[i] = temp;
        }
    }
}
```

4.1.5 Quick Sort

Quick sort is an algorithm based on the *divide and conquer* approach. In the divide and conquer problem-solving approach, a given problem is divided into smaller problems, and solve the smaller problems. The outputs of the smaller problems are then combined to provide the output of the bigger problem. In the divide and conquer based sorting algorithms, a bigger array is split into smaller arrays. The smaller arrays are then sorted. The sorted smaller arrays are then combined to get the bigger sorted array.

Given an array of data elements, quick sort divides the array into two smaller parts around an element called *pivot*. The process of dividing the input array into two smaller parts is generally called *partitioning*, and it is the main operation in quick sort. Before discussing quick sort algorithm, let us first try to understand the concept of partitioning an array around a pivot value.

Let `A` be an array with n number of elements, and let `x` be the pivot which can be one of the randomly picked up element from `A`. Then, the idea of partitioning `A` by `x` is to find the correct position of `x` in `A` such that all the elements preceding `x` are smaller than or equal to `x`, and all the elements succeeding `x` are larger than `x`. If i is the position of x returned by the partitioning algorithm, then after partitioning, all the elements from $A[0]$ to $A[i-1]$ will be smaller than or equal to `x`, and all the elements from $A[i+1]$ to $A[n-1]$ are larger than x, as shown below.

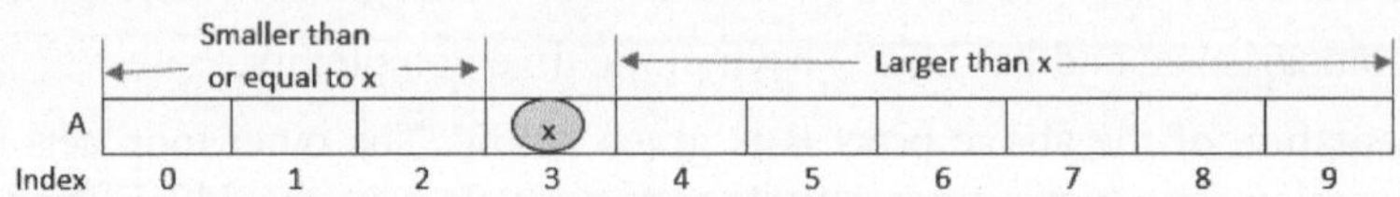

Different partitioning algorithms have been proposed in the literature. A typical partitioning approach which scans the array from two directions (left-to-right and right-to-left) is discussed in this book. Before describing the algorithm, we first explain the operational steps.

Let us consider an example array given below to describe the partitioning idea.

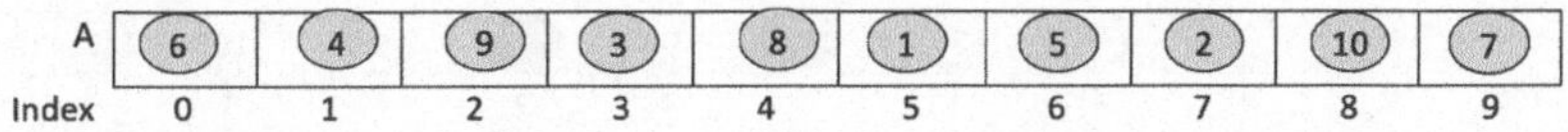

Let us consider the first element of the array i.e., $A[0]$ as the pivot. You may find different partitioning algorithms in different sources. Any algorithm that partitions the array into two around the pivot could be used. In principle, we should be able to select any random element as pivot, and devise an appropriate partitioning algorithm. For simplicity, the first element of the given array has been considered as pivot. The procedure adopted below also uses another two pointers - `left` and `right` to mark the beginning and end of the array, as shown below.

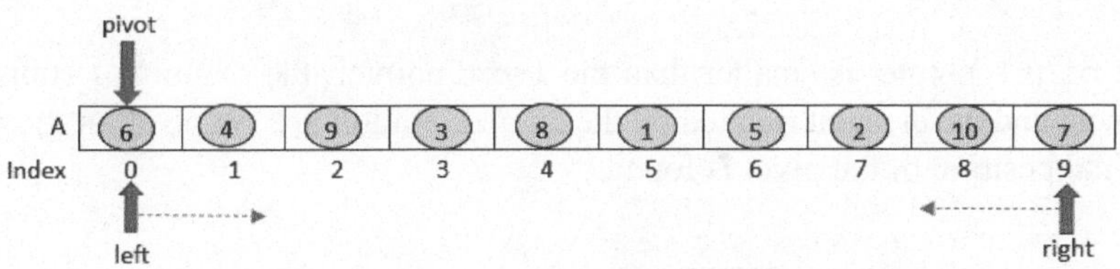

The `left` pointer scans the array from left to right direction, and the `right` pointer scans the array from right to left direction. Whenever the left pointer finds an element larger than the pivot, it stops scanning. Similarly, whenever the right pointer finds an element smaller than or equal to pivot, it stops scanning, as shown below.

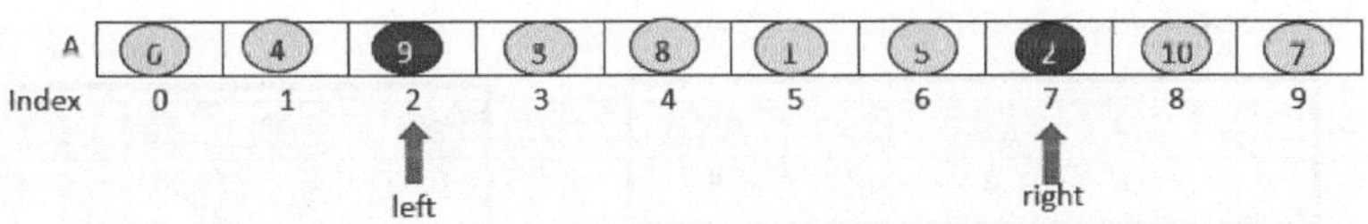

It then swaps the two elements pointed by `left` pointer and `right` pointer.

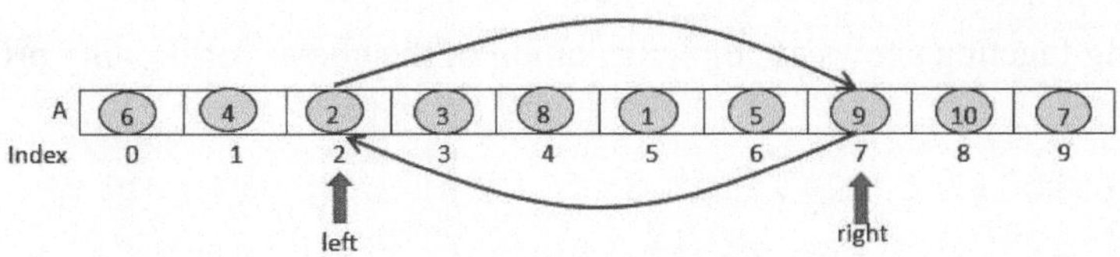

After swapping the two elements, repeat the above scanning process i.e., left pointer moves till it finds an element larger than pivot, and the right pointer finds an element smaller than or equal to pivot. It then swaps the two elements, and so on. The process continues as long as the left pointer is smaller than the right pointer.

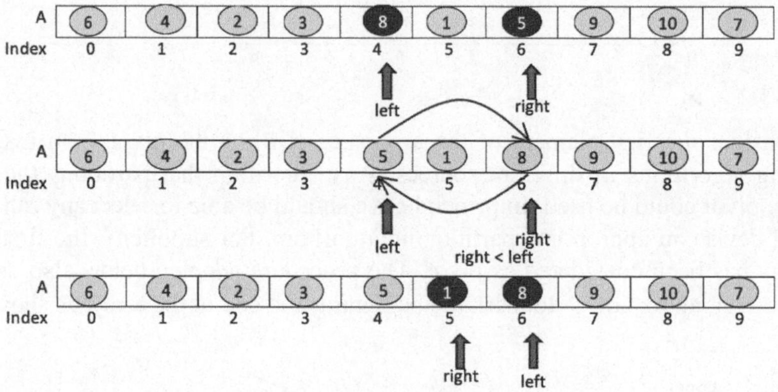

When the `right` pointer is smaller than the `left` pointer, the scanning terminates. Then, the pivot element and the element pointed by the `right` pointer are swapped, as shown below. With this, the final position of the pivot is found.

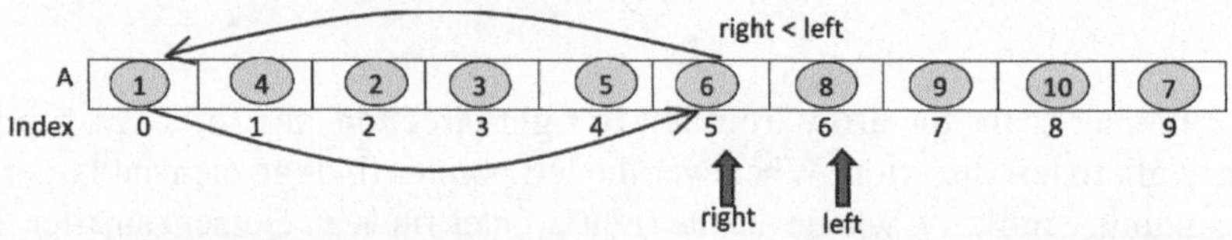

Now, the array is partitioned into two – left partition holds the elements smaller than or equal to pivot, and the right partition holds the elements larger than the pivot, as shown below.

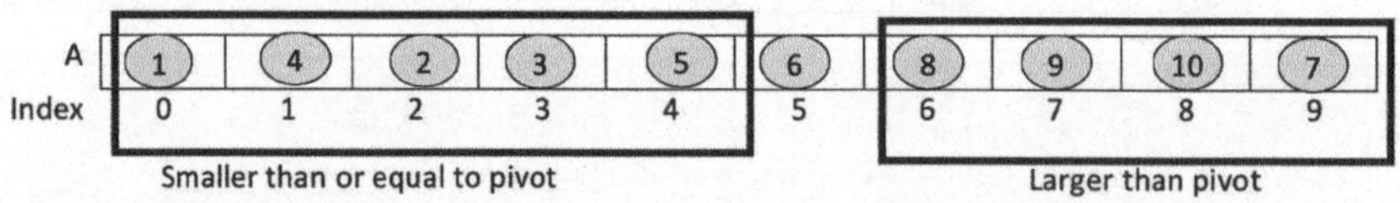

As the above partitioning algorithm scans the array in linear time, it has $\theta(n)$ time complexity. For any partitioning algorithm, as it needs to visit every element in the array at least once, it will have at least $\theta(n)$ time complexity.

The following function shows an implementation of the above partitioning procedure.

```
int partition(int A[], int left, int right){
    int l = left, r = right, temp;
    int pivot =A[left];
    while (l<r){
        /* Scan left to right as long as current element
           is smaller or equal to pivot */
        while((A[l] <= pivot) &&(l<= right))l++;
```

```
            /* Scan right to left as long as current element
            is larger than pivot */
            while(A[r] > pivot)  r--;

            /* move element smaller than pivot to the left side of
            the possible possible location of pivot, and larger
            element to the right side */
            if (l<r){
                temp = A[l];
                A[l] = A[r];
                A[r] = temp;
            }
        }
        // r has the location of the pivot
        temp = A[left];
        A[left] = A[r];
        A[r] = temp;
        return r;    //return the position of the pivot
}
```

Quick sort algorithm applies the partitioning algorithm recursively over the partitions obtained. The recursive quick sort algorithm can be defined as follows.

```
void quickSort(int A[], int left, int right){
    if (left < right){
        int p = partition(A, left, right);
        quickSort(A, left, p - 1);
        quickSort(A, p + 1, right);
    }
}
```

Time complexity: The *best-case scenario* will happen when partitioning algorithm always divides the array into equal halves. If $T(n)$ is the time taken by the algorithm to sort an array of size n, then the recurrence equation of quick sort algorithm in its best scenario can be defined as below.

$$T(n) = \begin{cases} 2T(n/2) + n, & if\ n > 1 \\ 1 \quad , & if\ n = 1 \end{cases}$$

where n is the time taken for the partitioning algorithm and combining results from recursion. As no cost for combining results from recursion involves, it is basically the cost for partitioning the array. If we expand the above recurrence equation, we get the expression defined below.

$$T(n) = 2T(n/2) + n = 2[2T(n/2^2) + n/2] + n = 2^2T(n/2^2) + n + n$$

$$= 2^2[2T(n/2^3) + n/4] + n + n = 2^3T(n/2^2) + n + n + n$$
$$= 2^3[2T(n/2^4) + n/8] + n + n + n = 2^4T(n/2^4) + n + n + n + n$$

....

....

$$= 2^kT(n/2^k) + n + \cdots + n + n + n + n$$
$$= 2^kT(1) + n + \cdots + n + n + n + n, \textit{ Assume that } n = 2^k$$
$$= n\log_2 n + n = O(n\log_2 n)$$

We can also visualize the estimate using recursion and estimate the running time of $T(n) = 2T(n/2) + n$ as follows. The computation cost at every level is n, and there are $\log_2 n$ number of levels.

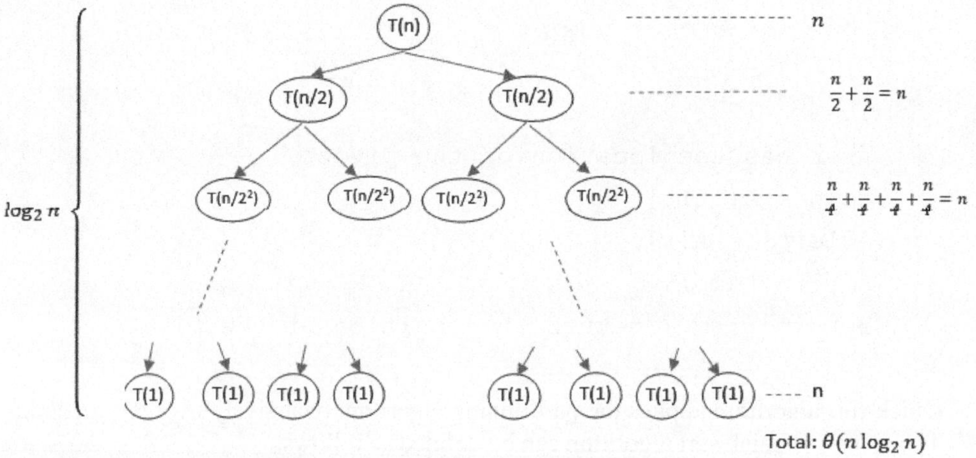

Therefore, the best time complexity of quick sort is $\theta(n\log_2 n)$. Likewise, *worst case time complexity* happens when the pivot partitions the array into an empty array and another array of size $n-1$. This situation will happen when the *smallest/largest element* is always selected as pivot. For the *worst-case scenario*, the recurrence equation can be defined as below.

$$T(n) = \begin{cases} T(n-1) + n, & if\ n > 1 \\ 1 \quad , & if\ n = 1 \end{cases}$$

We can expand the expression as follows.

$$T(n) = T(n-1) + n$$
$$= T(n-2) + (n-1) + n$$
$$= T(n-3) + (n-2) + (n-1) + n$$

....

$$= T(1) + 2 + 3 + \cdots + (n-2) + (n-1) + n$$
$$= \frac{n(n-1)}{2} = \theta(n^2)$$

Using recurrence tree, we can also estimate as follows.

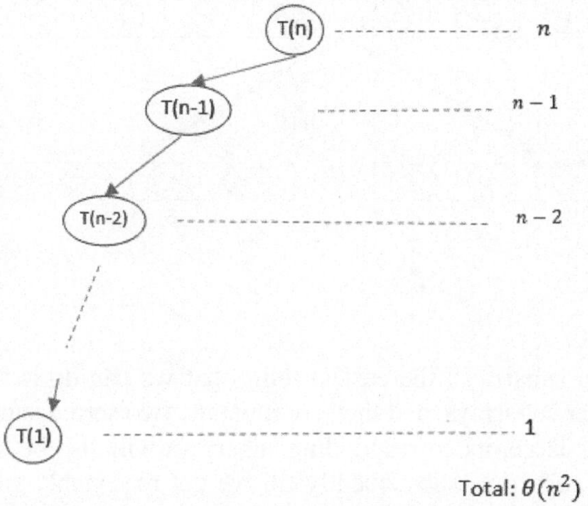

The average time complexity of quick sort is $\theta(n \log_2 n)$. Reader may check the reference material for average case analysis. The above quick sort algorithm is internal, in-place, non-adaptive, and non-stable. The above algorithm can also be modified to make it adaptive. However, the adaptive version of quick sort algorithm is left as an exercise to the reader.

4.1.6 Merge Sort

Like quick sort, merge sort is also a *divide and conquer* based sorting algorithm. It involves the following two basic steps.

Divide: Divide the input array into two almost equal halves.

Conquer: Sort the smaller subarrays (the two halves obtained from above divide operation), and merge the two sorted subarrays to produce a combined sorted array.

Merge sort performs the above divide and conquer steps recursively. The procedure of the algorithm is described below with an illustrative example. Let us consider the following array.

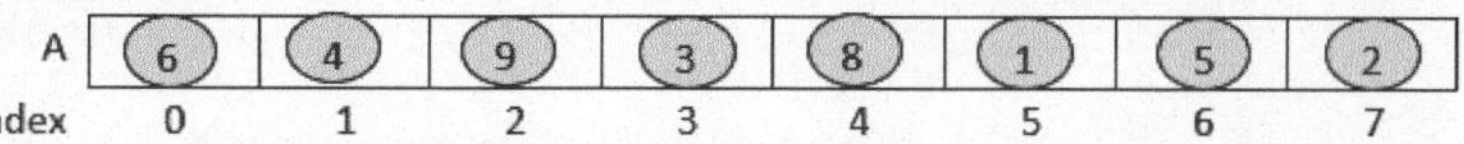

Given an array A with n elements, the algorithm takes two pointers defining the beginning index and the ending index of the array (*first* and *last*). Considering the beginning and ending index of the array, a middle index of the array is defined as below to partition the input array.

$$mid = \left\lceil \frac{last + first}{2} \right\rceil$$

The *middle index (mid)* partitions the given array A into two halves - $A[0 : mid - 1]$ and $A[mid : n - 1]$, as shown below.

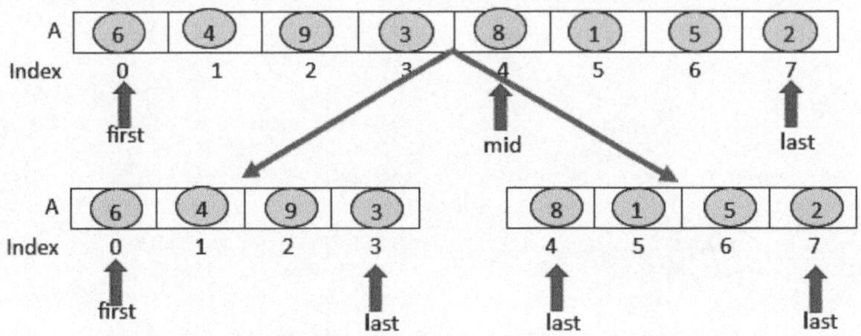

Once we get the smaller two subarrays, the easiest thing that we can do is to apply a sorting algorithm over the two smaller subarrays, and then combine the two sorted subarrays to produce the target sorted array. If n is large, its corresponding subarrays will also be large. So, we may further need to partition the subarrays subsequently till we get reasonably small subarrays. In merge sort, a bigger array will be partitioned into two halves in a hierarchical manner spanning many levels, till we obtain reasonably small subarrays. Once we get small subarrays which can be sorted in $O(1)$ time (probably single element), we hierarchically combine two sorted subarrays in the reverse order to generate the target sorted array. This process is illustrated pictorially below with an array of size 8. We have considered array size 8 in this example to obtain equal size partitioning. However, it is not necessary that the array size should be power of 2. The array is partitioned into two halves of size 4 in the first level. Then, these two subarrays are further partition in the middle to obtain four subarrays of size 2, in the second level. They are further partitioned into halves to obtain eight subarrays of size 1, in the third level. At this point, we stop partitioning the array, as shown below.

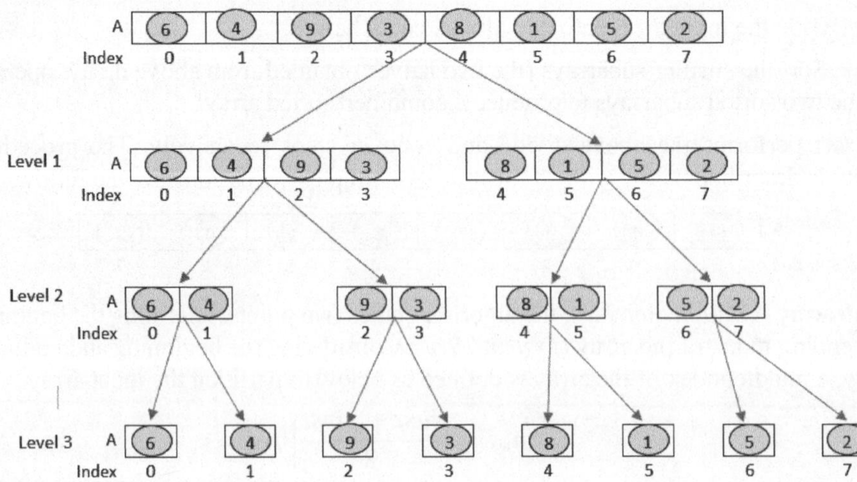

When an array has single element, it is sorted by default. Once we get the sorted subarray with single element, we then pick up two-two sorted subarrays of size 1 at a time and merge to generate another sorted array of size 2, in the first level. Then, in the second level, we pick up two-two sorted subarrays of size 2 and merge to generate another sorted array of size 4, Likewise, the merging process repeats hierarchically in the reverse order till we get completely sorted array.

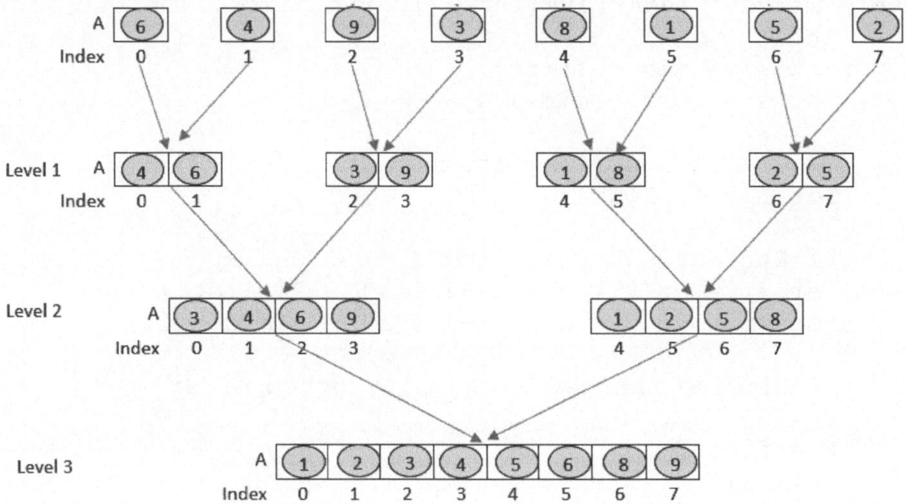

The above sorting process can be implemented either recursively or iteratively. It is simpler to implement and visualize the process of merge sort using recursive partitioning. The following algorithm/function puts the above procedure together to sort an array recursively, and defines the function for merge sort. It takes the array A, the first index and the last index as parameters. It then partitions the array into halves, and each half is then partitioned recursively, till the subarrays have single element (i.e., $first = last$). Once recursive partitioning reaches the last level, the `mergeSortedArrays()` function merge two sorted subarrays upon returning from the recursion.

```
void mergeSort(int A[], int first, int last){
    if(first < last){
        mergeSort(A, first, ⌈(first+last)/2⌉ - 1);
        mergeSort(A, ⌈(first+last)/2⌉, last);
        mergeSortedArrays(A, first, ⌈(first+last)/2⌉, last)
    }
}
```

Various ways can be adopted to merge two sorted arrays. One simple approach is to use auxiliary space to store the sorted subarrays, and then linearly merging them. If the sizes of two arbitrary sorted arrays are m_1 and m_2, combining these two arrays to produce a combined sorted array should ideally need scanning the arrays once. Therefore, we should be able to consider any algorithm which takes $O(m_1 + m_2)$ merging time. The merging algorithm given below extracts and temporarily stores the sorted subarrays from A into two auxiliary arrays. Then, the two sorted arrays in the auxiliary spaces are linearly scanned to generate combined sorted array, and to store back in A.

```
void mergeSortedArrays(int A[], int first, int mid, int last){
    int i, j, k;
    int sl = mid - first;
    int sr= last - mid + 1;

    // Create auxiliary space
    int L[sl], R[sr];

    // Extract subarray from A to L and R
    for (i = 0; i < sl; i++) L[i] = A[first + i];
    for (i = 0; i < sr; i++) R[i] = A[mid + i];

    // Combine the two arrays in sorted order
    i = j = 0;
    k = first;
    while (i < sl && j < sr){
        if (L[i] <= R[j]){
            A[k] = L[i];
            i++;
        }
        else{
            A[k] = R[j];
            j++;
        }
        k++;
    }
     while (i < sl){ // If R remains
        A[k] = L[i];
        i++;
        k++;
    }
    while (j < n2){ // If L remains
        A[k] = R[j];
        j++;
        k++;
    }
}
```

Unfolding the execution of the above recursive merge sort function over an example array, and time complexity estimation using a recurrence tree is illustrated as below.

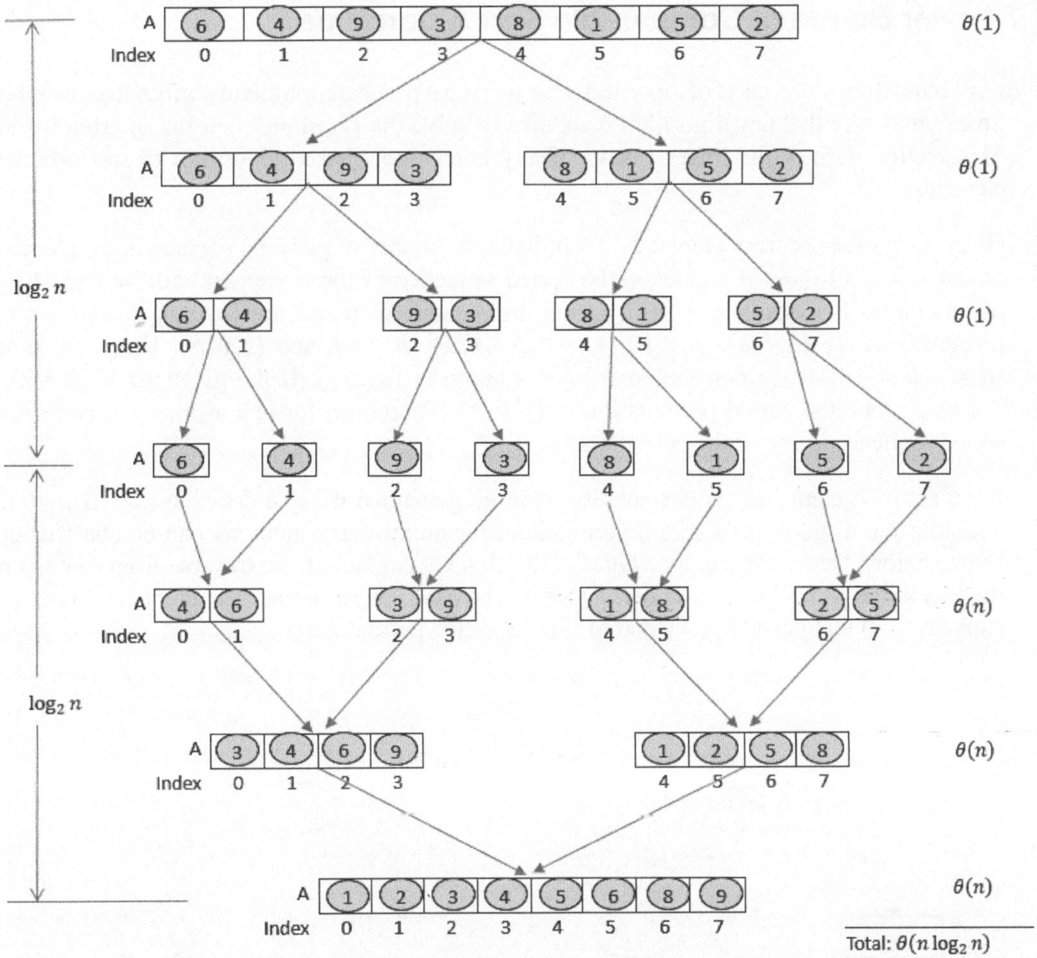

From the above figure, it can be seen that time complexity of merge sort is $\theta(n \log_2 n)$. Irrespective of the initial ordering of the given array, algorithm needs to call recursion till the subarrays have single element. Further, irrespective of the initial sorted orders, the `mergeSortedArrays()` function need to scan all the elements in the given array once. While partitioning is done in $\theta(1)$, merging two sorted arrays to a sorted array is done in $\theta(n)$. As the depth of the recursion is $\theta(\log_2 n)$, the total cost can be approximated as $\theta(\log_2 n) + \theta(n \log_2 n) = \theta(n \log_2 n)$, for all cases – *best case, average case*, and *worst case*. The above complexity can also be estimated using recurrence expression $T(n) = 2T\left(\frac{n}{2}\right) + cn$, which is equivalent to $\theta(n \log_2 n)$, as seen in quick sort. As different partitions of the merge sort can be stored, sorted, and merge using different arrays, which should not necessarily be present in RAM at the same time, merge sort is external. It uses auxiliary arrays to store intermediate partitions, it is an out-of-the-place algorithm. Merge sort is stable and non-adaptive.

4.1.7 Lower Bound of Comparable Sort Algorithms

The lower bound theory of a class of algorithms for solving a particular problem defines the lower bound time complexity that any algorithm must take to solve the given problem for an arbitrary input. This section defines the lower bound of any comparable-based algorithm to sort arbitrary n elements.

Given a set of n arbitrary elements, it will have $n!$ number of possible permutations. Depending on the values of these n elements, the sorted sequence of the n element will be one of the $n!$ permutations. For example, if n is 3, and the possible elements are $\{a, b, c\}$, then its possible permutations are $(a, b, c), (a, c, b), (c, a, b), (b, c, a), (b, a, c)$, and (c, b, a). If the given set is $\{a = 2, b = 5, c = 3\}$, then the sorted permutation is (a, c, b). If the given set is $\{a = 5, b = 1, c = 2\}$, then the sorted permutation is (b, c, a). Therefore, for any arbitrary n elements, its sorted sequence is one of the permutations.

For a set of n elements, its permutations can be generated using a decision tree. If $n = 3$, the decision tree to generate a sorted permutation for an arbitrary input set can be constructed, as shown below. Depending on the values of the elements in the set, we traverse from root to one of the leaf nodes to find its sorted permutation. The path length defines the number of nodes (i.e., comparisons) that need to be visited to find its sorted permutation.

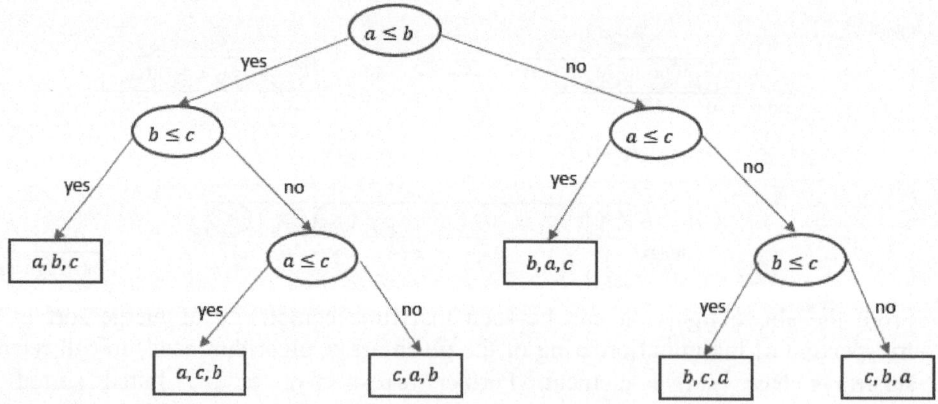

Theorem: The height $h \geq 0$ of a binary tree with $n \geq 1$ number of leaf nodes, where every non-leaf node has two child nodes, is at least $\log_2 n$.

Proof: (By induction on n) If $n = 1$, the tree has only root node, and it is also a leaf node. As the height of a leaf node is 0, it is true for $n = 1$. Let us assume that it is true for $n > 1$. It can be seen that at least one of the subtrees of root will have at least $\frac{n}{2}$ number of leaf nodes. That means, the height of the subtree with at least $\frac{n}{2}$ number of leaf nodes is at least $\log_2 \frac{n}{2} = \log_2 n - 1$. If we add one more leaf node, in one of the subtrees, the above condition will still hold for the subtrees as $\frac{n}{2}+1<n$. As the height of a binary tree is the height of the tallest child subtree plus one, the height of the binary tree with $n+1$ leaf nodes is at least $\log_2\frac{n+1}{2}+1=\log_2(n+1)$.

For an arbitrary set of *n* elements, there are *n!* number of permutations and all the permutations have an equal probability of being picked up as the sorted permutation. There may exist more than one decision trees for the same set of $n!$ permutations as leaf nodes. To define lower bound, we need to prove that the *expected height of any decision tree* for sorting n element is at least $\log_2 n\,!$.

Let T be a decision tree for sorting n elements. It has exactly $n!$ number of leaf nodes. Let $D(T)$ be the sum of the depths of all the leaf nodes in T. Let $M(T)$ be the minimum $D(T)$ over all possible decision tree with $n!$ leaf nodes. If i be the number of leaf nodes in the left subtree of the root of T, then there will be $(n!-i)$ number of leaf node in the right subtree. Then D(T) can be defined recursively as below.

$$D(T)=D(T_i)+D(T_{n!-i})+n!$$

The $n!$ in the above expression is additional depth of 1 from root to the roots of left and right subtrees for all the $n!$ leaf nodes. Now,

$$M(T)=arg\min_i\{D(T_i)+D(T_{n!-i})+n!\}$$

Now, our target is to prove that $M(T)\geq n!\log_2 n!$ for proving *the expected height of any decision tree* for sorting n element is at least $\log_2 n\,!$. We can prove it by induction on n. When $n=1$, $M(T)=0!\log_2 0!=0$. The condition holds for $n=1$.

Let us assume that the condition holds for $n-1$. For n elements, we can define $M(T)$ as $M(T)=\arg\min_i\{D(T_i)+D(T_{n!-i})+n!\}\geq\arg\min_i\{i\log_2 i+(n!-i)\log_2(n!-i)+n!\}$

The above expression will be minimum when $i=\frac{n!}{2}$. As $\frac{n!}{2}\leq(n-1)!$, we can write

$$M(T)\geq\frac{n!}{2}\log_2\frac{n!}{2}+\left(n!-\frac{n!}{2}\right)\log_2\left(n!-\frac{n!}{2}\right)+n!$$

$$=n!\log_2\frac{n!}{2}+n!=n!\,(\log_2 n!-1)+n!=n!\log_2 n!.$$

Now, there are n! number of leaf nodes in M(T). So, the expected height of the decision tree which constitutes M(T) is $\frac{M(T)}{n!}=\log_2 n!$. Therefore, the expected height of a decision tree for an arbitrary set of n elements is a least $\log_2 n!$.

Further, determining a sorted sequences from the decision tree with $n!$ number of leaf nodes, the expected number of comparisons will also be defined by expected height of the decision tree. Therefore, lower bound of any comparable sorting algorithm for an arbitrary input set of n elements is defined by the expected height of the corresponding decision tree i.e., $\log_2 n!$. We see below that it is equal to $\Omega(n \log_2 n)$.

Theorem: Any comparable algorithm to sort n number of arbitrary elements runs in $\Omega(n \log_2 n)$.

Proof: Since, for n number of elements, the decision tree will have $n!$ number of leaf nodes, the minimum height of the decision tree is $\log_2 n!$.

$$\log_2 n! \geq \log_2 \left(n(n-1)(n-2) \ldots \left\lceil \frac{n}{2} \right\rceil\right) \geq \log_2 \left(\frac{n}{2}\right)^{\frac{n}{2}} = \frac{n}{2}[\log_2 n - 1] = \frac{n}{2}\log_2 n - \frac{n}{2}$$

$$= \Omega(n \log_2 n).$$

4.1.8 Counting Sort

All the above sorting algorithms discussed so far are comparable-based algorithms, and their expected lower bound is $\Omega(n \log_2 n)$. *Can we do better? Counting sort* is a non-comparable sorting algorithm whose time complexity is asymptotic linear for all the cases. This algorithm is briefly described below with an example. This algorithm works only for *real numbers*.

Let us consider an input array A as given below.

A	1	2	0	3	0	1	4	2	3	1
Index	0	1	2	3	4	5	6	7	8	9

The algorithm needs an auxiliary array `Count` which stores the count of each element. The size of the auxiliary array is defined by the maximum value in the input array A. In the given array, the maximum element is 4. So, the size of `Count` array is 5 to store the values from 0 to 4. If the array has negative values, or minimum is larger than 0, accordingly the `Count` array and its indexes can be defined. For simplicity, we have considered positive values and index starting from 0. Each value in A corresponds to an index in `Count`. The ith index in `Count` will store the frequency count of i as element in A, as shown below.

Count	2	3	2	2	1
Index	0	1	2	3	4

`Count[0]` is 2. It means, the element 0 occurs two times in `A`. Likewise, the element 1 occurs three times in A, element 2 occurs two times in A , and so on upto element 4. Now, the counts in `Count` array are sequentially summed, so that `Count[i]` stores the cumulative sum from `Count[0]` to `Count[i]`, as defined below.

Count	2	5	7	9	10
Index	0	1	2	3	4

We define another auxiliary array B to store the elements in A in sorted order. Now, we scan the array A from right to left. It can also be done from left to right. In this example, we have scanned from right to left, to make the algorithm stable. The last element in A is 1. Now, go to index 1 of the `Count` array and get the frequency of 1 i.e., `Count[1]=5`. It means that this element will be the fifth element in the sorted array. As the index starts from 0, the element 1 is stored at B[4].

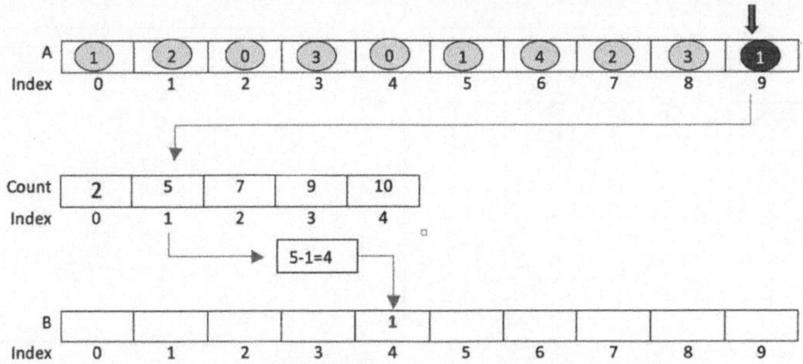

After storing the last element in B, the value of `Count[1]` is reduced by 1, i.e., one of the occurrences of the element is stored in its position B.

Count	2	4	7	9	10
Index	0	1	2	3	4

Now, repeat the same procedure for all the remaining elements, as shown below. At the end of the algorithm, the Count array will have the starting index of the respective elements in B.

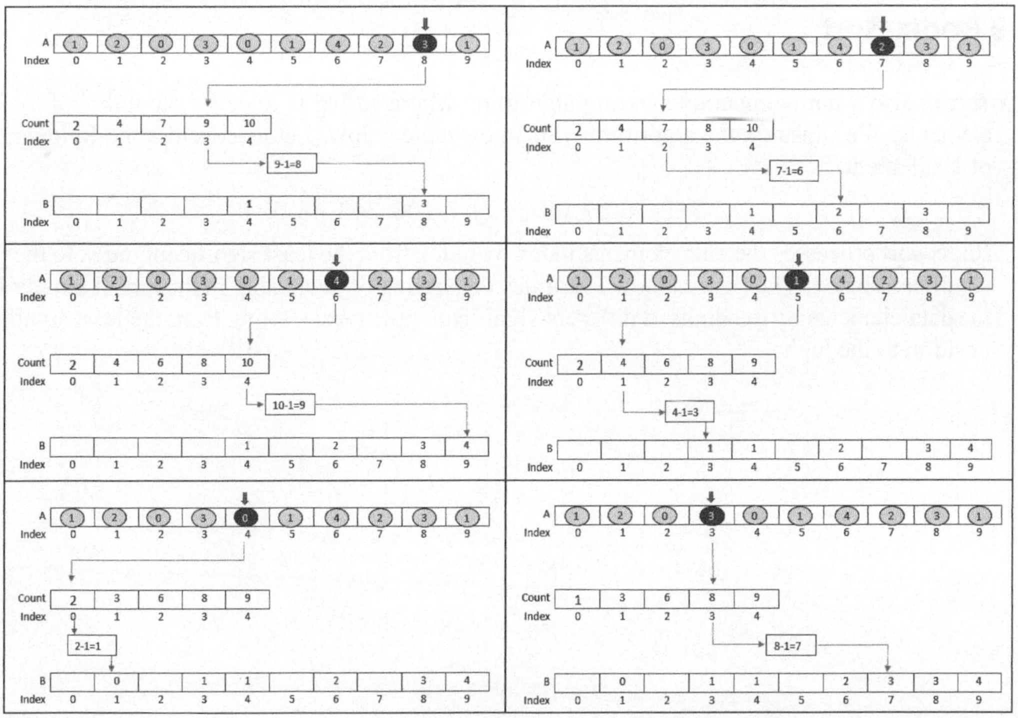

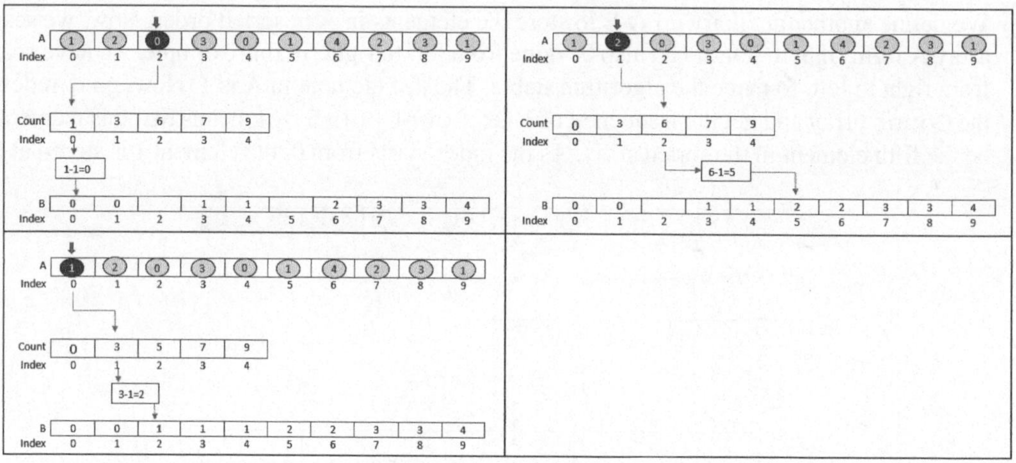

Once the sorted elements are obtained in B, copy them to A to obtain the final sorted array. As we need to scan the input array thrice – first for finding the maximum value, second for counting frequency, and third for scan the input array for final sorting. Similarly, the algorithm scans the `Count` array once for estimating cumulative values. Therefore, the running time for counting sort algorithm is $\theta(n + k)$, where n is the size of the input array and k is the size of `Count` array.

4.1.9 Radix Sort

Radix sort is also a non-comparable sorting algorithm, where soring is done by the index of the data elements. We illustrate the algorithm with an example below. Let us consider the following set of 10 elements.

$$312, 20, 87, 881, 402, 7, 100, 243, 68, 524$$

Radix sort processes the data elements index by index from the least significant index to the most significant index. The figure below illustrates the sorting of data using radix sort. It simply sorts the data elements by the digits at different significant positions, starting from the least significant position to the higher.

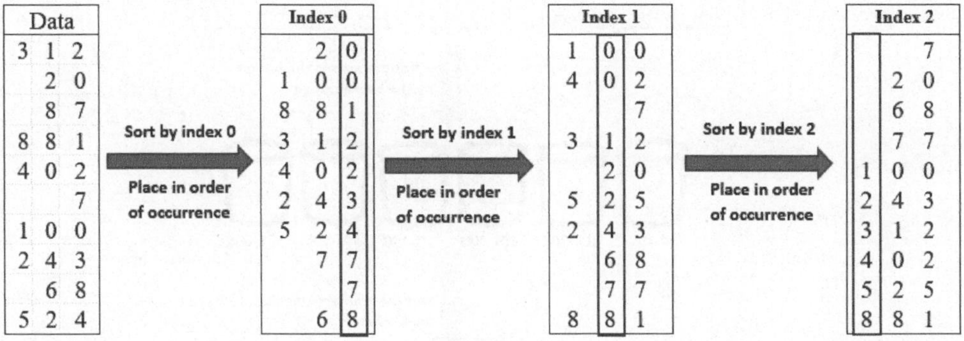

The time complexity of radix sort is $O(dn)$ where n is the number of elements in the array, and d is the number of digits of the largest element. It is because, sorting of the elements by an index position can be done in linear time i.e., $O(n)$ by temporarily storing the elements into b number of buckets (bucket sort), and we need to repeat the process for d times. To be specific, the time complexity is $O(d(n + b))$. As n is likely to be much larger than b, it is simplified as $O(dn)$.

4.1.10 Bucket Sort

Bucket sort distributes the data elements into different ordered buckets which can hold data within a defined range. The elements within each bucket are sorted using another sorting algorithm. Then the sorted list within each of the ordered buckets are simply concatenated to get a big sorted list.

Bucket sort is illustrated in the following figure using the set of data element listed below. The elements in the given list are distributed among six buckets, each bucket can hold 100 elements.

312, 20, 87, 581, 402, 317, 243, 213, 68, 524

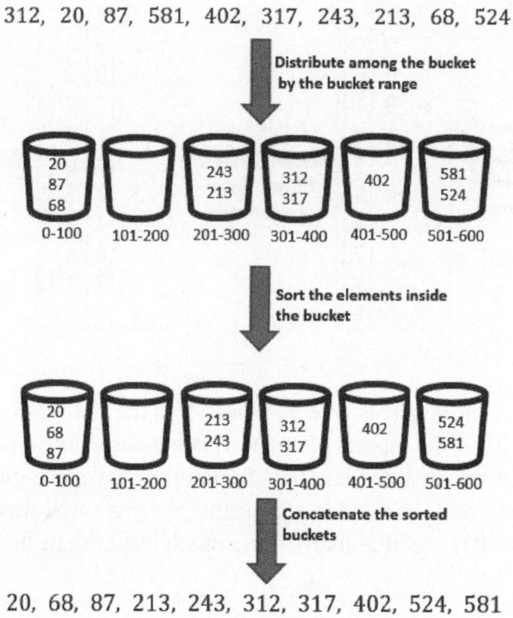

As evident in the above example, some of the buckets may be empty or may hold very few data elements. If the number of data elements is few and it has large value range, with non-uniform distribution, bucket sort may not be an efficient algorithm in terms of space as well as computation. Further, the time complexity of bucket sort algorithm depends on several factors such as distribution of elements to the buckets, the sorting algorithms employed for sorting elements in each bucket, and the number of buckets used, etc. For complexity estimate under different scenarios, reader may refer to the additional reading materials, cited by the QR code.

The classification of different sorting algorithms discussed in this section is listed below.

Algorithm	Internal	Stable	In-place	Adaptive	Comparison
Bubble	Yes	Yes	Yes	No (could be modified to be adaptive)	Yes
Insertion	Yes	Yes	Yes	Yes	Yes
Selection	Yes	No	Yes	No	Yes
Quick	Yes	No	Yes	No (could be modified to be adaptive)	Yes
Merge	External	Yes	No	No	Yes
Radix	Yes	Yes	No	No	No
Count	External	Yes	No	No	No
Bucket	External	Yes	No	No	No

4.2 HASHING

Search operation is one of the core fundamental operations required for any data structure. The running time of any search operation also depends on the position of the element to be searched in the data structure. For the traditional data structures such as array, linked list or tree, we have no clue of the expected position of the element to be searched, and end up searching the entire elements in the data structure in worst case, or half of the element on an average. The performance of the search operation improves by storing the data in an ordered manner by the value of the data, as we have seen in binary search or binary search tree. However, for all these approaches, we have no clue of the position of the data element in the data structure (through a vague idea can be guessed in the case of ordered data structure). Unlike the data structures that we have seen so far, *hash* is a data structure in which the location of the data element in the data structure is defined by the value of the data element itself. That means, if we know the value of the data element, we know the possible location where it might have stored in the data structure. Therefore, we can directly go the expected location and find the element.

Let us try to understand the concept through the following example. Let us assume that we have an array A of size 10, and we wish to store the following 10 elements 64, 31, 42, 55, 87, 78, 29, 43, 96, 20. Given an element, the idea is to estimate the index where the element will be stored in the array from the value of the element itself. That means, we need a function to estimate the index given the value of the element to be stored as parameter. This function is generally called *hash function*. Let us assume the following hash function.

$$f(key) = key \,\%\, S$$

where % denotes modulo operation and S represents the size of the array. Now, to store the first element 64, we perform $f(64) = 64 \,\%\, 10 = 4$. That means, 64 is stored at $A[4]$. Likewise, 31 is stored at $A[1]$ as $f(31) = 31 \,\%\, 10 = 1$, and so on. The figure below illustrates storing of the above elements in an array of size 10 using the above hash function.

Index	HASH	Hash function
0	20	$f(20) = 0$
1	31	$f(31) = 1$
2	42	$f(42) = 2$
3	43	$f(43) = 3$
4	64	$f(64) = 4$
5	55	$f(55) = 5$
6	96	$f(96) = 6$
7	87	$f(87) = 7$
8	78	$f(78) = 8$
9	29	$f(29) = 9$

Once the elements are stored into the arrays using the above hash function, we use the same hash function to search an element in the array. If we want to search the element 42, we estimate $f(42) = 42 \,\%\, 10 = 2$, and directly access the *A[2]* to find the element 42. From the above example, we can see that an arbitrary element can be found in $\theta(1)$ time, if the element is stored at the location defined by the hash function. In hashing, the above array is generally referred to as *table* or *buffer*. In the following discussion, we will refer it as table.

4.2.1 Hash Functions

A hash function should return a valid index in the table. Several hash functions have been used. This section presents a few of the commonly used hash functions. Let key denotes the element to be inserted into the hash, m be the size of the table, and $h()$ denotes the hash function.

Division Modulo: The hash function used in the above example is known as *modulo/division modulo* hash function, which is formally defined as follows.

$$h(key) = key \,\%\, m$$

This function returns the remainder when key is divided by m. In other word, $h(key) = key - \left\lfloor \frac{key}{m} \right\rfloor m$. It will always return a value between 0 to $m - 1$, inclusive, when both key and m are positive integers.

Given a set of arbitrary key values, there is a possibility that the hash function returns same values for more than one key. In such a scenario, more than one key will be competing for same storage index. This scenario is called *hash collision.* Collision is a problem in hashing. Details about collision will be discussed in Section 4.2.2. Collision reduces efficiency of hashing. In modulo hash function, it is important that m is chosen carefully to reduce the number of collisions. Studies reported that the number of collisions get reduced when key and m are coprime. To ensure that no integers evenly divide m except by 1 and m, m is generally considered to be a prime number.

Though the key is expected to be a positive integer, it can also be applied on non-integer values. Let us say, character, string, alpha numeric, etc. One simple way to convert a string to an integer could be sum of the ASCII values of the character present in the string. However, it is always a good idea to generate a large value to reduce possibility of collisions, say, multiplying by power of some constant and summing. One approach could be to multiply by power of m with each of the character value and then sum as defined below.

$$m^0 \times (first\ char) + m^1 \times (second\ char) + m^2 \times (third\ char) + \cdots$$

Though, the above expression may produce lesser number of collisions as compared to simply summing of the ASCII values, it will experience collisions for the words with same first character. Another commonly used approach to reduce collisions is to apply *multilevel hashing,* also known as *double hashing,* as defined below.

$$h(key) = (key \,\%\, d) \,\%\, m$$

for large prime $d > m$. Let us consider two keys 35 and 55. For a table size $m = 10$, both the keys return same index 5, i.e., $35\%10 = 5$ and $55\%10 = 5$, resulting in collisions with single level hash function. Let us assume d=15, and apply double hash function. Now, for the key value 35, $h(35) = 5$, and for the key value 55, $h(55) = 10$.

Folding: In folding, the given key is divided into multiple parts, then the parts are combined and then the combined value is passed to a hash function. Generally, the key will be divided into equal size, except for the last left over fold, if any. Let us say, $key = 513472881$, and the key is divided into three parts of equal size, say - (513), (472), (881). Then, the fold values are combined with some function, say addition, $513 + 472 + 881$. Then, the value is passed to a hash function, $h(513 + 472 + 881)$. Similarly, if the key is 51347288176, and is divided into parts consisting of three characters/digits, then the partitions could be (513), (472), (881), (76). Except the last one, all others have three characters/digits.

Folding can be generally of two types – *shift folding* and *boundary folding*. The above example is of shift folding type. In the boundary folding, the idea is that the key is written on a piece of paper and folded the paper at a defined boundary. Then, the parts of the key written on each side of the fold are seen in alternate reverse order, when they are looked at from top. For the $key = 513472881$, when it is divided into three parts of equal size, we get (513), (472), (881). When these parts are looked on a folded paper, they are seen as (513), (274), (881). Note that the digits in alternate folds are seen in reverse order. Now, they are added and passed to a hash function, $h(513 + 274 + 881)$.

Mid-Square Function: Mid-square function is considered to be one of the effective hash functions for integer keys. The idea is to generate an index by considering all the digits in the key, so that chances of generating two different indexes is higher for two different key values. In mid-square function, it takes the square of the key, and considers the middle digits as the index. As for example, let us consider a key with the value 6218. Take the square of 6218 to produce 38103904. If we consider a table of size 100, consider the middle two elements 03 as the index to store the key 6218.

Alternatively, we can also consider the size of the table as an integer with a power of 2, say $m = 2^k, k > 0$, and instead of considering the middle digits, consider binary representation of the square of the key, and then select middle k bits.

Extraction: In extraction methods, instead of considering the entire key element, consider only part of the key for generating hash value. As for example, consider the $key = 513472881$, and divide the key into parts, say (513), (472), (881). Now, consider one of the parts or a combination of a few parts to generate a value which will be passed to a hash function. Let us say, we consider the first part and used $h(513)$ to get the index, or combine few parts, say the first two digits from the first part and the last two digits from the last part, i.e., 5181, and pass it to a hash function to get index i.e., $h(5181)$.

Radix Transformation: In this method, a key value in one radix is transformed to another number with another radix. Then, the new value is passed to a hash function. For example, the key 6218 in decimal is transformed to 14112 in octal. Then, pass 14112 to a hash function, i.e., $h(14112)$.

4.2.2 Collisions Resolution

Like other data structures, *hash* data structure is also associated with *insertion, deletion and search operation*. The way the data structure is explored for the insertion operation and search operation are same. For better perception, we first discuss the insertion operation (or creating a hash from a set of data elements), before discussing the search operation.

For two different keys, if the hash function returns the same index, then collision happens. Let us consider the following sequence of keys – 21, 31, 41, 64, 34, 44, 54, 87, 78, 29, and a hash table T of size 10 to illustrate collisions. Let us consider modulo hash function for simplicity. When we insert the first key 21, the index is $h(21) = 21 \% 10 = 1$, and $T[1]$ is empty. So, 21 is stored at $T[1] = 21$. When we try to insert the next key 31, it has the index value $h(31) = 31 \% 10 = 1$. Since T[1] is already been occupied by 21, there is a collision. *How to resolve this issue?* Several methods have been proposed in the literature. Some of the commonly used methods are discussed below.

Open Addressing: Open addressing is one of the collision resolution methods. In open addressing, all the keys are stored in the hash table itself. Therefore, the size of the hash table should be larger than or equal to the number of keys that we wish to store. If there is a collision, when we try to insert a key, then starting from the hash index obtained using $h(key)$, an alternative available index in the hash table is searched (or, probed). Three commonly used open addressing methods are *linear probing, quadratic probing*, and *double probing*. All the probed sequence as defined by the respective probing methods will be looked. The direction of the probing can be either clockwise (smaller to larger index) or anti-clockwise in a circular fashion. The examples in this section consider clockwise probing direction. If m denotes the size of the hash table, and $p()$ denotes the probing function, the open addressing probing sequence at the event of a collision can be defined as $(h(k) + p(i)) \% m$, for $i = 0, 1, 2, 3 \ldots$ For all the probe sequences discussed below, this formula is applied, if not explicitly mentioned.

Linear probing: Linear probing is the simplest of three probing methods where $p(i)$ is defined as $p(i) = i$. That means, at the event of a collision, starting from the $h(k)$, all the consecutive indexes will be probed in a cyclic sequence, as shown below.

$$h(k), h(k) + 1, h(k) + 2, \ldots\ldots, m - 2, m - 1, 0, 1, 2 \ldots h(k) - 1$$

This probing sequence is illustrated with the key sequence - 21, 31, 41, 64, 34, 44, 54, 87, 78, 29, and $m = 10$. As discussed above, key 21 is stored at index 1 and needs only one probing. While inserting 31, there is a collision and need two probes to find the next available index. Then, we will start probing starting from index $h(31) = 1$, then $h(31) + 1 = 2$, then 3 and so on sequentially until we find an available free index or table is full. Since the index 2 is free, 31 is stored at index 2, i.e., $T[2] = 31$, and needs two probes. When the next 41 is inserted, as the index $h(41) = 1$ is already occupied, probing for next available index starts. Since $T[2]$ is already occupied, it goes to $T[3]$ and finds available (three probes). So, 41 is stored at $T[3]$. In the similar probing manner, all the remaining keys are stored as shown below.

HASH	29	21	31	41	64	34	44	54	87	78
Index	0	1	2	3	4	5	6	7	8	9

From the above figure, it can be seen that except for the keys 21 and 64, collisions occur for all the other keys (marked in red and bold) i.e., a total of 8 collisions out of 10 insertions. The total number of probes of all the keys is $(1+2+3+1+2+3+4+2+2+2) = 22$, and the average number of probes per key is 2.2.

Now, let us reorganise the sequence as 21, 64, 87, 78, 29, 31, 41, 34, 44, 54. From the figure below, it can be seen that the number of collisions reduces to 5 (marked in red and bold). From this, it is evident that the number of collisions depends on the sequence in which the keys are inserted. But, it has the same total number of probes $(1+1+1+1+1+2+3+2+3+7) = 22$, and average probes 2.2, as that of the first example.

HASH	**54**	21	**31**	**41**	64	**34**	**44**	87	78	29
Index	0	1	2	3	4	5	6	7	8	9

Let us further reorder the sequence as follows - 21, 64, 87, 31, 34, 55,41,96, 78, 29, and obtain the hash table as shown below.

HASH	**29**	21	**31**	**41**	64	**34**	**55**	87	**96**	**78**
Index	0	1	2	3	4	5	6	7	8	9

There are 7 collisions, but only $(1+1+1+2+2+2+3+3+2+2) = 19$ total probes and 1.9 average probes.

Another extreme case is illustrated below. Consider the key sequence – 20, 29, 31, 42, 43, 64, 55, 96, 87, 78. There is no collision for this sequence as shown below. In fact, as no two keys will return the same index value, there will not be any collision for any arbitrary order for the above set of keys.

HASH	20	31	42	43	64	55	96	87	78	29
Index	0	1	2	3	4	5	6	7	8	9

Let us assume that the key 29 is replaced by 10 to get the sequence 20, 10, 31, 42, 43, 64, 55, 96, 87, 78. For this sequence, except for key 20, there are collisions for all the keys i.e., 9 collisions out of 10 insertions. However, the total number of probes is 18 and an average probe 1.8.

HASH	20	**10**	**31**	**42**	**43**	**64**	**55**	**96**	**87**	**78**
Index	0	1	2	3	4	5	6	7	8	9

From the above examples, the following important points may be noted.

i. Number of collisions depends on the order of the keys in which the keys are inserted, provided at least two keys are mapped to a same index.
ii. The number of probes is not proportional to the number of collisions.
iii. A key will experience a minimum of 1 probe (no collision) and a maximum of m probes (every index is occupied except $h(key)-1$ in cycle). Therefore, the best case time complexity of inserting in linear probing is $\theta(1)$ i.e., no collision, and the worst case is $\theta(n)$.

Further analysis on Linear Probing: Let us consider the hash table shown below. The shaded cells denote already occupied cells. There are clusters of occupied cells (often referred to a *primary clusters*). Given an arbitrary sequence of keys, now, *what is the probability of filling up an empty cell?* When the hash table is initially empty, each cell has an equal probability of filling in. Once a cluster is formed, the probability of filling in an empty cell next to an occupied cluster is higher than that of an empty cell next to an unoccupied cells. That means, the probability of filling in

T[3] is higher than the probability of filling in T[7]. That is because the chances of occurring keys in an arbitrary sequence competing for the cells T[1] and T[2] together will be higher than that of T[7] only. The larger the size of the occupied cluster, the higher is the probability of occupying the adjacent available cell next, resulting in growing of the size of the existing cluster. The probability of filling an empty cell can be defined as $\frac{sizeof(cluster)+1}{m}$.

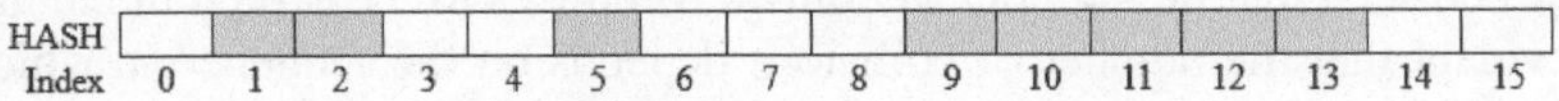

From the above discussion, it can be inferred that the number of probes required for inserting a key is proportional to the size of the cluster in which $h(k)$ lies. The cluster size distribution will in turn relate to the number of occupied cells in the table. The load factor α of a table can be defined as below.

$$\alpha = \frac{number\ of\ occupied\ cells\ in\ the\ table}{total\ number\ of\ cells\ in\ the\ table}$$

The average number of probes for inserting an arbitrary key into a hash table of an arbitrary occupied status is approximated, in the book Art of Computer Programming Vol 3, by Donald Knuth as below.

$$Avg\ number\ of\ probes = \frac{1}{2}\left(1 + \frac{1}{(1-\alpha)^2}\right)$$

Insertion is equivalent to unsuccessful search.

Searching in linear probing: The process of searching of a key in a hash table stored with linear probing is exactly the same as that of the probing process used. Given the key, estimate $h(key)$ and then start probing clockwise (assuming that insertion uses clockwise direction for probing) from the $h(key)$ till it finds a free cell, or all the cells are probed. Search operation may experience two cases - *successful search* or *unsuccessful search*. For a successful search, it will take $\theta(1)$ number of probing in the *best case*, if the key is found at $h(key)$ index, $\theta(n)$ in the *worse case* if the key is stored at $T[h(key) - 1]$, and the average of approximately $\frac{1}{2}\left(1 + \frac{1}{1-\alpha}\right)$ probes. For an unsuccessful search, while the best-case and worst-case complexities are same as that of the successful search, the average number of probes could be approximately $\frac{1}{2}\left(1 + \frac{1}{(1-\alpha)^2}\right)$ probing, as described in the book Art of Computer Programming Vol 3, by Donald Knuth.

Quadratic Probing: One of the problems with linear probing is its tendency to form bigger clusters. To take care of, we need a better probing function $p(i)$. *Quadratic probing* is one such choice in which the proving function is defined by the formula given below. The first probing is always $h(key)$. The following formula will be effective from $i = 1$.

$$p(i) = h(key) + (-1)^{i-1}\left(\left\lceil\frac{i+1}{2}\right\rceil\right)^2 \text{ for } i = 1, 2, 3, \dots, m-1$$

With the above probing function, the probing sequence of a key will be as follows.

$$h(key), h(key) + 1, h(key) - 1, h(key) + 4, h(key) - 4, \dots \dots, h(key) + \left(\frac{m}{2}\right)^2, h(key) - \left(\frac{m}{2}\right)^2$$

all with modulo m.

One problem with quadratic probing is that if m is not carefully chosen, the probing function will not cover all indexes of the hash table. For example, if m is even, it will cover only either the even indexes or odd indexes depending on $h(key)$ is even or odd. The ideal value of m is suggested to be a prime $4j + 3$ for an integer j in (Radke, 1970). For example, if $j = 4$, the value of m is 19. Assuming that $h(key)$ is 7, the sequence of probing is as follows

$7, (7+1), (7-1), (7+4), (7-4), (7+9), (7-9), (7+16), (7-16), (7+25), (7-25), (7+36), (7-36), (7+49), (7-49), (7+64), (7-64), (7+81), (7-81)$

which is equal to the index sequence - 7, 8, 6, 11, 3, 16, 17, 4, 10, 13, 1, 5, 9, 18, 15, 14, 0, 12, 2. It can be clearly seen that all the indexes of the table are covered. It can be noted that the above probing extends in both the clockwise and anti-clockwise direction. Extending in both directions is important. To illustrate the importance of extending the probes in both directions, we let assume that the probes happen only in clockwise direction, and define the probe function as $p(i) = h(key) + (i)^2$for $i = 1, 2, 3, \ldots, m-1$. Then, for the same index key i.e., h(key)=7, we get the following probe sequence – 7, 8, 11, 16, 4, 13, 5, 9, 14, 12, 12, 14, 9, 5, 13, 4, 16, 11, 8, 7. The second half of the sequence is exactly the reverse of the first half, i.e., missing half of the indexes from coverage.

Double Probing: Though quadratic probing is better than linear probing, it still forms secondary clusters (clusters formed by keys mapped to the same index). The idea behind *double probing* is to reduce the probability of forming secondary clusters. It is done using two hash functions, h_1 and h_2, where h_1 is used for finding the primary index and h_2 is used for resolving conflict. Given a *key*, the typical expression for probing the table is as defined below.

$$h_1(key) + i * h_2(key), \mathrm{i} = 0,1,2, \ldots, \mathrm{m} - 1.$$

It will generate the following probe sequence.

$$h_1(key), h_1(key) + h_2(key), h_1(ke) + 2 * h_2(key), h_1(key) + 3 * h_2(key), \ldots\ldots.$$

The primary hash function $h_1(key)$ produces a number from 0 to $m-1$. The secondary hash function $h_2(key)$ produces a number from 1 to $m-1$, which is *relatively prime* to m to ensure coverage of all the indexes of the hash table. Though in principle, the value of m could be any value, it is easier to get $h_2(key)$ which produces a relatively prime value to m, if m is either a prime number or power of 2.

If m is a prime member, a simple function $h_2(key) = 1 + (key \,\%\, (m-1))$ which produces any value between 1 to $m-1$, inclusive may be a good choice. Since m is prime and $m-1$ is an even number, it may face the problem of producing regular pattern with even number. Studies have also suggested other variants such as $h_2(key) = 1 + (key \,\%\, (m-2))$, $h_2(key) = 1 + \left(\left\lfloor\frac{key}{m}\right\rfloor \%\, (m-2)\right)$. Another convenient way to ensure the relative prime condition is to assume m to be a power of 2, and design $h_2(key)$ to produce odd numbers between 1 and m, inclusive. While the best case and worst case time complexities of double hashing are $\theta(1)$ and $\theta(n)$, the average number of probing of double hashing is reported as $\frac{1}{\alpha}\ln\frac{1}{1-\alpha}$ for successful search, and $\frac{1}{1-\alpha}$ for unsuccessful search (or insertion).

Chaining: Unlike open addressing, *chaining* (also known as *separate chaining*) does not store the keys in the hash table. Rather, hash table stores the address of a linked list which stores the set of keys with same hash index. Considering *modulo hash function,* and a hash table with size $m = 10$, hashing of the following key sequence - 21, 31, 41, 64, 34, 44, 54, 87, 78, 29 using chaining is illustrated in the figure below. In the figure below, the insertion of a new key in the chain of a particular hash index is inserted as the last node

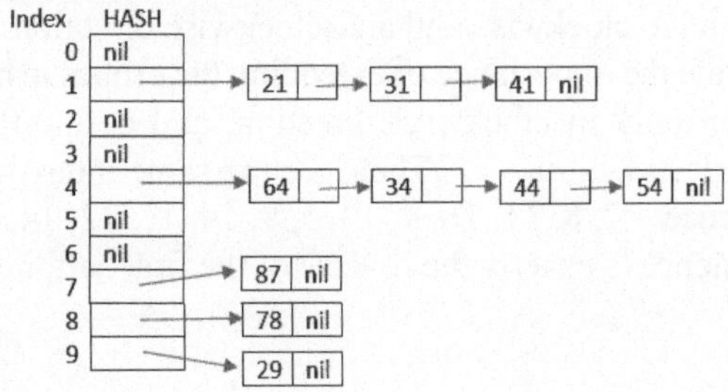

Let us assume that the insertion of a new key in the chain of a particular hash index is always inserted as the first node. Then the *worst case* time complexity of *inserting a key* into the hash is $\theta(1)$. However, the *worst case time complexity for search operation* is proportional to the length of the chain. If the particular chain has *n* number of nodes, the worst case time complexity for searching a key will be $\theta(n)$ plus the time of estimating hash function.

To estimate average case time complexity, let us assume a hash table of size m, n number of keys, and n_i number of nodes in i^{th} hash index, such that $n_0 + n_1 + n_2 + \cdots + n_{m-1} = n$. Further, we assume that any given key is equally likely be hashed to any index of the hash table. This assumption is also known as *simple uniform hashing.* Then, the expected number of nodes in the chain pointed by the pointer at $T[i]$ is $\frac{n}{m}$, which is nothing but the *load factor* α of the hash. For an unsuccessful search operation, we need to estimate $h(key)$ and scan the entire chain at $T(h(key))$. Therefore, the average time complexity of an unsuccessful search is $\theta(1+\alpha)$. As explained in [Cormen, 2001], the average time complexity of a successful search is also $\theta(1 + \alpha)$, though the estimates are different. Assuming that all the insertions in the linked lists are done as the first element, the number of nodes that will be scanned for a successful search is the number of keys inserted in the linked list of $T(h(key))$ before the target key plus 1. As we assume to follow simple uniform hashing, the probability that two keys - key_i and key_j have the same hash index (i.e., $\Pr\left(h(key_i) = h(key_j)\right)$ is $\frac{1}{m}$. Since a key in the sequence is also equally likely to be at any position in the sequence, the expected estimate of the event e_{ij} that the key_j is inserted after the key_i in the same hash index is also $\frac{1}{m}$ i.e., $E[e_{ij}] = \frac{1}{m}$. Therefore, the expected number of nodes inserted in the linked list before the node having key_i can be defined as follows.

$$E\left[\frac{1}{n}\sum_{i=1}^{n}\left(1+\sum_{j=i+1}^{n}e_{ij}\right)\right]=\frac{1}{n}\sum_{i=1}^{n}\left(1+\sum_{j=i+1}^{n}E[e_{ij}]\right)=\frac{1}{n}\sum_{i=1}^{n}\left(1+\sum_{j=i+1}^{n}\frac{1}{m}\right)$$

$$=1+\frac{1}{nm}\sum_{i=1}^{n}(n-i)=1+\frac{n-1}{2m}=1+\frac{\alpha}{2}-\frac{\alpha}{2n}$$

Considering $\theta(1)$ for estimating hash function and locating the index, the average time complexity is $\theta\left(1+\frac{\alpha}{2}-\frac{\alpha}{2n}\right)=\theta(1+\alpha)$.

Bucket Addressing: Bucket addressing is also one class of open addressing (or closed hashing) in which all the elements/keys are stored in the hash table. However, unlike traditional open addressing method discussed above, the hash table is divided into buckets and keys which return same hash index are stored in the same bucket. If the size of the hash table is m and the size of a bucket is B, then the hash table is divided into $\frac{m}{B}$ buckets with the bucket indexes 0 to $\frac{m}{B}-1$. In general, m is considered to be multiples of B. In bucket addressing, the hash function $h(key)$ returns a value between 0 to $\frac{m}{B}-1$, inclusive, instead of 0 to m-1. If we consider modulo hash function, the hash function will be defined as $h(key) = key\ \%\ \frac{m}{B}$. If more than one keys are mapped to same bucket, they are stored in the same bucket without any order. If the number of keys mapped to a same bucket index is more than B, then there is a *bucket overflow*. One way of addressing bucket overflow is to store the overflowed key to next available bucket using a probing method like linear probing or quadratic probing.

Another commonly used approach is to add additional overflow space in addition to the hash table of size m. Whenever an overflow happens, the overflow key is stored in the overflow space. In principle, overflow space is considered to be of infinite size. The probing based on overflow space-based bucket addressing are illustrated below with the key sequence - 21, 31, 87, 9, 19, 44, 25, 67, 78, 29. We assume $B = 2$, $m = 12$, and 5 overflow space.

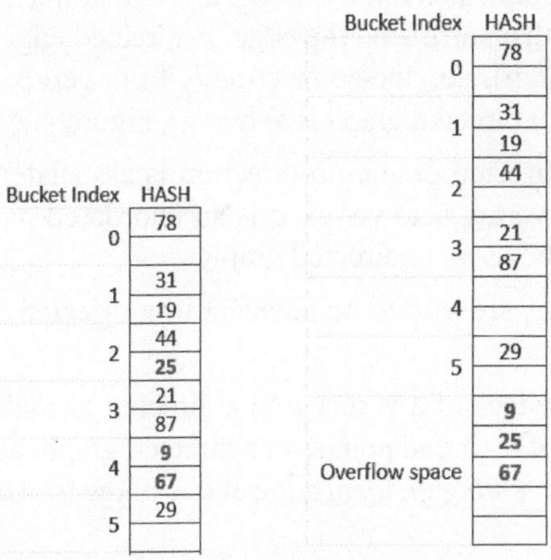

(i) With linear probing (ii) With overflow space

Additional topics on hashing such as universal hashing, delete operation, etc. are not within the scope of this book. Reader may refer to additional materials provided in the link cited by the QR code.

4.3 GRAPH

Graph is another *non-linear* data structure. A graph $G = (V, E)$ consists of a set V of *vertices* and a set E of *edges*. An example graph is shown below in Figure 4.2. The circles denote vertices, and the connections between the circles denote edges. There are seven vertices $V = \{A, B, C, D, E, F, G\}$ and eight edges $E = \{<A, B>, <A, C>, <A, E>, <B, D>, <D, F>, <D, E>, <D, G>, <C, E>\}$.

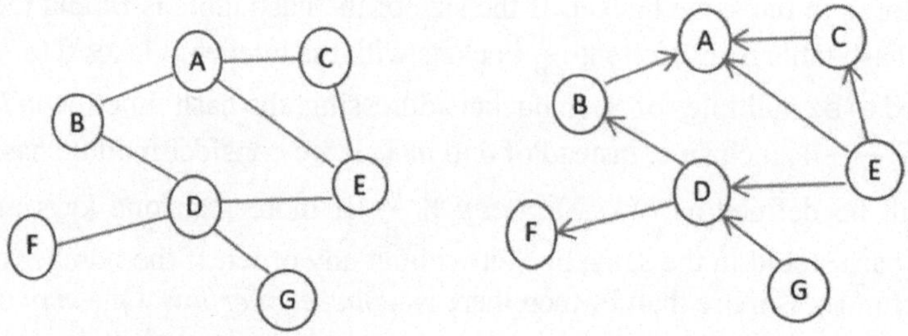

An Undirected Graph   A Directed Graph

Figure 4.2: An example of a graph.

4.3.1 Terminologies

Directed Graph: A directed graph also known as *digraph* is a graph in which the edges have a direction, generally indicated with an arrow on the edge. A directed edge from a vertex u to another vertex v is an ordered pair (u, v), i.e., the connection is from vertex u to vertex v. It is different from (v, u). An example of a directed graph is shown in Figure 4.2.

Undirected Graph: Unlike directed graph, no direction is associated with the edges in the graph. An undirected edge from vertex u to vertex v is an unordered pair (u, v) i.e., (u, v) and (v, u) are the same. Figure 4.2 shows an undirected graph.

Adjacent vertex: Two vertices are said to be adjacent in a directed or undirected graph, if there is an edge between them.

Incident edge: The incident edges of a vertex v in a directed or undirected graph are the edges which have v as at least one of their end points. In a directed graph, an *outgoing incident edge* of v is of the for (v, u), and an *incoming incident edge* of v is of the for (u, v) where u is one of v's adjacent vertices.

Degree: In an undirected graph, the degree of a vertex v is defined by *the number of its adjacent vertices*. In a directed graph, the degree of a vertex v is defined by the direction of the incident edges. The *out-degree* of a vertex v is the number of its outgoing incident edges, and the *in-degree* is the number of its incoming incident edges.

Weighted Graph: A graph is said to be weighted graph, if the edges in the graph carry weights. The weight of an edge denotes the strength of the connection between the participating vertices. The 0 weight indicates no connection.

Unweighted Graph: A graph is said to be unweighted graph, if the edges in the graph do not carry any weight.

Path: A path in a graph is a sequence of $k > 1$ vertices $\{v_1, v_2, \dots v_{k-1}, v_k\}$ such that two consecutive vertices $(v_i, v_{i+1}), 1 \leq i \leq k$ is an edge in the graph. The number of edges in the path is known as the *path length*. In a path, vertices may repeat, but not the edges. If the sequence has repeated edges as well, then it is called *walk*. A walk is just a traversal on a graph. A path may be considered as a special type of walk without repeated edges. A path is simple, if no vertices are repeated. If the first vertex and the last vertex are same, then it is called a *cycle*. If no vertices are repeated, except for the first and last, then it is a *simple cycle*. A simple cycle with only one edge is called *self-loop*. A path is a *tour*, if it consists of all the vertices in the graph. A tour with no repeated vertex is called the *Hamilton tour*.

Subgraph: A graph $S = (V_s, E_s)$ is a subgraph of another graph $G = (V_G, E_G)$, if $V_S \subseteq V_G$, and $E_S \subseteq E_G$.

Connected: A graph is said to be *connected* if there exists a path between every possible vertex pair in the graph, otherwise it is a *disconnected graph*. In other words, a graph is connected if there are no two disjoint subgraphs such that there are no edges from a vertex in one subgraph to a vertex in other graph. Otherwise, it is a disconnected graph. If a connected subgraph of a graph is disconnected from other subgraphs in the graph, then it is a connected component of the graph.

Traversal: It is a task of visiting every node in a graph.

Cyclic: A graph is called *cyclic graph*, if it has at least one cycle.

Acyclic: A graph without any cycle is known as *acyclic* graph. An acyclic connected graph forms a tree. If the tree has a designated node as root, then it is a *rooted tree*, otherwise *un-rooted tree*.

Spanning tree: A connected subgraph with no cycle is a tree. A collection of trees is a *forest*. A forest with a single tree, which consists of all the vertices in a graph, is known as the *spanning tree* of the graph.

Complete Graph: If every pair of distinct vertices of a graph is connected by a unique edge, then the graph is said to be complete. A complete subgraph is known as a *clique*.

4.3.2 Representing Graphs

Three commonly used methods for representing graphs are *adjacency matrix*, *adjacency list* and *edge list*.

Adjacency matrix is a matrix form of representing the edges in a graph. Given a graph with n vertices, its adjacency matrix is a two-dimensional matrix of $n \times n$. For an undirected graph, if there is an edge between vertex i and vertex j, then the entries in row i and column j, and row j and column i are 1s (i.e., $A[i][j] = 1$ and, $A[j][i] = 1$), otherwise 0. If it is a directed graph, the direction will be followed from row vertex to the column vertex, i.e., an edge from vertex i and vertex j will give $A[i][j] = 1$, but $A[j][i] = 0$. The figure below illustrates an example of an adjacency matrix of an undirected graph.

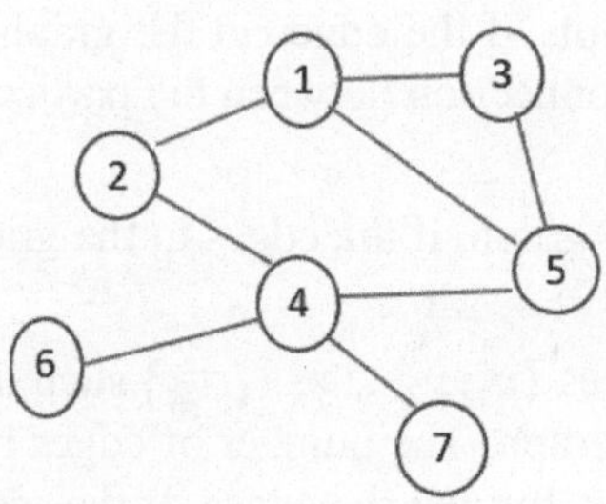

	1	2	3	4	5	6	7
1	0	1	1	0	1	0	0
2	1	0	0	1	0	0	0
3	1	0	0	0	1	0	0
4	0	1	0	0	1	1	1
5	1	0	1	1	0	0	0
6	0	0	0	1	0	0	0
7	0	0	0	1	0	0	0

Figure 4.3: Adjacency matrix of an undirected unweighted graph

Few of the important observations can be noted:

1. The adjacency matrix is symmetric i.e., $A[i][j] == A[j][i]$.
2. For a vertex i, the degree of the vertex i is the number of non-zero entries in the ith row vector or i^{th} column vector.
3. If there are m number of edges (excluding self loop), there will be $2m$ number of non-zero entries.

An example of an adjacency matrix of a directed graph is illustrated below. Unlike undirected graph, there are m entries for m number of edges. The adjacency matrix is not symmetric i.e., $A[i][j] \neq A[j][i]$. The number of non-zero entries in an ith row vector denotes the *out-degree* of the vertex i. The number of non-zero entries in an ith column vector denotes the *in-degree* of the vertex i.

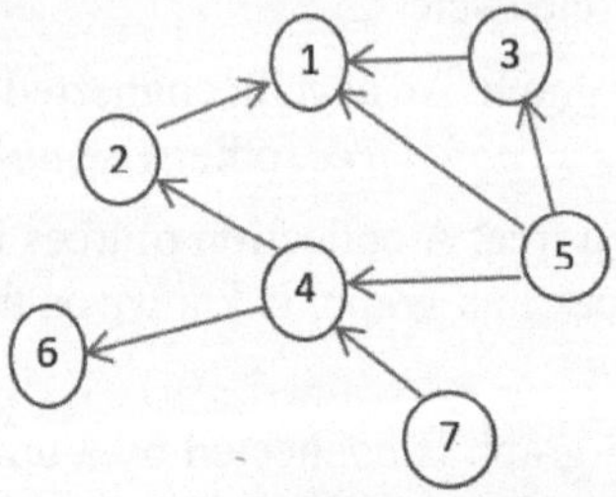

	1	2	3	4	5	6	7
1	0	0	0	0	0	0	0
2	1	0	0	0	0	0	0
3	1	0	0	0	0	0	0
4	0	1	0	0	0	1	0
5	1	0	1	1	0	0	0
6	0	0	0	0	0	0	0
7	0	0	0	1	0	0	0

Figure 4.4: Adjacency matrix of a directed unweighted graph

If it is a weighted graph, associated weights with the edges are entered instead of 0 or 1.

Adjacency List: For a graph with n vertices, its adjacency list will maintain an array of size n, where $A[i]$ points to a linked list storing all the vertices j (not in any particular order) such that (i, j) is an edge. The number of vertices in the linked list pointed by $A[i]$ denotes the degree of the vertex i. An example adjacency list is shown below.

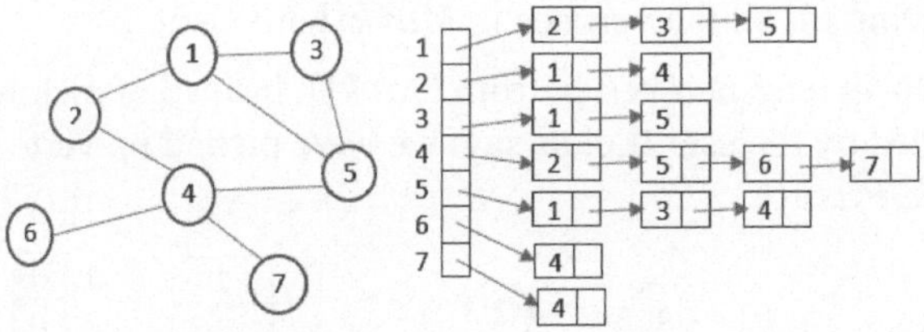

Figure 4.5: Adjacency list representation of a graph

Edge List: Edge list of a graph is an array (or a list) of the edges in the graph, as illustrated below.

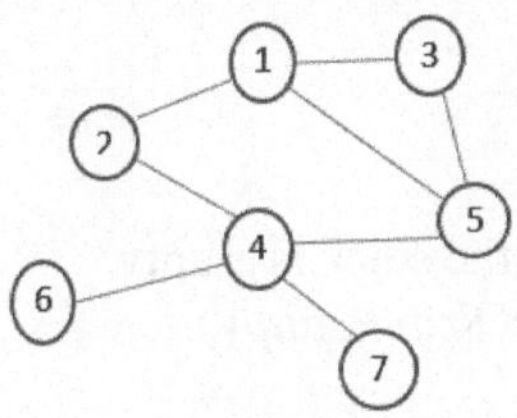

1	3
1	2
1	5
2	4
3	5
4	5
4	6
4	7

Figure 4.6: Edge list representation of a graph

4.3.3 Graph Traversal

Two types of traversals are commonly used in graphs namely *Depth First Search* and *Breath First Search.*

Depth First Search: Given a graph, the idea is to visit all the reachable vertices with higher depth from a selected vertex, before visiting another adjacent vertex. That means, if we visit vertex 2 from vertex 1, we should visit 4 (reachable from 1 through last visited node 2) before visiting vertex 3 or vertex 5 which are adjacent to vertex 1. After exhausting all the reachable vertices, it should pick up one of the unvisited adjacent vertices and repeat the above process till all the nodes are visited. This idea is illustrated with an example below. The algorithm discussed below uses two auxiliary data structures - *a stack (Stack)* and *an array (Mark)* to keep track of adjacent vertices to be explored and visited vertices. Given a graph, the depth first search algorithm works as follows.

Step - 1: Set all the vertices of the graph to 0 to denote *unvisited* i.e., $\forall i, Mark[i] = 0$.

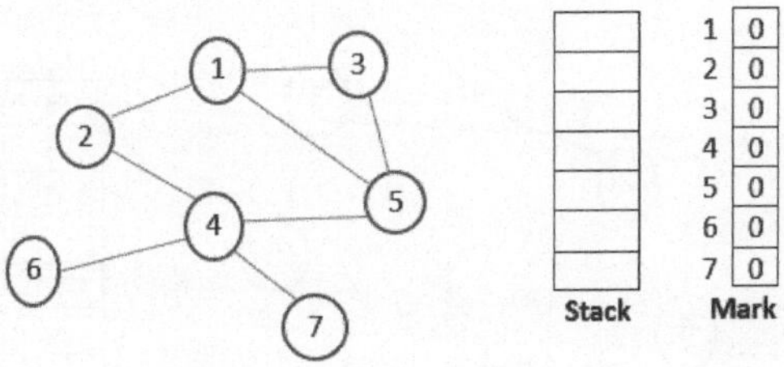

Step -2: Repeat the following till all the vertices in $Mark[]$ are visited.

a) Randomly pick up an *unvisited* vertex from $Mark[]$. Instead of picking up randomly, the vertex can also be decided by the user. Let us say, we have picked up vertex 1. *Push the vertex to the* $Stack$ i.e., $Stack.Push(1)$;

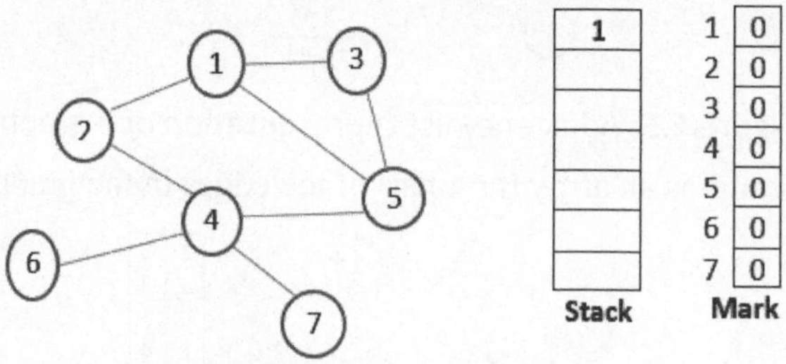

b) Repeat the following operation until the stack is empty.
   i. Pop the top of the Stack i.e., $v = Stack.pop()$.
   ii. Check if v is visited.
      a. If Yes, Go to 2.b).i.
      b. If No,
         [1] Visit the vertex v, and set $Mark[v] = 1$.
         [2] Push all the *unvisited adjacent vertices* u of v into the $Stack$ (not in any order), i.e., $Stack.Push(u)$.

Description:

Vertex 1 is pop from the stack. Visit vertex 1 (shown in green colour), as it is not already visited. Set $Mark[1] = 1$. Push all the unvisited adjacent vertices of 1 (i.e., 3, 5, 2) into the stack, i.e., $Stack.Push(3), Stack.Push(5)$, and $Stack.Push(2)$.

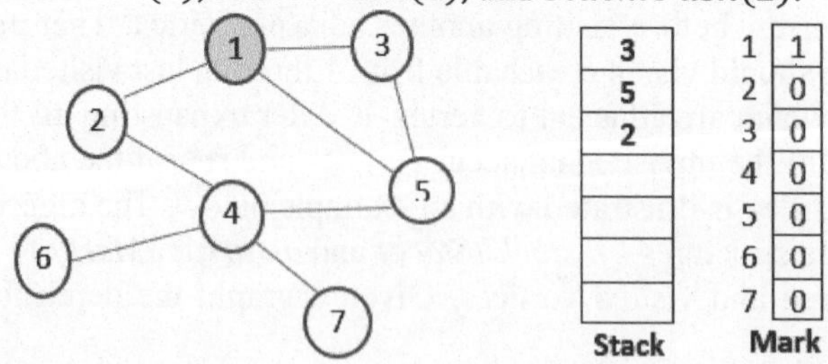

As the stack is not empty, pop the top vertex 2. Visit vertex 2, as it is not already visited. Set $Mark[2] = 1$. Push the unvisited adjacent vertices of 2 (i.e., 4) into the stack, i.e., $Stack.Push(4)$.

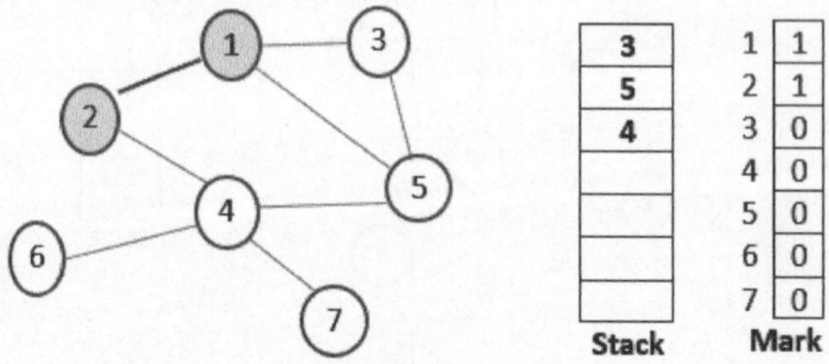

As the stack is not empty, pop the top vertex 4. Visit vertex 4, as it is not already visited. Set $Mark[4] = 1$. Push the unvisited adjacent vertices of 4 (i.e., 5, 7, 6) into the stack, i.e., $Stack.Push(5), Stack.Push(7)$, and $Stack.Push(6)$.

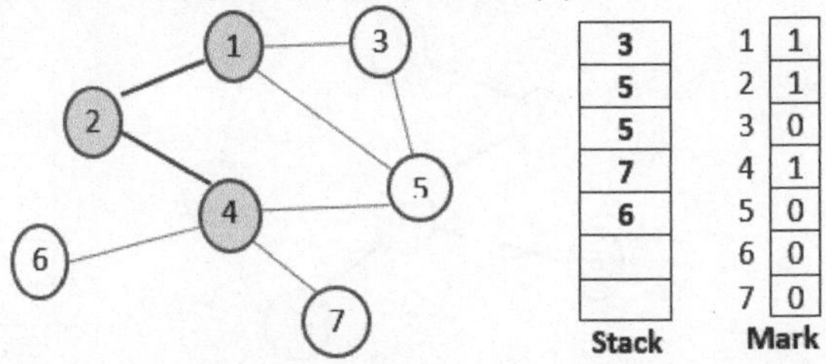

As the stack is not empty, pop the top vertex 6. Visit vertex 6, as it is not already visited. Set $Mark[6] = 1$. Push the unvisited adjacent vertices of 6. As there is no unvisited adjacent vertices of 6, no vertex is pushed.

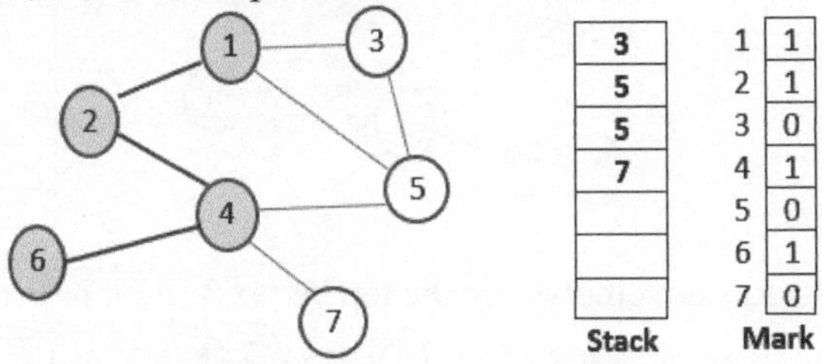

As the stack is not empty, pop the top vertex 7. Visit vertex 7, as it is not already visited. Set $Mark[7] = 1$. Push the unvisited adjacent vertices of 7. As there are no unvisited adjacent vertices of 7, no vertex is pushed.

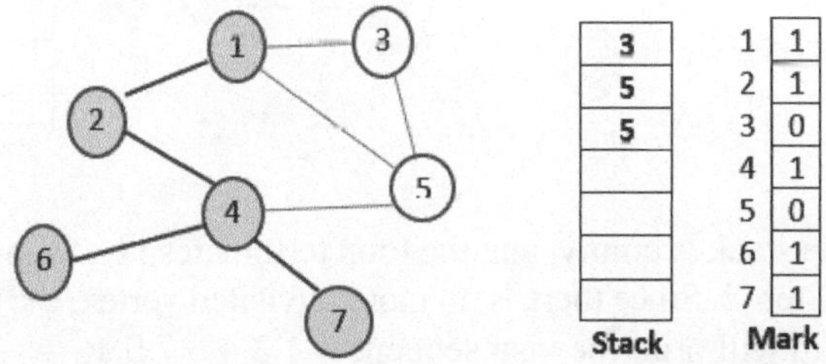

As the stack is not empty, pop the top vertex 5. Visit vertex 5, as it is not already visited. Set $Mark[5] = 1$. Push the unvisited adjacent vertices of 5 (i.e., 3) into the stack, i.e., $Stack.Push(3)$.

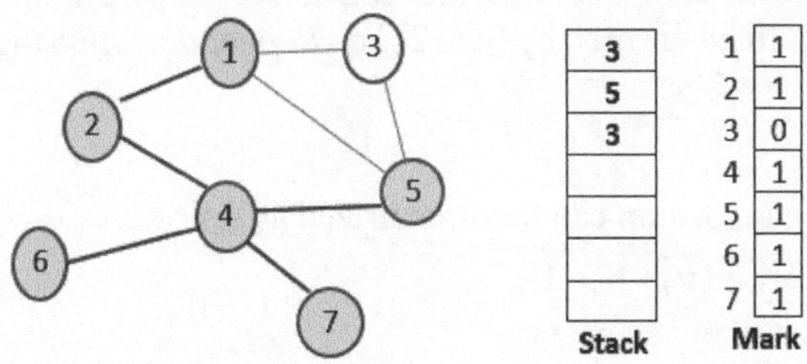

As the stack is not empty, pop the top vertex 3. Visit vertex 3, as it is not already visited. Set $Mark[3] = 1$. Push the unvisited adjacent vertices of 3. As there are no unvisited adjacent vertices of 3, no vertex is pushed.

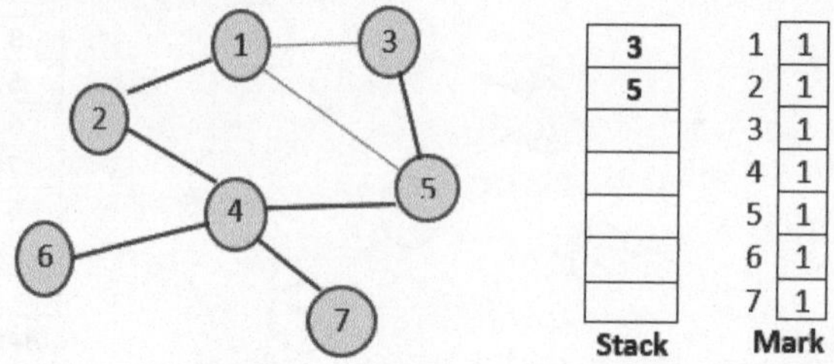

As the stack is not empty, pop the top vertex 5. As it is already visited, go to next iteration.

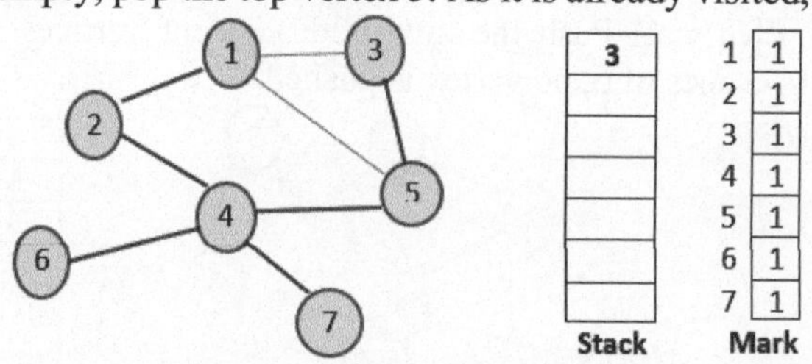

As the stack is not empty, pop the top vertex 3. As it is already visited, go to next iteration.

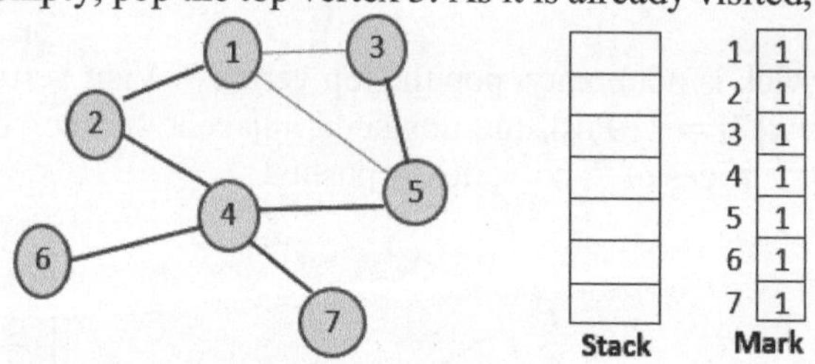

Now, the stack is empty, and the loop terminates i.e., Step-2.b terminates. Then, algorithm goes to Step-2. Since there is no more unvisited vertex, the algorithm terminates. The above algorithm will print the visit sequence -1 2 4 6 7 5 1.

In the above example, there is only one connected component. So, the algorithm runs Step-2.b only once for this example. The Steps 2.a and 2.b are applicable for only one component. If there are more than one component of the graph, the Steps 2.a and 2.b will be repeated for each component. It will be ensured by Step 2, i.e., *Repeat the following till there exists unvisited vertex in Mark*[].

Now, the above algorithm can be summarized as follows.

```
dfs-iterative(v, V, E) {
         Stack.Push(v);
         While(Stack.empty()==0){
            Set x = Stack.Pop();
            If (Mark[x] != 1){
                 Print x;
```

```
                        Set Mark[x]=1;
                        For each adjacent vertex y of x {
                              If(Mark[y]==0){
                                    Stack.Push(y);
                              }
                        }
                  }
            }
}
Depth-First-Search-Iterative(V, E) {
          For each v in V {
             Set Mark[v]=0;
          }
          For each v in V {
             If(Mark[v] == 0){
                   dfs-iterative(v, V, E)
             }
          }
}
```

The above `dfs-iterative()` function will perform depth first search on each connected component. Therefore, the time complexity of depth first search is defined by the time complexity of the `dfs-iterative()` function. The stack in the algorithm may hold multiple copies of the same vertex at a time. This phenomenon can be seen from the illustration above as well. At the same time, every vertex should have been inserted at least once before visiting. The inner loop defines the number of push operations into the stack. The total number of times the inner loop iterates to perform a push operation can not exceed the number of edges in the graph. Therefore time complexity of depth first search is $O(|V| + |E|)$.

The above iterative approach, and usage of stack can be simplified using recursive algorithm. In the following recursive version, the role of the above explicit stack will be maintained by the system-level stack for recursive function all.

```
dfs-recursive(v, V, E){
          Mark[v]=1;
          Print v;
          For each adjacent vertex u of v {
             If(Mark[u]==0){
                   dfs-recursive(u, V, E);
             }
          }
}
Depth-First-Search-Recursive(V, E){
          For each v in V{
```

```
            Mark[v]=0;
        }
        For each v in V{
            If(Mark[v]==0){
                dfs-recursive(v, V, E);
            }
        }
}
```

Breath First Search: Given a graph, the idea is to visit all the adjacent vertices of a selected vertex, before visiting reachable vertices with higher depth. That means, if we visit vertex 2 from vertex 1, we should visit vertex 3 and vertex 5 before visiting vertex 4. This idea is illustrated with an example below. The algorithm discussed below uses two auxiliary data structures - *a queue (Queue)* and *an array (Mark)* to keep track of adjacent vertices to be explored and visited vertices. Given a graph, the breath first search algorithm works as follows.

Step - 1: Set all the vertices of the graph to 0 to denote *unvisited* i.e., $\forall i, Mark[i] = 0$.

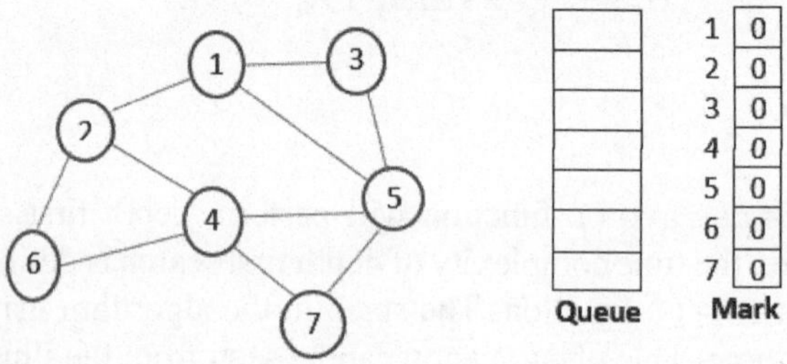

Step -2: Repeat the following till all the vertices in *Mark*[] are visited.

a) Randomly pick up an *unvisited* vertex from $Mark[]$. Instead of picking up randomly, the vertex can also be decided by the user. Let us say, we have picked up vertex 1. *Enqueue the vertex to the queue* i.e., $Queue.Enqueue(1)$;

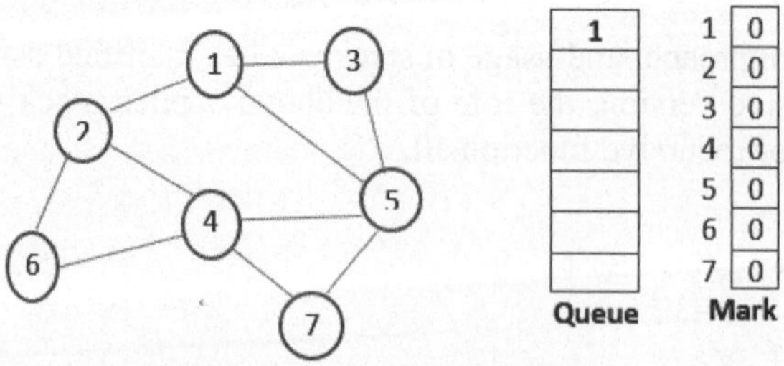

b) Repeat the following operation until the Queue is empty.
   i. Dequeue the front vertex from the queue i.e., $v = Queue.dequeue()$.
   ii. Check if v is visited.
      a. If Yes, Go to 2.b).i.
      b. If No,
         [1] Visit the vertex v, and set $Mark[v] = 1$.
         [2] Enqueue all the *unvisited adjacent vertices* u of v into the Queue (not in any order), i.e., $Queue.enqueue(u)$.

Description:

Vertex 1 is dequeue from the queue. Visit vertex 1 (shown in green colour), as it is not already visited. Set $Mark[1] = 1$. Enqueue all the unvisited adjacent vertices of 1 (i.e., 2, 5, 3) into the queue, i.e., $Queue.enqueue(2), Queue.enqueue(5)$, and $Queue.enqueue(3)$.

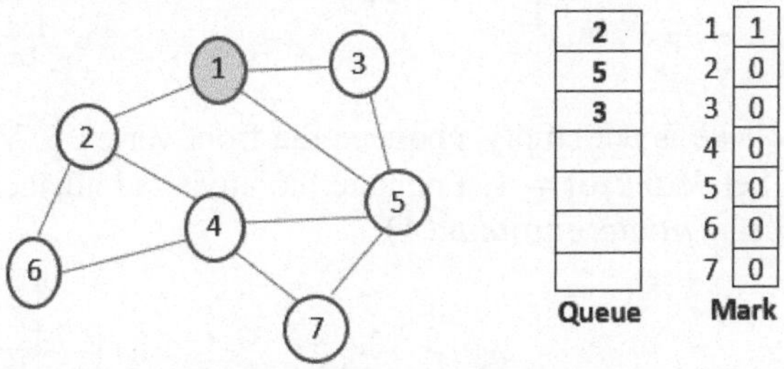

As the queue is not empty, dequeue the front vertex 2. Visit vertex 2, as it is not already visited. Set $Mark[2] = 1$. Enqueue the unvisited adjacent vertices of 2 (i.e., 6, 4) into the queue, i.e., $Queue.enqueue(6)$ and $Queue.enqueue(4)$.

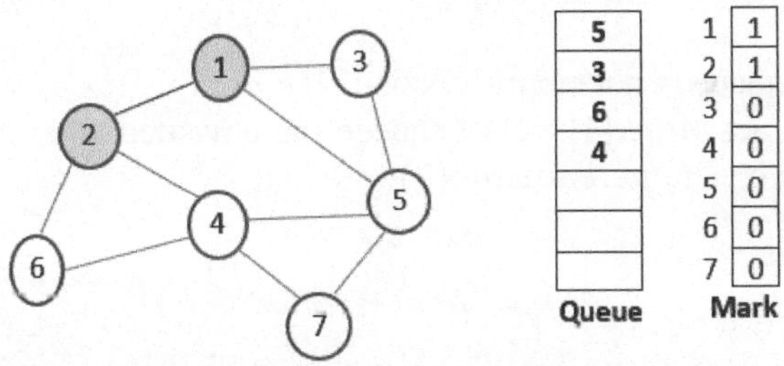

As the queue is not empty, dequeue the front vertex 5. Visit vertex 5, as it is not already visited. Set $Mark[5] = 1$. Enqueue the unvisited adjacent vertices of 5 (i.e., 4, 7, 3) into the queue, i.e., $Queue.enqueue(4), Queue.enqueue(7)$, and $Queue.enqueue(3)$.

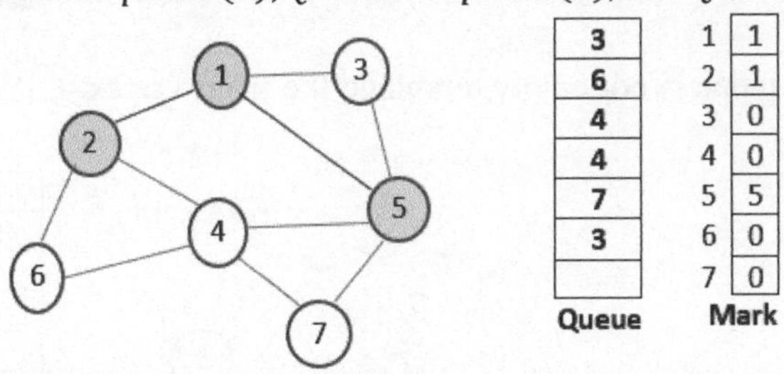

As the queue is not empty, enqueue the top vertex 3. Visit vertex 3, as it is not already visited. Set $Mark[3] = 1$. Enqueue the unvisited adjacent vertices of 3. As there are no unvisited adjacent vertices of 3, no vertex is enqueue.

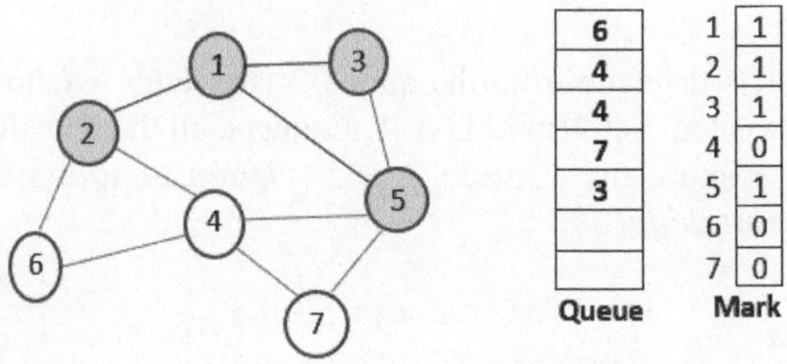

As the queue is not empty, enqueue the front vertex 6. Visit vertex 6, as it is not already visited. Set $Mark[6] = 1$. Enqueue the unvisited adjacent vertices of 6 (i.e., 4) into the queue, i.e., $Queue.enqueue(4)$.

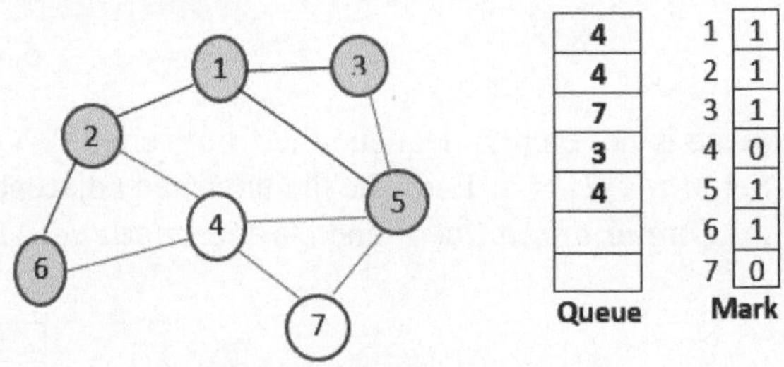

As the queue is not empty, enqueue the front vertex 4. Visit vertex 4, as it is not already visited. Set $Mark[4] = 1$. Enqueue the unvisited adjacent vertices of 4 (i.e., 7) into the queue, i.e., $Queue.enqueue(7)$.

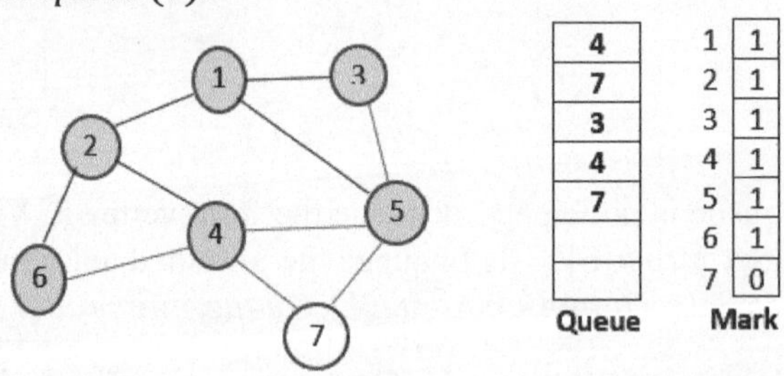

As the queue is not empty, enqueue the front vertex 4. As it is already visited, go to next iteration.

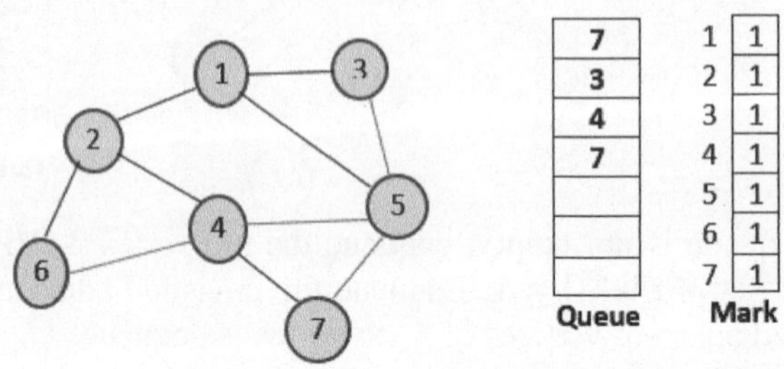

As the queue is not empty, enqueue the front vertex 7. As it is already visited, go to next iteration.

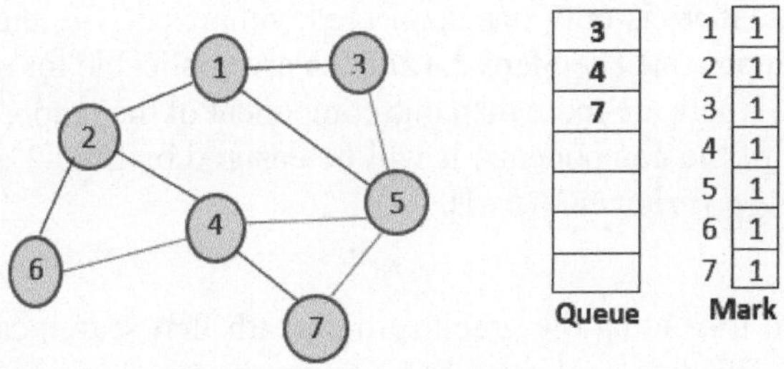

As the queue is not empty, enqueue the front vertex 3. As it is already visited, go to next iteration.

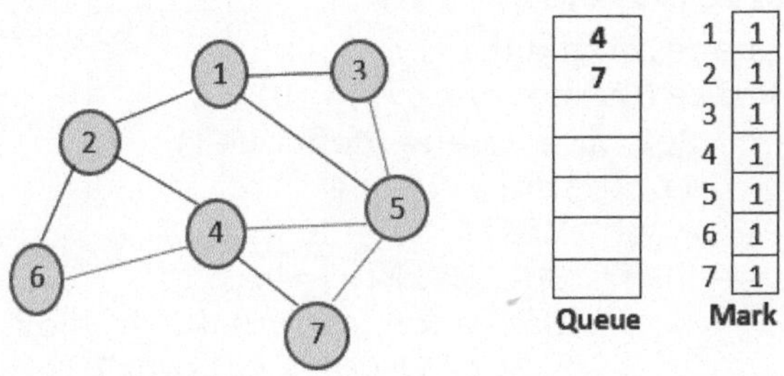

As the queue is not empty, enqueue the front vertex 4. As it is already visited, go to next iteration.

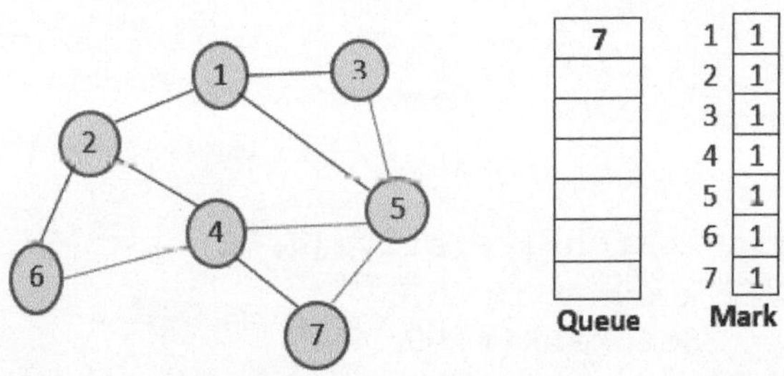

As the queue is not empty, enqueue the front vertex 7. As it is already visited, go to next iteration.

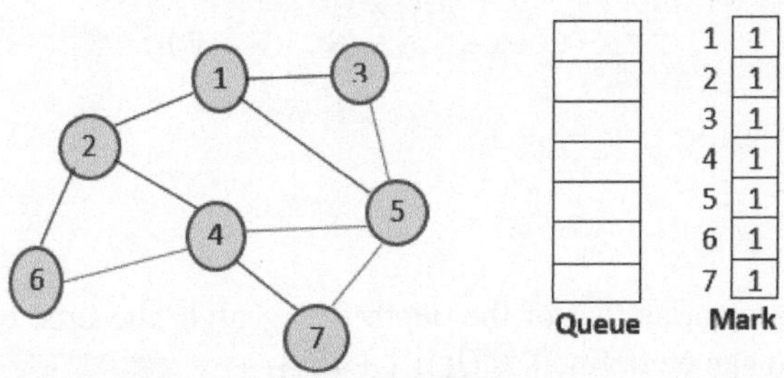

Now, the Queue is empty, and the loop terminate i.e., Step-2.b) terminates. Then, algorithm goes to Step-2. Since there is no more unvisited vertex, the algorithm terminates. The above algorithm will print the visit sequence -1 2 5 3 6 4 7.

In the above example, there is only one connected component. So, the algorithm runs Step-2.b only once for this component. The Steps 2.a and 2.b are applicable for only one component. Like in depth first search, if there are more than one component of the graph, the Steps 2.a and 2.b will be repeated for each of the components. It will be ensured by Step 2, i.e., *Repeat the following till there exists unvisited vertex in* $Mark[]$.

The above process of traversing the graph using breath first search can be summarized by the following algorithm. This traversal can also be done using a recursive algorithm. However, it is left as an exercise to the reader.

```
bfs-iterative(v, V, E) {
        Queue.enqueue(v);
        While(Queue.empty()==0){
            Set x = Queue.dequeue();
            If (Mark[x]!=1){
                Visit x;
                Set Mark[x]=1;
                For each adjacent vertex y of x {
                    If(Mark[y]==0){
                        Queue.enqueue(y);
                    }
                }
            }
        }
}
Breath-First-Search-Iterative(V, E) {
        For each v in V {
            Set Mark[v]=0;
        }
        For each v in V {
            If(Mark[v] == 0){
                bfs-iterative(v, V, E);
            }
        }
}
```

With the similar argument as that of the depth first search, the time complexity of the breadth first search algorithm can be defined as $O(|V| + |E|)$.

Other topics on graph such as shortest path, spanning tree, minimum spanning tree, etc. are not within the scope of this book. Reader may refer to additional materials provided in the link cited by the QR code.

UNIT SUMMARY

This unit discussed three important topics of data structures and algorithms namely sorting, hashing and introduction to graph. Among the different sorting algorithms, five comparable based and three non-comparable sorting algorithms are discussed. The complexity of these algorithms is also discussed. Further, we discuss various methods of hashing and hash functions. Efficiency of different hash functions and hashing approaches are also discussed in detail. Unlike sorting and hashing, only the introductory definition, representation and traversal of Graphs are discussed in this book. Reader may refer to additional reading materials for other topics on graphs.

EXERCISES

Multiple Choice Questions

Q1. In quick sort, for sorting n elements, the $\left(\frac{n}{4}\right)^{th}$ smallest element is selected as pivot using an $O(n)$ time algorithm. What is the worst case time complexity of the quick sort?

(a) $\theta(n)$ (b) $\theta(n \log n)$ (c) $\theta(n^2)$ (d) $\theta(n^2 \log n)$

Q2. Consider a binary max-heap implemented using an array. Which one of the following array represents a binary max-heap?

(a) {25, 12, 16, 13, 10, 8, 14}
(b) {25, 14, 13, 16, 10, 8, 12}
(c) {25, 14, 16, 13, 10, 8, 12}
(d) {25, 14, 12, 13, 10, 8, 16}

Q3. The degree sequence of a simple graph is the sequence of the degrees of the nodes in the graph in decreasing order. Which of the following sequence can not be the degree sequence of any graph?

(a) {7, 6, 5 4, 4, 3, 2, 1}
(b) {6, 6, 6, 6, 3, 3, 2, 2}
(c) {7, 6, 6, 4, 4, 3, 2, 2}
(d) {8, 7, 7, 6, 4, 2, 1, 1}

Q4. A hash table of length 10 uses open addressing with hash function $h(k) = k \ mod \ 10$, and linear probing. After inserting 6 values into an empty hash table, the table is as shown below.

0	
1	
2	42
3	23
4	34
5	52
6	46
7	33
8	
9	

Which one of the following choices gives a possible order in which the key values could have been inserted in the table?

(a) {46, 42, 34, 52, 23, 33}
(b) {34, 42, 23, 52, 33, 46}
(c) {46, 34, 42, 23, 52, 33}
(d) {42, 46, 33, 23, 34, 52}

Q5. Suppose we are given n keys, m hash table slots, and two simple uniform hash functions h_1 and h_2. Further suppose our hashing scheme uses h_1 for the odd keys and h_2 for the even keys. What is the expected number of keys in a slot?

(a) $\frac{m}{n}$ (b) $\frac{n}{m}$ (c) $\frac{2n}{m}$ (d) $\frac{n}{2m}$

Q6. Consider the following two statements:

i. A hash function (these are often used for computing digital signatures) is an injective function.

ii. encryption technique such as DES performs a permutation on the elements of its input alphabet.

Which one of the following options is valid for the above two statements?

(a) Both are false, (b) i true, but ii false, (c) ii true, but i false, (d) both are true

Q7 Assume that the algorithms considered here sort the input sequences in ascending order. If the input is already in ascending order, which of the following are true?

(a) Quicksort runs in $\theta(n^2)$ time
(b) Bubble sort runs in $\theta(n^2)$
(c) Merge sort runs in $\theta(n)$ time
(d) Insertion sort runs in $\theta(n)$ time

Q8. The worst case running times of Insertion sort, Merge sort and Quick sort, respectively, are

(a) $\theta(n \log n), \theta(n \log n), \theta(n^2)$
(b) $\theta(n^2), \theta(n^2), \theta(n \log n)$
(c) $\theta(n^2), \theta(n \log n), \theta(n \log n)$
(d) $\theta(n^2), \theta(n \log n), \theta(n^2)$

Q9. Which of the following data structure is used in breadth first search algorithm for traversing a graph?

(a) Stack (b) Queue

Q10. Which of the following sorting algorithms has the lowest worst-case complexity?

(a) Merge, (b) Bubble (c) Quick (d) Selection

Q11 Which one of the following in place sorting algorithms needs the minimum number of swaps?

(a) Insertion , (b) Bubble (c) Quick (d) Selection

Short and Long Answer Type Questions

Q1. What is the number of swaps required to sort n elements using selection sort, in the worst case?

Q2. What is the tightest lower bound on the number of comparisons, in the worst case, for comparison-based sorting?

Q3. A hash table contains 10 buckets and uses linear probing to resolve collisions. The key values are integers and the hash function used is key % 10. If the values 43, 165, 62, 123, 142 are inserted in the table, in what location would the key value 142 be inserted?

Q4. Given the following inputs in the given order (4322, 1334, 1471, 9679, 1989, 6171, 6173, 4199) and the hash function x mod 10, show the hash mapping using open chaining?

Q5. Breadth First Search is started on a binary tree beginning from the root vertex. There is a vertex v at a distance four from the root. If v is the nth vertex in this traversal, what is the maximum possible value of n?

Numerical Problems

Q1. An array of 25 distinct elements is to be sorted using quicksort. Assume that the pivot element is chosen uniformly at random. What is the probability that the pivot element gets placed in the worst possible location in the first round of partitioning (rounded off to 2 decimal places)?

Q2. Consider a double hashing scheme in which the primary hash function is $h_1(k) = k \ mod \ 23$, and the secondary hash function is $h_2(k) = 1 + (k \ mod \ 19)$. Assume that the table size is 23. Wjat is the address returned by probe 1 in the probe sequence (assume that the probe sequence begins at probe 0) for key value $k = 90$?

Q3. Given a hash table T with 25 slots that stores 2000 elements, What is the load factor α for T?

Q4. State the recurrence equation for the worst case time complexity of the Quicksort algorithm for sorting n (≥ 2) numbers. Estimate its time asymptotic time complexity.

Q5. An unordered list contains n distinct elements. Estimate the number of comparisons to find an element in this list that is neither maximum nor minimum.

PRACTICAL

Q1. Write an adaptive quick sort algorithm.

Q2. Write an iterative quick sort algorithm.

Q3. Write an iterative merge sort algorithm.

Q4. Given an array x with n objects colored red, white, or blue, sort them in-place so that objects of the same color are adjacent, with the colors in the order of red, white, and blue. We can use the integers 0, 1, and 2 to represent the color red, white, and blue, respectively.

Q5. You are given an integer array A. Sort the integers in the array in ascending order by the number of 1's in their binary representation and in case of two or more integers have the same number of 1's, order them in ascending order.

Q6. There are n cities. Some of them are connected, while some are not. If city A is connected directly with city B, and city B is connected directly with city C, then city A is connected indirectly with city A. A province is a group of directly or indirectly connected cities and no other cities outside of the group. Write a program to find the number of provinces.

Q7. Implement Rabin-Karp Algorithm for string matching.

Q8. Professor McGonagall teaches transfiguration at Hogwarts. She has given Harry the task of changing himself into a cat. She explains that the trick is to analyze your own DNA and change it into the DNA of a cat. The transfigure spell can be used to pick any one character from the DNA string, remove it and insert it in the beginning. Help Harry calculates minimum number of times he needs to use the spell to change himself into a cat. Hints: find the number of operations of deletion and insertion to change a string, say "GEEKSFORGEEKS", to another string, say "FORGEEKSGEEKS".

Q9. You are given an integer n. There is an undirected graph with n nodes, numbered from 0 to n -1. You are given a 2D integer array edges where edges[i] = [a_i, b_i] denotes that there exists an undirected edge connecting nodes ai and bi. Return the number of pairs of different nodes that are unreachable from each other.

Q10. You are given a 0-indexed integer array A. In one operation you can replace any element of the array with any two elements that sum to it. For example, consider A = [3,9,5]. In one operation, we can replace A[1] with 3 and 6 and convert A to [3,3,6,5]. It can then be converted to [3,3,3,3,5]. Write a program to return the minimum number of operations to make an array that is sorted in non-decreasing order.

KNOW MORE

Readers are encouraged to explore the following E-Books/E-Resources for additional examples, and discussions on related topics.

1. Sorting, Hash and Graph, Chapters 9, 10, and 11, Lecture Notes for Data Structures and Algorithms, John Bullinaria, School of Computer Science, University of Birmingham, UK. (https://www.cs.bham.ac.uk/~jxb/DSA/dsa.pdf)

2. Graph, and Sorting. Chapters 7, 8, and 9, Electronic Lecture Notes - DATA STRUCTURES AND ALGORITHMS, by Y. Narahari (https://gtl.csa.iisc.ac.in/hari/wp-content/uploads/2021/10/dsa.pdf)

3. Sorting. Chapter 8, Data Structures and Algorithms: Annotated Reference with Examples, Granville Barnett, and Luca Del Tongo, (https://www.mta.ca/~rrosebru/oldcourse/263114/Dsa.pdf)

4. Hashing, Sorting and Graph, Chapters 5, 7 and 9. Data Structures and Algorithm Analysis in C++, Weiss, Mark Allen, 4th Ed. (https://www.uoitc.edu.iq/images/documents/informaticsinstitute/Competitive_exam/DataStructures.pdf).
5. Sorting and Hashing. Chapters 2 and 5, Data Structures and Algorithms, N. Wirth. (https://people.inf.ethz.ch/wirth/AD.pdf)

REFERENCES AND SUGGESTED READINGS

- [Adamson, 1996] I. T. Adamson. (1996), Data structures and Algorithms: A first Course, Springer.
- [Aho, 1974] A. V. Aho, J. E. Hopcroft, and J D. Ullman. (1974), Design and Analysis of Computer Algorithms, Addison-Wesley.
- [Aho, 1983] A. V. Aho, J. E. Hopcroft, and J D. Ullman. (1983), Data Structures and Algorithms, Addison-Wesley.
- [Berge, 1962] Berge C., (1962) The Thesory of Graphs and Its Applications, Wiley.
- [Bondy, 1976] Bondy A. A. and Murthy U. S. R., (1976) Graph Theory with Applications, Elsevier.
- [Cormen, 2001] Cormen, T. H.; Leiserson, C. E.; Rivest, R. L. & Stein, C. (2001), Introduction to Algorithms , The MIT Press .
- [Donald, 2009] Donald E. Knuth. (2009), The Art of Computer Programming: Fundamental Algorithms, Vol. 1, 3rd Edition, Pearson.

- [Greene, 1988] D. H. Greene and D. E Knuth. (1988) Mathematics for the analysis of Algorithms, Birkhauser.
- [Hoare, 1962] Hoare, C. A. R., (1962) Quicksort, Comp. J, 5(1), pp: 10-15.
- [Hoare, 1971] Hoare, C. A. R., (1971) Proof of a recursive program: Quicksort, Comp. J, 14(4), pp: 391-395.
- [Horowitz, 1983] E. Horowitz and S Sahni. (1983) Fundamentals of data Structure, Computer Science Press
- [Horowitz, 1993] E. Horowitz, S Sahni and A. Freed. (1993) Fundamentals of data Structure in C, Computer Science Press.
- [James, 2009] James A. Storer. (2009), An Introduction to Data Structures and Algorithms, 1st Edition, Birkhauser Springer.
- [Kingston, 1990] J. H. Kingston. (1990), Algorithms and data structures, Addison-Wesley.
- [Kozon, 1992] D. C. Kozen. (1992), The design and Analysis of Algorithms, Springer.
- [Lewis, 1991] H. R. Lewis and L. Denenberg. (1991) Data Structures and Their Algorithms, Harper Collins.
- [Radke, 1970] C. E. Radke. (1970), The use of quadratic residue research, Communications of the ACM, 13(2), pp. 103-105.
- [Williams, 1964] Williams, J. W. J., (1970) Heapsort, ACM Communication, 7(6), pp: 347-48, 1964.
- [Wirth, 1976] Wirth, N. (1976), Algorithms + Data Structures = Programs , Prentice-Hall.
- [Van, 1970] Van Emden, M. H., (1970) Increasing the efficiency of Quicksort, ACM Communication, 13(9), pp: 563-566, 1970.

Dynamic QR Code for Further Reading

Scan the following QR Code to navigate to an external page for know more, additional reading materials, and additional exercises.

CO AND PO ATTAINMENT TABLE

Course outcomes (COs) for this course can be mapped with the programme outcomes (POs) after the completion of the course and a correlation can be made for the attainment of POs to analyze the gap. After proper analysis of the gap in the attainment of POs necessary measures can be taken to overcome the gaps.

Table for CO and PO attainment

Course Outcomes	Attainment of Programme Outcomes (1- Weak Correlation; 2- Medium correlation; 3- Strong Correlation)											
	PO-1	PO-2	PO-3	PO-4	PO-5	PO-6	PO-7	PO-8	PO-9	PO-10	PO-11	PO-12
CO-1												
CO-2												
CO-3												
CO-4												
CO-5												

The data filled in the above table can be used for gap analysis.

INDEX